Marketing in Travel and Tourism

Marketing in Travel and Tourism

Victor T. C. Middleton

Butterworth-Heinemann Ltd
Linacre House, Jordan Hill, Oxford OX2 8DP

 PART OF REED INTERNATIONAL BOOKS

OXFORD   LONDON   BOSTON
MUNICH   NEW DELHI   SINGAPORE   SYDNEY
TOKYO   TORONTO   WELLINGTON

First published 1988
Reprinted 1988, 1989, 1990, 1992

British Library Cataloguing in Publication Data
Middleton, Victor T. C.
    Marketing in travel and tourism
    1. Tourism.   Marketing
    I. Title
    658.8′09′91

ISBN 0 7506 0359 3

Printed and bound in Great Britain by
The Bath Press, Bath, Avon

Contents

v

Figures

vii

Foreword

There can be few in the tourist industry in Britain and other parts of the world who would disagree that there is a need for more professional marketing in many large organizations as well as in the thousands of small businesses which the industry comprises.

Marketing is not, of course, just a bolt-on specialism which can be added to existing management structures, but an integrated approach to the whole conduct of profitable business, within an overall corporate culture focused on long run customer orientation.

To be successful in competitive conditions, businesses must think strategically as well as tactically, be pro-active, not reactive, and make key decisions ahead of competitors. To do this effectively requires a deep knowledge of customers and their changing needs and expectations, focused on product satisfaction and value for money.

To be successful also means being cost efficient in operations and marketing and this requires the careful specification of objectives and the evaluation of performance over time – always in the context of securing the best available return on assets employed.

These and many more issues vital to profitability in travel and tourism are addressed in this comprehensive, cohesive book which is clearly relevant to the needs of marketing managers in all sectors of the industry, as well as to the hundreds of students aiming each year to gain entry and make career progress in the tourist industry of the future.

Sir Colin Marshall
British Airways PLC
March 1988

Preface

This book is written in the belief that the marketing of travel and tourism is still in the early stages of a development, which will influence travel and tourism to an increasing extent for the remaining years of the twentieth century. Marketing is seen as a dominant management philosophy or culture, a systematic thought process, and as an integrated set of techniques focused on customer needs and aspirations. Combined, the application of the thought process and techniques may be used in marketing orientated organizations to guide the way they understand, respond to, and influence their target markets, in a continuously changing business environment.

As an integrated approach to business in commercial and non-commercial sectors of travel and tourism, marketing is presented as a proactive management response, especially to industry conditions of excess capacity of production and volatile market demand, which are commonly found in international travel and tourism. Marketing perishable products in such conditions inevitably produces highly aggressive competition for market share and growth and it is easy to predict that competition will intensify rather than diminish over the next decade. The rapid growth of tourism demand around the world from the 1950s to the 1970s served to cushion many producer organizations in travel and tourism from the full effects of competition and delayed the full application of marketing in many organizations. As travel markets approach maturity in many countries, and as the rate of growth slows, competition will be further stimulated by the growing marketing professionalism of the many large-scale producer organizations, which developed so strongly in all sectors of the travel and tourism industry over the last decade.

Marketing is not viewed, however, as the only focus of business management. Throughout the book the requirement of meeting customers' needs is balanced against the essential need of organizations to make the most profitable use of existing assets, and to achieve integration of management functions around customer orientated objectives. Nor does marketing necessarily determine the nature of an organization's long-run goal or mission, although its approach and techniques are always an essential input to specifying revenue earning objectives, which are precise, realistic and achievable in the markets in which an organization operates. In this sense the adoption of a marketing approach can be as relevant to museums responsible to non-profit making trusts, and to local government tourist offices, as it is to airlines, hotels, or tour operators in the commercial sector.

The rigorous application of the modern marketing concept can also provide the route to achieving the marginal extra business volume and revenue, on which the difference between profit and loss so often depends in the travel and tourism industry. Systematically applied, marketing can also secure the marginal increases in the cost effectiveness of promotional and related budgets. This is a most important aspect of marketing which this author terms *marketing the margin*. The concept is relevant both to strategy and tactics, and it is reflected throughout the book.

ix

Marketing as a body of knowledge is international; like travel and tourism it observes no geographical boundaries. While many of the principles and techniques were developed originally in North America and Europe in the context of manufactured consumer goods, they are now being practised and developed all around the world in service industries too. For reasons which are set out in Chapter 3, this author believes that it is possible to construct an overall understanding of travel and tourism marketing based on three essential points. First, that the fundamental principles of consumer marketing are common to all its forms. Second that service industries display particular generic characteristics, which do not alter the principles but must be understood before marketing can successfully be applied in practice. Third that there are important common characteristics of travel and tourism, which require particular forms of marketing response.

It is certainly too much to claim that a theory of travel and tourism marketing exists. Yet the increasing consistencies of approach in marketing, adopted in the different sectors of travel and tourism to the opportunities and threats they perceive, do point to a coherent, systematic body of knowledge within the overall framework of marketing, which is capable of being developed.

The aim of the book and its intended market

The book has three aims, which are to provide:

- a basic but comprehensive text about what marketing means in the travel and tourism industry,
- a balance of concepts and principles drawn from the study of marketing, with illustrations of recent practice,
- a necessary companion volume for all concerned with travel and tourism marketing,

but not a substitute for the many excellent texts, which explain marketing principles in their overall context.

On both sides of the Atlantic, the better of the standard texts on marketing are now substantial volumes, many of them having developed over four or more editions. This book makes no attempt to replace them. It is intended instead to fit fully within a framework of internationally accepted marketing principles, which have stood the test of time, and develop the ideas in travel and tourism. Suggested readings, indicating chapters in books which are typically recommended to students in the USA and in Britain are noted at the end of each chapter where relevant. Such books have the added advantage of dealing with the important principles in the wider industrial context in which marketing developed, and students in particular will profit from the breadth of understanding this conveys.

The book is written to meet the needs of students of travel and tourism and hospitality courses, and related leisure industry programmes. For all of them marketing is likely to be a very important influence in their careers, whether or not they are directly involved in marketing practice. The contents are developed from lecture material originally prepared for students, and judged to be suitable for all preparing for examinations in further and higher education courses with a travel and tourism component. It provides much material relevant to those on other courses, in which service industries are an important element.

But marketing is also a very practical subject, and the book is equally aimed at the great majority of managers in travel and tourism in the 1980s who have some responsibility for aspects of marketing but who have not studied the subject formally. Much of the contents have also been exposed to the critical reaction of managers in the industry and modified in the light of their responses. The book is not an attempt to tell the practitioner how to make instant improvements to his marketing efforts, and to increase sales revenue, and reduce marketing expenditure over night. Nor does it contain any 'golden rules'. But if people in the industry read the book with care, and relate its principles to the particular circumstances which their own organization faces, most should perceive many useful insights and ways to improve the effectiveness of their marketing decisions. If they do not, the author will have failed in his purpose.

The structure of the book

The book is presented in five parts. The structure is designed to follow a logical development of the subject but, as every manager will understand, marketing is a circular rather than a linear process. So far as possible, the parts are designed to be reasonably self explanatory with the intention that lecturers and students can fit the chapters into whatever pattern the logic of their courses suggests.

Briefly, Part One defines travel and tourism and the sectors within the industry, which are referred to throughout the book. The subject of marketing is introduced, especially for those who are coming new to the subject, and

Chapter 3 sets out the characteristics of travel and tourism to which marketing responds. Part One also explains the factors in the external business environment which influence demand and customers' purchasing behaviour.

Part Two explains the four Ps of the marketing mix in travel and tourism and notes their significance for all marketing managers involved in both strategic and tactical decisions. Part Three focuses on planning for marketing, and deals with marketing research, marketing strategy and tactics, and with the procedures involved in putting together and budgeting for a marketing campaign. Issues of organization and the role of marketing managers are included in this part of the book. Part Four deals with each of the main tools or functions used in marketing, and emphasizes the role of print, distribution, and direct response marketing which are especially important in travel and tourism.

Using a broadly common format, Part Five analyses separately the meaning and application of marketing in five of the main sectors of travel and tourism. The Epilogue looks ahead at prospects for travel and tourism marketing in the year 2000.

Victor T. C. Middleton
Farnham, Surrey

Acknowledgements

It is for the readers of this book to decide whether or not it achieves the goals set out in the preface. To the extent that the author succeeds, it will certainly reflect the very many helpful insights and views contributed over recent years by more people than can be fully acknowledged here. To the extent that he fails, it will be his sole responsibility, together with the onus for all errors and omissions.

Generally, because of their involvement and interest in much of the material of this book, I wish to acknowledge the hundreds of undergraduate and postgraduate students to whose views I paid rather more attention than many supposed at the time. For stimulating my thoughts and improving so many of them for over a decade, I owe a special debt of gratitude to my friend, and former colleague at the University of Surrey, John Burkart.

Specifically, because they read and much improved particular chapters, I am indebted to Ken Robinson, Managing Director of Ventures Consultancy, Beaulieu, whose comments did much to enhance whatever is direct and to the point; David Airey, a former colleague and now an HM Inspector at the Department of Education and Science; Michael Beaumont, Marketing Director of the National Trust; Christopher Dunn, Managing Director of Superbreak Mini-Holidays; Roger Heape, Managing Director of Intasun Holidays; Philippa Watt, Marketing Director of Trusthouse Forte Hotels; and Stephen Wheatcroft, formerly a director of British Airways.

For their contributions at different times to typing parts of the manuscript I am very grateful for the support of Joanna Terry, Rachel Helyer and Sue Kitching.

My greatest debt of gratitude is owed to Professor Rik Medlik, who, as advisor on hotel, catering and tourism books for Heinemann, read and enormously improved my draft chapters, employing greater tact and patience than they truly deserved. In particular, over three difficult years, he steadfastly encouraged, goaded, and not infrequently shamed me into completing the task, albeit two years late.

Part One

The Meaning of Marketing in Travel and Tourism

1

Introducing travel and tourism

This chapter introduces and defines the subject matter of this book. The intention is to identify the essential nature of travel and tourism, and the industry it supports, for practical purposes in marketing.

In essence, travel and tourism represents a total market, which is of interest worldwide because of its recent growth and current size; its potential for further growth; its economic contribution measured in terms of investment, employment and balance of payments; its effects on host communities; and its impact on the physical environment of visited destinations. Marketing is of interest because it is one of the principal management influences which can be brought to bear on the size and behaviour of the market.

Within the total market there are many submarkets, or segments, and many products designed and provided by a wide range of organizations which are categorized in Figure 1.1. Because travel and tourism is defined as a market, it is best understood in terms of demand and supply. Marketing is subsequently introduced in Chapter 3 as a vital part of the linking mechanism between supply and demand, focused on *exchange transactions*, in which consumers exercise preferences and choices, and exchange money in return for the supply of particular travel experiences or products. For reasons discussed subsequently, the practice of marketing is also highly relevant to visitor attractions and other tourism resources for which no market price is charged, and to the role of national tourist offices and other area organizations, most of which are not directly involved in the sale of products.

The chapter commences with an overview of travel and tourism demand, its international dimensions, and main components. A working definition of the subject is provided which comments on the distinction between *tourism*, and *travel and tourism*; often a source of confusion to students. The components of demand and supply and the linking role of marketing are put together in diagrammatic form (Figure 1.2), which serves also to identify the main categories of supply within the travel and tourism industry. Suggestions for further reading will be found at the end of the chapter.

An overview of travel and tourism demand

In defining travel and tourism for the purposes of this book it is useful to follow the basic classification system, which is used in nearly all countries where measurement exists. This system is discussed in detail in most introductory texts; see, for example, Burkart and Medlik: (1981/41): it is based on three categories of visitor demand, with which any country is concerned; each is a different sector of the total market:

1 International visitors, travelling to a country, who are residents of other countries (inward tourism)
2 Residents of a country, travelling as visitors to other countries (outward tourism)

3   Residents visiting destinations within their own country's boundaries (domestic tourism).

In line with internationally accepted definitions discussed for example by Holloway (1985: p. 1), it is normal to speak of:

visitors to describe all travellers who fall within agreed definitions,
tourists to describe visitors who stay overnight at a destination,
excursionists, or *day visitors*, to describe visitors who arrive and depart on the same day.
Excursionists are mostly people who leave home and return there on the same day, but may be tourists who make day visits to other destinations away from the places where they are staying overnight.

As outlined above these categories are easy to understand. In practice, the technicalities of achieving precision in measuring visitor categories are extremely complex and, despite various international guidelines, no uniformity yet exists in the measurement methods used around the world. For example, should visiting diplomats be treated as tourists? Should airline crew be included? Should nationals of a country who are resident abroad be treated as foreign visitors for statistical purposes? At what point, measured in distance covered away from home, or time travelled, or activity followed, should a resident of a city be counted as an excursionist, or day visitor, as distinguished from a resident pursuing his or her normal daily activities? In cities, for example, some shopping trips are evidently tourist or recreational excursions, but other trips to make routine purchases, are not.

Whilst the definition of travel and tourism outlined in this chapter will be adequate for the working purposes of those involved in marketing, this book does not set out to be a detailed study of the nature of tourism. Readers seeking further elaboration of concepts and measurement issues are referred to the reading suggestions noted at the end of the chapter. Marketing managers will, of course, require their own definitions of the market segments with which they are involved, and these will be far more precise than the broadly indicative international categories referred to here (see Chapter 7).

International tourism

People who travel to and stay in countries other than their country of residence are normally described as international tourists. They are usually treated as the most important market sector of tourism because, compared with domestic tourism (see next section), typically they spend more, stay longer at the destination, use more expensive transport and accommodation, and bring in foreign currency which contributes to a destination country's international balance of payments.

Around the world, measured as *arrivals* or *trips*, the numbers of international tourists and their expenditure have grown strongly since the 1950s, notwithstanding temporary fluctuations caused by the international energy and economic crises of the 1970s. The overall growth pattern is revealed in Table 1.1, and the reasons for it are discussed later in some detail in Chapters 4 and 5. For the purposes of this introduction it is suf-

Table 1.1 *Growth in international tourist arrivals, and expenditure, 1950–1985*

Year	International arrivals (millions)	International expenditure ($ millions)
1950	25.3	2,100
1960	69.3	6,867
1970	159.7	17,900
1980	284.0	102,363
1985	340.0p	115,000p

Note: p = provisional
Source: World Tourism Organization, *Yearbook of Tourism Statistics*, Vol. 1, p. 1, 1986.

ficient to note the recent growth and current size of the international market, and to be aware of consistently confident projections in the mid 1980s that international tourism will continue to grow for the rest of the twentieth century. Although annual fluctuations in volume, reflecting economic and political events, are virtually certain, current expectations are for annual growth of the order of at least 5 per cent per annum over the next two decades (see for example Edwards: 1985 p. 3).

At the present time, in Northern Europe, it is common for over half of the adult population to have made one or more international tourist trips during the previous five years, mostly on vacation. Experience of international travel is very much less for Americans, reflecting the size of the USA and the distances involved for most of them in making international trips. US interstate tourism, for example between the North East and Florida, should perhaps be viewed as similar in principle to European tourism over similar distances.

Although not included in Table 1.1, international excursionism is an important market sector in countries with common land frontiers, such as the USA and Canada, the Netherlands and West Germany, and Malaysia and Singapore. Because of the speed and efficiency of cross-Channel ferries, excursionism between Britain and France, and Britain and Belgium, is also important.

Domestic tourism

People who are tourists travelling within the boundaries of their own country are classified as domestic tourists. Estimates of the size of this sector of the market vary because in many countries domestic tourism is not adequately measured at the present time. In the case of the USA and Britain, where good measurement does exist, Americans take only one trip abroad for every 100 domestic trips defined as travel to places more than 100 miles distance from home.

Even for longer trips of over ten nights duration, international trips were no more than 3 per cent of the total. For the British in the mid 1980s, reflecting the shorter distances involved in travelling abroad, there were some six domestic tourism trips (including overnight stays) for every one that involved foreign travel. The comparative growth figures over the last fifteen years are shown in Table 1.2.

Table 1.2 *Growth in domestic tourist arrivals and expenditure in the USA and Britain, 1972–1985*

	USA*		Britain†	
Year	Trips (millions)	Expenditure ($ millions)	Trips (millions)	Expenditure (£ millions)
1972	458ᵉ	na	132	1,375
1980	1,029	162,000	130	4,550
1986	1,092	256,000	128	7,150

Note: na = not available, e = estimate
*USA data includes trips of 100 miles or more away from home, for any purpose, whether or not an overnight stay is involved.
†British data includes trips, for any purpose, involving overnight stays away from home, irrespective of distance travelled.
Sources:
Economic Review of Travel in America, US Travel Data Center.
†*British Tourism Survey* – Monthly, English Tourist Board.

Evidence from surveys of the vacation market in Europe and North America in the mid 1980s indicates that in most countries, between a half and three-quarters of the adult population took holidays in any twelve-month period. This proportion covers international and domestic holidays, although the latter are the largest category. Increasing numbers of people take more than one vacation trip a year; a factor of great importance to marketing managers, for reasons to be discussed later.

Precise data analysing the tourism experience of individuals over periods of more than one year are rarely available, but excluding the very old, the sick, the severely disabled, and those facing particular financial hardship, recent and frequent experience of some form of tourism and excursionism now extends to over nine out of ten people in most economically developed countries.

Within the overall total, domestic excursions, or day visits taking place within a country's frontiers, are the most difficult sector of travel and tourism demand to quantify. In most economically developed countries the frequency of day visits is already so great that it is not easily measured by traditional survey techniques because people find it hard or impossible to remember the number of trips they have taken over a period of months or even weeks. There is in the mid 1980s, however, a rough but useful estimate for economically developed countries, that there are at least as many domestic day visits for leisure purposes within a country, as there are tourist days or nights spent away from home for all purposes. Thus, for example in Britain in 1985, 126 million domestic tourist trips generated 500 million nights away from home. An additional 500 million day visits or excursions are estimated, by this author, to have taken place for leisure purposes. With a population of some 55 million in Britain, this is the equivalent of around twenty visitor days per person for leisure purposes over a year. No estimates of day visits for business and social purposes, which fall within the definitions of travel and tourism, are known to exist, although such visits are obviously a very large market for transport operators in particular.

To summarize, the total market for travel and tourism comprises three main elements. These are: international visits inwards to a country; visits made to foreign destinations by a country's residents; and domestic visits including day trips. The total market has grown rapidly in recent years and it is very large indeed, involving the great majority of the populations of economically developed countries. Frequent, repeat purchases of travel and tourism products in any period of twelve months, are already a normal experience for many travellers. Whether travel and tourism will emerge as the largest sector of international trade by the year 2000, as some authors claim, is debatable. On current evidence it is certain that it will be a very important industry in all parts of the world, and that marketing within it will be a subject of growing significance and interest.

A working definition of travel and tourism

Before drawing the previous discussion of the main markets of travel and tourism into a working definition, one important potential source of confusion needs clarification. What, if any, are the differences between *tourism*, and *travel*, used on their own as single terms, and *travel and tourism* used as a combined term? What can a definition of tourism mean if it does not include travel? this book proceeds in the belief that an acceptable definition of tourism necessarily covers all relevant aspects of travel. In other words *tourism*, and *travel and tourism*, are terms which relate to exactly the same market and they are used interchangeably.

Travel and tourism tends to be the term used most often by managers, especially in North America, because it is convenient, practical, and widely understood. Accordingly, this usage is adopted generally throughout the book. As the US Travel Data Center puts it, 'Tourism is synonymous with travel' (USTDC: 1987: Appendix B). Where, for the sake of convenience, *tourism* is used alone, it also means travel and tourism: students should be aware that no conceptual difference is implied between the two expressions.

The view of the British Tourism Society is adopted to define the total market for travel and tourism; it is based on the work of Burkart and Medlik (1981), which in turn draws on earlier definitions and is widely accepted. The Tourism

Society statement has the added advantage of endorsement by several hundred managers working in all sectors of travel and tourism.

'Tourism is deemed to include any activity concerned with the temporary short-term movement of people to destinations outside the places where they normally live and work, and their activities during the stay at these destinations,' (Tourism Society: 1979; p. 70).

There is nothing particular to Britain about this definition. It is comprehensive; it holds good for all countries; it encompasses all the elements of visitor categories noted earlier in the chapter; and it serves as the working definition of the total market which is relevant throughout the book.

The definition pulls together three main elements of all travel and tourism products:

1 Visitor activity is concerned only with aspects of life outside normal routines of work and social commitments, and outside the location of those routines.
2 The activity involves travel and, in nearly every case, some form of transportation to the destination.
3 The destination is a focus for a range of activities, and a range of facilities required to support those activities.

Five important points should be noted in relation to the definition.

1 There is nothing in it which restricts the total market to overnight stays; it includes excursionism or day visits.

2 There is nothing in it which restricts the total market to travel for leisure or pleasure and it includes travel for business, social, religious, educational, sports or any other purpose – provided that the destination of travel is outside the normal place of residence or work.

3 By definition all tourism includes an element of travel but all travel is not tourism. The definition excludes commuter travel and purely local travel, such as to neighbourhood shops, schools or theatres.
4 Travel and tourism includes large elements of individual leisure time and also recreation activities, but it is not synonymous with them because the bulk of all leisure and recreation takes place in or around the home.

5 By definition all travel and tourism trips are temporary movements; the bulk of the total market comprises trips of no more than a few nights duration.

One of the greatest difficulties in understanding and dealing with travel and tourism as a total market, distinguishing the industry from most others with which marketing managers deal, is the extent to which so many of the supplying organizations see tourism as only a part of their total business operations. For example, trains, buses, tourist attractions, restaurants and hotels, all deal with a wide variety of market segments, many of which do not fall within the definition of travel and tourism. Hotels have local trade for bars and meals, transport operators carry commuters, many attractions serve local residents, and so on. This mixture of products, designed to serve both tourism and other markets, has great significance for marketing decisions; it is discussed in some detail in Part Five of the book which considers marketing applications in the component sectors of the industry.

The component sectors of the travel and tourism industry

Travel and tourism was discussed at the beginning of this chapter from the demand side, as a total market comprising three main sectors, of international tourism, domestic tourism, and

```
┌──────────────────────────────────────────────────────────────────────────────┐
│  ┌──────────────────────────────────┐        ┌──────────────────────────────┐ │
│  │ Accommodation sector             │        │ Attractions sector           │ │
│  │ Hotels                           │        │ Theme parks                  │ │
│  │ Guest houses                     │        │ Museums                      │ │
│  │ Farmhouses                       │        │ National parks               │ │
│  │ Apartments/villas/flats          │        │ Wildlife parks               │ │
│  │ Condominiums/time share          │        │ Gardens                      │ │
│  │ Vacation villages                │        │ Heritage sites               │ │
│  │ Conference/exhibition centres    │        └──────────────────────────────┘ │
│  │ Static and touring caravan/camping sites │                                  │
│  │ Marinas                          │                                          │
│  └──────────────────────────────────┘                                          │
│                                                                                │
│              ┌──────────────────────────────┐                                  │
│              │ Transport sector             │                                  │
│              │ Airlines                     │                                  │
│              │ Shipping lines               │                                  │
│              │ Railways                     │                                  │
│              │ Bus/coach operators          │                                  │
│              │ Car rental operators         │                                  │
│              └──────────────────────────────┘                                  │
│                                                                                │
│  ┌──────────────────────────────────┐                                          │
│  │ Travel organizers sector         │   ┌──────────────────────────────────┐   │
│  │ Tour operators                   │   │ Destination organization sector  │   │
│  │ Tour wholesalers/brokers         │   │ National tourist offices (NTOs)  │   │
│  │ Retail travel agents             │   │ Regional/State tourist offices   │   │
│  │ Conference organizers            │   │ Local tourist offices            │   │
│  │ Booking agencies (e.g. accommodation) │ Tourist associations           │   │
│  │ Incentive travel organizers      │   └──────────────────────────────────┘   │
│  └──────────────────────────────────┘                                          │
└──────────────────────────────────────────────────────────────────────────────┘
```

Figure 1.1 *The five main sectors of the travel and tourism industry*

excursionism. It is appropriate to complete the introduction by discussing briefly the sectors on the supply side, which are loosely, but meaningfully, known as the *travel and tourism industry*. From Figure 1.1 it is obvious that the 'industry' comprises the products or outputs, not of one but of several different industry sectors, as these are conventionally defined and measured in most countries' economic statistics. In practice, convenient though the concept is for all working within it, travel and tourism is not an industry which is recognized as such by economists. In assessing the performance of industry sectors, it is normal for economists and statisticians to measure the outputs of transport, accommodation, and catering, for example, but they cannot easily distinguish what proportion of each output is generated by tourist spending. Whilst this is a topic of almost infinite debate for statisticians and economists, and for complicated visitor survey techniques, it is fortunately not a matter of concern for marketing managers. Accordingly, the term travel and tourism industry is used throughout this book in the broad sense that it is recognized without difficulty in practice.

The five component sectors of the industry discussed in Figure 1.1 are reflected in the chapter headings adopted in Part Five of the book. Each of them comprises several sub-sectors, all of which are increasingly involved in marketing activities, both in the design of their products and the management of demand. There are many ways to classify the components of the industry, but for reasons set out in Part Five, this author considers that the classification in Figure 1.1 is justified by the existence within the sectors of certain common, integrating, principles which underlie the modern practice of marketing. Such principles greatly facilitate the understanding of the subject and help to explain the common interests in marketing which practitioners recognize. Students may find it a useful exercise to extend the list in Figure 1.1, using the same five sector headings and aiming to produce up to fifty sub-sectors involved altogether in the *travel and tourism industry*.

It can be seen that some of the sub-sectors are fully commercial, operated for profit; some are operated commercially for objects other than profit; and some in the public sector are operated mainly on a non-commercial basis. To illustrate, in the first category are most hotels; in the second category, many attractions, such as safari parks and heritage sites; and in the third category are many state-owned operations such as national museums, national parks, and most of the operations undertaken by tourist offices.

The systematic links between demand and supply and the role of marketing

Figure 1.2 is provided to show the vital linkages between demand and supply in travel and tourism, which are fundamental to an understanding of the role of marketing. The figure shows the relationship between market demand, generated in the places in which visitors normally live (areas of origin), and product supply, created in areas of destination. In particular it shows how the five main sectors of the industry set out in Figure 1.1, combine to influence visitors' demand through marketing influences. Noted as the *marketing mix*, in the centre of the diagram, the meaning of this important term is fully explained in Chapter 6.

Readers should note that the linkages in Figure 1.2 focus on visitors in the left-hand box. A detailed knowledge of their customers' characteristics and buying behaviour is central to the activities of marketing managers in all sectors of the industry. Knowledge of the customer, and all that it implies for management decisions, is generally known as *consumer orientation*; a concept developed in the next chapter.

It should be noted also, in the lower half of the diagram, that not all visitors' trips to a destination are influenced by marketing activity. For example, domestic visitors travelling by private car to stay with their friends and relatives, may not be influenced by marketing in any way. On the other hand, first-time buyers of package tours to exotic destinations in the Pacific area may find almost every aspect of their trip is influenced in some way by the marketing decisions of the tour operator they choose. The operator chooses the destinations to put into a brochure, the accommodation, the range of excursions, the routes, choice of airline, and prices. In between these two examples, a traveller on business selects his own destinations according to business requirements but may be influenced as to which hotel he selects. The range of influences, noted as 'marketing mix', is obviously very wide, and it is varied according to visitors' interests and circumstances.

There are, of course, many other linkages

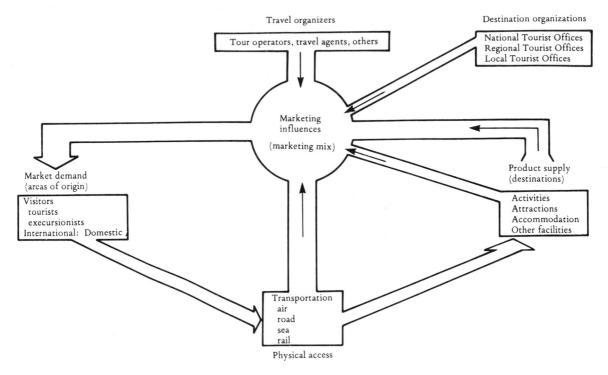

Figure 1.2 *The systematic links between demand and supply and the influence of marketing*

between the five sectors of the travel and tourism industry, not least for marketing purposes, but these linkages are not drawn into Figure 1.2 to avoid unnecessary confusion in this introduction. The linkages are noted subsequently in all parts of the book.

Chapter summary

This chapter introduces travel and tourism, as a nationally and internationally important market, in which the natural focus of management activity is on exchange transactions between visitors (demand) and producers (supply). The overall dimensions of the market are set out and key definitions provided in a form which is

suitable for marketing purposes. The travel and tourism industry is outlined as five main sectors, the marketing practices of which subsequently form the subject matter of Part Five of the book. The chapter emphasizes that there are no conceptual differences intended between the use of the terms *tourism*, and *travel and tourism*, which are used interchangably throughout the book. All the definitions are based on principles which are valid for all countries, whether they are economically well developed or not, and whether their tourist industry is mature or just emerging.

The five sectors of the industry are brought together in the important diagram in Figure 1.2 which traces the main linkages between supply and demand and, in particular, indicates the area of marketing influence which is analysed in depth in later chapters.

For students who wish to consider the definitions of travel and tourism in greater depth, although this is not necessary for marketing purposes, further readings are given.

Further reading

Burkart, A. J. and Medlik, S., *Tourism: Past, Present, and Future*, Heinemann, 1981, Chapters 4 and 7.

Gee, C. et al., *The Travel Industry*, Part 1 AVI, 1984.

Holloway, J. C., *The Business of Tourism*, Macdonald and Evans, 1985, Chapter 1.

Murphy, P. E., *Tourism: A Community Approach*, Methuen, 1985, Chapter 1.

2

Introducing modern marketing: The systematic thought process

This chapter explains the meaning of modern marketing as it is applied internationally to goods and services of all types. The intention is to define the essential characteristics common to all forms of marketing, whilst Chapter 3 considers the special characteristics of travel and tourism marketing.

In explaining the meaning of marketing, it is necessary to distinguish between the familiar word in everyday use, and the term as it is used professionally by marketing managers. Popular notions of marketing are probably more of a hindrance than a help to those studying the subject for the first time because, before reading any marketing texts, readers will be aware already of the continuous and competitive process of persuasion and inducements of every kind, to which we are all routinely exposed in the conduct of our lives. All of us are daily the targets of massive and sustained marketing activity in a variety of forms, which range from advertising on television and radio, in the press, on posters, on drink mats and on milk bottles, through promotional literature of all types, and through special offers and price reductions in retail stores. If we pause to think about it, the evidence of marketing activity surrounds us on every hand like the air we breathe and take for granted. We are continuously exposed to persuasion and inducements, not only from national and international commercial organizations, but also from governments and their agencies.

However imprecise their initial understanding of the subject, most people approach marketing with the view that it is important both commercially and socially; many are suspicious about its potential influence on their lives. Marketing, as an approach to the conduct of business has, of course, developed most strongly in countries in the Western world with highly developed economies, but the concepts are also found increasingly in less developed countries. Interestingly, in the mid 1980s, marketing activity is being injected into the centrally planned economies of China and the Soviet bloc, in which for many decades competition and promotional activity were seen as wasteful of resources and against the public interest. What consumers see of promotion and persuasion is, of course, only the visible tip of an extensive iceberg of marketing management activities of which most consumers are completely unaware.

This chapter begins by explaining the essential idea of voluntary exchange between two parties, which underlies all marketing theories of the conduct of business. It proceeds to discuss what *marketing orientation* means in terms of management attitudes, and this leads into formal definitions of marketing, from which five propositions are derived. The most important of these is that marketing is a system comprising a series of stages, which are represented in an important diagram shown in Figure 2.1. The final part of the chapter discusses the other propositions,

12

which together help to explain the growing significance of marketing in the late twentieth century. Whilst every aspect of this chapter is relevant to travel and tourism marketing, the intention is to introduce the subject as it applies to transactions generally for all types of goods and services.

Marketing means exchanges

Chapter 1 explains that travel and tourism is best understood in terms of overall demand and supply within a total market. At its simplest, marketing can be explained as a process of achieving voluntary exchanges between two individual parties:

1 customers who buy or use products,
2 producer organizations who supply and sell them.

In terms of buyers, marketing is concerned with understanding their needs and desires (why they buy), which products they choose, when, how much, at what price, how often, and where they buy them from. In terms of producers, marketing focuses on which products to produce and why, how many, at what price, when and where to make them available.

Not all products are exchanged for money. For example, many tourist attractions are made available to visitors free of admission charges, but provided such visitors have choices as to how to spend their time, the central notion of exchange remains valid.

From this simple introduction it follows that marketing involves a *management decision process* for producers, focused on a *customer decision process*, with the two sets of decisions coming together in an *exchange transaction* – money for products in the case of commercial operators. Assuming that customers have choices between different products, which is nearly always the case in travel and tourism markets, it is easy to see that producers have a

strong motivation to *influence* prospective customers to choose their products rather than a competitor's.

Management attitudes and the business environment

To get below the surface of promotional activity, which is all the typical customer ever sees of marketing, it is helpful to focus first on the attitudes of managers in producer organizations. The spirit of marketing; its driving force; and the reason that its professionals find the subject enormously stimulating, exciting, and satisfying, lies in the way in which it is carried out in practice. Important though they are, marketing skills and techniques do not explain what marketing is; attitudes do. In a few lines it is impossible to communicate the excitement and energy which surround successful marketing operations. Most managers will recognize the enthusiasm the subject inspires; students will have to take it on trust, though they should be aware that the subject has to be experienced 'live' before it can be fully understood.

Above all other things, marketing reflects a particular set of strongly held attitudes, or sense of commitment on the part of senior managers – not just marketing managers – which are common to all marketing led organizations. Together, the guiding principles which affect the whole of an organization are known as a management orientation or corporate culture and, in the particular case of a *marketing orientation*, there are four key elements, as follows:

1 a positive, innovative, and highly competitive attitude toward the conduct of exchange transactions (in commercial and non-commercial organizations),
2 a continuous recognition that the conduct of an organization's business must revolve around the long-run interests of the customers it serves,

3 an outward looking, responsive attitude to events in the external business environment, within which an organization operates,

4 an understanding of the balance to be achieved between the need to earn profits from existing assets, and the equally important need to adapt an organization to secure future profits.

With these pro-active attitudes integrated as the driving force in a management team, marketing techniques may be implemented with success and vigour, although it is never easy. Without the driving force, the most professional skills are unlikely to succeed because their practitioners will typically lose heart and seek more productive working environments. Management attitudes are partly learned, and partly a response to external circumstances, especially the current balance between the capacity of supply and the volume of demand in the markets which an organization serves. The next section considers some important effects of this changing balance or relationship between supply and demand.

A *marketing orientation* described above, is not the only choice for managers. At the risk of over-simplifying it is possible to comment on two other orientations, which at different times and in different market circumstance, serve managers as the guiding set of principles, or corporate culture, in the conduct of their businesses.

Production orientation

This is a term often used to summarize the attitudes and responses of businesses whose products are typically in strong and rising demand, and profitable. Because demand does not present problems, there is a natural management tendency to focus their main attention on more pressing decisions, such as those concerning production capacity, quality and cost controls, finance for increasing production, and maintaining the efficiency and profitability of operations generally. In the short run, where demand is buoyant and growing, an emphasis on production and financial controls appears both logical and sensible.

Consider the example of a small town with two hotels and one car rental operator. If the town's business community is prosperous and growing, it is likely that the hotels and the car rental operation will be profitable businesses and they are very likely to be production orientated. Such demand conditions are quite commonly found in travel and tourism, even in the late twentieth century. Readers should note that the focus of production orientation is *inward looking* toward operational needs.

Sales orientation

This is a term often used to summarize the attitudes and responses of businesses whose products are not enjoying growth in demand, or for which demand may be declining to levels which reduce profitability. Production is not now the main problem; surplus capacity is. The natural management tendency in these conditions is to shift the focus of attention to securing sales. Increased expenditure on advertising and on sales promotion is a logical response in an attempt to secure a higher level of demand for available production capacity.

In the small-town example, noted above, suppose a third hotel of similar size and quality were built. The occupancy of the existing two would probably suffer an initial fall, and a sales response from their managers would appear to be logical and sensible. Such changes in demand conditions are also frequently met in travel and tourism in the late twentieth century. Readers should note that the focus of sales orientation is still essentially *inward looking* toward the needs of operations and their surplus capacity.

Marketing orientation

This term can now be defined as summarizing the attitudes and responses of businesses which adopt the four key principles noted earlier in this section. Readers should note that the focus of marketing orientation is essentially *outward* looking toward the needs of customers and the effects of a changing business environment on their operations. A marketing orientation is typically a response to business conditions in which there is strong competition and surplus capacity for the available level of demand. In the notional small-town example, suppose there were now five hotels of a similar standard for a current demand which will fill only three of them at profitable levels of room occupancy. In these conditions, an inward looking concern with production and operational efficiency will not make much impact on demand, especially if competitors' products are of a similar standard and price. Similarly, a strong sales drive with its emphasis on increased promotional expenditure will not increase demand significantly if competitors quickly follow suit with matching expenditure, whilst the increased expenditure will erode profitability. Reducing prices to increase demand will not succeed if competitors are able to match the reductions, and profit will again be eroded.

In the competitive business conditions noted above, which are typical of those faced by most operators in the travel and tourism industry, survival and future success lies in rethinking the whole business from the customers' standpoint, in order to secure and sustain an adequate *share* of the available demand. Since customers' needs and market conditions are in a state of constant change, the involvement of managers with marketing also has to be continuous. Identifying, responding, and adapting to market changes ahead of competitors is the essence of a successful marketing approach, and the focus of this book.

Defining marketing

For a student approaching the subject for the first time, it would be highly convenient if there were one standard definition of marketing, with which all authors agree. But, although the subject has been studied and taught in academic courses for over seventy years (Bartels: 1976), it is still evolving and most consider it still as much an art as a science. There are literally dozens of definitions. Crosier, for example, recently reviewed over fifty (see Baker: 1979: p. 5). Fortunately, most of these definitions are individual variations within a broad consensus that the marketing concept is consumer and profit orientated. Consumer orientation does not mean giving customers what they want, but understanding consumers' needs and wants in order to respond more efficiently in ways which make business sense for organizations, both in the short term of six months to a year, and in the long term of several years.

Kotler, the author familiar to most marketing students on both sides of the Atlantic, defines the marketing concept as follows:

> The marketing concept holds that the key to achieving organizational goals consists in determining the needs and wants of target markets and delivering the desired satisfactions more effectively and efficiently than competitors (Kotler: 1984: p. 22).

The British Institute of Marketing defines marketing as:

> The management process responsible for identifying, anticipating and satisfying customer requirements profitably (Thomas: 1986: p. 81).

Both of these definitions hold good for any form of consumer or industrial product marketing, whether of goods, such as soap powders or pianos; or services, such as hotel rooms, theme parks or airline travel. The Kotler definition is equally relevant to the marketing of people, ideas and places, and to any exchange process where target markets and organizational goals exist. It also covers the products of non-profit organizations such as trusts responsible for museums, or charities established to provide particular products on a subsidized basis, such as holidays for the disabled or elderly.

Whilst this book is about marketing in travel and tourism, readers must appreciate that tourism marketing is not a separate discipline but an adaptation of basic principles, which have been developed and practised across a wide spectrum of consumer products for more than three decades.

Both definitions noted above provide a basis for developing five important propositions which are entirely relevant to travel and tourism marketing, but which are not derived from it.

Five marketing propositions

Marketing:

1   is a management orientation or philosophy,
2   comprises three main elements linked within a system,
3   is concerned with long-term (strategy) and short-term (tactics),
4   is especially relevant to late twentieth century market conditions,
5   facilitates the efficient conduct of business.

The first proposition (management orientation) was discussed earlier; each of the other four is developed below.

Three main elements linked within a marketing system

It is implicit in Kotler's view above and all other definitions, that marketing comprises the following elements:

1   The attitudes and decisions of consumers (target markets) concerning the perceived utility and value of available goods and services, according to their needs and wants and ability to pay.

2   The attitudes and decisions of producers concerning their production of goods and services for sale, in the context of their business environment and long-term objectives.
3   the ways in which producers distribute or provide access to their products and communicate with consumers, before, during, and after the point of sale.

In other words, the key elements in any marketing system are the attitudes and thought processes of the two parties – buyers and sellers – involved in any exchange process or market transaction.

It should be noted that there exists no natural or automatic harmony between what consumers want and will pay for, and what producers are able or willing to provide. In practice, there is usually continuing tension between a producer's need for profit and the customer's search for value and satisfaction. Marketing managers will typically have to use judgement in balancing between the conflicting needs of the parties in the exchange process, and to do so with imprecise knowledge about their customers and about the decisions of other producers marketing competitive products. Their judgement is most easily seen in the third element of the system, distribution and communication, on which the bulk of marketing expenditure is spent.

The better the balance between the interests of the two parties in the exchange process, the smaller the marketing expenditure will need to be as a proportion of sales revenue, and vice versa. For example, if a tour operator has accurately designed, priced, and judged the capacity of his programme, sales will be achieved at a relatively low promotional cost. If, for whatever reason, the price is too high or the capacity excessive for the available demand, only massive promotional expenditure and discounting will bring supply and demand back into balance. (Chapter 24 develops this point in more detail.)

In short = 1) attitudes + decisions of managers
2) " " of customers
3) way in which 2 parties communicate

The marketing system for service products

The three elements in the marketing system are shown in more detail in Figure 2.1. This is an important diagram, which in addition to introducing all the main processes or stages involved in any form of marketing, also serves as a framework for the contents of this book.

In the diagram, the logical flow and linkages between the main processes are shown within an integrated system relevant to all forms of service products. The process begins with a detailed analysis of the external business environment, and works through marketing and campaign planning to produce business strategies and operational plans, which identify the marketing activities to be undertaken. The research and planning stages of the process incorporate all that an organization knows about its customers and potential customers, their attitudes and buying behaviour. Business strategies express an organization's attitudes and decisions over a specified time period. As the stages proceed, plans are turned into costed action programmes, which express how an organization will communicate with its potential customers. The marketing process ends with further research into customers' feelings about the satisfaction and value for money they received from the purchases they made.

To simplify the explanation, the marketing system is shown in Figure 2.1 as a series of logical steps with an obvious beginning and an end. In practice, as explained in subsequent chapters, the steps do not proceed in a straight line; they comprise a continuous cycle, or rolling programme of decisions, actions and research, which incorporate many feedback loops and are under constant management review.

Because this book is concerned with services rather than goods, production capacity is shown as being held within an inventory/reservation system. For an airline this would be a computerized reservations system for seats on flights, for an hotel a reservation system for beds, and so on. For manufacturers of physical goods, all the main stages in the marketing system are essentially the same, but transport, warehousing, and related physical distribution systems would be the relevant considerations for inventory.

The summary of the marketing system below is intended to be read with Figure 2.1 and it notes the main chapters in which each of the stages is explained and discussed in detail.

Process	Description	Main chapter reference
Marketing research and analysis	Continuous, detailed appreciation of the historic and projected trends in the external business environment; includes consumer research and evaluation of previous marketing expenditure and results	4, 5 and 11
Business strategy and marketing planning	Developing the research and analysis into overall business and marketing strategies and operational plans; includes product and capacity plans	12 and 13
Campaign planning and budgeting	Producing costed operational programmes to integrate the four main marketing mix elements of products, prices, promotion and distribution	6 and 14
Action programmes	Detailed programmes of weekly and monthly activity for all forms of promotion and distribution	15 to 18
Evaluation and marketing research	Monitoring and evaluating the results of completed marketing activity; includes customer research. Feeds data into the next cycle of the marketing process	11 and 14

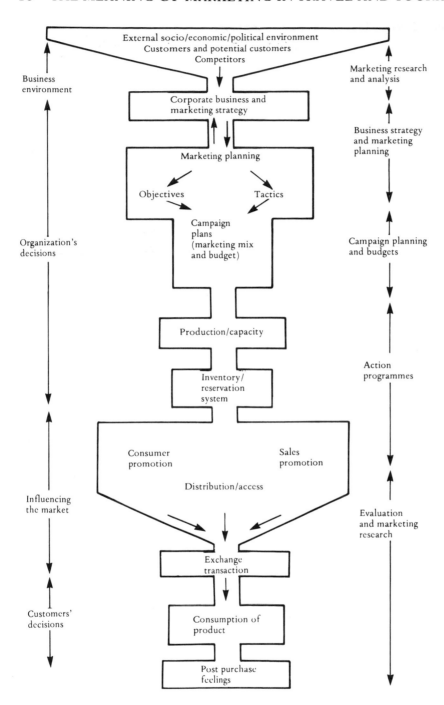

Figure 2.1 *The marketing system for service products.*

Concerned with long term and short term (strategy and tactics)

The meaning of strategy and tactics are discussed in Chapters 12 and 13, but in understanding marketing orientation it is always important to distinguish the time scale within which marketing decisions are taken. The short term (or short run) may be defined as the period of time in which an organization is able to make only marginal alterations to its product specifications and published price ranges. In other words, in the short run, an organization has no choice but to offer its goods or services for sale within the limits of a set of constraints, which were established, in part at least, by its own earlier decision process. In the long run, according to its view of future markets and customers' requirements, an organization may decide to alter product specifications, introduce new products or phase out old ones, alter its pricing strategy, or change its position within a market.

In the short run, organizations frequently find themselves unable to adapt their products quickly to changes in customers' needs. In order to survive, they have to stimulate the available demand through all the techniques of sales promotion, merchandising and advertising they can command. For example, if a rival airline gains permission to operate a scheduled route and reduces its competitors' seat occupancy (load factor) from, say, 64 to 54 per cent in the first six months of a new service, the immediate task for the competitor's marketing is to regain share and volume through aggressive sales tactics. What always distinguishes the marketing-led organization, is not the objectives of its short-term tactics, but the speed and the way in which it uses and exploits its deep knowledge of customers to achieve its objects, while at the same time developing strategies aimed at long-run con-

sumer orientation and satisfaction. Readers should note that most marketing definitions, (including the Kotler version quoted in this chapter) are relevant primarily to the long run, while most marketing practice takes place in the tactical context of the short run. The constraints imposed by marketing highly 'perishable' service products with a fixed capacity on any one day, make short-run marketing decisions especially important in travel and tourism, a point which is explained in the next chapter.

It is not possible to set a precise time scale for either short or long run, because it varies from product to product. Suffice it to say that the short run typically means six months to a year ahead, and the focus of decisions is on this year's and next year's marketing campaign. The long run typically means not less than three years ahead, and the focus of decisions is on marketing strategy.

In the ideal world of textbooks, products are mostly designed to meet customers' needs, and they generate satisfaction and profit. In the real world of travel and tourism marketing, products are mostly less than ideal in one or more respects and marketing managers have to live with the results of decisions, which looked right when they were made some months or years previously, but which have since been overtaken by unpredicted (and often unpredictable) events. Marketing performs a vital compensating function for the gaps and mis-matches between demand and supply, which occur inevitably when markets do not move in the ways predicted by managers.

Especially relevant to late twentieth century conditions

There is really nothing new in a marketing concept based simply on recognizing the need to satisfy customers, understand market trends, and exploit demand efficiently. As they are defined in many marketing textbooks, the essential characteristics of marketing have been practised by small businesses throughout history. No one survives long, especially in small service businesses, unless they understand their customers' needs, and provide satisfactory service at competitive prices. What distinguishes markets in the late twentieth century from those in any previous era, is a combination of:

1 Large, growing, highly competitive businesses with standardized products and relatively large shares of the markets they serve.
2 Capacity of supply considerably in excess of what markets can absorb naturally (without stimulation).
3 Large numbers of consumers in countries with highly developed economies, who have sufficient disposable income and leisure time to indulge in non essential purchases; many of them choosing to engage in frequent travel for leisure purposes.

These circumstances are obviously not unique to travel and tourism, but they are highly relevant to what is happening in marketing in the industry in the last part of the twentieth century. Large service organizations on both sides of the Atlantic and in other parts of the world, are increasingly able through their marketing decisions, to influence customers' expectations of products and prices on the one hand, and lead the way in the development of marketing skills on the other. In this they are aided by modern information technology, which has greatly facilitated the speed and efficiency with which it is possible to manage and control large, multi-site operations. Amongst hotels, fast food restaurants, airlines, other transport operators, retail travel agencies, and tour operators, the conduct of operations in many different locations spread over a wide geographical area is already common. In each of these sectors a greater share of operations is becoming concentrated into fewer large-scale organizations. Many of them are major national and international corporations.

This process has already produced giant organizations such as Holiday Inns, Trusthouse Forte, Hyatt, Quality Inns, or Sheraton in the hotel sector; United, Eastern, Japan Air Lines and British Airways in the airline sector; Hertz, Avis and Budget in car rental; and McDonald's, Burger King, Wimpy and Little Chef in fast food catering. These, of course, are only a few of the better-known major corporations competing for shares of travel and tourism markets, and students may find it a worthwhile exercise to expand this list around the industry sectors shown in Figure 1.1 in Chapter 1.

The emergence of large organizations in manufacturing industries has been well quantified in recent years in the USA, Britain and in Continental Europe. The economic arguments of economies of scale, and the search for lower unit costs of production through the operation of larger capacity machines and equipment, are also well covered (see, for example, Pickering: 1974). Less well analysed for the travel and tourism industry, the trends to larger scale appear to be in the same direction, for the same main reasons.

Without in any way denying the importance and future role in marketing of the many thousand small businesses, which still account for the largest part of travel and tourism supply in most countries, the recent emergence and growth of large organizations justifies the view that their marketing practices will be increasingly influential. They will tend to dominate customer expectations, product design, prices, and marketing techniques in all sectors of travel and tourism markets. The emergence of these corporations and their plans for expansion, has greatly added to the excess production capacity available and, therefore, to the pressures of competition. As Baker puts it for industry as a whole, '... in the modern advanced industrial economy we have arrived at the point where the basic capacity to produce exceeds the basic propensity to consume' (Baker: 1979: p. 379). The same point, based on the capacity implications of technological innovation and slower growth in more mature markets, is highly relevant to travel and tourism in many countries now, and will be more so by the end of the century.

This author believes, and the view is reflected throughout this book, that the nature of modern international competition, and the continuous need to fill thousands of under-utilized beds, seats and other supply components, provides the most powerful motivating force now forcing the pace of modern marketing in the travel and tourism industry. There is no equivalent phenomenon on this scale in any previous period of history; it is the driving force which explains the current and future importance of marketing orientation and the need for improved marketing techniques.

Facilitates the efficient conduct of business

It has been stressed already that a marketing orientation is effectively forced upon businesses in competitive markets as a necessary method of survival. It is less clear from the definitions of marketing exactly how this orientation leads to the more efficient conduct of a business. The reasons lie in the ways in which the processes outlined in Figure 2.1 are planned and co-ordinated. It is not the processes themselves which are characteristic of marketing led organizations, but the way in which they are integrated and managed within an overall management orientation, around long-run customer needs. All commercial organizations plan, promote and distribute products. Marketing orientated businesses are characterized by the systematic organization of their planning processes, the speed at which they act in relation to com-

petitors, and their knowledge of the effects of their actions on their customers.

Throughout the book it is stressed that cost effective marketing is always based upon systematic planning and the specification of precise objectives and action programmes, which can be closely monitored and evaluated. Precise marketing objectives also serve in practice as an integrating mechanism for all the operational departments in a business, and as a control system for measuring actual performance against planned targets. Tactical objectives may be evaluated against strategic marketing objectives and, if the organization is large enough, subsidiary objectives may be set for the profit performance of particular products or subdivisions of a business, providing further ways to check on operational and marketing efficiency.

Chapter summary

This chapter defines the meaning of modern marketing, first as a management orientation, sometimes referred to as a management philosophy, and secondly as a systematic process comprising the techniques used by marketing managers to influence demand. To be effective in practice the orientation and the techniques must be integrated and co-ordinated within the overall management team. Whilst the practice of marketing is most easily understood in commercial operations, the orientation and the techniques may be applied in non-profit-making sectors also.

A marketing orientation is defined in contrast to other orientations based on production or sales, both of which tend to be inward looking and responsive to the needs of an organization and its operational requirements, rather than outward looking and pro-active to the changing business environment, and the needs, expectations and behaviour of customers. In distinguishing conceptually between production, sales, and marketing orientations, the differences appear quite clear. In practice no such clarity exists and evidence of all three types of management orientation may be encountered within parts of the same organization at the same time.

Students of travel and tourism are reminded that the marketing approach to business is a response to business conditions, especially competition, and that such conditions are increasingly common to all producers of consumer goods and services in the latter part of the twentieth century. The particular conditions of severe competition between large scale multi-site organizations, often with a considerable surplus of capacity of highly perishable products and seeking to influence available demand, are those which are now found frequently in travel and tourism markets in many parts of the world. The chapter stresses the role of these larger organizations because of their influence over modern markets, but the importance of small businesses is not ignored. Competition between large organizations seems certain to leave many gaps and niches, which are too small to be profitable for big firms with their standardized operations but can be highly profitable for smaller ones practising the same marketing orientation and techniques without competing head-on in large volume markets.

Figure 2.1 provides a step by step diagram of the modern marketing process, which also serves as a framework for the contents of the book. The diagram is one of the most important in the book and should repay careful consideration. It is applicable to all types of organization in the travel and tourism industry.

Above all, this chapter stresses that marketing is a responsive approach to business, conducted at best in a marvellously stimulating and positive spirit of competitive enthusiasm which no textbook can convey. There are three elements within it, the attitudes and decisions of managers, the attitudes and decisions of customers and the way in which the two parties communicate. Marketing focuses on exchange transactions and product sales, which yield satisfaction and value for money to one party, and a profitable long-run return on assets employed to the other.

Further reading

Because Baker in Britain, and Kotler in the USA and Britain, are commonly used marketing textbooks, these two authors are recommended for the chapters in this book which deal with basic marketing principles. Chapter 2 recommended reading is:

Baker, M. J., *Marketing: An Introductory Text*, Macmillan, 1985, Chapters 1 and 2.
Kotler, P., *Marketing Management: Analysis, Planning and Control*, Prentice-Hall, 1984, Chapter 1.

3

Special characteristics of travel and tourism to which marketing responds: Managing demand

Drawing on the contributions of widely recognized authors, Chapters 1 and 2 introduced the essential concepts of travel and tourism as a market, and of marketing as an approach to the conduct of modern business. This chapter focuses on the special characteristics of supply in travel and tourism, in response to which modern marketing is increasingly being adopted throughout the industry. Organizations in travel and tourism are a part of the services sector of an economy, as distinguished from manufacturing, construction, and primary sectors, by economists internationally. Understanding the special characteristics of travel and tourism services, which are common to all the sectors noted in Chapter 1, helps to explain the way in which marketing decisions are made in the industry and they merit very careful consideration. Travel and tourism operations are by no means unique in marketing terms but they do present a series of structural considerations, which combined, determine marketing responses.

This chapter begins by drawing some vital distinctions between the marketing of goods, on which much of the theory of marketing has been traditionally based, and the marketing of services. It notes the growth and importance of large scale service operations in travel and tour-

ism and identifies the general characteristics common to most forms of services marketing before proceeding to identify the particular characteristics distinguishing travel and tourism services. The response of marketing managers to these characteristics and the implications for demand management are noted, and the chapter ends by stating the basic differences between marketing as a set of principles relevant to all forms of exchange transactions, marketing for services generally, and marketing for travel and tourism in particular.

Marketing goods and services

The origins of marketing theory are generally attributed to the USA in the first part of the twentieth century (Bartels: 1976). The early contributions to the study recognized the growing importance of sales and distribution functions for manufacturers of consumer goods, reflecting opportunities provided by rapid improvements in transport and communication systems, and the consequent growth in the size of markets which businesses could reach with their products. For over fifty years the emerging theories focused almost exclusively on the marketing of physical goods; especially on the marketing of items manufactured on a mass production basis for consumption by the general public.

Until quite recently service industries generally were largely ignored on both sides of the Atlantic, or discussed in crude simplifications which lumped together as one broad category, personal services such as domestic cleaning and hairdressing; commercial services such as banking, transportation, restaurants and tour operation; professional services such as medical and legal services; and public services such as education and health care. Yet in countries with highly developed economies, the proportion of the working population employed in all forms of services has been rising rapidly in the last half of the twentieth century, to current levels of half or more of all employment in many areas. Employment in the service sector, is more than twice that in the manufacturing sector in the USA (Lovelock: 1984: p. xiii), and similar proportions now exist in most Northern European countries.

It was the rapid growth in the 1960s and 1970s of large-scale commercial service operations, such as banking, insurance, and retail distribution, as well as transportation, accommodation and catering, which prompted the recent shift of emphasis in marketing studies towards services. The first American Marketing Association Conference devoted specifically to service industries took place as recently as 1981, and there has been a massive volume of articles and books on services marketing since the late 1970s. Whilst it is beyond the scope of this book to trace and analyse the growth of service industries, the causes are mainly economic and related to increasing levels of consumers' disposable income, the development of rapid communications within and between countries, the growth of telecommunications, and the emergence of computerized systems for management information and control purposes. Most importantly, associated with improved communications and control processes, the recognition of economies of scale in service operations has triggered much of the recent growth, and such economies are especially important in marketing. Developments in franchising and management contracts for services have also facilitated the speed of growth in large commercial organizations in service industries, both nationally and internationally.

Large-scale service operations

It is not easy to define the point at which a service producer becomes a large-scale operator; it tends to vary in different sectors of industry according to the nature of their operations. Large-scale operations in all parts of the world, however, typically display the following common characteristics, all of which have important implications for marketing in travel and tourism:

1 marketed as standardized, repeatable, quality controlled products,
2 typically branded with the producer's name and bearing standard prices (with variations by place and time),
3 available at many places (multiple outlets),
4 continuously produced and available, mostly on a daily basis, throughout the year,
5 mostly marketed by head offices which control and direct the activities at individual outlets.

These characteristics are common to most supermarket chains, fast food chains, post offices, banks, car rental and hotel corporations; they are not restricted to travel and tourism services.

Given the characteristics noted above, it should be appreciated that there are some strong similiarities between the operating needs of large scale service organizations, and manufacturers of goods produced on a continuous mass production basis. Levitt, for example, pushed this similarity to its logical conclusion in discussing the need to 'industrialize service production systems'. He suggested that this could be achieved by reducing the level of discretion available to service staff through the use of standardized procedures, and the use of what he calls 'hard', 'soft' and 'intermediate technologies' (Levitt: 1981: p. 37). Levitt cites McDonald's Corporation as an excellent illustration of the successful blending of industrial processes in food production, distribution, and quality control over every aspect of standardized operations, including the performance of the staff who provide service in the restaurants. The whole thrust of McDonald's international operations are firmly market orientated as described in the previous chapter. Most airlines, hotel groups, tour operators, retail travel agency chains, and the larger tourist attractions, are striving currently to organize, control and deliver their continuous production capacity in equivalent ways, for the same reasons.

Recent developments in modern service industries, noted above, explain why the concept of services marketing set out in this book is primarily orientated around the marketing of large scale, widely distributed, standardized products. It has to be stressed that production on a large scale does not necessarily imply the mass production of undifferentiated products for all markets. All the complexities of market segmentation and product differentiation are as relevant to service producers as they are to manufacturers of physical goods; there is also ample room for market niches to be filled by the many small entrepreneurial businesses, which are important in travel and tourism in all tourist destination countries.

From an operational efficiency standpoint, the essential requirement of continuous production on a large scale lies in effective product design and quality control of operations. But, once the technical problems of production have been solved, the ability to sustain production at efficient levels of utilization of premises and equipment, forces management attention on the systematic promotion of continuous consumption. In other words, ensuring that there is balance between the volume of demand and the volume of supply. If sufficient demand cannot be generated, massive financial losses are inevitable. Recent examples are the losses sustained internationally by airlines in the years 1979–1982, and by American car manufacturers over the same period. The larger the operator, the more important it is to secure and sustain a regular flow of customers to purchase the available capacity. This explains much of the modern focus on the role of marketing by these larger organizations.

It is interesting to speculate that the *size* of business operations is, in fact, more important in determing marketing responses, than the nature of goods or services. As this author put it some years ago:

It is a reality of large-scale continuous production of many service products, which provides the essential like with like comparison with manufactured products. Of course, this characteristic has little if anything to do with lawyers, undertakers, cobblers or beauticians. But then neither has it any relevance to basket weavers, jobbing potters, saddle makers or gunsmiths. A dentist and a street corner shoe shiner have more in common (in marketing terms) with each other and with bakers and candlestick makers, than any of them have in common with mass produced goods or services (Middleton: 1983).

Services and their characteristics

The essential difference between goods and services, as noted by Rathmell in one of the earlier contributions to the subject, is that 'Goods are produced. Services are performed' (Rathmell: 1974). Goods are products purchased through an exchange transaction conferring ownership of a physical item, which may be used or consumed at the owner's choice of time and place. Services are products purchased through an exchange transaction that does not confer ownership but permits access to and use of a service at a specified time in a specified place. Thus, for example, the buyer of a ready-to-wear suit takes it from the store and wears it when and where he pleases. The producer need have no further involvement unless the article is faulty. The buyer of a hotel room agrees to arrive alone or with a specified group, on a particular night or nights, and may forfeit a deposit if he fails to appear. Throughout his stay the traveller is closely involved with the hotel and its staff, and may participate directly in aspects of the service product by carrying his own bags, serving himself from a restaurant buffet, making his own tea, and in other ways.

The manufacturer or retailer of suits can put his products into warehouses and shops, and it may not be a vital concern if six months or more elapse between the completion of production and sale to the customer. But an hotel can perform its services once only on, say, the 31st January, and if customers are not available on that day, products are lost and cannot be resold the following day.

From this short introduction the principal characteristics of service products may be summarized as:

inseparability, and
perishability.

From these two flow most of the distinguishing differences between goods and services, which influence marketing.

Inseparability

This means that the act of production and consumption must be simultaneous. The performance of the service requires the active participation of the producer and the consumer *together*. In the context of this book it also means that production and consumption takes place on the premises, or in the equipment (such as aircraft or hire cars) of the purchaser, and not in the consumer's home environment.

It means too that most services production or operations staff have some consumer contact and are seen by the customer to be an inseparable aspect of the service product. Factory workers, managers and distributors, typically do not meet customers; their attitudes, and the way they look and behave in the factory, are not necessarily relevant to product performance and customer satisfaction. Physical items can be tested and guaranteed and precise product performance can be enforced by consumer protection laws. For services, a wide range of product performance is determined by employees' attitudes and behaviour, for which there can be none of the normal guarantees and no prospect of legal enforcement.

Inseparability of production and consumption is thus a vital concept in marketing services, but it does not mean that consumption and purchase cannot be separated. A primary aim of services marketing is to create ways to distance the act of purchase from product performance. An hotel or an airline, for example, which has only 20 per cent of its capacity booked twelve hours before the scheduled performance of its particular service, becomes highly dependent upon passing traffic for last-minute purchases. The same hotel or airline, if it is 85 per cent pre-booked three months before the specified date of service production, is clearly in a much stronger position.

Perishability

It is convenient to treat perishability as a separate characteristic of services, although it follows from the fact of inseparability that service production is typically *fixed in time and space*. This means that if service capacity or products are not sold on a particular day, the potential revenue they represent is lost and cannot be recovered. Services production, therefore, is better understood as a *capacity to produce*; not a quantity of products. Capacity can be utilized only when customers are present on the producers' premises.

To illustrate the point, consider the example of a museum, which has an effective visitor capacity (assessed as space in which to move in comfort around the exhibits) of, say, 500 visits per hour. This could mean 2,000 visits on a typical busy day, when open from 10 a.m. to 6 p.m., making allowance for peak and slack times of the day. If the museum closes one day per week it has a nominal 'production' capacity of 313 (days) × 2,000 visitors = 626,000 visits over twelve months. In practice such a museum is unlikely to exceed around 150,000 visits per annum and, on say ten days, it may be overcrowded with 3,000 visits per day, while on 100 days in the winter it may never exceed 200 per day. If 10,000 visitors want to visit the museum on a particular day, they cannot do so because the display space cannot be expanded, and the inevitable queues would simply cause most prospective visitors to go elsewhere. A Sunday visitor is unlikely to be impressed by the fact that he could visit on Monday if he is going to be back at work on that day.

Hotels with a fixed number of rooms, or transport operators with a fixed number of seats, face identical problems of matching available demand to perishable supply, although they can calculate their available capacity with much more precision than museums or other visitor attractions. Perishability is linked in the case of travel and tourism services with seasonality, which is discussed later in this chapter.

No possibility of creating and holding stocks

It follows from the characteristics of inseparability and perishability that it is not possible for a services producer to create a stock of products, which can be used to satisfy daily fluctuations in demand. By contrast, manufacturers of Christmas goods, for example, are able to manufacture their products around the year and create stocks, most of which are sold to customers in December. The process of stock creation and physical distribution between factories, warehouses and retailers is expensive, but it does create a relative stability and continuity in the production process, which is not available to service producers.

Perishability and the impossibility of stock holding does not mean that inventory systems for services cannot be created, or that distribution processes are not a vital concern for services producers. On the contrary, one of the most interesting developments of the 1970s in services marketing was the refinement of systems making it possible to retain details of each year's production capacity in a computerized inventory, and then to treat the inventory in exactly the same ways that physical stocks are treated by producers of physical goods. Thus, an hotel may keep an inventory of its production capacity for conferences for two or more years ahead of the actual performance of services, and market that capacity through contracts to deliver products at specified times.

Two other characteristics are sometimes said to distinguish products based on services from those based on physical goods; one is *heterogeneity* and the other is *intangibility* (see, for example, Stanton: 1981). Taken literally, heterogeneity means that every service performance is unique to each customer and service producer. Strictly, because human beings are not machines, this is true. But in practice it is a totally academic concept and it is absurd to apply it to frequently used service products such as those marketed by banks, transport operators, fast food chains, and all other large-scale service operators, all of whom are committed to standardization and quality control of service performance.

Intangibility is an important characteristic of service products in the sense that most services cannot easily be measured, touched or evaluated at the point of sale prior to performance; it means, in other words, that many service products are 'ideas' in the minds of prospective buyers. But many physical goods, such as motor cars, perfumes or expensive leisure wear, are also 'ideas' in customer's minds at the point of sale, even though they can be inspected and guaranteed. On the other hand, bus services, fast food restaurants and even hotels, are hardly less tangible to those who use them regularly, than are cigarettes or washing powder. Accordingly, although the intangibility of travel and tourism products requires careful understanding by marketing managers, and a particular response in the promotion and distribution of products, it is not a generic difference between goods from services of the same order as inseparability and perishability.

Figure 3.1 summarizes the main generic characteristics which distinguish most goods from most services.

Particular characteristics of travel and tourism services

Associated with the basic or generic character-istics common to all services, there are at least three further features, which are particularly relevant to travel and tourism services. These are seasonality, the interdependence of tourism products, and the high fixed costs of operations.

Seasonality and demand fluctuations

It is a characteristic of most tourism markets that demand fluctuates greatly between seasons of the year. Residents of Northern Europe and the Northern States of the USA tend mostly to take their main holidays of the year in the summer months of June to September because the winter months of December to March are generally cold and wet, and hours of daylight are short. Whilst such climatic variations are not so relevant to many Mediterranean, Middle Eastern, Pacific or Caribbean tourism destinations, their main markets are still accustomed to think of summer and winter months, whilst schools and many business year cycles reinforce such traditions. As a result, many tourism businesses fluctuate from peaks of 90 to 100 per cent capacity utilization for sixteen weeks in a year, to troughs of 30 per cent or less for twenty weeks in the year.

On a weekly basis, city centre restaurants may

Goods	*Services*
Are manufactured	Are performed
Made in premises not open to customers (separable)	Performed on the producers' premises with customer participation (inseparable)
Goods are delivered to places where customers live	Customers move to places where services are delivered
Purchase means right of ownership to use at will	Purchase confers temporary right to use at a fixed time and place
Goods possess tangible form at the point of sale; can be inspected	Services are intangible form at the point of sale; often cannot be inspected
Can be stocked, physically	Perishable, cannot be stocked physically
Note: These characteristics are those which apply generally to most services and most goods	

Figure 3.1 *Generic characteristics distinguishing services from goods*

fluctuate from 80 per cent occupancy on Thursdays to 20 per cent (if they open) at weekends. On a daily basis, seats on a scheduled airflight may be 95 per cent full at 0800 hours, whilst seats on the following flight at 1000 hours may be only 45 per cent occupied. These demand variations are all the more acute because of the fact of perishability discussed previously and it is always a major preoccupation of marketing managers to generate as much demand in the troughs as market conditions permit.

Interdependence of tourism products

Most tourists combine in their travel purchase decisions, not one service or product, but several. A vacationer chooses attractions at a destination together with the products of accommodation, transport and other facilities such as catering. The sales of tourist accommodation suppliers at a destination are, therefore, influenced to some extent by marketing decisions made by tour operators and travel agents, attractions, transport interests and tourist boards, which together or separately promote the destination and its activities and facilities.

Over time, there is a relationship underlying the capacity of different travel and tourism products at a destination, and a potential synergy to be achieved in their marketing decisions, if the different suppliers can find ways to combine their respective efforts. There will often be opportunities for joint marketing of the types discussed in Part Five of this book.

Interdependence can best be understood when a new resort, for example a ski resort, is being planned. The basic capacity estimate is the number of skiers per peak hour who can be accommodated comfortably on the slopes. With an estimate of skiers and non skiers, and of day and staying visitors, it is possible to determine the optimum capacity of ski lifts, the number of beds needed, and the required restaurant facilities, car parks and so on. Each visitor

element in the resort is a component related to other components and, even if they are separately owned, their fortunes are certainly linked. This vital interdependence was designated 'complementarity' by Krippendorf (1971).

High fixed costs of service operations

When the profit and loss accounts of most businesses in the travel and tourism industry are analysed, it is generally the case that they reveal relatively high fixed costs of operating available capacity, and relatively low variable costs. This is most easily seen in the case of a visitor attraction, in which the following main costs must be incurred in order to be open to receive visitors:

> premises (capital costs and annual maintenance costs),
> equipment (including repairs and renewals),
> rents and rates,
> heating, lighting and other energy costs,
> insurances,
> wages and salaries of permanent employees,
> management overheads and administrative costs.

The point to note is that these costs, mostly committed over a twelve-month period, have to be met whether the attraction draws in fifty visitors, five hundred or five thousand on any day. Whilst there is a significant element of variable cost involved in operating catering and shops, and in the numbers of part-time staff employed, the variable cost of admitting one additional visitor is virtually nil. The same basic fact of operations is true for room sales in hotels, seats in transport operations, and all forms of visitor entertainments.

To illustrate the same point with a transport example, whether an airline operates a particular flight with 20 per cent or 80 per cent of seats occupied, its aircraft maintenance costs are the same, its airport dues are the same, it pays the same wages to cabin and flight deck staff and to its airport and other personnel, and its fuel charges vary only marginally. In other words, to perform the service at all involves a high level of fixed cost regardless of how many passengers are carried. Although operating costs are mainly fixed regardless of seat occupancy, the revenue side varies dramatically. For a seat price of say £100 (average), sales of forty seats produces a basic gross revenue contribution of £4,000. If 200 seats are sold, contribution is £20,000. If the fixed costs of operating the flight are £10,000, then forty occupied seats produces a loss of £6,000 and 200 occupied seats produces a surplus of £10,000.

The facts of high fixed costs of operation force all service operators' attention on the need to generate extra demand, especially the additional, or marginal sales, a very high proportion of which represents revenue gain with little or no extra cost. Kotas, for example, has argued the connection between the high fixed cost structure of hotel and restaurant businesses and their need to be market- rather than cost-orientated (Kotas: 1975: p. 18.). The same point is even more important in some of the other sectors of the travel and tourism industry.

The marketing response to the characteristics of supply

In reviewing the distinctive characteristics of services operations generally and of travel and tourism in particular, this chapter has focused on six very important structural aspects of supply, summarized below. These aspects strongly influence the attitudes and decisions of management in all sectors of the travel and tourism industry as they seek to respond to, and influence, prospective customers' demand for their products – the marketing response. Further reference to these structural influences will be found in all parts of this book, especially in Part

Five, which considers the application of marketing in each main sector of the industry:

inseparability	seasonality
perishability	high fixed costs
interdependence	fixed in time and place

This chapter also stresses that these characteristics are found in an industry, in which the supply of standardized products by large-scale organizations is taking an increasing share of total demand, and increasingly dominating customer expectations of products, prices and satisfactions. The larger an organization is, the more vulnerable it is to any shortfalls in demand, and the more emphasis it puts on ways to influence its customers; in other words, on marketing.

Simply put, the marketing response to the six characteristics is to manage or manipulate demand. The more an organization knows about its customers and prospective customers – their needs and desires, their attitudes and behaviour – the better it will be able to design and implement the marketing efforts required to stimulate their purchasing habits. This calculated response has strategic, long-run implications, and tactical aspects related to the short term.

To understand the enormous continuous pressure which the six characteristics impose on operators in all sectors of travel and tourism, students in particular will find it helpful to consider operations in terms of daily capacity. To illustrate this point, if the task is to organize marketing for a hotel, of say, 150 rooms, the first step is to express its total capacity over the year. Thus, 150 rooms × 365 days × 2 (average beds per room) × say, 65 per cent (target bed occupancy average over a year) = 71.175 bed-nights to be sold. The marketing task is to break up that total into the estimated number of bookings to be achieved per days of each week, and by the different groups of customers which the hotel services; for example, customers for business and leisure.

If the task is to market an airline, one jumbo jet represents, say, 450 seats × 350 days (in operation allowing for routine servicing) × 3.4 (average seat utilization per 24 hour period, assuming optimum number of hours in the air) × 70 per cent (target seat occupancy average over a year) = 374,850 seats to be sold. The marketing task is to break up that total by the estimated number of bookings to be achieved on a daily basis, and by the different groups which the airline serves; for example, first class, club class, and economy class passengers.

It cannot be stressed too often that the role of marketing in the travel and tourism industry in response to the six factors noted in this section is:

to manage or manipulate sales, (customer purchasing behaviour) on an orderly, continuous, daily or weekly basis,

(a) to utilize the regular daily flow of available, inseparable capacity,
(b) to generate the extra or marginal sales, which generate revenue at very little extra cost.

The better the product is designed to meet customers' needs and expectations, the easier the overall task will be. The better the knowledge of customers, the more effectively the demand management task can be carried out.

How does marketing in travel and tourism differ from other forms of marketing?

Students of travel and tourism often find it difficult to appreciate clearly the way in which the marketing of travel and tourism differs from other forms of consumer marketing practice. Standard texts on marketing principles are not much help in this problem. Generally speaking, however, it appears to be common ground that the *principles* of the body of knowledge about marketing, and its main theoretical elements, can

be applied in all industries and in commercial and non-profit sectors of an economy. Differences occur in the *application* of the theory.

To the extent that there is an internationally recognized theory of marketing, its principles should hold good for all types of product. In other words, the basic or core principles of marketing must be relevant to all products, whether they are based on services or manufactured goods. Marketing managers at senior levels of responsibility can, and frequently do, switch between industries with little difficulty, and this is only possible because of the integrity of the body of knowledge. In travel and tourism in particular, many marketing managers have been 'imported' from manufacturing industries to bring their expertise to bear as firms grow faster than the level of expertise available from within their own organizations.

Against this evidence of common ground, however, experience convinces many in the industry that there are some characteristics of travel and tourism services, which are so dominant in their implications, that standard marketing principles must be considerably adapted to ensure success in an operational context. If this is true, it is clearly a very important consideration indeed.

This author believes that the body of knowledge about marketing in travel and tourism must be based firmly on five aspects of demand and supply in the industry, each of which has important common characteristics that combine to give marketing practice its particular approach and style. These are:

1 nature of demand (see Chapters 4 and 5),
2 nature of supply (discussed in this chapter),
3 products and prices, which respond to 1 and 2 (see Chapters 8 and 9),
4 characteristics of promotion used to influence demand (see Chapters 15 to 17),
5 characteristics of distribution used to facilitate demand (see Chapters 18 and 19).

Marketing practice, reflecting these five aspects of demand and supply, is discussed throughout Part Five of this book.

On the basis of the characteristics of these five aspects of demand and supply, it is possible to make three propositions about marketing in travel and tourism, which are relevant to all the forms which it takes:

1 In the context of opportunities and constraints arising from the business environment of a major national and international market, products in tourism are designed, adapted and promoted, to meet the long-run needs and expectations of prospective customers. This is the common ground with all forms of consumer marketing, and the cornerstone of all marketing theory.

2 Service products have particular characteristics of inseparability and perishability, which involve a different application of the marketing mix variables. This is the common ground with those who advocate, properly, that marketing of services is different in practice from that of physical goods.

3 The marketing of travel and tourism services is shaped and determined by the nature of the demand, and the operating characteristics of supplying industries. The forms of promotion and distribution used for travel and tourism products also have their own particular characteristics, which distinguish their use in comparison with other industries. These characteristics form the common ground on which marketing for travel and tourism is based.

It is the *combined* effect of these three propositions, which distinguishes marketing in travel and tourism from marketing in other industries. The full meaning of the propositions, and the ways in which they determine and influence marketing decisions at strategic and tactical levels, are the subject matter of this book.

Chapter summary

This chapter explains the characteristics of services production influencing marketing generally, and the importance of modern large-scale service operations. The main characteristics of travel and tourism operations are noted, and the implications for demand management are stressed. While none of the aspects discussed is unique to travel and tourism operations, it is the combined effect of the characteristics which influences marketing in the industry.

Inseparability and perishability are shown to cause inflexibility in the supply of product capacity, which allied to seasonality, make tourism businesses very vulnerable to short-run fluctuations in demand. Marketing managers are, therefore, usually pre-occupied with the need to manage or manipulate short-run demand around the fixed capacity of supply. The chapter notes that the marketing task is easier if long-run strategic decisions have created products which match customer needs, and if marketing managers have detailed knowledge of their customers, with which to undertake short-run demand management efficiently.

The high fixed costs of operating most service businesses are highlighted, and the fact that additional customers can often be accommodated at the margin, at little or no extra cost to the business, underlies many of the short-run marketing methods used in travel and tourism, especially the widespread use of price discounting. All of the characteristics together help to explain why much of travel and tourism is considered to be a high risk business, in which entrepreneurs with a strong intuitive understanding of rapidly changing market-place trends, and a willingness to make the difficult adjustments in capacity faster than competitors, have so often thrived in the industry with spectacular success.

Students of marketing will be aware that the simple distinctions drawn here between goods and services are open to dispute, and there is much evidence that many physical goods require extensive services to support their sales. For the purposes of this book, however, the distinctions summarized in Figure 3.1 should be helpful in clarifying differences which profoundly influence the nature of the marketing responses discussed in Parts Four and Five.

Further reading

Cowell, D., *The Marketing of Services*, Heinemann, 1984, Chapters 1, 2 and 3.

Lovelock, C. H., *Services Marketing: Text, Cases and Readings*, Part 1, Prentice-Hall, 1984.

4

The changing business environment : Aspects of demand for travel and tourism

Chapter 2 identifies the marketing process common to all businesses and explains that a marketing orientation is an outward looking set of management attitudes, sometimes known as a corporate culture. Organized around a detailed knowledge of existing and prospective customers, outward looking means being highly responsive to the general business environment within which any organization operates. Figure 2.1, which represents the systematic marketing process, has at the start of the process an appreciation of the external environment, on which all strategy and subsequent marketing decisions are based.

The external environment of any business contains a number of elements which require careful analysis, some of which are also discussed in Chapter 6. First and foremost among them for any marketing led organization must be a continuous, systematic study of market demand and customer behaviour, normally based on market research. Within an overall recognition that total demand and many of the shifts which occur in market patterns are outside the control of individual commercial operators or tourist boards, it is the business of marketing managers to influence demand to the maximum extent possible and to adapt their products and operations to it. Marketing is, therefore, both

responsive to what it cannot change in the external environment, and pro-active in adapting operations to ever changing circumstances.

Typically, other than in tourist boards and major international organizations, most marketing managers are not concerned directly with measuring the factors which influence *total* market movements. But they are invariably involved with interpreting such movements and deciding how their organizations should respond. Accordingly, the discussion which follows is relevant to all engaged in marketing decisions, regardless of their actual direct involvement in any of the market research processes.

Overall market demand and customer behaviour for travel and tourism reflects two separate dimensions, characterized by Burkart and Medlik as 'determinants and motivations' (Burkart and Medlik: 1981: p. 50). Determinants are the economic, social and political factors at work in any society, which set limits to the volume of a population's demand for travel, whatever individuals' motivations may be. For reasons discussed in this chapter, a country such as India for example, cannot generate the same level of travel demand per capita as the USA, primarily because the average personal income in India is only a fraction of that in America. Within any particular country, economically depressed regions do not generate the same volume of travel as affluent ones, and so on. Motivations are the internal factors at work within individuals, expressed as needs, wants and desires, which lead some people to place a much higher value on leisure travel than others. Motivations are not necessarily related to economic factors and students, for example, may set a much higher priority on international travel than many older, much more affluent people.

This chapter focuses on the main determinants of travel and tourism, which are external to any individual business and beyond their direct control, and the next discusses motivations. The chapter begins by noting that the factors which influence the total demand for travel and tourism are common to all countries and are the same, in general terms, for all supplier organizations. Eight principal factors are identified and discussed separately. A framework is provided in Figure 4.1 which summarizes the factors associated with high and low propensities to engage in travel and tourism. The chapter concludes with a brief note on the implications of the determinants for marketing managers.

The determinants of demand are common to all countries and suppliers

Fortunately for students and others wishing to understand the market demand for travel and tourism, the basic factors which underlie demand and determine what its total potential size will be, are common to all countries. Whilst the demand and the particular patterns generated by the population in each region within any country are unique to the area, the underlying factors are the same. The factors are also relatively easy to measure and the measurement methods used by researchers in all countries are essentially the same.

The same external determinants of market demand affect all individual operators such as hotels, tour operators and airlines, although the responses which marketing managers make will certainly differ according to their understanding of the factors at any time.

Categorizing the main determinants of demand

It is possible to summarize the main determinants of demand for travel and tourism under eight broad headings, as follows:

- Economic
- Demographic
- Geographic
- Socio-cultural
- Comparative prices
- Mobility
- Government/regulatory
- Media communications

All of these are identified as determinants of travel and tourism demand because all are external and beyond the control of individual suppliers, and changes occurring in any of them exert an influence over the size and patterns of travel markets. In the last part of the twentieth century these determinants are changing rapidly, requiring constant study by those whose job it is to understand and anticipate market shifts.

Of course, demand responds also to changes in the supply of products so that supply is an important determinant of demand as well as vice versa. For example, a significant volume of demand for leisure travel from the USA to Australia, or from Britain to Spain, could not have been developed until a supply of products was available based on new technology of transport capable of undertaking the journeys involved at a speed and cost that the market could afford. Such products were the result of commercial decisions taken by suppliers in the light of their appreciation of demand and supply factors; a central aspect of marketing decisions in any field. At the level of the individual operator, making supply or product decisions in relation to changes in demand are a constant theme throughout the book, and for this reason they are not discussed separately in this chapter.

Economic factors

Wherever travel and tourism markets are studied, it is invariably the economic variables in the countries or regions in which prospective tourists live, which are the most important set of factors influencing the total volume of demand generated. In the 1980s, some three-quarters of the world's international tourism arrivals are generated by twenty countries of origin (Edwards: 1985: p. 10). Obviously, it is no accident that these twenty include those with the highest income per capita and often the most rapid economic development, such as the USA, Japan, and West Germany.

Developed and growing economies sustain large numbers of trips away from home for business purposes of all kinds. Business meetings, attendance at conferences and exhibitions, and travel on government business are all important parts of the travel and tourism industry. In Britain in 1984, for example, domestic business and conference tourism accounted for an estimated 25 million trips in 1984, with an expenditure approaching 30 per cent of domestic tourism revenue for all purposes.

The influence of economic variables is more obviously seen in leisure travel where, in many countries with advanced, developed economies, average disposable income per capita has grown over the last two decades to a size large enough to enable two-thirds or more of the total population in any year to take holidays staying away from home. If allowance is made for day visits from home, this proportion rises typically to over 90 per cent of the population in a year.

Using published statistics of tourist trips and of national economic trends, it is possible to trace the relationship over time between changes in real disposable income (measured in constant prices) and the volume of trips and expenditure away from home. For the bulk of the population in countries with developed economies, notwithstanding the world energy crises of the 1970s and early 1980s, steadily rising real incomes over the last two decades have led to a proportionately higher expenditure on travel and tourism. This relationship between incomes and expenditure on travel and tourism is known as the *income elasticity* of *demand*. If, for example, in any measured group in a population there is a greater than 1 per cent increase in expenditure on travel and tourism, in response to a 1 per cent increase in disposable income, the market is known as income elastic. If demand changes less than proportionately to income, the market is known as inelastic. In the travel and tourism industry, the total demand for vacation travel has so far typically proved to be very income elastic, whilst the demand for visits to friends and relatives has been relatively inelastic.

If the other determinants remain unchanged there is a very clear direct relationship between the performance of a country's economy, especially the average disposable income of its population, and the volume of demand which it generates for holidays and leisure trips. For over a quarter of a century it has proved generally to be the case that travel and tourism have been very income elastic, although projections now being made for the rest of the century, indicate that future growth of demand in the main generating countries is more likely to change only in line with disposable income.

One important implication for marketing managers, of the continuing rise in disposable incomes in countries with developed economies, is that the people most likely to engage in travel and tourism are also those most likely to have increased their standards of living as expressed in their home environments. As a consequence, the quality standards of furnishings and fittings in hotels, for example, and other forms of accommodation, have had to improve to keep pace with customers' rising expectations. Sound proofing, adjustable heating and ventilation, bathroom facilities, size of rooms and lighting, are all aspects of product provision influenced by rising levels of relative affluence, to which marketing managers in the travel and tourist industry have to respond with new and modified products.

Demographic factors

The term 'demographic factors' is just a convenient way to identify the main characteristics of the population which influence demand for travel and tourism. Mostly operating much more slowly than economic variables, which can change rapidly from year to year, the main characteristics determining tourism markets are household size and composition, age, and the experience of further and higher education. The actual number of people involved in each population group is, obviously, the base from which any market volume projection is calculated.

Over the last two decades, in countries with developed economies, smaller households have emerged as the norm with fewer young children in them, and a much greater proportion of married women in full or part time work. The number of households including couples and one or more children in Britain is now only just over a quarter of the total, and the number of children under the age of 15 fell by over two million between 1971 and 1991. The growing incidence of divorce has created many single person and single parent households, and has a major impact on the nature of demand. Obviously these changes have affected producers who traditionally provided family holiday products based on the needs and interests of children. Smaller households also means more households and more reasons to visit family and friends living outside the home environment.

At the other end of the age scale the increasing number of people over the age of 55 who are retired or near retired, has been identified as a vitally important population trend, which will increasingly influence travel and tourism markets by the end of the century. In the USA there were some 39 million people over the age of 55 in 1970, 46 million in 1980, and there will be over 50 million in 1990. In Western Europe it is estimated that one in four people will be aged 55 or over by the year 2000 (de Rooij: 1986: p. 17). Apart from the size of the market, these retired and near retired people are quite different from any previous generation of senior citizens, in the sense that most of them are far more active, fit, and affluent than before. By the year 2000 many of them will have been brought up in a civilization accustomed to high levels of personal mobility, and most will have established patterns of leisure activities and holidays, which they will be able to afford to continue into their seventies and eighties. Marketing managers around the world are studying ways to develop their shares of this expanding market, and there are obvious profit prospects for those who design products which older people want to buy.

The influence of education as an important determinant of travel is not easily separated from associated changes in income and household composition. But it is clear that, the higher the level of education achieved, the greater the involvement in travel, both for business and leisure purposes. This tendency reflects a greater knowledge of what travel opportunities are available and also the experience of travel as a normal part of college and university life, especially for those living away from home.

Geographic factors

For populations living in Northern climates, weather effects are undoubtedly one of the principal determinants of travel demand for leisure purposes, and explain destination patterns of travel flows. For the population living in Northern Europe, Spain and other Mediterranean countries offer the most accessible locations for warmth and sunshine. Florida provides much the same amenity for many Americans in the North-Eastern states of the USA.

Next to weather, another important geographic factor is the size of the community in which populations live. Large urban and suburban communities, reflecting also the factors of relative wealth and education previously discussed, typically generate more tourism per capita than the populations of smaller, especially rural communities. Large urban centres are also catchment areas for day visitors to attractions within accessible distance, which is typically defined in Britain as one to one and a half hour's drive. Beyond that distance the volume of day visits drawn from any place of origin dwindles to a small proportion, even for large nationally known attractions.

In the nineteenth century, the geography of seaside resorts in Northern Europe can be explained in terms of population centres and railway journeys lasting typically no more than an hour and a half. In the twentieth century, the geography of Mediterranean resorts is explained by a combination of weather factors, the location of large urban areas in Northern Europe, and air transport journeys of up to around one thousand miles, which can be accomplished in up to two hours' flying time.

For operators of all kinds of tourist attractions, and for accommodation suppliers, the choice of location for their businesses in relation to their intended markets is the most important decision to be made. For hotels, for example, as for retail supermarkets, it will normally be possible to calculate with precision the probable level of business to be achieved at any given site, purely on an analysis of locational factors and their experience of demand in similar locations.

Socio-cultural factors

Socio-cultural factors is a term used to describe the broad trends in any society's attitudes, which influence individual motivations, but have a wider national or regional impact in the sense that they represent commonly held beliefs and notions, with which people are brought up as children. Such a belief, for example, is that holidays are necessities rather than luxuries, and that trips abroad for business or pleasure are symbols of economic and social status, which serve to indicate the value of one's position in society. Related to this is the belief by many that the amount of paid holiday entitlement of those in work should increase. Supported by trades union pressure, there was a remarkable growth in the amount of paid leave enjoyed by most British employees in the 1970s. At the start of the decade, 28 per cent of British manual workers received two weeks paid holiday, with only 4 per cent receiving three to four weeks or more. By the end of it, none was receiving two weeks or less and more than nine out of ten received over three weeks; a half achieving four or more weeks paid holiday. Similar trends in increased amounts of paid holiday time can be observed in other countries, although not usually at such speed.

Large numbers of people in Northern countries with developed economies clearly believe that second homes, and sunshine holidays, are important attributes of a satisfactory life style. There are many surveys confirming the strength of these beliefs, which are also widely communicated in the popular press and on TV.

The full marketing implications of this extra time available for holidays and the most appropriate product responses, do not appear to be fully understood at the end of the 1980s. The change has certainly helped to encourage the development of additional short holiday products taken at most times of the year, and has made it possible for tour operator companies to increase the capacity of products offered in shoulder months, confident that there are sufficient people with the necessary holiday entitlement and flexibility in their arrangements to travel outside what were traditional peak summer months of July and August. The growing number of retired people able to travel when they wish, and the decline in the number of families committed to school holiday periods, has also helped to support this new flexibility in demand patterns. Yet the pricing policies adopted by most operators towards peak and off peak periods still largely reflect the traditional summer demand patterns, which are far less relevant than they were a decade previously.

Comparative prices

There is convincing evidence in the large British market for package tours that the price of products, compared with those of competitors and from one year to the next, is the most important short-run determinant of the volume of demand. Price, which represents value to customers and is relative to their spending power, reinforces the economic determinants previously discussed and is related to socio-cultural attitudes. For international tourism, price is complicated by the combined effects on holiday prices of exchange rates between countries of origin and countries of destination, and of the comparative level of inflation in the destination area, compared with the area in which tourists live. The cost of fuel, which is especially important in all forms of air transport, adds a third variable to these price complications. The concept of comparative prices is highly complex in practice and the effects are far from easy to predict with any precision, partly because customers' perceptions may differ from reality. In the short run at least, price appears to be the strongest single influence on many forms of market demand in the leisure sector.

The influence on demand of just one of the price factors, the variability of exchange rates, is well illustrated by the following data:

Relationship of the US dollar to the British pound

£1 = $ (US) (all rates at year end)

1980	= $2.39
1981	= $1.91
1982	= $1.62
1983	= $1.45
1984	= $1.16
1985	= $1.45
1986	= $1.48
1987	= $1.86

With these changes affecting the price of travel products, it is hardly surprising that British holiday tourism to the USA, which had increased massively in 1981, fell back year by year to 1985 when it was only 40 per cent of the 1981 level; it recovered very strongly in 1986 as a result of the stronger pound. In the other direction across the Altantic, for Americans visiting Britain on holiday, 1985 was a record volume year with the number of trips recorded more than double the 1982 total. Effective marketing, of course, aims as far as possible to work with the grain of external events affecting demand, and to exploit all the opportunities which occur.

In Europe the growth of British holidays abroad, which increased by 50 per cent between 1982 and 1986, was largely influenced in that period by the comparative strength of the pound against currencies in tourist destination countries, and the beneficial effects of a fall in the price of fuel oil. In the case of Spain, the largest destination for British holiday makers travelling abroad on package tours, the number of packages fell by just over one million in 1985 (nearly 30 per cent of the total) when prices for that year were increased relative to other destinations. The following year, with substantial price reductions (estimated at around 15–20 per cent), Spain recovered more than a million extra holidays in the third quarter alone (Middleton: 1986: p. 17).

Personal mobility factors

The personal mobility provided by private motor cars has become a prime determinant of the volume and nature of tourism for many producers over the last two decades, especially those primarily involved with domestic tourism. In the USA, the private car has for decades been the dominant holiday transport choice, and between European countries sharing land frontiers the car is the preferred mode of transport for leisure tourism, and for much of business travel too. Car ownership is highest in the USA (1982 data) with over 550 cars per thousand population; West Germany has 385, Britain 286, and Japan 217 cars per thousand.

Ownership and access to cars increased significantly in Europe over the last decade. In the late 1980s, most hotels, nearly all self catering establishments, most tourist restaurants and the great majority of visitor attractions and entertainments, are highly dependent on travellers by car for their business. Looking toward the end of the century there is currently no reason to anticipate any lessening of the demand for personal mobility and the convenience and comfort which it provides.

Overall, the use of surface public transport invariably declines as car ownership increases. Apart from non leisure travel, such as much of inter city transport by road, rail and air, there remain some important segments of the travel and tourism market, which use public transport on longer journeys for economic reasons, or through preference. Accordingly, transport operators have responded with a wide range of marketing schemes to provide attractively priced products for target market segments, such as those over sixty, or young people such as students still in full time education. Coach and bus operators have found many niches to exploit, especially for international tourists and groups in the private hire market as well as for the more traditional holidays based on coach tours.

Government/regulatory factors

Although government and regulatory factors are rather different in kind from the other factors determining the likelihood of populations to participate in travel and tourism, the influence over demand by governments and their agencies is usually highly significant in the travel industry. Commercial firms and tourist offices generally organize lobbies in attempts to influence government decisions, but they are frequently obliged to respond to decisions which reflect political aspirations, rather than the commercial or other interests of any particular sector of the industry.

The decision of President Carter's Administration in 1978 to de-regulate domestic air transportation in the USA had massive repercussions on airlines and their markets. In terms of their prices, routes flown, capacity offered, competition, and thus on the volume and type of demand for air travel, it is taking years for the full effects on air transport marketing to emerge. The same process of liberalization is expected to influence the operations and marketing practice of European airlines in the last part of the twentieth century, following a ruling of the European Court in April 1986 concerning the application of the competition rules of the Treaty of Rome (Wheatcroft and Lipman: 1986: p. 3). The implications of this ruling for the travel and tourism industry were not clear at the time of writing but the pressure for de-regulation of airline operators is not likely to lessen. Any move toward liberalization is likely to benefit those who market tourism products using air travel and could significantly increase the size of some markets.

In Britain, regulation of the domestic bus and coach industry has been much reduced since the early 1980s, producing increased competition and much improved equipment and marketing practices. The improvements in standards of comfort offered may increase the size and type of markets which use bus transport, especially private groups for whom coaches offer many advantages.

Mass media communications

The last of the factors in the external environment to be discussed in this chapter also has a powerful and relatively recent influence over the demand for travel and tourism. The principal influence is that of television, especially colour television, to which the populations in countries with developed economies are by now virtually universally exposed. Television watching emerges as the most popular leisure-time pursuit in many countries, with an estimated thirty-five hours a week per household in the USA and around nineteen hours a week for the average adult in Britain (the figures are not directly comparable). No other leisure activity accounts for the number of hours spent in front of the small screen.

Over the last decade, land based and space satellite transmitters have provided the populations of economically developed countries with instantaneous international images of places and events, as well as a continuous stream of films identifying places and standards of living, promoting activities such as golf and tennis, patterns of behaviour, and exotic resorts. The cumulative effect of television over the years in shaping the travel and tourism expectations of the major demand generating countries, cannot be over-estimated. Television is, of course, also a main medium for advertising many products in travel and tourism, and sometimes the two influences come together, as in the promotion of Australia in the USA in the mid 1980s. Initially, considerable impact was scored by Paul Hogan commercials for Australia as a destination, which were followed by massive exposure of Australia during the America's Cup races of 1986/7. At the same time, initially in the cinema, the Hogan film *Crocodile Dundee* became a major box office draw. The combined effect of all this publicity on

travel from the USA to Australia is impossible to quantify, but is known to have had a considerable impact on general attitudes and awareness of a previously little known destination. The media coverage of visits by the British Royal Family to the USA has an equivalent impact on attitudes to travel to Britain.

The cumulative impact of thousands of hours of TV watching must have a major social influence on travel demand. No generations prior to the 1960s ever had such massive, continuous exposure to events, people and places outside their normal places of residence and work. In the year following the Chernobyl nuclear disaster in Russia and the American punitive raid against Libya (1986), one can only speculate on the full effect which the massive exposure had on the travel plans of Americans in 1986 and 1987.

Not least of the influences exerted by the mass communication media is the effect achieved by regular TV travel programmes, which review and expose a wide range of tourist products on offer and provide critical evaluations of their quality and value for money. Such programmes achieve a level of authority and exposure which no individual organization's advertising budget could match. For individual products covered, the programmes have the power to reduce demand for the businesses or destinations which are criticized, or create it for those they approve.

At a lower level in terms of mass impact, the exposure of prospective travellers to books, films, newspapers, magazines and radio, contributes to awareness and attitudes in addition to TV programmes. But the other media cannot reproduce the sense of colour and action conveyed by TV or command the same hours of attention.

The ability of TV to expose and draw attention to the things which go wrong for tourists is also part of the overall effect on demand. It includes, for example, the coverage given to airline disasters, the stories of muggings of British tourists in Spain in 1985 or the disaster to the Townsend Thorenson ferry that sank in the English Channel in the early part of 1987. Where the majority of a population participates regularly in travel and tourism, the industry is of great interest to the media, and is certain to generate stories which the public wish to see and read. The full effect on demand of wide media coverage is not well understood in the late 1980s but there can be no doubt of its importance.

Characteristics associated with high and low demand for tourism

Because the underlying factors determining the volume of demand for tourism are common to all countries, it is possible to summarize the influence of the main determinants in a *scale of propensity* to travel away from home, which applies for all purposes. Propensity is a useful term, frequently used in the study of travel and tourism to define the extent of participation in travel activity in a given population. Using national or other tourism surveys of trips taken, it may be quantified with precision.

Holiday propensity is a measure of the proportion of a population which takes holidays in a year. Of course, some people take one holiday only, whilst others take three or more. Accordingly it is useful to distinguish between gross propensity and net propensity, defined as follows:

- net propensity is the proportion of a population which takes at least one holiday in a twelve month period,
- gross propensity is the total number of holidays taken, expressed as a proportion of a population (proportion taking any holidays multiplied by the average number of holidays taken).

To illustrate the point, in 1985 61 per cent of British people aged 16 or more are estimated to have taken at least one holiday of four or more nights away from home to any destination in Britain or abroad. Net propensity is, therefore, 61 per cent. On average, those travellers took 1.6 holidays each, so gross propensity is $61 \times 1.6 = 97.6$ per cent.

Measured annually over a decade or so, it is possible to assess the extent to which a market for travel and tourism is increasing its size due to increased penetration, (more of a population taking trips away from home) or because of increased intensity (the same people taking more trips in a year). Both of these are important measures for marketing managers, especially when related to specific market segments, for example to measure the holiday propensity of people aged 55 or more, or of a particular social class. For countries with highly developed economies such as Switzerland or Sweden, net propensity already exceeds 75 per cent and gross propensity exceeds 150 per cent.

Figure 4.1 is based on the main determinants of demand discussed in this chapter, especially the socio-economic aspects. The determinant effects of comparative prices, government/regulatory and communication factors are not separately identified in the figure, but each would have the effect of accelerating or retarding the propensities established by the other determinants.

The response of marketing managers

The role of marketing managers in response to the determinants of travel and tourism can be put simply. First it is their business to research and monitor the factors which influence overall movements in the particular markets with which they are concerned. Second, based on this knowledge, it is their business to forecast the direction and speed of change in the determinants, and the implications of such forecasts for the travel patterns in their markets. The techniques for monitoring change in marketing are aspects of marketing research discussed in Chapter 11.

	Low propensity	*High propensity*

Low propensity	*High propensity*
low income per household	high income per household
single parent household	two parents (employed) household
rural community dweller	large-city dweller
educated to minimum age	high level of qualifications
older people (70+)	younger people
no private transport	2 or more cars in household
2 or less weeks' paid holiday	4 or more weeks' paid holiday

Note: In cases where all the determinants combine, such as a 75-year-old retired farm labourer living alone without an occupational pension, the propensity to engage in any form of travel and tourism in a year may be zero. At the other end of the scale, a young, professional couple without children, both working, and living in a city apartment, may well generate ten or more leisure trips of one night or more away from home, over a year. Such a couple would be likely also to make several business trips in a year.

Figure 4.1 *The scale of propensity to engage in travel and tourism*

An important part of the marketing managers' task is to identify, through research, opportunities and threats emerging in the external environment, of which the demand determinants are always a vital element. Both opportunities and threats require a management response through products and promotion and the other elements which are known collectively as the 'marketing mix' and discussed in Chapter 6.

In the long and short run, investment and operating decisions in marketing led organizations will always be based firmly on an understanding of market patterns. This is true in all circumstances, but especially true where markets are no longer growing rapidly, and are changing structurally. In British tourism in the 1980s, for example, there was a massive structural shift away from traditional one and two week summer seaside holidays taken within Britain. The shift is largely explained by the effects of the determinants discussed in this chapter, to which tour operators offering holidays abroad, reacted with great speed and energy.

Chapter summary

This chapter focuses on the marketing implications of eight variables in the economic, social, and cultural environment, which are common to all the countries with developed economies currently generating the bulk of the world's tourism. It has been stressed that such variables are part of the external business environment within which all firms operate; they are not under the control of any commercial organization and only partly influenced by government decisions.

Some of the determinants, such as income per capita, geographic factors and population changes, have long-run implications for marketing. Such factors tend to produce fairly stable relationships with demand, for example income elasticity ratios, and they are the basis of most of the forecasting models used to project tourism flows. These long-run determinants are summarized in Figure 4.1 in the scale of propensity to engage in travel and tourism.

Other determinants, such as exchange rates,

regulatory changes and the impact of mass media, have a much more immediate effect on the volume of tourism demand and market patterns, which it is often impossible to predict.

Marketing led organizations will always base their strategic decisions on a carefully researched analysis of the determinants of demand and their associated market patterns, and will adjust those decisions tactically in the light of short-run trends. The importance of understanding the determinants underlies the commitment of marketing organizations to market research, as discussed in Chapter 11.

Further reading

Baker, M. J., *Marketing: An Introductory Text*, Macmillan, 1985, Chapter 3.

Burkart, A. J., and Medlik, S., *Tourism: Past, Present and Future*, Heinemann, 1981, Chapter 5.

Kotler, P., *Marketing Management: Analysis, Planning and Control*, Prentice-Hall, 1984, Chapter 3.

5

The changing business environment: Travel motivations and buyer behaviour

The previous chapter discussed the elements of the social, economic and political environment, which are essentially *external* influences on individual customers, but which collectively tend to determine the volume and patterns of travel and tourism generated within any country. The determinants of demand certainly explain why residents of countries such as Germany, USA and Sweden have very high propensities to participate in travel and tourism; whereas others, such as India, Egypt and China, have low propensities. In discussing determinants it is generally assumed that customers in large numbers respond in predictable ways to variations in income, leisure time, price and other factors discussed in Chapter 4. Indeed, the study of macroeconomics could not be sustained if these cause and effect linkages did not operate with reasonable consistency within an economy.

High propensities to participate in travel and tourism, however, are also strongly correlated with the propensity to purchase hi-fi equipment, theatre and opera tickets, fashion goods, eating out and purchases of a whole range of non essential goods and services, which compete for shares of disposable income. A discussion of motivations is required to throw light on why consumers choose to spend significant amounts of their disposable income on travel and tourism, rather than on other forms of puchase.

Even more importantly, within an overall context established by the largely external determinants, it is necessary for marketing managers to be clear how *internal* and psychological processes influence individuals to decide the choice of a particular vacation destination, and a particular type of product within the destination of choice, or vice versa. These internal and psychological processes are known within marketing as aspects of buyer behaviour. This important subject lies at the very heart of marketing theory, and has been the subject of extensive literature in recent years. The understanding marketing managers have of the way in which consumers make their product decisions, influences the way in which all the subsequent decisions in the marketing process are made.

This chapter deals, therefore, with issues which are fundamental to the understanding of modern marketing, defined as centred on customer needs and behaviour. The chapter

45

covers the main issues in three parts. First, the internal, personal influences and motivations affecting buyer behaviour are introduced and summarized in an overall classification of travel motivations. Next, a simple input-output model of the buyer behaviour process is explained with a diagram shown in Figure 5.1. The diagram explains the relationship between the influences which are brought to bear on buyers (inputs); the personal factors, which reflect an individual's position in society, his personality, attitudes and needs, wants and goals (buyer characteristics); and the outputs shown as purchase decisions. The diagram also illustrates how buyers process inputs to arrive at their decisions. The chapter concludes with a discussion of the way in which all products can be placed on a spectrum or scale reflecting the complexity of the buying decision seen from the customer's viewpoint. In travel and tourism there is a wide range of products, some of which require only routine decisions, and others such as annual vacations, which customers see as complex and demanding purchases. The place a product occupies on the scale, greatly influences the way in which it is marketed.

Behaviour influenced by internal processes

The internal and pyschological influences which affect individuals' choices are commonly known as 'motivations'. Internal motivating processes effectively operate on individuals' purchase choices within the framework already set by the determinants of demand. For marketing managers, an understanding of the motivations affecting behaviour will usually be more important than measuring the determinants because marketers are directly concerned with choices buyers make between competitive products. They can influence those choices through promotion and other marketing decisions.

To illustrate the important distinction between the external and internal influences on buyers, consider the vacation decisions of a young, professional, unmarried person, living in a rented apartment in New York, with two vacation weeks to plan. The choice is wide, because disposable income is high; the time is available; distance by air is no problem for a relatively affluent New Yorker; and the technology of air transport and travel organization is sophisticated enough to make Europe, the Far East, or anywhere in North or South America, easily accessible. In terms of demand determinants discussed in Chapter 4, this prospective travel buyer has one of the highest propensities to travel.

What motivating factors will influence the choice, for example, between a Club Mediterranée village in the Caribbean, culture seeking in Thailand or Bhutan, an adventure holiday in Canada, or a vacation at a sports resort in Florida? What will be the conscious and unconscious influences on the decision which is made? How far will this prospective traveller make his or her own decision or be influenced by the preferences of possible companions for the trip? Even more basic, why should, say, two and a half thousand dollars be spent on a vacation when it could be spent on furnishings or equipment for the apartment? No marketing manager has anything like a full or satisfactory answer to all these questions or their equivalents affecting any form of vacation decision. But the more he finds out about what sort of people choose particular products, what needs they seek to fulfil through each type of vacation, and their activity preferences once in a resort, the better he will be able to formulate an appealing product and communicate its benefits and attractions to a target audience of prospective visitors.

Before listing the wide range of possible motivations that exist in travel and tourism, as a starting point for the discussion of buyer behaviour, it should be obvious that the customer decision or buyer behaviour process in travel and tourism is likely to be highly complex.

Classifying travel motivations

For convenience, to illustrate the wide range of possible travel and tourism motivations, it is possible to draw on the work of others. What is listed below, however, are not motivations for individuals in the sense that psychologists and authors of behavioural marketing texts would understand them, but simple groupings of the reasons for different types of travel, which share some common characteristics. A more precise discussion of individual motivation has to be related to needs and personal goals, and will be found later in this chapter. The groupings below provide a broad structure within which buyer behaviour operates and may serve a useful function as an introduction to the behaviour model.

McIntosh and Gupta (1980) outlined four 'basic travel motivations':

physical motivators
cultural motivators
interpersonal motivators
status or prestige motivators

Hudman (1980) lists ten 'motivations':

health	visiting friends and relatives
curiosity	professional and business
sports (participation)	pursuit of 'roots'
sports (watching)	self esteem
pleasure	religion

Schmoll (1977) lists five 'general travel motivations':

educational and cultural
relaxation, adventure and pleasure
health and recreation (including sport)
ethnic and family
social and competitive (including status and prestige)

Any visit to a large travel agency and a look through the brochures will confirm the wide range of primary reasons for travel and tourism currently catered for by producers.

Stimulus and response concepts in buyer behaviour

The broad groupings of motivations noted in the previous section serve a purpose in outlining the wide range of possibilities, but they do nothing to indicate the reasons why individuals have such motivations, nor how their travel decisions are made. To throw light on this it is necessary to put the individual, metaphorically, under the microscope, drawing on the analysis originally developed in the study of economics and more recently in other behavioural sciences.

Classical economic models of buyer behaviour operate on the well tested assumption that buying decisions (demand) are primarily governed by price. Other things being equal, the lower the price, the higher the volume of demand, and vice versa. Economic concepts of price response and price elasticity of demand are still highly relevant in travel and tourism, but from a marketing management standpoint, other behavioural influences are equally important considerations in making marketing mix decisions.

For those considering buyer behaviour for the first time it may be helpful to imagine that, in some important ways, consumers' minds work rather like microcomputers. Every computer has a given range of functions determined by its designed characteristics; every buyer has a personality which is partly inherited at birth and partly developed by experience. Computers can perform certain tasks very rapidly through built-in programmes, whilst other tasks require extensive additional programming in order to produce the required output. Buyers perform some buying decisions by habit and with hardly any conscious thought, whilst other purchases require careful consideration and extensive information gathering.

Both computers and consumers' minds can only process information, which has been fed into their decision systems at the right time, working within the limitations of their design (or personality constraints) and memory capacity. If an operator fails to input vital data to a computer, then for that computer the information simply does not exist. Similarly if an 'ideal' product exists and is available to a prospective purchaser, but the purchaser is not aware of it, then for that consumer the product does not exist. In other words, computers and buyers' minds receive inputs, which they process according in their inbuilt capacities and programmed 'states'. Both produce outputs which are a resolution of all the input variables. Obviously, machines are totally predictable and consistent in their outputs, whilst people clearly are not. But the basic principle of inputs, information processing and outputs, is to be found at the heart of all models of buyer behaviour.

Marketing is very much concerned with supplying prospective buyers with factual and persuasive inputs of information about specific attributes of particular products. To be effective, it is necessary for marketers to have some understanding of how and to what extent that information is likely to be received and processed and how the purchasing decision is made. In the next section a simple input-output model of buyer behaviour is explained.

A buyer behaviour model for travel and tourism

The stimulus response concept discussed in the previous section is shown diagrammatically in Figure 5.1. The diagram has four interactive components with the central component identified as 'buyer characteristics and decision process', which incorporates motivation. The first two components are inputs, most of which can be manipulated by marketing managers, whilst the final component represents the purchase out-puts of the travel decision process. The four components within the diagram are explained below. The communication filters, shown in the shaded part of the diagram, are discussed separately towards the end of the chapter.

Product inputs

These comprise the whole range of competitive products and product mixes which are made available to the prospective customer. In Britain, for example, there are dozens of tour operators offering trips abroad to potential vacationers, and dozens of domestic British destinations and operators also seeking the travellers' purchase. Across the USA a prospective tourist is faced by a similar choice, amounting to literally thousands of possibilities, if they could all be counted.

Communication channels

These are in two parts. There are the formal communication channels or media, aimed at persuading prospective buyers through advertising, brochures, sales promotion techniques and public relations (PR) activity. There is also information which is accessible to individuals through their family, friends and the groups of people with whom they interact at work and socially. Much research suggests that these informal channels of information, noted in the diagram as 'friends, and reference groups', are at least as influential on purchase decisions as the formal channels, and are sometimes referred to as 'word of mouth' communications.

Buyer characteristics and decision process

Grouped around the central focus of needs, wants and goals, there are three main interacting elements, which determine an individual buyer's disposition to act in certain ways. These three elements act sometimes as constraints upon purchase decisions and sometimes to provide or reinforce the motivation. The three elements are discussed below; communication filters are discussed later in the chapter:

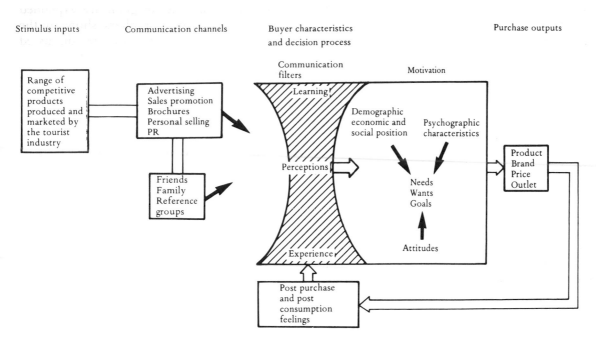

Figure 5.1 *A stimulus-response model of buyer behaviour*

1 *Demographic/economic/social* position. These are the easily quantifiable characteristics such as age, sex, occupation, region of residence, household size, and social class, some of which were dealt with under determinants in Chapter 4. They are also relevant here since they act as constraints or limits within which individuals' motivations and buying behaviour take place. Included in these characteristics is stage in the life cycle, meaning whether a person is a child, young adult living at home, adult married but without children, retired person, and so on. These aspects are developed in Chapter 6 on segmentation.

2 *Psychographic attributes* or 'personality traits' as they are often referred to, indicate the type of person the buyer is and strongly influence the types of product which are bought. These attributes also determine the sort of advertising and other communication messages to which buyers respond. Psychologists and marketing researchers measure people's psychographic characteristics using dimensions, such as confident or diffident, gregarious or loner, conscientious or happy-go-lucky, assertive or submissive, neurotic or well balanced, tense or relaxed, adventurous or unadventurous. These dimensions can be used in product formulation and in promotional messages.

3 *Attitudes*. All people adopt conscious and unconscious attitudes towards ideas, people, and things, of which they are aware. An attitude was defined by Allport as 'A mental state of readiness, organized through experience, exerting a directive influence upon the individual's response to all objects and situations with which it is

The basic capacity estimate is the no. of divers per peak hour who can be accompanied sufficiently in the water by instructors, the amount of equipment able to be hired, the no. of beds required, restaurant facilities, internal transportation and so on.

related' (Allport: 1935). Attitudes extend to beliefs and knowledge of products as well as to people and events. Attitudes also cover feelings, such as likes and dislikes aroused, and a disposition to act or not because of such beliefs and feelings.

It should be noted that there is nothing necessarily right, wrong, or rational about attitudes, and also that people do not have to have direct experience of products in order to form an attitude. Consider, for example, Club Mediterranée. There are those who consider the Club offers an ideal holiday for discriminating young people, whilst others consider the idea of being in close proximity to hundreds of others, a daunting and disagreeable prospect. For some people cruise ships are an ideal form of vacation, whilst others prefer fishing and hunting in the wild. Some people have a favourable response to casinos and gambling, which others find repellent and morally wrong.

Modern marketing research methods and the power of computer processing have made a considerable contribution to the measurement of attitudes and their relationship to product purchasing. Whilst this is far from an exact science, most large organizations in air transport, accommodation, and tour operating, as well as national tourist organizations, have had at least some involvement in attitude measurement in recent years, and the research techniques are improving. The understanding of attitudes is also an essential aspect of product positioning, which is discussed in Chapter 8.

Needs, wants, goals

Individuals have a range of needs extending, in the well known hierarchy established by Maslow in 1954, from immediate basic physical needs for food, warmth, shelter and sleep, through safety and social needs for affection and love, to self esteem and status needs, and the most sophisticated level of self development needs (self actualization in Maslow's terms). Self development needs relate to people's preoccupation with their own happiness, fulfilment of their potential as individuals, and concern for their image as received by others. Of course, self development needs are unlikely to become very important until most if not all the lower order needs are satisfied on a reasonably regular basis. Individuals with a high propensity to participate in travel and tourism, as measured by the determinants discussed in Chapter 4, are also those most likely to be in a position to focus on their own self development.

For centuries travel has been associated with a broadening of awareness and self recognition, through added knowledge and exposure to other cultures and human circumstances. Vacations in particular, and their associations with rest and recreation (in a literal sense of being renewed in mental and physical ways), have a stimulating effect upon people's minds and are clearly linked with self development. The tensions of living in the late twentieth century are often associated with a longing to escape for a while, into forms of self indulgence and self development, usually with family or chosen companions. The increasingly frequent links between travel and personal hobbies, sport and other recreation activities, combine to associate leisure travel and tourism with the fulfilment of self development needs. It is this powerful association which helps to explain why vacation travel tends to be regarded, among those who can afford it, as more of a necessity than a luxury. As a 'necessity' travel and tourism clearly competes for disposable income with other goods and services. It is essential for marketing managers to recognize that their products are valued only to the extent of satisfying underlying needs, wants, and goals, many of which are highly sophisticated.

Personal goals influencing behaviour patterns include, for example, the respect of friends, the influencing of peer groups, the achievement of a happy domestic life or achievement, and status in employment or voluntary work. Travel and tourism can be used, in part at least, as a means of achieving many personal goals.

Motivation, the dynamic process in the model

Psychological theory holds that needs, wants and goals generate uncomfortable tension states within individuals' minds and bodies, which cannot be released until the needs are satisfied. States of tension, including hunger, fatigue, and loneliness as well as self development wants, are thus the *motivators*, which produce actions to release tension states. Motivations, therefore, are the dynamic process in buyer behaviour, which bridge the gap between the felt need and the decision to act or purchase. Most readers will recognize in themselves many less important needs, which are not satisfied primarily because the felt motivation is not strong enough to overcome the inertia against decision choices. A powerful motivator is one which triggers urgent action. In a marketing sense motivation bridges the gap between a general interest in a product, and a decision to go out and buy it. It is in this sense that products can be designed and marketed as solutions to customers' needs (tension states). A marketing manager who has taken the trouble to understand his customers' needs and attitudes will clearly be better able to trigger their decisions by targeting his communication on their motivating influences, than one whose knowledge in this area is inadequate.

Purchase choices/decisions/outputs

In the final stage of the diagram are listed outputs of the decision process of most direct concern to producers, including which type of product, what brand, what price, at what time, and through what distribution outlet. These decisions are all related to the individuals' personal circumstances and are systematically monitored by many large companies through the marketing research procedures discussed later in this book. The point to be understood here is that action on purchases is linked directly to motivations, which in turn are linked to the buyers' characteristics defined earlier. Motivations may be influenced through marketing decisions, especially through product design and promotion.

Filters in the buying decision process

Experience, learning and perceptions, influenced strongly by attitudes, are shaded in Figure 5.1 to draw attention to the fact that the information shown as inputs to buyers is not necessarily received by individuals as its marketing originators intended. All inputs pass through a sieve, or series of filters, which serve to suppress most of the available information and to highlight specific parts, very probably distorted in the reception process. Perception is the term used to cover the way individuals select and organize the mass of information they are exposed to, and perception is a function of attitudes. The exact way in which information is received and processed remains the most obscure area of all behaviour models. Knowledge of an individual's demographic, psychographic and attitudinal characteristics will obviously enable a producer to communicate in suitable terms with prospective buyers. But it will not enable that producer to predict how much, or how accurately, his information messages will penetrate the filters and stimulate action.

Consumers' perception is influenced by personal attitudes, by motivations, knowledge, and interest in products, based on experience, advertising and hearsay. It changes over time through a constant learning process. Whilst no advertiser is ever likely to gain the ultimate secrets of perception and manipulate prospective customers against their will, there is obviously scope to make improvements to communications and product design aspects at the margin. If the perceived positive aspects of product design and promotion can be enhanced, and the perceived negative aspects can be reduced through consumer research which throws light on perception processes, more cost effective marketing expenditure should result.

Post purchase feelings

If, having found a specific product considered likely to satisfy his needs, a consumer is sufficiently motivated to buy it, the experience of consumption will affect all future attitudes towards it. If the product is highly satisfactory, the probability of repeat purchase will be high, the likelihood of good 'word of mouth' is high, and the customer will have 'learned' that satisfaction is associated with that product. If the experience is highly unsatisfactory the opposite will occur, and depending on the importance of the purchase, the consumer may never buy that product again. For example, a good experience of an airline, with a punctual flight and friendly service, is highly likely to influence future choices. A long delay, surly service or an overbooked flight can create tensions and frustrations, which are observable on any day at any large airport. In other words it is not enough to secure a sale. Good marketing aims to secure subsequent sales through harnessing product satisfaction as often the most powerful means of influencing future buyer behaviour. It achieves this through the learning process which conditions an individual's perceptions.

Personal and situational variables in buyer behaviour

Thus far, travel and tourism buying decisions have been treated as though they all occupied equal significance in the minds of customers. In practice, of course, this is obviously not true and it is necessary to consider a classification, which makes it possible to distinguish simple purchases, such as routine car rental or motel accommodation, from complex purchases such as a two-week vacation abroad or a world cruise. In marketing texts the basic distinction between *convenience* and *shopping* goods, originally

Spectrum of buyer behaviour characteristics – goods or services

Convenience products	Shopping products
mainly low unit value/price	mainly high unit value/price
mainly perceived necessities	mainly non-essentials

$$\longleftarrow \qquad\qquad\qquad\qquad \longrightarrow$$

Convenience products	Shopping products
low problem solving	high problem solving
low information search	high information search
low customer commitment	high customer commitment
high purchase frequency	low purchase frequency
high brand loyalty	low brand loyalty
high speed decision process	low speed decision process
high rapidity of consumption	low rapidity of consumption
extensive distribution expected	limited distribution expected

This spectrum of behaviour characteristics may be applied equally to goods and services and some examples of both are shown below.

Spectrum of products associated with the spectrum of buyer behaviour

Convenience products	Shopping products
$\longleftarrow$	$\longrightarrow$

Convenience products	Shopping products
urban bus transport	holidays
commuter train transport	hotel accommodation
bank services	air transport
post office services	private education
take-away foods	motor cars
washing powder	freezers
cigarettes	carpets
branded chocolates	furniture
beer	

Source: Middleton VTC, in *Quarterly Review of Marketing*, Vol. 8, No 4, 1983.

drawn in 1923 by Copeland, is a standard element of marketing theory. A convenience good is a manufactured item, which typically has a relatively low price, is bought frequently, is widely available and satisfies basic routine needs. A shopping good typically has a relatively high price, is bought infrequently and it may be necessary to travel some distance, and make some effort to buy it. Shopping goods usually satisfy higher order needs in the Maslow hierarchy noted earlier in this chapter. This distinction can be applied to service products, which may be categorized on a scale or spectrum with simple convenience items at one end and extensive shopping items at the other. The terms *routinized* and *extensive problem solving* were used by Howard and Sheth in one of the seminal papers on buyer behaviour models in 1967. They are clearly relevant to the buyer behaviour process explained in Figure 5.1. This author summarized the spectrum of behaviour as follows:

'The place a product occupies on the spectrum of buyer behaviour will tend to determine the way in which it is marketed. For example, both car rental and city hotel accommodation are essentially convenience products for many American business travellers, who comprise the principal buyers for these products. They involve, therefore, only routinized behaviour and a secretary or a travel agent may make the purchase so that the user has only to collect his key. Car rental in this context matches every one of the convenience characteristics listed. For European vacationers on the other hand, hotel selection and car rental are often shopping products, and a quite different marketing approach is needed.'

Chapter summary

Chapter 2 notes that one of the three key elements in the marketing system comprises the 'attitudes and decisions of consumers concerning the perceived utility and value of available goods and services according to their needs and wants

and ability to pay'. This chapter has sought to justify that statement, and to provide some practical indications of what is involved in achieving a better understanding of buyer behaviour. An understanding of consumer motivations and behaviour is at the heart of all modern marketing theory and practice. It underlies the techniques of market segmentation discussed in Chapter 7.

Whilst the behaviour model included in this chapter is descriptive rather than predictive, its principal practical value lies in explaining the range of variables likely to be involved in any travel and tourism purchase decision, and the linkages between them. The model can serve also as an aide memoire in drawing up marketing programmes, and as a framework for organizing marketing research.

Complicating any simple classification of travel motivations is the fact that within the total market for travel and tourism, many customers perform more than one role as buyers. The businessman in the executive suite this month, may be a vacationer in two weeks' time using budget accommodation; the hang gliding expert may also be a regular business class traveller, or a back-packer seeking the cheapest range of accommodation; the hamburger eater at lunchtime may be visiting a top restaurant in the evening, and so on. Often the buying decision in travel and tourism is not made for the individual's sake, but for the sake of others such as family or friends.

Finally there is the difference to consider between buyer behaviour which is 'routinized', involving little conscious decision effort, and that which is 'extensive problem solving' and may take weeks of careful deliberation and information searching and analysis before a decision is made. Such differences have great significance for the way in which marketing is undertaken.

If, notwithstanding the attempt to simplify the explanation of buyer behaviour, the reader concludes this chapter somewhat alarmed at the enormity of the subject, that is no more than a measure of its significance. It is all too easy to say that marketing is about understanding consumers' needs and matching them. Achieving it in practice is both difficult and uncertain, but the rewards to those who achieve even marginal improvements can be great in terms of marketing efficiency and added profitability. Effective marketing in competitive conditions is impossible without an understanding of buyers' motivations and decision processes.

Further reading

Baker, M. J., *Marketing: An Introductory Text*, Macmillan, 1985, Chapter 4.

Kotler, P., *Marketing: Analysis, Planning and Control*, Prentice-Hall, 1984, Chapter 4.

Part Two
Understanding the Marketing Mix in Travel and Tourism

6
The four Ps:
Focus of the marketing mix

This chapter outlines the four principal variables with which marketing managers are concerned in their efforts to manage consumer demand in relation to perishable, inseparable products (see Chapter 3). Known collectively as the 'marketing mix', these four variables reflect and express in practical decision terms, the second of the three elements in the marketing system referred to in Chapter 2, as 'the attitudes and decisions of producers concerning their production of goods and services for sale, in the context of their business environment and long-term objectives'.

This chapter is in two parts. The first part explains the meaning of each of the four variables in the marketing mix, and provides examples of the decisions involved in Figure 6.1. The second part of the chapter explains where the mix decisions fit within the overall marketing system for travel and tourism organizations, which is represented diagramatically in Figure 6.2.

The marketing mix concept is central to understanding modern marketing, and the key variables discussed in this chapter are subsequently developed and referred to throughout this book. In particular the planning of the marketing mix is discussed in detail in Chapter 14.

Marketing mix defined

The marketing mix may be defined as 'the mixture of controllable marketing variables that the firm uses to pursue the sought level of sales in the target market' (Kotler: 1984: p. 68).

The concept implies a set of variables, which are akin to levers or controls that can be operated by a marketing manager to achieve a defined goal. By way of illustration the controls may be likened to those of an automobile which, to reach a chosen destination, has four main controls. There is a throttle or accelerator to control engine speed; there is a brake to reduce speed or stop; there is a gear shift to match the engine speed to the road speed required, or to reverse direction; and there is a steering wheel with which to change the direction of travel. As any driver will recognize, movement of the controls must be synchronized and used in a way which is relevant to constantly changing road conditions and the actions of other drivers. Progress from one point to another is, for the driver, a continuous manipulation of the four basic controls.

In commercial organizations marketing managers are also 'driving' products towards chosen destinations. The four controls are *production formulation*, which is a means of adapting the product to the changing needs of the target customer; *pricing*, which in practice tends to be used as a throttle to increase or slow down the volume of sales according to market conditions; *promotion*, which is used to increase the numbers of those in the market who are aware of the product and are favourably disposed towards buying it; and *place*, which determines the number of prospective customers who are able to find convenient places or ways to convert their buying intentions into purchases. These four controls are manipulated continuously according to the market conditions prevailing, especially with regard to the actions of competitors.

While it is not sensible to push the car driving analogy too far, the central concept of continuously adjusting and synchronizing the controls according to constantly changing market conditions, is the important point to grasp about marketing mix decisions. Continuous in this context could mean daily decisions, but in practice is more likely to mean weekly or monthly adjustments in the light of market intelligence about progress being achieved. Marketing is always a dynamic process.

The destinations or goals towards which products are being 'driven' by the four controls, are set by strategic decisions taken by organizations about their desired futures (see Chapter 12).

It will be noted that the four variables all begin with the letter 'p', hence the name 'the four Ps' originally used to describe the marketing mix in 1960 by McCarthy (1981: p. 42).

The four Ps

As the focus of marketing management decisions, each of the Ps, product, price, promotion and place warrants a separate chapter in this book. Here the object is to introduce and explain them in an integrated way, which also serves as an introduction to market research, and planning for marketing strategy and tactics.

Product

Product covers the shape or form of what is offered to prospective customers; in other words, the characteristics of the product as designed by management decisions.

Product components include its basic design, such as the size and facilities of a hotel; presentation, which for service products is mainly a function of the atmosphere and environment created on the producer's premises; the service element including numbers, training, attitudes and appearance of staff; branding, which identifies a particular product with a unique name; and image, which is a synthesis of all the product elements as well as the focus of promotional activity.

In a modern marketing context, products in travel and tourism are designed for, and continuously adapted to match target segments' needs, expectations, and ability to pay.

Price

Price denotes the published or negotiated terms of the exchange transaction for a product, between a producer aiming to achieve predetermined sales volume and revenue objectives, and prospective customers seeking to maximize their perceptions of value for money in the choices they make between alternative products.

Almost invariably in travel there is a regular or standard price for a product, and one or more discounted or promotional prices reflecting the needs of particular segments of buyers, or particular market conditions such as seasonality.

Promotion

The most visible of the four Ps, promotion, includes advertising, sales promotion, merchandising, sales force activities, brochure production, and PR (public relations) activity. Promotional techniques, explored in detail in Part Four of the book, are used to make prospective customers aware of products, to whet their appetites, and stimulate demand. They also provide information to help customers decide, and generally provide incentives to purchase, either directly from a producer or through a channel of distribution. The range of promotional techniques is so wide that the term 'promotional mix' is frequently used in practice.

In this introductory chapter it is important for the reader to appreciate the relationship between this P and the other three Ps to which it is integrally linked in the marketing process. However important and visible it is, promotion is still only one of the levers used to manage demand. It cannot be fully effective unless it is co-ordinated with the other three.

Place

For marketing purposes, place does not just mean the location of a tourist attraction or facility, but the location of all the points of sale which provide prospective customers with *access* to tourist products. For example, 'place' for Disney World is not only Orlando, Florida, but also the numerous travel agents located in the North-East of USA (and elsewhere inside and outside the USA) selling products which include Disney World admission. As a result of marketing decisions, prospective visitors to Florida can obtain promotional information and buy a range or products, which either include Disney World admission, or make such visits probable in terms of vacation locations and motivation. Travel agents are, of course, only one of the ways in which 'place' or access is created for Disney World customers, or indeed for most other products in travel and tourism.

Mixes mutiplied and confused

Because each of the four Ps includes within it so many important sub-elements it is not surprising that subsequent authors have developed many variations of the original four, especially for service products. Cowell (1984: p. 69) for example, reviewing recent American contributions and drawing in particular on work by Booms and Bitner, recommends a 'revised marketing mix' for services which comprises:

- product
- price
- promotion
- place

- people (numbers, training, attitudes)
- physical evidence (furnishings, colour, lighting, noise)
- process (customer involvement, procedures in service delivery)

Closer scrutiny suggests that the proposed additional three mix elements are in fact all integral elements of travel and tourism *products*. It is, of course, a matter for judgement whether or not it makes sense to sub-divide the product elements as shown. Certainly the nature of service products compared with those based on physical goods heightens the importance of the sub-divisions. But product design decisions, which do not incorporate these elements explicitly, make little sense in practice. This author is not convinced that the understanding of marketing is advanced by the proposed revisions.

Readers will also encounter terms such as 'product mix', 'communication mix', 'promotional mix', 'presentation mix', and 'distribution mix'. In a hospitality marketing context, Reneghan discussed the definitional problems of the 'marketing mix' in some depth (Reneghan: 1981). There is no recommended definition or agreed usage of these terms but, provided the central concept of designing a marketing mix around the needs of identified customers is clearly understood, the variations and extensions should not create difficulties. The practical use of the mix concept is most clearly seen in the way in which marketing campaigns are planned and executed (see Chapter 14).

The four Ps, with illustrations drawn from hotels and airlines, are further explained in Figure 6.1. Readers may find it a worthwhile exercise to complete their own illustrations for tourist attractions, tour operators, a cruise ship or a car rental operation.

Marketing mix cost and revenue considerations

It is important to understand that all marketing mix decisions involve costs to an organization

	Hotel	Scheduled airline	Museum
Product Designed characteristics/ packaging	Location/building size/ grounds/design/room size/facilities in hotel furnishings/decor/ lighting/catering styles	Routes/service frequency Aircraft type Seat size/space Decor, meals, style,	Building size/design/ facilities Types of collection Size of collection Interior display/ interpretation
Service component	Staff numbers/uniforms/ attitudes	Staff numbers, uniforms e.g. TWA, PAN AM,	Staff numbers, uniforms e.g. Tate Gallery (London)
Branding/positioning	e.g. Holiday Inn, Crest, Savoy	British Airways, Virgin Atlantic	Metropolitan Museum (New York)
Image/reputation	e.g. upmarket, down market	e.g. reliable, exotic food, badly managed	e.g. dull, exciting, modern
Price Normal or regular price Promotional prices (for each product offered)	Rack rates Corporate rates Privileged user rates Tour operator discount rate	First class/business/ tourist APEX Standby Charter	(assuming charge made) Adult rate, senior citizen rate Party rates Children rate Friends of the museum pass rate
Promotion (solo and collaborative) Advertising (TV/radio/ press/journals) Sales promotion/ merchandising Public relations Brochure production and distribution Sales force	Examples not provided since these are generally self evident and specific to individual organizations (See Parts Four and Five)		
Place Channels of distribution including reservation systems	Central reservation system Other hotels in group Travel agents Tour operators Airlines 800 telephone lines	Central reservation system City offices Airport desks Travel agents Other airlines 800 telephone lines	Other museums Tourist information offices Hotel desks Schools/colleges

Figure 6.1 *Examples of the marketing mix in travel and tourism*

and have implications for sales revenue. Consideration of Figure 6.1 will suggest that three of the Ps involve significant expenditure, which has to be *committed in advance* of the revenue it is expected to generate. Changes to the product, advertising, sales promotions, brochure production, and the organization and servicing of distribution channels, all represent financial commitments made in the expectation of sales results. While pricing decisions do not involve costs in advance of sales, they obviously determine the level of revenue achievable, and in the case of price discounting to sell unsold capacity, they represent revenue foregone.

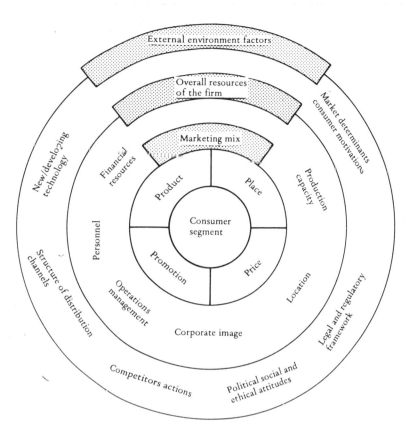

Figure 6.2 *The marketing mix in context of the marketing system* Adapted from Stanton, W. J., 1974

To illustrate this important point, if a tour operator decides to develop his existing product range by adding new destinations, there will be set up costs in investigating the options and contractual obligations created, months before the first customers make full payment. Advertising and brochure costs will also be committed months ahead of the first sales. To give a different example, a decision by a hotel group to provide improved access for customers by investing in a new, on-line computer reservation system, may be made up to three years before the advantages of the new system secure additional customer bookings, and contribute revenue to pay back the cost and add to profit.

Marketing mix in context of the marketing system

Figure 6.2 expresses the marketing system in three concentric rings, which is an *alternative* way to represent the marketing process. Readers should compare this diagram with Figure 2.1 in Chapter 2. The two diagrams are completely compatible, but illustrate the same process from a different stand point. Figure 6.2 is designed to demonstrate how marketing mix decisions operate around the core focus of selected consumer segments.

As discussed earlier in the chapter, the four Ps in the *inner ring* are under the direct control of marketing managers, but subject to the other resources and management of the firm shown in the middle ring.

The *middle ring* elements are influenced by and influence marketing decisions, but are not typically under the direct control of marketing management. For example, initial choice of location and capacity for an hotel, as well as its general corporate image, will be heavily influenced by marketing inputs to project appraisal, but thereafter these aspects will be difficult or impossible to change in the short run. The management of personnel and operational systems, for example in an airline, will place constraints or limits for manoeuvre on marketing management. The size and scope of marketing budgets in all organizations will be governed by financial resources.

In the *outer ring*, summarized under six headings, are the factors external to a business, which are not controlled by, or even much influenced by marketing managers of any one organization. The powerful effect of some of these external factors on business decisions has already been made clear in Chapter 4 dealing with market determinants, and in Chapter 5 on buyer behaviour. The combined influence of the six factors in Figure 6.2 provides the context of opportunities or threats, within which strategic and tactical marketing mix decisions have to be made. Brief notes are provided below to explain what is meant by legal and regulatory framework, political, social and ethical attitudes, new and developing technology, structure of distribution channels, and competitors' actions.

Legal and regulatory framework covers the whole range of statutory and voluntary rules, within which decisions on the four Ps are made. Both advertising and brochures, for example, are surrounded by detailed consumer protection legislation covering the way in which products may be communicated to customers. Legal requirements for price notification in travel and tourism affect pricing decisions and limit the room for manoeuvre. Much of the regulatory

framework is common to all consumer industries, but some is specific to sectors of travel and tourism, such as the de-regulation provisions for US domestic airlines noted in Chapter 4. Other examples can be seen in the legal or voluntary requirements for registration, classification and grading, which in many countries are applied to hotels and other forms of tourist accommodation.

Political, social and ethical attitudes normally take years to evolve but, for example, British social attitudes towards alcohol licensing laws (especially permitted hours of opening of licensed premises) are evidently changing in the 1980s. Modern European attitudes to nude bathing have provided marketing opportunities for so called naturist resorts, such as Cap d'Agde in Southern France. The traditional concepts of non-charging museums in North America and Britain are presently changing fast in the face of cost pressures and evident opportunities for revenue generation from visitors. Skilled marketing involves a careful assessment of political and other social attitudes in order to take advantage of and exploit emerging trends ahead of the competition.

New and developing technology in travel and tourism applies in different ways to all sectors of the industry. For example, when the first generation of Boeing 747 and other 'jumbo' jets appeared in the early 1970s, they made a significant difference to airline seat mile costs and, through their influence on speed of journeys as well as prices over long distances, opened the markets for long-haul leisure travel in ways previously not possible. New information technology, for example, international computer networks for hotel reservations, linked by space satellites, has provided powerful new marketing tools, first exploited by Holiday Inns in the late 1970s, and now adopted by most large hotel groups. At a different, but still highly significant level for marketing in the sector, the nature and quality of the tourist products provided by the caravan park sector of accommodation has been transformed in recent years by the production technology applied to new caravans and trailers, and also to the provision of facilities such as swimming pools and other leisure equipment.

The structure of distribution channels may appear relatively stable on first consideration, but taken over a decade or so, the changes are considerable. In the USA, for example, the number of travel agency outlets more than doubled from just over 12,000 to over 28,000 between 1976 and 1986. In Britain, the rapid regrouping of many retail agencies into six large, national, multi-site networks took place over less than a decade, and has altered the structure of distribution channels and distribution strategies for most large producers in the tourist industry. The combination of changes in information technology and organizational structure in distribution channels, is one of the most important developments for marketing in travel and tourism, and likely to influence marketing mix decisions significantly over the remaining years of the twentieth century.

The actions of competitors provide the most immediately powerful of all the external factors affecting marketing managers' decisions. With very few exceptions, commercial organizations in travel and tourism are typically locked in continuous 'battle' with their competitors, many of whom offer very similar products, at similar prices, and use the same distribution channels. Where non-commercial organizations are engaged in marketing to achieve additional revenue, they are inevitably involved in a similar competitive struggle. In terms of long-run strategies as well as short-term tactics, competitors are engaged, quite literally, in a battle of wits, for which the principal weapons or tools available for use are the four Ps. The prizes in the struggle are expressed as market share, sales revenue, and profit.

Chapter summary

In this chapter the essential components of the marketing mix are introduced as the four Ps. They are discussed as the main levers or controls available to marketing managers in their continuous endeavours to achieve planned objectives and targets, expressed as sales volume and revenue from identified customer groups. The mix decisions are based on a mixture of marketing research, marketing planning procedures, and judgement of individual managers engaged in a battle of wits with their competitors.

This chapter sets the four Ps in the wider context of non-marketing resources within organizations, and the continuously changing external influences to which marketing managers have to respond. This very important concept of marketing response is succinctly summarized by Stanton's view that:

'A company's success depends on the ability of its executives to manage its marketing system in relation to its external environment. This means (1) responding to changes in the environment, (2) forecasting the direction and intensity of these changes, and (3) using the internal controllable resources in adapting to the changes in the external environment' (Stanton: 1981: p. 32).

In terms of this quotation there is no difference whatever in principle, between what is required of marketing managers in travel and tourism, and those in any other industry selling products to the general public. Such differences as do occur in marketing practice are based on the nature of the products offered, the particular implications of price manipulation in an industry distinguished by highly perishable production, and the nature of the distribution channels available. These differences are fully discussed in later chapters of this book.

Finally, it is stressed that marketing mix decisions mostly imply significant costs, which have to be met in advance of the revenue such decisions are expected to achieve. Later chapters will emphasize the need for integration and co-ordination of marketing mix decisions, in which even small improvements in the effectiveness of marketing expenditure can make a significant difference to profitability.

Further reading

Kotler, P., *Marketing Management: Analysis, Planning and Control*, Prentice-Hall, 1984, pp. 68–73 and Chapter 3.

7

Segmenting travel and tourism markets

For marketing purposes, apart from national tourist organizations (NTOs), no individual producer is ever likely to be much concerned with the whole of any country's tourist markets. They will typically be closely involved with particular sub groups of tourists within the total market, or 'segments' as they are known, which they identify as the most productive targets for their marketing activities. Even NTOs find it necessary to segment the total market of potential tourists in order to carry out marketing campaigns, although they may have to provide facilities such as information services for all visitors.

Chapter 3, reviewing the implications of the characteristics of travel and tourism, noted that the role of marketing managers is to manage and influence demand. 'The more an organization knows about its customers and prospective customers – their needs and desires, their attitudes and behaviour – the better it will be able to design and implement the marketing efforts required to stimulate their purchasing habits'. As explained in this chapter, market segmentation is the *process* whereby producers organize their knowledge of customer groups and select for particular attention, those whose needs and wants they are best able to supply with their products. In other words, since it is usually impossible to deal with all customers in the same way, market segmentation is the practical expression in business of the theory of consumer

orientation. It is certainly the most basic of all the practical marketing techniques available to marketing managers and it is normally the logical first step in the marketing process involved in developing more acceptable products to meet customers' needs. Segmentation is also the necessary first stage in the process of setting precise marketing objectives and targets, and the basis for effective planning, budgeting, and control of marketing activities.

This chapter is in three parts. The first part introduces the wide range of segments which typically exist for most producers of travel and tourism products. The second part defines the process of segmentation and outlines the criteria to be applied to any grouping of customers. The third part describes the principal ways used in travel and tourism to divide up markets for marketing purposes. The meaning of segmentation for a tour operator is illustrated in Figure 7.1.

Multiple segments for producers in travel and tourism

Before considering the techniques used to segment markets, it may be helpful to indicate the range of sub-groups with which operators in the different sectors of the travel and tourism industry are concerned. For each of the main sectors identified in Chapter 1 (excluding destination organizations which tend to be involved at least indirectly with every segment), five different consumer segments are listed below.

Hotels	Transport operators
1 Corporate/business clients	1 First class passengers
2 Group tours	2 Club class passengers
3 Independent vacationers	3 Tourist class passengers
4 Weekend/midweek package clients	4 Charter groups
5 Conference delegates	5 Domestic/ international travellers

Tour operators	Destination attractions
1 Young people 18–30	1 Local residents in the area
2 Families with children	2 Day visits from outside local area
3 Retired/senior citizens	3 Domestic tourists
4 Activity/sports seekers	4 Foreign tourists
5 Culture seekers	5 School parties

The segments listed above are not comprehensive but simply an illustration of the range of possibilities which exist for each sector. Readers may find it a useful exercise to extend these lists to around 15 segments for each sector, using the analysis discussed later in this chapter.

Even the minimum list above should make clear a very important point: *most businesses deal with not one but several segments*. Some markets are largely dictated by the location in which a business operates; others may be generated through products designed for identified segments and marketed to them.

A marketing and operations view of segmentation

At first sight, it may appear obvious that businesses create a range of products and market them to identified customer groups or segments. In practice, there is often a real conflict between the needs of operations management and the view of marketing managers.

From an operations standpoint it is usually most cost effective if a single, mass produced product, such as a standard airline seat, or a standard bedroom, can be marketed to all buyers. In that way unit costs can be cut to the minimum and operational controls can be standardized and more easily implemented. In such conditions, segmentation is still relevant as the basis for separate promotional campaigns, but it does not interfere with the smooth operation of production processes. Some marketing led organizations, most notably McDonald's family restaurants, major theme parks, and other attractions, do provide standard products for their customers, but they tend to be the exceptions in the tourist industry rather than the rule. Increasingly, under competitive market conditions in which several producers are competing for shares of the same markets and aiming their products at more than one group of the same prospective customers, the need to create and deliver *purpose designed products* for each group becomes more urgent. For reasons discussed in earlier chapters, the essence of a marketing approach is to adapt an organization's operations to satisfy identified customer requirements. If groups of prospective customers are found to have different needs, wants and motivations, competition makes it essential to design products which meet those needs, and to promote and distribute them accordingly.

In an ideal world each separate customer would receive special personal service or a custom-built product. To a great extent they may still do so in travel and tourism if they are able to pay the necessary price, as in luxury hotels. It may be possible also in very small businesses, such as farmhouses taking in a few visitors to stay, in which the level of personal contact

Because small groups required, Personal tuition.

between visitor and host is very high. In the real world of large-scale marketing of standardized products, however, such individual attention is not possible at the highly competitive prices which customers are willing and able to pay. There is, therefore, often a considerable level of tension, between the interests of marketing managers in offering products designed to cater for sub-groups in the market, as the best way to secure their custom, and the interests of the operations managers responsible for holding down or reducing unit costs, and controlling the quality standards of product delivery.

If significant product differentiation is required to meet the range of needs of different market segments, there is also likely to be management problems in servicing the needs at the same time on the same premises. To provide an example, a hotel may find it difficult or impossible simultaneously to meet the needs of business people and coach parties of packaged tourists in the same restaurant; museums have similar problems with noisy school parties, and older visitors requiring peace and quiet to achieve their satisfaction with a visit. The problems are very clear in the case of conference halls, which may be separately marketed as the venue for a pop concert one day, a political meeting next day, and a sales conference on the subsequent day. In each case a different segment with different needs is involved but they are not compatible on the same premises on the same day. Considerable strain and careful sequencing is imposed on those who manage such operations.

Management concerns with reconciling the requirements of segmentation and product differentiation with economies of scale, is not a new problem. As Alderson put it some thirty years ago, marketing is to be seen essentially as a multi-phase sorting process, which 'makes mass production [standardization] possible first by providing the assortment of supplies needed in manufacturing [production] and then taking over

the successive transformations which ultimately produce [deliver] the assortments [products] in the hands of consuming units [to customers]' (Alderson: 1958: p. 59). By inserting the words in brackets as shown, it is easy to adapt Alderson's original sorting concept intended for manufacturing industry, to a travel and tourism context. As such, the sorting concept neatly explains the essence of a segmentation approach to marketing today.

In other words the task of marketing management, in close liaison with operations management, is to identify compatible products, which meet the needs of compatible target segments. This has to be achieved on the same premises in a way which permits economies to be achieved in both operational and marketing processes, so as to achieve optimum income from the selected customer and product mix. Such optimization is never easy to achieve in service businesses and readers should be aware of the conflicting management interests which often exist in practice.

Segmentation defined

Segmentation may now be defined as a process of dividing a total market, such as all tourists, into manageable sub-groups or segments of the total. Its purpose is to facilitate more cost effective marketing, through the design, promotion and delivery of purpose built products aimed at satisfying the identified needs of target groups. In other words, segmentation is justified on the grounds of achieving greater efficiency in the supply of products to meet identified demand, and in the marketing process. In most cases producers in travel and tourism will typically deal with several segments over a twelve-month period but not necessarily simultaneously.

In the tourist industry, most established producers will often have no practical choice but to deal with certain segments because of the location and nature of their ongoing business.

Usually there will be other segments which could be chosen as targets if they meet the producer's needs. These new or optional segments are likely to change over a period of, say, 5 to 10 years, as the determinants of travel and tourism change. For example, as a normal part of monitoring market trends and observing competitor's actions, a tour operator may decide to develop a range of specific products for segments of people over the age of 55. If the operator is successful, the over-55s product may grow from a small base to, say, 20 per cent of total turnover over a period of years. The operator will have changed its segment/product mix as a result of a marketing decision.

Most businesses will have scope and opportunities for altering the current mix of their business as generated by the existing structure of segments, through manipulating the marketing mix around new segments. The criteria for choosing new segments for marketing development will stem either from the producer's needs to utilize assets, for example to develop offseason business, or from attractive characteristics of the segments themselves, for example high relative expenditure per capita of some groups compared with others.

Actionable market segments

Drawing on the contributions of Kotler (1984) and Chisnall (1985) it is possible to focus on four main criteria, which must be applied to any segment if it is to be usable or actionable in marketing. Each segment has to be:

- discrete,
- measurable,
- viable, and
- appropriate.

Discrete means that the selected sub-groups must be separately identifiable using some dimensions such as purpose, income, location of residence, or motivation, as discussed later in this chapter.

Measurable means that the dimensions which distinguish the sub-groups must be measurable using available marketing research data, or with such new data as can be obtained within acceptable budgets. Research is normally expensive and segmentation must be affordable within available budgets. Segments which cannot be adequately measured on a regular basis cannot be properly targeted. If targeting is not measurably precise, it will be difficult or impossible to evaluate the effectiveness of marketing activities over time.

Viable means that the long run projected revenue to be achieved from a targeted segment exceeds the full cost of designing a marketing mix to achieve it, by a margin which meets the organization's objectives. In the short run it may be necessary to ignore segment viability in order to achieve other organization objectives. Viability, therefore, is a function of the costs of designing products for segments, promoting to target groups, and ensuring that prospective customers can find convenient access to such products, once they have been persuaded to buy.

Appropriate reflecting the inseparability of service product delivery (see Chapter 3), it is essential that segments to be supplied on the same premises are mutually compatible and contribute to the overall image or position in the market adopted by a producer. An economy car with a Rolls-Royce label would be absurd, even if the company wished to make it. Similarly, down-market coach tour business to the Savoy Hotel in London or to Crowne Plaza hotels, could only damage those companies' reputations for exclusiveness and luxury, at a price which maintains the expected standards.

To summarize thus far, market segments are identified target groups within a total market, chosen because they are relevant to an organization's interests, skills and particular capabilities. In other words, selected segments have particular needs, which a producer feels especially competent to satisfy with relevant products.

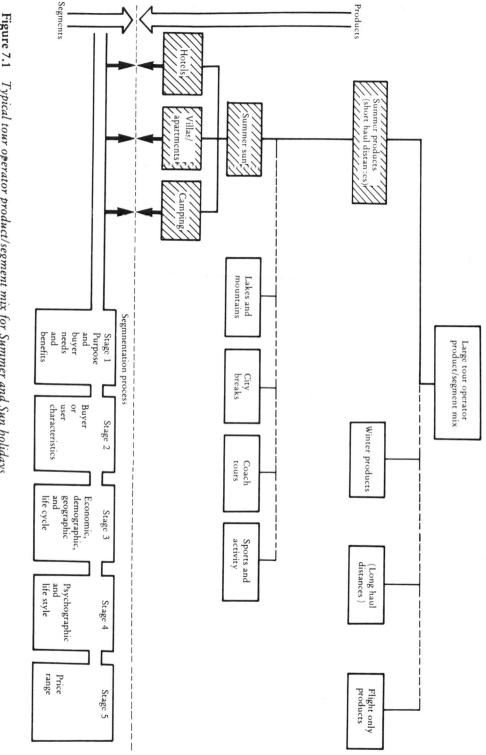

Figure 7.1   *Typical tour operator product/segment mix for Summer and Sun holidays*

To be actionable in a marketing sense, segments must meet the four criteria noted in this section which are as relevant to producers of manufactured goods as to service producers. The next section discusses the ways, sometimes known as 'modes', by which target groups may be identified and measured.

In considering the modes, it may be found helpful to relate them to the context of a product/segment mix for the Summer Sun holidays of a large tour operator, shown in Figure 7.1.

Methods used to segment markets

There are six main methods or ways of dividing up markets for segmentation purposes, all of which are used in practice in the travel and tourism industry. These methods are usually based on some form of marketing research and a commitment to segmentation normally implies a commitment to market research.

The methods are listed below and subsequently discussed. The sequence in which they appear is not the sequence commonly found in marketing texts but if reflects an order of priority which will be found most relevant to travel and tourism markets.

Segmentation by:

1 Purpose of travel
2 Buyer needs, motivations, and benefits sought
3 Buyer or user characteristics
4 Demographic, economic, and geographic characteristics
5 Psychographic characteristics
6 Price

These six methods are not to be seen as alternative choices for segmentation, but rather as overlapping and complementary ways by which it is possible to analyse a consumer market in order to appreciate, and select from it, the range of segments it comprises. Many businesses in travel and tourism will use at least three of the methods for any particular segment; all of them could be used if the segment being analysed is important enough to a business.

Segmentation by purpose

For most producers in travel and tourism, practical marketing segmentation begins with a careful analysis of the purposes for which customers travel, and use their (and their competitors') products. For example, if the purpose of travel is mainly for business, this obviously requires a range of business orientated travel products. Within the broad category of business travel there are many aspects of purpose, which determine the nature of the products offered and the promotional approach to be used. For example, conference markets require different products to those supplied to other business travellers; meetings for groups of different sizes may require special provision; some travellers may require secretarial services, and so on. The range of segments noted under the main sectors of travel and tourism earlier in this chapter reflect some of the more obvious purposes. A little thought will indicate a broad range of possibilities and, provided the customer groups associated with any purpose meet the four essential criteria for effective segmentation, a detailed understanding of each purpose of visit is likely to be useful in practice. For smaller businesses in travel and tourism, segmentation and simple analysis of purpose may be adequate for all practical or actionable purposes.

For any producer organization in tourism approaching a new market for the first time, segmentation by purpose of travel is likely to be the most logical way to start the process. For a tour operator in the holiday market, typical purposes may include:

1 to enjoy beach type holidays in the sun,
2 to participate in active water sports,
3 to meet new people,

4   to participate in cultural activities.

For a tour operator with an existing successful business, the grouping of products currently provided is likely to be an accurate reflection of customer purposes served. In other words, and this is an important point

> market segmentation and product formulation, are mirror images if they are correctly matched.

The other segmentation methods discussed below are ways to sharpen the focus of segments, which already exist in outline through the identification of travel purpose. Figure 7.1 which shows an example of segmentation for tour operators will help to make this point clear.

Segmentation by buyer needs and benefits sought

Within purpose, and obviously an aspect of it, the next logical consideration for segmentation is to understand the needs, wants and motivations of particular customer groups, as discussed in Chapter 5. For reasons which are developed in a later chapter on products, it is generally accepted in marketing that customers are typically seeking particular benefits when they make their product choices. For example, some business travellers may identify luxury and high levels of personal service, as the principal benefits they seek when travelling away from home. Others may identify speed of service and convenience of particular locations as their principal benefits. Some business travellers, if they are paid a standard sum of money for their travel expenses, may seek economy products, especially if they are able to retain the difference between their travel allowance and the actual cost they pay. Some travellers prefer to stay in large, modern, international hotels, while others choose older, more traditional establishments, which may offer a more personalized service.

In the case of tourist attractions, the benefits sought by family groups may relate to children's interests rather than those of the adults who purchase the admission tickets. In the case of museums, the benefits sought by most visitors are likely to be understood in terms of an hour or two's general interest and amusement, because they have only a limited knowledge of the subject matter's intrinsic merit. Many a museum has been misled by its own enthusiasm for its precious collection, into believing that average visitors are also very interested in the subjects displayed. Typically they are not, and their threshold of patience is very easily crossed if the collections are not displayed in ways designed to appeal to general interest. In most sectors of travel and tourism, the range and perceived importance of the benefits sought by customer segments are not necessarily apparent to marketing managers. Usually they may be discovered only through the conduct of market research among identified target groups. Segmentation by benefits makes it possible for marketing managers to fine tune their products within the broad requirements of purpose noted earlier.

Segmentation by buyer or user characteristics

Within purpose and benefits sought, there is ample scope for refining the segmentation process according to the types of behaviour or user characteristics which customers exhibit. One obvious example is the frequency of usage of products. Business users may be very frequent users of hotels, with perhaps twenty or more stays in hotels in a year, and even more frequent users of airlines and car rental companies. Frequent users may represent only 10 per cent of individual customers in a year, but up to 60 per cent of revenue for producers such as hotel groups and airlines. As such they are usually a key segment for marketing attention. The benefits sought by frequent users for particular purposes are an obvious focus for marketing research.

Tourist expenditure per capita, not necessarily directly associated with levels of income or socio-economic status, is another dimension of behaviour or user characteristics which is highly relevant to segmentation decisions. For example, many British holidaymakers in Spain outspend German and Swedish visitors, although their per capita income is very much less. Other things being equal, high expenditure segments are seen as attractive targets in all sectors.

Some buyers tend to use the same hotel group, airline or travel agent on each or most occasions, a buyer characteristic known in marketing as 'brand loyalty'. Others may choose their purchase on each occasion according to price, convenience and availability. 'Loyal' customers are highly attractive to producers for obvious reasons and a combination of high spending, high frequency and high loyalty would be the best of reasons for designing products and promotional campaigns aimed at securing and retaining such valuable buyers.

A little thought will soon indicate that there is a wide range of user characteristics which could be relevant for identifying particular segments. The characteristics may be divided according to the timing or sequence of buyers' decisions, before, during, or after using any travel and tourism product. The table below explains this point.

The aspects of behaviour noted below, are not fully comprehensive but they cover main aspects, and can be adapted to the specific context of any producer in travel and tourism. Pre-booking characteristics, for example, would not be very important to museums (but still relevant for group visitors), whereas details of 'in use' circulation patterns, exhibits visited, division of time within the museum during the visit, would be highly significant in management terms.

Measuring and monitoring the user characteristics noted in the table is the basis of many surveys of customers and prospective users (see Chapter 11). In their various forms, user surveys are the most widely practised type of market research used in all parts of the travel and tourism industry.

Segmentation by demographic, economic, geographic and life-cycle characteristics

If producers commence their segmentation process with an analysis of customer needs and benefits sought, within purpose of travel, they are likely to have a clear understanding of the type of products their chosen customer groups want. If that understanding is backed up by information obtained by user surveys of the type noted in the preceding section, their knowledge of target groups will already be considerable. For the purposes of efficient promotion and distri-

Buyer behaviour/usage characteristics by sequence of purchase and usage

Pre-booking	Booking process	In use	After use
media habits	via travel agent	length of stay	customer satisfaction level and perceived value for money
awareness/use of brochures	via central reservation office	party size and composition	
sources of travel information used	booking direct with producer	transport mode	
previous usage/ experience	package/independent arrangements	expenditure per head	
frequency of usage	credit terms required		

bution of products, however, especially to prospective new customers rather than existing ones, they will also need detailed knowledge of the demographic and other physical characteristics of their selected target groups.

At the simplest level of analysis, which will be familiar to most readers, customer segments may be defined in terms of basic facts about their age, sex, occupation, income grouping, and place of residence. Known collectively as customer 'profiles', such facts are often easily obtained for existing customers in travel and tourism as a byproduct of booking records, registration procedures, and regular customer surveys such as the in-flight studies undertaken by airlines. Descriptive information about buyers of travel products generally, are usually also available in many countries from various forms of national tourist office sponsored, and commercial surveys of travel and tourism markets, commonly available for purchase in countries with developed tourism industries. In Britain, the British Tourism Surveys (monthly and yearly) published by national tourist boards, provide a wealth of standard demographic data. In the USA, the US Travel Data Center in Washington is the source of similar data.

Simple descriptive profiles have their uses in segmentation, and in deciding which media to choose for advertising purposes. In the 1980s many producers in travel and tourism go no further. But on their own, without the prior analysis of purpose, benefits and user characteristics, demographic profiles will seldom be an adequate basis for organizing effective marketing campaigns. Producer organizations which rely solely on such simple data run the risk of being out-manoeuvred by their competitors.

At a slightly more complex level of analysis of consumer profiles, it is possible to group together a number of physical characteristics of people to form what is usually termed 'lifecycle analysis' based on the stages through which all people progress in life, from infancy to old age.

The travel behaviour of people aged 18 to 35 may not vary much according to whether they are single or married, but it is likely to vary enormously according to whether or not they have children. Those with young children under the age of four are likely to have different travel needs from those with older children between the ages of 10 and 15. At the other end of the age scale, the travel activities of those aged between 55 and 70 will vary enormously according to whether or not they are retired or still at work.

In Britain since the early 1980s, a very interesting and powerful segmentation tool has been developed through the combination of census data with the postal area codes used to identify every group of households in the country. Allied to the power of modern computers to store and analyse data, the major development was the classification of household types into a total of thirty-eight different groups, more usually summarized under eleven groups, each with clearly defined characteristics of housing types, which in turn correlate closely with population characteristics of age, family structure, and income. The housing types include, for example, *modern family housing, higher incomes; better off council estates;* and *affluent suburban housing.*

Known as ACORN, which stands for *a* classification *of* residential *neighbourhoods,* the census data is now supplemented by data from major commercial surveys of purchasing patterns, including travel behaviour. By the late 1980s, provided suppliers record the names and addresses of their customers, it is now possible for research companies to trace and map the typical household types and the areas in which buyers with similar characteristics may be found throughout Britain.

These *geodemographic* segmentation tools, as they are known, are capable of targeting individual buyers with great precision and they clearly have 'particular relevance to direct marketing, leaflet distribution, and local media selection' (Chisnall: 1985: p. 280). Since 1986, the ACORN targeting techniques have been increasingly used by tourist boards in Britain, and appear to offer great scope for cost effective direct response marketing based on precise segmentation. (See also Chapter 19.)

To illustrate the usefulness in practice of the demographic, economic, geographic, and life-cycle analysis of segments, it is interesting to consider one of the typical target groups for weekend package holidays in hotels in Britain. These products have enjoyed a significant growth market in the 1970s and 1980s. The target groups of buyers are typically married, professional people, college educated, living in their own homes (not rented) in cities or suburbs, in the age range 35–60, either without children living at home or with children over the age of about 10 who can be left with friends or relatives. It is also possible to define the typical distance in miles which such couples would drive to reach their weekend destinations, so that the catchment areas of target customers can be targeted from the location of any hotel. With such a profile, which draws on most of the descriptive characteristics referred to in this section, supplemented by the ACORN analysis, it would not be difficult to develop a broadly relevant promotional campaign and choose the type of media best calculated to reach the target audience. This profile is not the only one for weekend package breaks, but it is generally applicable to the market as a whole. To refine the segmentation further, market research would be needed to assess for any particular hotel and its location, customers' reasons for taking breaks, their personal motivations, and benefits sought.

Segmentation by psychographic characteristics and life style

'Psychographics' is a term used to denote measurement of an individual's mental attitudes and psychological make-up, as distinguished from demographics, which measures the objective dimensions of age, sex, income and life cycle, noted in the preceding section. Always involving sophisticated marketing research techniques, psychographics aim to place consumers on psychological rather than physical dimensions. The reason for segmenting buyers on psychological dimensions is the belief that common values can be found among groups of consumers, which tend to determine their purchasing patterns. For example, some individuals are mentally predisposed to seek adventure, enjoy risks and active vacations. Typically, their values and goals are those of competitive people for whom measures of achievement, such as winning races or gaining proficiency certificates, are important. Others are risk avoiders, choose passive and unstressful vacations, often at familiar destinations unlikely to present any unknown threats.

The measurement of consumer attitudes and their values has been a preoccupation of market researchers on both sides of the Atlantic for decades. The methods of measurement, typically involving consumers in making complex ratings of items included in multiple choice questions, were greatly enhanced by the availability of computers in the 1960s and 1970s. A range of computer programmes is now available to measure the extent and strength of any correlations which exist between people's attitudes and values, and their behaviour patterns as buyers of travel and other products. Such measurements may be further refined by including questions about attitudes to and perceptions of individual companies in the industry, and the products they supply. This type of research underlies the modern concept of product positioning which is discussed later in this book.

Related to their demographic characteristics and life cycle, the links which exist between attitudes, perceptions and actual buyer behaviour, combine to determine the life style which individuals adopt. An understanding of the life style of target customers has obvious advantages when formulating new products or creating messages designed to motivate such people. Among international operators in travel and tourism, Club Méditerranée, for example, clearly understand and have single-mindedly adopted a life-style segmentation approach, as any consideration of their product brochures will confirm.

Life-style segmentation is based on an understanding of individuals' needs, benefits sought and motivations; it normally involves a significant expenditure on marketing research and it is used within the basic segmentation by purpose of visit.

Segmentation by price

Price ranges are often used in the early stages of segmenting markets in travel and tourism, as in most other consumer markets. For any given purpose of travel there are typically segments of customers to be found at the high priced, luxury end of a market and others at the low priced, economy end of the market who will usually be highly price elastic. When deciding to market new products, or enter a market for the first time, producers have to make a fundamental strategic choice as to where on the prevailing price spectrum they should aim their marketing effort. That choice largely determines which segments they will be dealing with, and has immediate implications for the nature of the products to be provided and the form of any promotion and distribution.

Prices communicate expectations of product quality and value to customers; they also communicate images of producer organizations which customers are likely to relate to their own images of the sorts of people they think they are. Once made, in the context of chosen target segments, pricing strategy governs all subsequent decisions in the marketing mix. For example, if a tour operator decides to compete in the luxury price range, all its services must be organized to deliver the high quality which is implied. Brochures, advertising and all forms of sales promotion, as well as the products and ancillary services available when customers reach their destinations, have to live up to the target market's expectations. As indicated earlier in this chapter, compatibility between segments is essential for service businesses which bring customers together in the same premises and price structures are usually a major element in achieving this. A full discussion of pricing will be found in Chapter 9.

Chapter summary

This chapter focuses on the role of market segmentation as a set of techniques which enable marketing managers to divide total markets into component parts, with which they can deal more effectively and more profitably for marketing purposes. As Chisnall puts it, '. . . market segmentation recognizes that people differ in their tastes, needs, attitudes, lifestyles, family size and composition, etc. . . . It is a deliberate policy of maximizing market demand by directing marketing efforts at significant sub-groups of customers or consumers' (Chisnall: 1985: p. 264).

The more that people differ, and the greater the level of competition between producers seeking to maintain or increase their shares of the same market, the more important segmentation becomes to business success. It is usually impossible in practice to promote to, and satisfy all customers, in the same way. The case for segmentation increases as markets grow in total volume and sub-groups are identified, around whose particular needs it becomes cost effective (viable) to focus particular marketing activity. Even where, for operational reasons, the basic product is essentially the same for all customers, as is usually the case for many tourist attractions, there are different ways to promote to sub-groups in the market and opportunities to enhance the basic product around a segment's needs. The promotion of special group facilities for educational visits to museums, and the creation and use of special information materials for school visitors, illustrates this point.

'There is no single way to segment a market. A marketer has to try different segmentation variables, singly and in combination, hoping to find an insightful way to view the market structure' (Kotler: 1984: p. 254). This chapter outlines six variables in the order of importance considered relevant to most producers in travel and tourism. In particular, this chapter emphasizes the importance of segmentation by purpose of travel, and of understanding the benefits different groups of customers seek. The implications for segmentation of researching user characteristics, before, during and after purchasing and using travel products is also stressed.

Segmentation in a rapidly changing business environment is never a static process. New segments emerge as some older ones disappear or are no longer viable as a result of market change. At any point in time, most organizations in travel and tourism will deal with several different segments at the same time. All of them are likely to be in a state of continuous change, partly in response to shifts in the external market determinants, and partly to changes in customers' internal needs, attitudes and motivations. In almost every case there will be opportunities for marginal improvements in what a business knows of its customers and, therefore, how best to satisfy their product needs marginally better than the competition. For these reasons, except for the smallest of businesses, segmentation normally justifies a considerable and continuous commitment to marketing research; an important consideration developed in Chapter 11.

Further reading

Kotler, P., *Marketing Management: Analysis, Planning and Control*, Prentice-Hall, 1984, Chapter 8.

Baker, M. J., *Marketing: An Introductory Text*, Macmillan, 1985, Chapter 6.

8

Travel and tourism products: Product formulation

In Chapter 6, products are introduced as one of the four basic elements in the marketing mix to be geared to the needs of identified customer groups. The process of identifying customer segments is covered in Chapter 7. In practice, the way in which products are put together (product formulation) is the most important response which marketing managers make to what they know of their customers' needs and interests. Product decisions, with all their implications for the management of service operations and profitability, reflect all of an organization's management policies, including long-term growth strategy, investment and personnel policy. They largely determine the corporate image which an organization creates in the minds of its existing and prospective customers.

To a great extent, the design of products determines what prices can be charged, what forms of promotion are needed, and what distribution channels are used. For all these reasons it is realistic to identify customer-related product decisions as 'the basis of marketing strategy and tactics' (Middleton: 1983: p. 2). As the most important of the four Ps in the marketing mix, product formulation requires careful consideration in any branch of marketing. Because of the particular nature and characteristics of travel and tourism, the subject is especially complex in the tourist industry.

This chapter is in four parts. The first part introduces the existence of two different di-

mensions or aspects of tourism products, one of which is the total product as perceived by customers, and the other is the view of products taken by marketing managers of individual producer organizations. Products are explained in terms of their component parts and the benefits which they offer to customers. The second and third parts discuss these two dimensions of products separately, and the fourth part introduces the meaning of product positioning.

A components view of travel and tourism products – from two standpoints

It follows from the definitions discussed in Chapter 1 that any tourist visit to a destination comprises a mix of several different *components*, including travel, accommodation, attractions and other facilities such as catering and entertainments. Sometimes all of the components are purchased from a commercial supplier, for example when a customer buys an inclusive holiday from a tour operator, or asks a travel agent to put the components together for a business trip. Sometimes customers supply some of the components themselves, for example when a tourist drives his own car to stay with friends at a destination.

The total tourist product

Developing the components view from the

standpoint of the tourist, Medlik and Middleton noted (1973) that, 'As far as the tourist is concerned, the product covers the complete experience from the time he leaves home to the time he returns to it.' Thus, 'the tourist product is to be considered as an amalgam of three main components of attractions ... and facilities at the destination, and accessibility of the destination.' In other words the tourist product is 'not an airline seat or a hotel bed, or relaxing on a sunny beach ... but rather an amalgam of many components, or a package.' The same article continued, 'airline seats and hotel beds ... are merely elements or components of a total tourist product which is a composite product.' This concept of the product was used subsequently by Wahab *et al*., (1976), and Schmoll (1977), and appears to be widely accepted internationally.

The product of individual producers

Without detracting in any way from the general validity and relevance of the total view of tourist products noted above, it has to be recognized that airlines, hotels, attractions, car rental and other producer organizations in the industry, typically take a much narrower view of the products they sell, which often focuses exclusively on their own services. Many large hotel groups and transport operators employ product managers in their marketing teams and handle product formulation and development entirely in terms of the operations they control. Hotels refer to 'conference products' for example, or 'leisure products', airlines, to 'business class products and so on. For this reason, the total product concept sets the context in which tourism marketing is conducted but it has only limited value in guiding the practical product design decisions, which managers of individual producer organizations have to make. A components view of products still holds good, however, because it is in the nature of service products that they can be divided into a series of

specific service operations, which combine to make up the particular products customers buy. Thus, for a visitor to a hotel, the hotel product covers the complete accommodation experience from the point of first contact, which may be made by a travel agent or direct to the hotel's reception desk, through checking-in procedures, all the services used during the stay and in checking out.

It is usually highly instructive to analyse any service producers' operations in terms of the full sequence of contacts between customer and operator, from the time that they make initial enquiries (if any), until they have used the product and left the premises. Even for a product such as that provided by a museum, there is ample scope to analyse all the stages of a visit and potential points of contact that occur from the moment the customer is in sight of the entrance until he leaves the building, say two hours later. Putting the components view in slightly different terms, individual service producers designing products 'must define the service concept in terms of the bundles of goods and services sold to the consumer and the relative importance of each component to the customer' (Sasser *et al*.: 1978: p. 14).

To bring the two distinctive aspects of tourist products together; the total view and that of individual producer organizations; it is possible to consider them as two different dimensions. The total view is a horizontal dimension in the sense that a series of individual products are included in it, from which customers, or tour operators acting as manufacturers (Chapter 24), make their selection to produce the total experience. By contrast the producers' view is a vertical dimension of specific service components organized around the identified needs and wants of target segments of customers. Producers typically have regard for their interactions with other organizations on the horizontal dimension, but their principal concern is with the vertical dimension of their own operation (this point is developed later in this chapter).

A benefits view of products

Before discussing the components of the two dimensions of travel and tourism products in more detail, it is important to keep in mind the customers' view of what businesses of all types offer for sale. Levitt's statement is succinct; 'People do not buy products, they buy the expectation of benefits. It is the benefits that are the product' (Levitt: 1969). Developing this point, Kotler noted 'the customer is looking for particular utilities. Existing products are only a current way of packaging those utilities. The company must be aware of all the ways in which customers can gain the sought satisfaction. These define the competition' (Kotler: 1976: p. 25).

Researching targeted customers' perceptions of product benefits and utilities, and designing or adapting products to match their expectations, lies of course at the heart of marketing theory. There is no difference in principle between a benefits view of products applied to travel and tourism and any other industry producing consumer goods.

Components of the total tourism product

From the standpoint of a potential customer considering any form of tourist visit, the product may be defined as a bundle or package of tangible and intangible components, based on activity at a destination. The package is perceived by the tourist as an experience, available at a price.

There are five main components in the total product, which are discussed separately below:

- Destination attractions
- Destination facilities and services
- Accessibility of the destination
- Images of the destination
- Price to the consumer

Destination attractions

These are elements within the destination's environment, which largely determine consumers' choice and influence prospective buyers' motivation. They include:

Natural attractions	landscape, seascape, beaches, climate and other geographical features of the destination.
Built attractions	buildings and tourist infrastructure including historic and modern architecture, monuments, promenades, parks and gardens, marinas, ski slopes, industrial archaeology, managed visitor attractions generally, golf courses, speciality shops and themed retail areas.
Cultural attractions	history and folklore, religion and art, theatre, entertainment and museums. Some of these may be developed into special events, festivals, and pageants.
Social attractions	way of life of resident population, language and opportunities for social encounters.

Destination facilities and services

These are elements within the destination, or linked to it, which make it possible for tourists to stay, and in other ways enjoy and participate in the attractions. They include:

Accommodation units	hotels, apartments, villas, campsites, caravan parks, hostels, condominia.

Restaurants, bars and cafes	ranging from fast food through to luxury restaurants.
Transport at the destination	taxis, coaches, car rental, cycle hire.
Sports/activity	ski schools, sailing schools, golf clubs.
Other facilities	craft courses, language schools.
Retail outlets	shops, travel agents, souvenirs, camping supplies.
Other services	hairdressing, information services, tourist police.

For some of these elements, the distinction between attractions and facilities may be blurred. For example, a hotel may well become an attraction in its own right and a prime reason for selecting a destination. Nevertheless, its primary function of providing facilities and services remains clear.

Accessibility of the destination
These are the elements which affect the cost, speed and the convenience with which a traveller may reach a destination. They include:

Infrastructure	of roads, airports, railways, seaports.
Equipment	size, speed and range of public transport vehicles.
Operational factors	routes operated, frequency of services, prices charged.
Government regulations	the range of regulatory controls over transport operations.

Images and perceptions of the destination
For reasons outlined in Chapter 5, the attitudes and images which customers have towards products strongly influence their buying decisions. Destination images are not necessarily grounded in experience or facts but are powerful motivators in travel and tourism. Images, and the expectations of travel experiences, are closely linked in prospective customers' minds.

For example, of the millions of people in America and Europe who have not so far visited Las Vegas, there will be few who do not carry in their minds some mental picture or image of the experiences that destination provides. Through the media and through hearsay, most people have already decided whether they are attracted or repelled by the Las Vegas image. All destinations have images, often based more on historic rather than current events, and it is an essential objective of destination marketing to sustain, alter or develop images in order to influence prospective buyers' expectations. The images of producer organizations within destinations (for example the hotels in Las Vegas) are often closely related to the destination image.

Price to the consumer
Any visit to a destination carries a price, which is the sum of what it costs for travel, accommodation, and participation in a selected range of services around the available attractions. Because most destinations offer a range of products and appeal to a range of segments, price in the travel and tourism industry covers a very wide range. Visitors travelling thousands of miles and using luxury hotels, for example, pay a very different price in New York than students sharing campus style accommodation with friends. Yet the two groups may use adjacent seats in a Broadway theatre. Price varies by season, by choice of activities, and internationally by exchange rates as well as by distance travelled, transport mode, and choice of facilities and services.

Some marketing implications of the total product concept
With a little thought it will be clear that the elements comprising the five product components, although they are combined and integrated in the tourist's experience, are in fact

capable of extensive and more or less independent variation over time. Some of these variations are planned, as in the case of the Disney World developments in previously unused areas around Orlando, Florida, or in the former mosquito infested coastline of Languedoc Roussillon in France. In both those cases, massive engineering works transformed the natural environment and created major tourist destinations in recent years. By contrast, in New York, London, or Paris, the city environments have not been much altered for travel and tourism purposes although there have been massive planned changes in the services and facilities available to visitors.

Many of the changes in destination attractions have not been planned, however, and in Northern Europe the decline in popularity of traditional seaside resorts since the 1960s has been largely the result of changes in the accessibility of competing destinations in the sunnier South of the Continent. Changes in the product components often occur in spite of, and not because of the wishes of governments and destination planners. They occur because travel and tourism, especially at the international level, is a relatively free market with customers free to pursue new attractions as they become available. Changes in exchange rates, which alter the prices of destinations, are certainly not planned by the tourist industry but have a massive effect on tourist volumes, as the movements between the UK and the USA since 1978 have demonstrated.

It is in the promotional field of images and perceptions where some of the most interesting changes occur, and these are marketing decisions. The classic recent example of planned image engineering may be found in the 'I Love New York' campaign which, based on extensive preliminary market research, created a significant improvement to the 'Big Apple's' appeal in the early 1980s. At a very different level, industrial cities in Britain such as Manchester and Bradford, are working hard on their image projection to achieve the same type of change in tourists' perceptions.

The total view of the product taken by customers, whether or not they buy an inclusive package from a tour operator or travel wholesaler, is essentially the same view or standpoint as that adopted by tour operators. Tour operators act on behalf of the interests of tens or hundreds of thousands of customers, and their brochures are a practical illustration of blending the five product components discussed in this section (see also Chapter 24).

The total view is also the standpoint of national, regional and local tourist organizations, whose responsibilities usually include the co-ordination and presentation of the product components in their areas. This responsibility is an important one even if the destination tourist organizations are involved only in liaison and joint marketing, and not in the sale of specific product offers to travellers.

In considering the total product, it should be noted that there is no natural or automatic harmony between components, such as attractions and accommodation, and they are seldom under any one organization's control. Even within the component sectors there will usually be many different organizations, each with different, perhaps conflicting objectives and interests. Indeed, it is the dispersion or fragmentation of overall control, and the relative freedom of producer organizations to act according to their perceived self interests, at least in the short term, which makes it difficult for national, regional and even local tourist organizations to exert much co-ordinating influence either in marketing or in planning. Part of this fragmentation simply reflects the fact that most developed destinations offer a wide range of tourist products and deal with a wide range of segments. In the long term, however, the future success of a destination must involve coordination and recognition of mutual interests between all the components of the total tourist product. Achieving such co-ordination is the rationale for much of the marketing work undertaken by NTOs (see Chapter 20).

Specific products – the producer's view

The total view of tourist products is highly relevant to the marketing decisions taken by individual producers, especially in establishing the interrelationships and scope for co-operation between suppliers in different sectors of the industry, for example between attractions and accommodation, or between transport and accommodation. But in order to design their product offers around specific service operations, there are other dimensions of products for marketers to consider, which are common to all forms of consumer marketing and part of widely accepted marketing theory. Marketing managers 'need to think about the product on three levels' (Kotler: 1984: p. 463).

Using Kotler's terminology, which is based on earlier contributions by Levitt, these three levels are:

- Core product
- Tangible product
- Augmented product

The core product is the essential service or benefit which is designed to satisfy the identified needs of target customer segments; the tangible product is the specific offer for sale which states what a customer will receive for his money; the augmented product is all the forms of added value, which producers may build into their tangible product offers to make them more attractive to their intended customers.

Although the labels applied to these three levels of any product are not very informative, the value of the thought process the levels reflect is potentially very great indeed. They reflect a thought process which can be applied by producers in any of the tourist industry sectors and are equally applicable to large and small businesses.

The following example of an inclusive weekend break in a hotel will help to explain what the three levels mean in practice. The product offer covers two nights accommodation and two breakfasts, and may be taken at any one of a chain of hotels covering several different locations. Because of the bedroom design and facilities available at the hotels, the package is designed to appeal to professional couples with young children. The product is offered for sale at an inclusive price through a brochure, which is distributed at each of the hotels in the chain and through travel agents. It is in competition with the products of other very similar hotels, which are promoting to the same market at similar price levels. Products of this type are now widely available in many parts of North America and Europe and the total market for them grew substantially in the 1970s and 1980s.

Core product – comprises the essential need or benefit as perceived and sought by the customer, which may be expressed in words and pictures designed to motivate purchasing responses. In the example under discussion, the core benefit may be defined as relaxation, rest, fun, and self fulfilment in a family context.

It should be noted that the core product reflects characteristics of the target customer, not the hotel. The hotel may, and does aim to design a need satisfying core product better than its competitors, through its delivery of the sought benefits, but all its competitors are typically aiming at the same basic customer needs and offering virtually identical benefits. Typically, customers' core needs tend not to change very quickly, although a hotel's ability to identify and better satisfy such needs can change considerably. Since customer perceptions are never precisely understood, there is ample scope for improvement in this area.

Tangible product – comprises the formal offer of the product as set out in a brochure, stating exactly what is to be provided at a specified time at a specified price. In the example under discussion, the tangible formal product is two nights and two breakfasts at a particular location, using rooms of a defined standard, with bathroom, TV, telephone, etc. The provision (if any) of elevators, coffee shops, air conditioning and swimming pool are all within the formal product and the name of the hotel is also included.

In the case of hotel products generally, and certainly in the example cited, there is often very little to choose between competitors' tangible product offers and price may become a principal reason for choice. Blindfolded and led to any one of say twenty competitors' premises, most hotel customers would not easily recognize the identity of their surroundings. The description of the tangible product in the brochure forms the basic contract of sale, which would be legally enforceable in most countries.

Augmented product – Augmentation is harder to define with precision. It comprises the *difference* between the contractual essentials of the formal product and the totality of all the benefits and services experienced in relation to the product by the customer, from the moment of first contact in considering a booking, to any follow-up contact after delivery and consumption of the product. The augmented product expresses the idea of value added over and above the formal offer. It represents a vital opportunity for producers to differentiate their own products from those of competitors.

In the example under discussion, there may be up to twenty 'add ons'; some fairly trivial such as a complimentary box of chocolates on arrival, and some significant item such as entrance tickets to local attractions or entertainments. Some of the added benefits are tangible as indicated, but some are intangible such as the quality of service provided and the friendliness of staff at reception, in the bars and so on. Also intangible is the image or 'position' which the product occupies in customers' minds, which in the case of an hotel group, will be closely related to the corporate image of the group. In the example under

discussion, the augmented elements would be designed and developed around the core product benefits in ways calculated to increase the appeal to the target segment's needs.

There is, inevitably, an area of overlap between the tangible and augmented elements of the product, which cannot be defined with any precision. For example, if only one hotel group offers jacuzzi pools, that is a form of product augmentation. If all hotels offer jacuzzis, the pools are simply part of the tangible product.

Competitive product formulation

To stay ahead of the competition, pro active marketing managers are constantly involved in product innovation. There are clearly no secrets once brochures are published but there is normally considerable scope for creative innovation and for experimentation in the area defined as product augmentation. The one augmented element which cannot be easily copied is the image the hotel creates in prospective customers' minds, and image is, therefore, often one of the principal reasons for choosing between alternative products.

Frequent research into the perceptions and purchasing characteristics of segments, in order to define the core product, the formal product and to identify the scope for product augmentation with some precision, are necessary aspects of consumer orientation in the travel and tourism industry.

In the example used to illustrate the three levels of the product, it is interesting to note the degree of overlap between the particular accommodation product offer discussed (vertical dimension) and other components of the total product (horizontal dimension). Attractions at the destination in which the hotel is located may be part of the hotel users' total experience, whether or not the hotel forms links with the attractions as part of an augmented product. Similarly, hotel users may use public transport links to the destination, whether or not the hotel forms links with transport operators to include fares as part of the tangible product.

Product positioning

In this chapter, image as perceived by customers, is identified as one of five components in the total tourist product and as a vital element within the augmented product developed and marketed by individual businesses in the industry. In common with most services, the benefits provided by travel and tourism products are essentially intangible and, for vacationers in particular, products are strongly identified with personal goals and aspirations at levels which Maslow termed 'self actualization' (see Chapter 5).

Accordingly, the image or identity chosen for the purposes of promoting tourist products is a matter of the greatest importance to marketing managers. As Reisman put it, 'knowing what the customer wants isn't too helpful if a dozen other companies are already servicing his or her wants' (Reisman: 1979). In such circumstances, producers are not just concerned with satisfying customers' needs, but doing so in ways which are recognized as unique or very strongly identified with a particular organization, and which cannot be easily copied by any other producer. Images provide identities both for products and for the organizations (or destinations) which produce them.

The modern approach to product positioning is based on the well-tested hypothesis that products, companies and tourist destinations have images or perceptions, with which they are identified in the minds of existing and potential customers. By measuring these perceptions and images, it is possible to compare one product's image with that of its competitors. It is equally possible to compare different organizations or different destinations in terms of what customers believe about them, and to identify image strengths and weaknesses. By tackling any weaknesses which emerge among key segments – using the product formulation methods noted in this chapter – or focusing on strengths, it is possible for organizations to 'steer' their products using the techniques of the marketing mix. For airlines and hotel groups especially, the positioning of products and corporate images has emerged at the centre of marketing management decisions in recent years.

The measurement methods used to identify images and positions involve relatively complex statistical techniques and are usually handled by market research agencies acting on behalf of marketing managers. Product positioning is a strategic issue and it is discussed further in the chapters on marketing strategy annd advertising (Chapters 12 and 15).

Chapter summary

This chapter emphasizes a components view of travel and tourism products at two separate but related levels. At both levels the components view implies an ability, given adequate marketing research and product knowledge, to 'engineer' or formulate products to match the identified needs of target segments. Because needs are continuously shifting and competitors' abilities to supply needs is constantly changing, product formulation is a continuous process. This holds good for new, purpose-built products, which may be designed years before they are in operation, and for existing products, which may be adapted over time through re-arranging product components.

Product formulation has two sides, reflecting concerns with demand and supply. In terms of demand, the approach involves market research focused on customer needs, behaviour and perceptions, in order to define target segments and to identify strengths and weaknesses of product images. In terms of supply, product formulation involves analysing product components and elements and identifying the range of existing and potential products which could be improved or developed profitably to meet customer needs. These demands and supply implications apply equally to tourist destinations and to individual producers. Matching supply to demand is, of course, the cornerstone of the modern marketing approach. Integration between the two levels of the product is often an essential part of the matching process in travel and tourism.

In practice, the ability to 'engineer' intangible service products on paper and to promise satisfactions in brochures and in advertising, often exceeds a destination's or a producer's ability to deliver the satisfaction at the time of consumption. Because tourist products are ideas at the time of purchase, it is relatively easy to oversell such products, especially to first-time buyers. Any significant dissatisfaction experienced during consumption may destroy the vital word of mouth recommendations and decisions on repeat purchase, on which long-term business profit and survival are likely to depend.

Most tourist attractions and individual producers provide several products to match the needs of their several segments. Some of their products are likely to be relatively new and growing in market share, some will be well established or 'mature', and some are likely to be relatively old and may be declining in popularity and market share. The idea that organizations have a mixture of products and segments – usually known as a 'market/product portfolio' – is a very important one in travel and tourism.

Portfolio analysis is the basis for much of marketing strategy and this point is developed in later chapters.

Overall, this chapter seeks to develop the concept of the marketing mix in its most important dimension; that of the product in the context of market segmentation, reflecting a knowledge of customer motivations and their propensity to engage in travel and tourism. Marketing is nothing if not an integrated approach to business and students in particular should note the overlapping structure of the chapters thus far.

Further reading

An understanding of product concepts in travel and tourism is crucial to effective marketing in the industry. Accordingly, the limited space in this book is allocated deliberately to tourism aspects in preference to other important, widely used, standard product concepts, which are fully explained in most text books of marketing principles. For an understanding of the concepts of product life cycles, product mix decisions and product classifications, the following reading is recommended:

Baker, M. J., *Marketing: An Introductory Text*, Macmillan, 1985, Chapters 3 and 12.

Kotler, P., *Marketing Management: Analysis, Planning and Control*, Prentice-Hall, 1984, Chapters 10, 11, and 15.

9

The role of price

In Chapter 6 dealing with the 'Marketing Mix', price was introduced as one of the four Ps. Price denotes the terms of the voluntary exchange transaction between customers willing to buy and producers wishing to sell. Through the agreed terms of exchange, customers are attempting to maximize their perceptions of benefits and value for money as they select from competing products on offer. Producers are aiming to achieve targeted sales volume, sales revenue, market shares, and return on investment.

This chapter aims to show the significant and complex role that pricing plays in the marketing mix decisions, which marketing managers in commercial travel and tourism organizations are required to make. The contents focus first on the crucial role of price in manipulating demand and, therefore, sales revenue. The characteristics of travel and tourism influencing pricing decisions are then outlined and followed by a discussion of pricing strategy and tactics. The latter half of the chapter identifies the main influences on pricing decisions and comments separately on each of them.

Manipulating price in order to manage demand

It is easy to appreciate that the volume of products sold × average price paid = sales revenue. It is also easy to see that the potential influence on profit of relatively small changes in price may be massive. For example, if a hotel of 150 bedrooms operates at 70 per cent room occupancy, with an average price across its segments and products of $100 per room night, 150 rooms × 365 nights × 70% × $100 = $3,832,500 (annual room sales revenue). If, by more effective use of marketing techniques, the same hotel could increase its average room rate by 5 per cent to $105 without loss of volume, the annual sales revenue would be 150 × 365 × 70% × $105 = $4,024,125. The difference is $191,625 which, if fixed costs were held constant, would certainly represent a significant percentage of gross operating profit earned by this hotel. The role of a marketing manager in achieving such an average increase in room rates through more effective deployment of the marketing mix to stimulate demand, would reflect many separate decisions spread over the whole year. Continuous judgement would be required as to the price which each of the hotel's segments could bear at a given time.

Whilst most tourist businesses publish standard prices and many are required by law to display them, there are usually many opportunities to vary the published price in practice. The reasons for this are made clear in this chapter. Typically over a year's trading, the sales revenue generated in any except very small businesses is a function of many decisions on the optimum price to be charged to the range of segments involved, on a week by week basis. For some businesses, such as tourist attractions, average prices are relatively stable over a year but for others, such as tour operators, and scheduled airlines, prices may vary widely as managers seek to optimize their short-run revenue. The use of price changes to manage demand is common throughout the industry, and is often a daily concern for many marketing managers.

The characteristics of travel and tourism services which influence pricing

Whilst price is a vital decision in the marketing of all types of goods and services, the characteristics of travel and tourism products explain the industry's preoccupation with price. The main characteristics of services, introduced in Chapter 3, are summarized below and further discussed later in this chapter.

- High price elasticity in the discretionary segments of leisure, recreation, and vacation travel markets.
- Long lead times between price decisions and product sales. Twelve months or more are not uncommon lead times when prices must be printed in brochures to be distributed months before customer purchases are made, as is typically the case for tour operators.
- No possibility of stock holding of service products, so that retailers do not share with producers the burden and risk of unsold stocks and tactical pricing decisions.
- High probability of unpredictable but major short-run fluctuations in such cost elements as oil prices, and currency exchange rates.
- Near certainty of tactical price cutting by major competitors if supply exceeds demand.
- High possibility of provoking price wars in sectors such as transport, accommodation, tour operation and travel agencies, in which short-run profitability may disappear.
- Extensive official regulation in sectors such as transport, which often includes elements of price control.

- Necessity for seasonal pricing to cope with short-run fixed capacity.
- High level of customers' psychological involvement, especially with vacation products, in which price may be a symbol of status as well as value.
- The high fixed costs of operation, which encourage and justify massive short-run price cuts in service operations with unsold capacity or perishable products.

A major tour operator such as Thomson Holidays, for example, has to cope with each of these characteristics in its pricing policies. Traditionally, in the British market, Thomson has also established itself as the first large operator to publish its summer prices in the preceding autumn. As such it has tended to establish price leadership for much of the rest of the British tour operating industry, a position which has disadvantages as well as advantages.

Strategic and tactical prices

A very important way in which travel and tourism businesses respond to their highly complex pricing circumstances, is to operate prices at two levels.

The first level, which corresponds broadly with marketing strategy, is the price structure which an operator is obliged to publish months in advance of production, in brochures, guides, on admission tickets, and so on. For hotels, this price is the so-called rack rate, for airlines it is the published fare structure. This price structure reflects strategic marketing decisions concerning product positioning, value for money, long-run return on investment requirements, and overall corporate objectives such as growth, market share, and profit levels set for the operation.

The second level, which corresponds to marketing operations or tactics, is the price at which an operator is prepared to do business on a weekly, daily or hourly basis. It changes as the date of production approaches and in the light of bookings and expectations at the time. This often may be many weeks or months after the published price decisions were made. The tactical price may be widely known, advertised and published, as are the 'sale' offers regularly put out by tour operators as they seek to achieve additional last minute bookings. Alternatively, the price may be a closely guarded commercial secret, as happens when tour operators undertake deals with hoteliers facing cash flow crises or bankruptcy unless they can generate additional revenue from otherwise empty rooms. Unofficial 'dumping' of airline tickets for sale at heavily discounted prices is a common place activity around the world, which is frequently criticized but not stopped because discount fares provide a tactical, daily service of great value to the airlines. In Britain, the daily and Sunday press regularly publish pages of unofficial discount fares, well below published rates. Members of the public willing to bargain with half empty hotels in the late evening, may well find that they are able to achieve significant reductions from the published room rate.

Travel and tourism sectors are not alone in practising these two-level pricing approaches. Heavy discounting, for example of new car sales or computer equipment, is also frequent and undertaken for the same reason – to secure additional sales which it is believed would not otherwise occur. In the case of manufactured goods, discounting is used also to release money tied up in expensive stocks so that the fixed costs of operation can be paid.

The role of price in strategy and tactics

Chapters 12 and 13 discuss the meaning of strategic and operational planning. In this chapter it is necessary only to distinguish between the role of price as a management tool to achieve strategic business objectives, and as a tactical tool to manipulate short run demand. In pricing, as in all other elements of the marketing mix, the tactical or operational decisions have to be made within an overall strategic framework, which steers the business toward its chosen goals.

The main distinctions can be summarized as follows:

Strategic role (regular or published prices)

1 Reflects corporate objectives such as maximum growth, or maximum profit.
2 Communicates chosen positioning and image for products among target segments.
3 Communicates expectations of product quality, status, and value to prospective customers.
4 Reflects stage in the product life-cycle.
5 Determines long-run revenue flows and return on investment.

Tactical role (discounted/or promotional prices)

1 Manipulates marginal demand through incentives, which may be general or restricted to particular segments.
2 Matches competition by the quickest route.
3 Promotes trial for first-time buyers.
4 Provides a short-run tool for crisis management.
5 Determines short-run cash flows.

At the strategic level, growth strategies in price sensitive markets are often based on relatively low or 'budget pricing' in order to make a rapid impact on a large number of potential buyers. Such strategies typically aim for a high volume of sales at low profit margins per unit sold. The lifecycle stage of a product is also very much a strategic consideration and older, mature products will often be more price sensitive because of the competition they face from newer, developing products in high demand. Because service products cannot be seen or easily evaluated before purchase, the product's image and implications of quality have added significance for prospective buyers. Price is a highly relevant symbol in signalling or communicating what buyers should expect in terms of product quality and value for money.

The strategic decision of an organization to operate in the de-luxe end of a market rather than the budget end, immediately commits it to a relatively high cost structure, which can only be met by relatively high prices. In this sense, the decision to occupy a certain price band in the market precedes and determines the other three Ps of the marketing mix. The strategic price band decision is, therefore, also an operational decision. For hotels, restaurants and airlines especially, it determines the level of investment required for buildings and equipment. For all these reasons, strategic price decisions have implications beyond marketing, and necessarily involve the other senior managers of an organization. It is, of course, the role of marketing managers to research and interpret what price levels are realistic and achievable among the consumer segments whose needs an organization aims to satisfy.

Important as pricing decisions are in a strategic sense, they are even more important in a tactical sense, because of the inseparable and perishable nature of service production and consumption, and the inability of service producers to carry over unsold stocks as a buffer to cope with future demand. Thus, whilst a hotel with 150 rooms in the budget end of the market has a capacity of 54,750 room nights to sell in a year, the marketing requirement is to organize budget level demand in 'blocks' of 100–150 room buyers per night. To achieve this feat involves managers in what amounts to a continuous obsession with demand manipulation in which tactical price cuts are usually the most important and often the only available tool.

The typical seasonal and daily variation in demand for most travel and tourism products,

and the seasonal pricing structure devised to respond to it, also heighten the concern with tactical pricing decisions.

The influences on price setting

From the foregoing discussion it will be obvious that there are many influences which determine price setting in practice. Figure 9.1 shows the range of influences which marketing managers in travel and tourism have to take into account in setting prices, especially at the strategic level. At the tactical level, the considerations focus more narrowly on day-to-day demand management in relation to competitors' actions. The remainder of this chapter comments on each of the influences separately.

It should be noted that there are two circles of influence surrounding pricing decisions. The *inner circle* reflects primary influences:

1. corporate strategy and positioning,
2. marketing objectives for the period over which prices are set,
3. segments with which a business is concerned,
4. operating cost constraints,
5. competitors' actions.

The *outer circle* reflects wider influences of

1. characteristics of products and capacity,
2. non price options,
3. legal and regulatory constraints.

Corporate strategy and positioning

The first and dominant influence on product pricing is that of strategic business decisions concerning image and product positioning (such as deluxe or budget) and strategies for growth, market share, and return on investment. These decisions set the context for marketing operations over a three to five year time span or longer, and effectively set realistic upper and

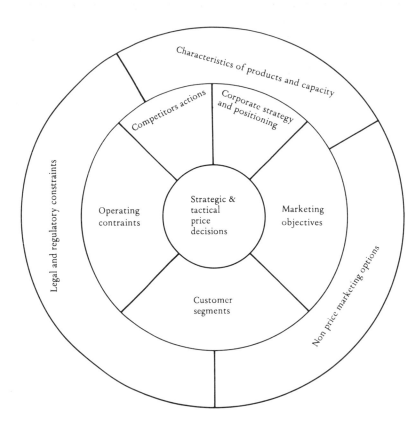

Figure 9.1 *The network of influences in pricing decisions*

lower limits within which product prices are likely to move.

Marketing objectives

In modern, marketing led organizations in any industry, business strategy has to be implemented systematically on a year to year basis, through operational decisions focused on specific targets for sales volume and sales revenue. Price is a highly influential component of the marketing mix, which is adjusted to meet particular short-run objectives for each product/market sector of a business. For reasons developed in Chapters 13 and 14, objectives for particular campaigns will be a critical input to price setting decisions.

Market segments

Since marketing in practice revolves around an understanding of consumer behaviour and profiles, it follows that every pricing decision has to be realistic in the context of the expectations and perceptions of chosen market segments, and their capacity and willingness to pay. Through consumer research and experience gained from results of previous price changes, marketing managers are expected to know what price level each segment can bear, and to what extent price signifies value for money and product quality. Knowledge of segments also reveals practical ways in which pricing may be made relevant to one group of customers but inaccessible to others. Senior citizen rail cards designed to promote cheap travel on railways outside commuting times, or hotel weekend prices designed to appeal to non business segments, are examples. In the context of airline travel, Shaw provides an excellent illustration of the principles of pricing by segments (Shaw: 1982: p. 153).

Operating costs

As noted earlier, in order for a business to survive over the long run, the average prices charged must be high enough to generate sufficient revenue to cover all fixed and variable costs and provide an acceptable return on the assets employed. Operating costs, expressed as average costs per unit of production, are therefore a primary input to pricing decisions.

Many catering establishments, hotel restaurants and bars, still fix prices according to the basic cost of production per unit sold, plus a 'mark up' percentage to cover return on investment and profit. Unfortunately for tourist businesses with a significant volume of turnover from leisure segments, such as airlines, tourist attractions, accommodation suppliers and tour operators, the so-called 'cost plus' methods are not very useful in practice. This is partly because most tourism markets are highly competitive and price sensitive so that operators are often forced for tactical reasons to accept prevailing market prices regardless of mark-up. It is also because of the influence on operations of high fixed costs and low variable costs. It costs an airline very little extra, for example, to operate an aircraft with 60 per cent seats occupied rather than 50 per cent. In principle, at least, it would be preferable to charge a fare of say $50 one way across the Atlantic than to forego the revenue and fly empty seats. The $50 would be much less than average seat cost but it would at least provide some revenue to contribute to an otherwise certain loss. Obviously there are dangers of upsetting regular customers with very low prices not

accessible to all. One common way around this for airlines is to offer 'stand by' seats with last minute availability and no guarantee that customers will fly.

Unit costs typically provide a target floor for prices, below which they should not fall except in the short-run circumstances previously noted.

Competitors' actions

It is at the level of tactical marketing that price competition becomes a dominant influence. For example, for summer 1985, reflecting increased costs of hotels abroad and unfavourable exchange rates, the average published price of package tours from Britain to destinations abroad rose by around 15 per cent over 1984. The result was tens of thousands of unsold seats, massive late price cutting between competitors, and a flood of last minute bookings stimulated by very low prices. For 1986, with more favourable exchange rates, falling oil prices and reduced hotel prices, Thomson Holidays reduced its average prices by over 15 per cent and increased its capacity significantly. As a result, Intasun immediately matched its main competitor and most other smaller operators were forced to follow suit. By July 1986, both Thomson and Intasun, with over 3 million package holidays between them on offer, achieved sales volume increases of up to 50 per cent above 1985 levels.

In all countries generating or receiving tourist flows, the travel trade press is likely to contain frequent examples of competitive, tactical, pricing decisions. It is a useful exercise to select some of these examples for examination and discussion.

Characteristics of products and capacity

When products have close substitutes and producer organizations have surplus capacity, it is highly likely that price will be an especially dominant consideration in marketing tactics. Many resort hotels find themselves in this position. In Britain, sea ferries operating across the channel are similarly placed, and airlines in deregulated conditions also are forced into price competition. Across the travel and tourism industry generally the close substitutability of products, coupled with the need to secure daily patterns of customer purchases, heightens the level of marketing dependency on pricing tactics.

Substitutability of products is one of the reasons why leisure products in travel and tourism typically demonstrate high price elasticity. Other things being equal, a small increase in the price of one product provokes a considerable shift in demand to other similar products, which are then relatively less expensive. Analyses of price against volume of sales data confirm that many travel and tourism markets do respond in accordance with traditional economic models of price elastic demand and supply. Many managers are well aware of the effects of price elasticity, although they can rarely predict exactly how any given market will respond in a forecast period. In practice, therefore, likely market responses to changes in price have to be guessed at, relying heavily on judgement and market intelligence to interpret such mathematical models as may exist, although these are usually based on historical data. Moreover, prices are usually set with only limited knowledge of competitors' actions, which when known, may require a matching response, regardless of the elasticity implications in the short run.

On the other hand, some products, even with large capacity, are able to secure a unique niche or position within the minds of potential customers, which reduces perceived substitutability and lessens their dependency on price. For example, the Ritz or Savoy hotels in London, Disney World in Florida, and Center Parcs in Northern Europe, have developed product concepts which, for marketing purposes, are unique. Marketing managers have a primary responsibility for developing such product niche positions, unless of course an organization's strategy is deliberately based on lowest prices.

Non price options

From the foregoing discussion of the main influences on price setting decisions, it should be obvious that the principal requirement for marketing managers is to understand fully what the influences are and how they work, because the real room to manoeuvre is often limited. Often, especially as a result of competitors' actions, the initiative in pricing may be lost in the short run. Ideally no business aims to be a price follower, responding to what the market place dictates; in practice it often happens in many travel and tourism markets, and cannot always be avoided.

There are, however, other marketing ways in which it is possible to limit the intensity of price competition by reducing the effects of substitution between products. Most of these ways are aspects of adding value to the services offered through product augmentation, which was described in detail in Chapter 8. Through augmentation focused on target segments, it is possible significantly to enhance the benefits which products provide, and therefore the reasons for choosing according to product attributes rather than lowest price. For example, to meet the needs of frequent business customers, many privileged user card schemes have been designed and promoted in Britain by the major hotel groups since the early 1980s. Such cards sometimes provide price discounts but almost invariably offer attractive services such as rapid check-out facilities or credit billing. The holder of a card may use it, in preference to simple price switching to a competitor, for reasons of convenience, familiarity and the status of recognition and special treatment on arrival. These card schemes are also designed to promote loyalty among targeted business visitors and represent an excellent and cost effective marketing method for securing additional sales revenue either at, or very near, 'rack' rate.

There are also numerous ways of disguising price cuts as consumer benefits in the guise for example of offering spouse accommodation (but not meals) 'free', or one 'free' night for every three paid for at the full rate and so on. The link between sales promotion and tactical pricing considerations is an interesting one which is further discussed in Chapter 16.

For hotels, the advantages of a particular location, such as city centres for business persons, may confer a benefit in the minds of users which justifies a premium price. For an airline, the careful cultivation and promotion of a particular image for service and efficiency may constitute a benefit, for which customers are willing to pay a premium price. For visitor attractions, most of which are already unique in their own intrinsic qualities, the route out of price substitutability lies in enhancing the quality of their sites or the enjoyment benefits conferred by a better presentation of the experiences offered. The Jorvik Viking Exhibition in York, for example, offered a new way to present historic artefacts in the early 1980s. As a result, the visitor interest in what was offered made it possible to charge relatively high prices for a relatively short, but intense, experience. All of these are consumer orientated marketing routes to avoid head-on price competition between products, which may otherwise be seen by customers to be close substitutes.

Legal and regulatory constraints

Whilst pricing is essentially a decision based on commercial influences, travel and tourism prices are often also subject to government regulation. For reasons of public health and safety, and to ensure consumer protection, governments in all countries frequently intervene in or influence pricing decisions. For example, for most international scheduled air routes, air fares must be ratified by official agreements between governments. In some countries, in which accommodation is officially registered and classified, price categories are fixed annually and can be varied by individual businesses only within given limits.

Sometimes, as in Britain in the 1960s and 1970s, governments take national decisions to limit permissible annual price increases for all businesses in the interests of securing agreements on wages and salaries. Whilst these decisions are not usually aimed at any one industry, the effect is especially strong in volatile markets such as travel and tourism.

Administrative friction

Not an influence in the same context as those in Figure 9.1, an argument against frequently changing prices is the administrative problem which arises, as well as possible inconvenience and irritation caused to customers and retailers. Shaw notes in relation to the bewildering array of airline fares, 'Simplicity – or rather the lack of it – is becoming a major concern of pricing ... complexity in the tariff will involve airlines in costs of staff training, and costs of staff time and passenger delay whilst fares are worked out and the details of the different price options explained' (Shaw: 1982: p. 154). If one adds to this the difficulties of communicating changes to consumers and retailers, the problems of administrative friction are clear. In practice, the imperative need to generate revenue often overcomes longer-run concerns about harmful effects upon consumers, but the dangers of over-frequent fluctuations cannot be ignored.

Chapter summary

Managing relatively volatile demand around a relatively fixed capacity of highly perishable product supply is identified in previous chapters as one of the principal characteristics of travel and tourism marketing. The use of price as one of the four main levers in the marketing mix is particularly important in managing demand. But its successful use involves reconciling customer interests and operational constraints within a strategic framework of business objectives. As stressed in Chapter 6, price must be integrated with the other three Ps to achieve the most cost effective results.

Two levels of pricing are discussed, strategic and tactical, and these are themes developed in Chapters 12 and 13. Summarized in Figure 9.1, this chapter identifies and discusses the main influences which have to be taken into account in setting prices in practice. The chapter lays particular stress on the importance of non price marketing options in tourism markets, through the use of which, marketing managers may be able to reduce the sometimes dominating effects of price elasticity and product substitution.

Price is a central concern in marketing all types of goods and services. It is often an obsession in many travel markets, especially those concerned with leisure segments, and it is essential that it should be kept in its proper perspective. It is one of four levers to be co-ordinated, not the only one. The implications of strategic and tactical pricing are further developed in Part Five of this book.

Further reading

Baker, M. J., *Marketing: An Introductory Text*, Macmillan, 1985, Chapter 14.

Kotler, P., *Marketing: Analysis, Planning and Control*, Prentice-Hall, 1984, Chapter 16.

Part Three

Planning Strategy and Tactics for Travel and Tourism Marketing

10

Organization for marketing: The role of marketing managers

Successful marketing requires the skills of people to plan marketing strategy and tactics, implement the marketing mix, and evaluate results. But marketing is only one part of business operations and it is only likely to be effective in practice if it is well organized and integrated with all other business activities.

Effective marketing decisions in travel and tourism have to be integrated and co-ordinated with the management of service production operations, with personnel management, and with financial management and control. Because customers are present on the premises of service producers, even greater attention has to be given to the co-ordination of marketing and operations than is necessary in the production of physical goods manufactured by staff in factories away from the customer's gaze and participation.

Because marketing is involved with so many aspects of corporate strategy and co-ordination with other departments of a business, effective organization for marketing extends well beyond the simple internal aspects of how best to arrange the work load and reporting structure of the marketing and sales team responsible for the marketing budget. Marketing organization extends into the management structure as a whole. As Medlik expressed it for hotels, 'Organization is the framework in which various activities operate. It is concerned with such matters as the division of tasks within firms . . . , positions of responsibility and authority, and

relationships between them' (Medlik: 1980: p. 71).

For small businesses, such as guest houses, small hotels or visitor attractions, marketing is the responsibility of the proprietor or general manager. Larger businesses will normally employ a marketing manager or director with one or more executive staff according to the size of the operations. Special considerations apply where a large, multi-site organization, such as a chain of hotels, employs a head office marketing team as well as marketing executives in each of the individual hotel units.

This chapter first identifies the tasks which are undertaken by marketing managers and have to be integrated with the other common tasks (or *functions* as they are known), such as operations, finance and administration. It notes two dimensions in organization and describes how businesses are traditionally organized according to functions, a pattern which is still found in many sectors of travel and tourism. The main problems with traditional ways to organize are noted from a marketing viewpoint, and the need for splitting businesses into manageable components, usually grouped around customers and their needs, is explained. A modern form of matrix organization for effective marketing is shown in Figure 10.2. The chapter discusses the personal qualities of successful marketing managers and ends by noting some of the marketing implications of organization for larger, multi-site groups with headquarters marketing staff.

Summary of marketing tasks to be organized

Undertaking successful marketing programmes for any size of business involves management and executive actions, which may be grouped into three areas. The object of the list below is to identify the main tasks but not to discuss them, since each is covered later in the book:

planning and control tasks
> marketing research, including undertaking or commissioning studies, gathering marketing intelligence, and interpreting the results (see Chapter 11),
> marketing planning: strategy; tactics; and marketing mix decisions (Chapters 12 and 13),
> planning product presentation and promotion,
> planning marketing campaigns and budgeting (Chapter 14),
> monitoring and evaluating marketing results.

executive tasks
> attending workshops and exhibitions,
> making and following up sales calls,
> briefing agencies, or undertaking the functions of advertising, PR, print, and sales promotion,
> (these tasks are discussed in Chapter 15–19).

co-ordinating tasks
> liaison with operations, personnel, financial and other management to ensure that the delivery of products in terms of quality, timing and costs, is matched with promotion and presentation.

If a firm markets only one or two products to one or two segments, the needs of marketing organization are minimal, although the tasks must still be carried out and co-ordinated in a logical sequence. Where there are several products for multiple markets, the problems of organizing the many tasks increase. It becomes essential to find ways to *group* operations and other business functions, in order to plan and control them effectively.

How best to group business functions and co-ordinate them, is the issue to be resolved through particular forms of marketing organization.

Two dimensions of marketing organization

As noted in the introduction to this chapter, there are two levels of marketing organization which have to be put together in practice.

At the lower level, organization means establishing a framework of responsibilities for undertaking the tasks summarized in the previous section. This is essentially an internal problem for the marketing team. At the simplest it may concern just one person, whose main problem is how best to organize his or her time.

At the higher level, organization means establishing a much wider framework of responsibilities, designed to ensure effective co-ordination links between marketing and the other essential functions of a firm. This requires some consideration of what the other business functions are. At its simplest, Kotler notes that 'all companies start out with four simple functions. Someone must raise and manage capital (finance), produce the product . . . (operations), sell it (sales), and keep the books (accounting)' (Kotler: 1984: p. 717).

To these four basic functions it is necessary to add some refinements in order to bring the discussion up to date. Larger businesses in the travel and tourism industry have a personnel function (or operational responsibility) to recruit, train, pay and manage staff in accordance with legal requirements. Many have a pro-

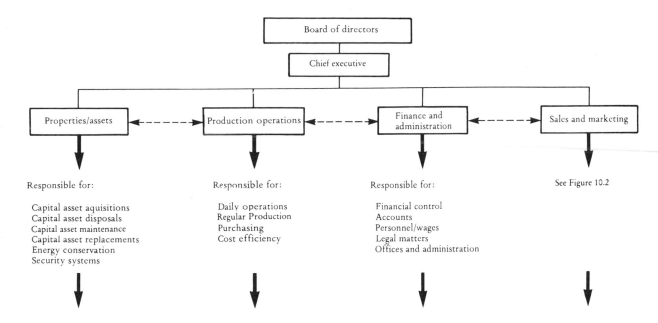

Figure 10.1 *Traditional functional organization of a service business in travel and tourism*

perties/capital equipment management function, to purchase, develop and maintain the capital assets. Most have marketing functions extending far beyond the narrow concern for sales. These functions can be represented in a simple chart, relevant in principle to most large service businesses in travel and tourism. See Figure 10.1.

The traditional, functional structure of business organization

In Figure 10.1, in each of the four main functions, there are managers, executives and operational staff, who are specialists in their particular roles. Specialists, for example, in purchasing, in finance, and in personnel. In larger firms, the specialists are represented typically by a senior manager or a director for each of the functions, who report through a chief executive to a board of directors. Co-ordination may occur informally in this organization structure through consultation and meetings between managers, or formally through scheduled co-ordinating meetings and the board. As commercial firms and public sector bodies increase in size, the need for specialists tends to increase. The specialist focus is denoted in Figure 10.1 by the vertical arrows under each main function.

Understandably, the operations division of service businesses (the equivalent of manufacturing production for makers of physical goods), has traditionally tended to be seen as the most important of the management functions. Operations produce the products, handle the customers, receive the revenue and are also responsible for most of a firm's costs. The efficiency of the operations division is, therefore, often perceived as the basis of business success or failure. An operations focus is, of course, just another way of describing production orientation (see

Chapter 2). When markets are growing, operations are understandably the principal focus of management attention. If the growth in demand levels off, competition increases and the focus of attention shifts to sales and then to marketing. Such a shift of focus typically forces changes in organization within a firm.

Figure 10.1 reflects a traditional orientation in service companies, in which sales and marketing is typically perceived and used as a service function required to support the operations division. As the most recent of the four business functions to emerge, and it is still emerging in many parts of the travel and tourism industry, sales and marketing are still often seen as an extra or 'bolt on' specialist service, not an integral part of the business. Marketing people in production orientated firms tend to be treated primarily as specialists in various processes (or functions) such as advertising, sales promotion, and marketing research. In such a traditional structure the value of marketing people is often only understood in a tactical, reactive sense of generating customer demand when it is needed. But, even if the essentially pro-active and strategic role of marketing outlined in this book is recognized in such firms, its full potential is unlikely to be achieved because the organization structure is not conducive to it.

'Because the concept of a formalized marketing function is still relatively new to most service businesses, it is often difficult to define where marketing specialists should be positioned in the organization structure, what their responsibilities and authorities should be, and precisely what should be expected of them beyond a somewhat reactive advertising or public relations role.' (Lovelock: 1984: p. 413).

The need to divide and group business operations into manageable components

Figure 10.1 reflects the fact that any service business, large or small, comprises operational or production processes, and supporting functions, which range from routine asset management and accounting, to office administration, sales and marketing. For a hotel, production processes include food and beverage management, front of house operations, housekeeping, room services. For a managed tourist attraction, production processes include reception and ticket issuing, cleaning and maintenance of exhibits and buildings, operation of shops, cafés, cloakrooms, provision of information and security services.

As businesses grow and become more competitive, senior managers normally have to examine the efficiency of their production processes and other functions more closely. Often, the most effective way to do this in practice is to divide a total business into its component parts, or 'mini-businesses'. This is normally done by identifying particular groupings of operations having costs and revenues which can be separately calculated. Cost and revenue 'centres', as they are normally known, are typically associated with particular products aimed at particular market segments.

For a tour operator with winter and summer products, it is usually possible to split the costs and revenues associated with the operation of summer sun packages from the equivalent data for winter sun products. By analysing the figures it may emerge that summer business is far more profitable per unit of staff, marketing, and office overheads, than the operation of winter packages. Examining the specific winter business in terms of all its direct costs and revenues may reveal areas of weakness which can be rectified, possibly with a different approach to marketing. Such analysis is only possible once the relevant costs and revenues have been identified.

Although it may appear simple, it is often far from obvious how best to define the cost and revenue centres of a total business. Analysing the main customer groupings or segments which a business serves, provides a logical basis for dividing most businesses. It is customer orientated and thus provides the basis for a marketing rather than an operations based division.

Grouping business processes by purpose

Of the various ways in which businesses may be sub-divided and organized by purpose, Baker notes the three main groupings which are alternatives to the traditional organization by functional specialisms (1979: 104). These are:

Product based	business operations or processes are grouped into the main products provided. But this type of grouping does *not necessarily* imply production orientation.
Market based	business operations are grouped around the main markets which a business serves.
Area based	business operations are grouped around the regions, territories or countries which a business serves.

To give brief examples, a large hotel may organize its production processes according to products such as banqueting, conferences, exhibitions, executive suites, or short stay leisure packages. Each of these groupings represents one or more products offered to one or more customer segments.

A tour operator may organize its operations according to the types of customer it serves, such as winter sports enthusiasts, senior citizens, or young people in the age group 18–35. Each of these is a segment to which may be offered one or more products.

A national tourist office, or an airline with an overseas network, will typically tend to organize its processes according to the geographical areas it serves. Within each of the areas, it may discern

several segments for which one or more products will be required.

Dividing up businesses as described above leads logically into the point that separate marketing activity is required for each of the cost revenue centres identified. Effective marketing has to be organized around the needs of product/market groupings, and may not easily be provided as a functional specialism on the centralized basis noted in Figure 10.1.

Potential conflict between grouping by purpose and grouping by process

For reasons discussed under segmentation (Chapter 7) and product formulation (Chapter 8), businesses in all kinds of consumer industries increasingly find it necessary to group or organize their production or operational processes around identified, targeted market segments. In practice, this means that operations have to be packaged and presented to customers as products designed to meet their specific needs. Only through such groupings of business processes is it possible to plan specific programmes of marketing activities, which are essential for effective marketing management.

In other words there are two sets of interests to be served by an organization structure; those of managers responsible for *production and other* processes, and those of managers responsible for *customer groups*. In discussing these interests, Piercy suggests that the critical problem facing any large organization is how to achieve 'a compromise between grouping [business activities] by purpose . . . and grouping by process . . . , in an attempt to retain the advantages of a functional specialism at the same time as gaining the strengths of a sharper focus on the market segment.' He identifies purpose with market segments, or products, or projects; processes are functions, specialisms or disciplines (Piercy: 1985: p. 159).

This brief discussion of the underlying reasons why businesses are increasingly being split up into manageable components, can only hint at a most important management debate. Around the world, large commercial organizations and others in the public sector, are finding it more efficient to manage and control their operations on the basis of cost/revenue centres, rather than through centralized headquarters planning and control. This change of emphasis amounts to a managerial revolution which goes much deeper than marketing and draws on all aspects of modern management techniques. In the last decade, the process of decentralization and sub-division has been greatly facilitated by the emergence and sophistication of information processing technology which creates the continuous information flows needed to identify and control the new groupings. Since the new divisions of business usually have marketing origins or implications, marketing managers are at the forefront of this modern managerial revolution. The sub-divisions of businesses has strategic and tactical implications for marketing, which are discussed in Chapters 12 and 13.

Modern purpose based organization structure for marketing

Earlier in the chapter, Figure 10.1 noted a

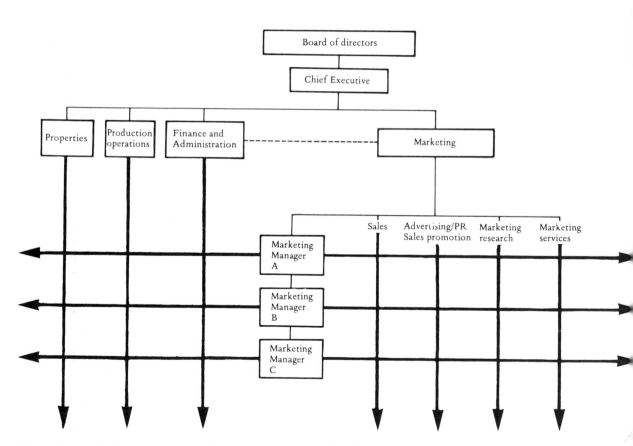

Figure 10.2 *Modern purpose based matrix organization for effective marketing*

traditional function or process based organization structure, in which marketing is seen as a set of specialisms providing services to the other major business functions. By contrast, Figure 10.2 shows a modern purpose based organization structure, in which all the business functions, including marketing, are grouped around particular purposes shown as A, B, and C.

Figure 10.2 shows a matrix organization, so called because it highlights the interaction between columns (management functions and specialisms), and rows (groupings of the business, which cut across all columns.) The lateral arrows in Figure 10.2 illustrate how the management of the sub-groups of the business (including marketing) extends sideways, through co-ordination, across the responsibilities of the main operational functions. It can be seen that they cut across the specific specialisms within the marketing function too.

To illustrate what this matrix organization means in practice, consider the case of an international airline which has decided to split its total operations into cost/revenue centres for first class travel, business class travel, and charter operations. The marketing manager appointed for business travel is directly responsible for all the tasks noted at the beginning of this chapter, summarized as planning, implementation and coordination. The job involves researching into the market, forecasting business traffic flows, agreeing the seat capacity to be operated (in the context of all other operational constraints), and agreeing the levels and quality of service to be provided to the customers by the cabin staff. He will also be involved in negotiating the size of the budget to be spent on marketing business travel, and the way in which that budget is spent. The manager reports to a marketing director, who has to co-ordinate the budgets and activities of the other marketing managers, and resolve any conflicts which may arise with the operations division.

At the end of the budget year, a marketing manager is expected to evaluate the results of marketing efforts in detail and to account for the success or failure of the programmes that were recommended. He may well have salary bonuses tied to results achieved. In this illustration, the marketing manager can be seen to be 'unlike other employees who apply a special expertise to all company [products]' because he 'is concerned with every aspect of a single [product]' (Davidson: 1975: p. 96). In his book, Davidson refers to brands rather than products because he was writing in the context of fast-moving consumer goods. But the principle of generalist rather than specialist interests of marketing managers remains equally valid for service producers.

Davidson also noted that 'the marketing department is the link between the firm and the market place. It represents the views of consumers to the company, and works out, with other departments, how to transfer these views into profitable products' (1975: p. 79). Davidson and others stress that, without marketing managers to represent the customer point of view internally within the firm, there is no natural process whereby this happens automatically. In market conditions in which customer needs, attitudes and expectations change very rapidly, as is often the case in travel and tourism, this internal function of customer representation is vital in achieving fast effective responses on the part of general management.

Product, brand or marketing managers?

It creates much confusion, but there is no agreement in practice on the job titles given to marketing executives. There are three basic choices used in travel and tourism:

- brand manager
- product manager
- market or marketing manager

In hotels in particular, job titles often incorporates sales, as for example sales and marketing manager.

It is possible to attribute to each of these titles a separate meaning, and many marketing texts do so. This author finds the distinctions drawn are largely irrelevant in travel and tourism practice where titles often reflect traditional practice or current fashion. All that matters for the purposes of understanding what a job entails is, does the marketing person (by whatever title) carry out the tasks of marketing set out in this chapter? In particular, is the marketing person responsible for the tasks of co-ordination and implementing marketing programmes in collaboration with others? If the answer is yes, it is simpler to use the generic title of marketing executive or marketing manager than to worry about the niceties of product, brand or market management. In this author's experience there is many a so-called advertising manager or sales manager, who is responsible in practice for the full range of marketing functions, and many a so-called brand or product manager who is not.

If a manager or executive is responsible for only one of the functions, such as advertising or sales, then it is better to use the functional title, as in sales manager.

Apart from disagreements over the titles, there is a continuing academic debate over the extent to which marketing managers actually 'manage', and are less relevant in the 1980s than they were in the 1960s. Certainly it is incorrect to see a marketing manager as having executive power over the specialists who manage operations processes: his primary role is one of persuasion, liaison and co-ordination rather than one of control. But as long as it is necessary to split up large businesses into smaller components for management and marketing purposes, and over that issue there appears to be no disagreement, it will be necessary to find adequate arrangements to plan, implement and control marketing programmes. That involves marketing managers

acting as generalists rather than specialists, and their future role, whatever their titles, appears quite secure.

Personal qualities for successful marketing managers

As many readers of this book are likely to be, or aspiring to be marketing managers (by whatever job title their employers use), it may be helpful to indicate the principal qualities which are common to successful practitioners. These qualities are not specific to travel and tourism, but applicable to any form of marketing. They are as follows:

energetic   very active, competitive, and aggresive rather than passive by nature.

creative   in thought processes and in seeking out opportunities to develop and exploit, especially at the margins of revenue generation so vital to the profitability of service businesses. Artistic creativity is not an essential attribute, since this is normally achieved through the use of advertising and other promotional agencies.

good communicator

(a)   as an advocate for his product (or market) interests, at meetings, in presentations and in documents.

(b)   in securing vital co-operation and goodwill among managers whose actions he may influence, but cannot control.

numerate   not necessarily competent in statistical methodology, but very confident and intuitive in analysing and appreciating meaning from the mass of data which flows continuously across marketing desks.

good administrator

  able to handle and organize the

numerous administrative and progress chasing details involved in managing any marketing programme.

Finally, in this list of desirable characteristics, should be added the quality of judgement. Impossible to define with precision, judgement is an ability to weigh the many imponderables in any marketing decision and decide on a course which is bold in the context of evaluated risks, but not unnecessarily risky. Judgement is also an intuitive sense of knowing when to change previous decisions, either to limit the damage caused by inevitable mistakes or to back a hunch. Because so many marketing decisions have to be made ahead of the customer decisions which are their only final validation – you don't know if it works until the customers pay or stay away – the ability to take balanced judgements of events is crucial.

The reader may observe many military analogies in the language of marketing; strategies, campaigns, tactics, pre-emptive strikes (against competitors), targeting, loss leaders, logistics, and so on. Not for nothing does Davidson describe product managers as the 'storm troopers of marketing' (Davidson: 1975: p. 95). The qualities of successful marketing managers are certainly akin to those of successful military leaders. Good judgement, confidence, and steady nerves are as essential in generals as they are in marketing directors of large companies, and for much the same reasons.

Organization for group marketing of multi-site corporations

Any individually owned business, such as a car rental firm based on one garage, a proprietor owned hotel, or a retail travel agent with one office, will be solely responsible for organizing and implementing its own marketing activities. But if a business such as an hotel group contains many individual units, totally different organizational considerations for marketing apply. For example, Avis, in car rental, Hyatt in hotels, and Thomas Cook in tour operation and travel retailing, all have corporate marketing staff at their headquarter offices, who are responsible for group marketing policy. To operate effectively as a group, products and operational processes – including marketing – have to be standardized as far as possible, so that customers can purchase the same reliable products, at any of the group's locations under the same corporate image.

Standardized marketing programmes are typically designed to cover the promotion of group images and the deliberate 'branding' of group products. Brochures and other sales literature tend to be identical, or at least clearly identified with group logos and themes; sales promotions are often the same and co-ordinated between units; and prices, product presentation and customer services are as closely standardized as possible.

Obviously, group policy restricts the room for individual units to exercise marketing discretion and it is not unusual for unit managers to have very little influence over the external marketing of the units for whose profits they are nominally responsible. In the case of group hotels, the unit manager's discretion may be limited to promoting functions in the local catchment area of the hotel, liaising with local businesses to promote the use of the hotel, undertaking local public relations, and direct mailing particular product offers to addresses of existing customers. Unit managers retain principal responsibility for 'in house' promotions, but even these may be organized with materials provided by head office. Whilst the percentages vary from one unit to another, it is unlikely that many unit managers of nationally promoted groups are responsible for generating more than about a fifth of their unit's total sales revenue. The balance of marketing power has shifted from the unit to the group, increasingly organized around cost and profit centred groupings of products and segments.

Chapter summary

Organizing for effective marketing in larger businesses means establishing a framework in which marketing managers and executives can use their skills to best effect. This framework has two levels, of which the most important is that which facilitates integration between marketing functions and the other business functions of any commercial firm or public sector body.

The traditional type of function based organization, often encountered in travel and tourism, is shown in Figure 10.1. In such an organization structure, 'although marketing has assumed greater importance in recent years, the operations function still dominates line management in most service industries' (Lovelock: 1984: p. 415). Traditional organization structure is contrasted with a modern form of matrix organization, summarized in Figure 10.2. This latter type of structure enables marketing to play its full role in the conduct of business operations, especially where large businesses are split into cost/profit centres, usually reflecting particular groups of products and segments.

Successful marketing requires skilled professionals who need the special blend of personal characteristics noted in this chapter. Because many marketing managers are managers in title only, it is stressed that the skills of persuasion and co-operation are always important.

Organization is a function of purpose. The purpose of marketing organization is to group, integrate, and co-ordinate business functions in ways best calculated to satisfy customers' needs, and meet producers' requirements for return on assets employed over the long run.

Further reading

Baker, M. J., *Marketing: An Introductory Text*, Macmillan, 1985, Chapter 7.

Kotler, P., *Marketing Management: Analysis, Planning and Control*, Prentice-Hall, 1984, Chapter 23.

11

Marketing research: The information base for effective marketing

What managers know of market trends, consumer segments, buyer behaviour, product performance, and of consumers' response to all aspects of marketing campaigns, is mostly derived from one or more aspects of marketing research activity. The planning processes at both strategic and operational levels, discussed in Chapters 12 and 13, are research based. This chapter, therefore, focuses on techniques which are essential in successful marketing practice.

In relation to computer programmes, most readers will be aware of the maxim, 'garbage in, garbage out'. In other words, if the information or data fed into a computer is inaccurate or inadequate, one cannot hope for useful results. There is a marketing research parallel because the whole of marketing strategy and operations are also calculated responses using information input. Some authors draw distinctions between market research, consumer research and marketing research but, for all practical purposes, the term *marketing research* can be used to include all research based information used in making marketing decisions.

Commencing with an initial definition, this chapter identifies the six main types of marketing research. It next describes ten kinds of marketing research activity widely used in travel and tourism, which readers can expect to find in

practice. The next section explains a typical 'menu' of marketing research choices available to operators and illustrates it in a travel and tourism context. The final part of the chapter indicates what is involved in using a market research agency, and comments on test marketing and monitoring for travel and tourism products.

Marketing research defined

Marketing research is an organized information process which 'has to do with the gathering, processing, analysis, storage and dissemination of information to facilitate and improve decision making' (Seibert: 1973: p. 128). The value of this definition is that it is sufficiently broad to encompass the whole range of systematic information inputs, from regular analysis of press cuttings taken from the travel trade press, through 'intelligence' gathered by a sales force, to full-scale sample survey research on a national or international scale.

Most authors stress that marketing research cannot, as is commonly supposed, provide solutions to management problems. Research can seldom ensure correct decisions. What it can do is reduce the amount of uncertainty and risk associated with the results of marketing decisions, and focus attention on the probable implications of alternative courses of action. As Luck *et al.*, put it, 'Imagination, judgement and courage remain important qualities for the successful decision maker. Research is the handmaiden of competent management but never its substitute' (Luck *et al.*: 1970: p. 8).

From wide experience of the industry internationally, it appears to be a distinctive feature of travel and tourism that the use of marketing research is significantly weaker in the 1980s in this industry than in any other major industry dealing with consumer products. International airlines, a few hotel groups, and some national tourist boards are exceptions. The reason for this weakness is rooted in the traditional, but increasingly irrelevant assumption that producers with customers on their premises have little further need of market research. This may still be true for guest houses and individual neighbourhood travel agencies but it is increasingly not true for larger businesses, especially those with multi-site operations. The presence of customers on site is, however, a most important marketing asset to be exploited systematically by producers, and this point is developed at the end of the chapter. The reasons for using marketing research, and the techniques available, are essentially the same in travel and tourism as in any other form of consumer marketing.

Judgement or research?

In practice it is frequently the case that managers have to take most decisions with less than adequate information. The cost of obtaining additional information has to be measured in time as well as money, and must always be relevant to the prospective gain or loss at risk in the decisions that are made. For example, faced with a decision between two alternative designs for a brochure cover, a marketing manager for a tour operating company has either to exercise judgement, or commission a survey to evaluate target customers' responses to the two designs.

Where millions of brochures are involved, a 10 per cent better customer reaction to one of the designs could pay off in thousands of additional bookings. Research in this case would be justified provided that waiting for results did not delay production and distribution. For smaller operators the expense would rarely be justified by the potential extra business, and close attention to the print design brief (itself research based) would have to suffice, together with experience and judgement gained with other brochures.

By contrast, a strategic decision by a business, such as a tourist attraction, to re-structure its product by major investment in new facilities, would always justify marketing research studies at a cost related to the size of the investment. Such research would be needed to inform decisions about the scope and range of the new facilities, and the design of the new product in terms of identified market needs, behaviour patterns, and visitors' capacity to pay. For example, if research indicated that visitors would spend only an hour at a new attraction and not two hours, the implications for car parking, prices, display and content, would be critical. In practice there is always a requirement to balance the need to know, against the cost in time and money.

Six main categories of marketing research

It would be possible to draw up a list of several dozen different types of research investigation. Such a list would not be helpful to the student of marketing, and an understanding of the six main categories of marketing research noted in Figure 11.1 will be adequate for most purposes. The six categories correspond exactly with the information needs required to make efficient decisions for marketing mix programmes, and the strategic and operational plans within which they are implemented. The categories in Figure 11.1 are

Research category	Used in	Typical marketing use
1 Market analysis and forecasting	Marketing planning	Measurement and projections of market volumes, shares and revenue by relevant categories of market segments and product types
2 Consumer research	Segmentation and positioning	(a) Quantitative measurement of consumer profiles, awareness, attitudes and purchasing behaviour including consumer audits (b) Qualitative assessments of consumer needs, perceptions and aspirations
3 Products and price studies	Product formulation, presentation and pricing	Measurement and consumer testing of amended and new product formulations, and price sensitivity studies
4 Promotions and sales research	Efficiency of communications	Measurement of consumer reaction to alternative advertising concepts and media usage; response to various forms of sales promotion, and sales force effectiveness
5 Distribution research	Efficiency of distribution network	Distributor awareness of products, stocking and display of brochures, and effectiveness of merchandising, including retail audits and occupancy studies
6 Evaluation and performance monitoring studies	Overall control of marketing results	Measurement of customer satisfaction overall, and by product elements, including measurement through marketing tests and experiments

Figure 11.1 *Six main categories of marketing research*

common to any marketing organization dealing with consumers, although the uses are specific to travel and tourism.

Ten kinds of marketing research commonly used in travel and tourism

Because marketing research has become a large and complex sector of economic activity in its own right, it has inevitably produced its own technical vocabulary. This chapter makes no attempt to cover the full range of technical terms but ten, which are commonly used in practice to denote different research methods, will be found helpful and are discussed below.

Marketing research methods

continuous	:	*ad hoc*
quantitative	:	qualitative
primary	:	secondary
omnibus	:	syndicated
retail audit	:	consumer audit

Continuous and *ad hoc*

Commercial organizations are finding it increasingly necessary to measure certain key trend data on a regular, or 'continuous' basis. 'Continuous' in this context may mean daily, weekly or monthly. Data covering market volume, market shares, customer satisfaction, hotel bed occupancy and booking patterns, are typical examples of 'continuous' marketing research measures in travel and tourism. For reasons developed later in Chapter 19, continuous information may be integrated within a data base, which provides a fertile source of information for marketing mix decisions generally.

Specific problems also frequently occur in marketing, which require research relevant to a particular circumstance. For example, could a redesigned guide book at a tourist attraction, with a print life of say three years, produce extra

sales revenue? Would the introduction of a buffet style instead of full service lunch reduce customer satisfaction or increase it? Does the market size warrant investment in a new hotel, and what size and level of service is justified? To inform such management decisions a specific or *ad hoc* investigation would be needed.

Most marketing research programmes involve a mixture of continuous research to monitor trends, and *ad hoc* surveys to illuminate identified problems or opportunities as they occur.

Quantitative and qualitative

Traditionally, most marketing research studies involve questions asked of random samples of existing or potential customers, to establish the relevant proportions possessing particular characteristics of interest to marketing managers. For example, a coach tour operator may need to know that 60 per cent of adults took a holiday in a given year, of whom a third travelled abroad, stayed an average of 12.4 nights away from home, and spent £400 per capita. The operator would also want to know what proportion used coaches and cars, and how that proportion varied year by year, month by month, by type of client, and so on. All of these are quantifiable dimensions which, with due allowance for statistical variation, can be projected into tens or hundreds of thousands of people comprising total market volume. Hence, quantitative research, meaning studies to which numerical estimates can be attached. Quantitative research is always based on 'structured' questionnaires in which every respondent is asked identical questions. Mostly, the range of possible answers is also printed on questionnaires, based on previous experience, and variations to suit individual respondents are not possible.

Quantitative methods are less suitable for exploring consumer attitudes, feelings, desires or perceptions, because often the researcher cannot predict the ways in which people think about different products. It is always possible to construct hypothetical answers and ask people to agree or disagree, but these may not get at what really matters to prospective buyers. For example, Wales as a destination has many surveys quantifying likes and dislikes in terms of scenery, heritage, villages, beaches, weather etc. To dig deeper the Wales Tourist Board commissioned group discussions of target travellers in 1984, who were invited in groups of 6 to 8 to talk informally about holidays in general and Wales in particular. The discussion leader, trained in social psychology, was responsible for introducing the subjects for discussion and encouraging views, but did not impose his or her own pre-conceived ideas. What emerged, recorded for analysis on tape, was a discussion in consumers' own words concerning what mattered to them. In the case of Wales, a fairly widespread concern emerged among prospective visitors that possible dislike of the English by the Welsh could create a negative, cold, or even hostile atmosphere, which is obviously not conducive to holiday motivations. Other research among people who had recently visited Wales, indicated that in fact, the welcome they received was generally warm and friendly. Responding to this perception problem became an aspect of WTB communications. The research was also used as the basis for communicating the need for friendly attitudes to the tourist industry in Wales. By definition, such surveys cannot be quantitative because the ideas are not tied down to structured questionnaires or based on adequate samples of the target group. They can be used to structure subsequent quantitative surveys, or they can be used in their own right to help marketing managers understand the ways in which travellers think, and what matters to them.

In recent years, given adequate quantification of the main patterns of visitor behaviour, qualitative studies have been more widely used. They are especially useful in designing advertising messages and brochure contents, in ways best calculated to communicate with prospective customers in their own terms.

Primary and secondary

Primary data is a label applied to marketing research specifically commissioned by a business to contribute to its own decisions, involving the gathering of data not available from any other (secondary) source. For example, a survey commissioned by one airline, to study business travellers' current attitudes towards other airlines competing on the same route, would be primary data.

Secondary data is information gathered originally for a purpose not related to the specific needs of a business, but which may be used by it as part of its information search. All published sources, including government statistics, trade association surveys and commercial publishers' market surveys, represent secondary data.

It is common sense that it will always be quicker and cheaper to obtain and use secondary rather than primary data. For any decision requiring research information, initial investigation should always commence at the secondary level before proceeding, if necessary, with primary research.

Omnibus and syndicated

Not only in travel and tourism but in consumer markets generally, there has been a growing tendency for market research companies to operate their own regular (continuous) sample surveys and sell space in them to a range of customers. Such surveys are known technically as 'omnibus' surveys because they are open to all users. Where an organization seeks answers to say four or five key questions, it may be possible to get access to a nationally representative sample of 2000 adults for a tenth of the cost of commissioning its own survey. For the price, a client would not only get answers to his questions but also fully cross tabulated data using profile data, such as age and readership of media, which are a standard part of any 'omnibus'. The British Home Tourism Survey (BHTS), now British Tourism Survey – Monthly (BTS–M), is probably the best known survey of British tourism. It is in fact a series of questions regularly asked on a National Opinion Polls Ltd (NOP) omnibus study. There are many other omnibus surveys available, covering not only adults but many segments such as motorists, doctors, business travellers, and so on.

Syndicated surveys serve much the same purpose as omnibus surveys but typically are commissioned by a group of clients on a cost sharing basis. Frequently one major user draws in others on the basis, for example, of dividing costs by the number of questions asked. The British National Travel Survey (BNTS) now BTS–Y is not an omnibus but a syndicated survey commissioned annually.

Both syndicated and omnibus studies provide cost effective research, especially for smaller businesses, for whom the costs of an *ad hoc* survey would usually be prohibitive. By using such studies, firms can also obtain technical assistance from research agencies with the wording of questions and interpretation of results. The omnibus method is especially suitable for achieving quantified results much faster than would be possible with *ad hoc* surveys.

Retail audit and consumer audit

In many sectors of consumer goods marketing, but to a much lesser extent in travel and tourism, the most common forms of continuous marketing research are consumer and retail audits. It is no accident that the two largest international marketing research companies, AGB Ltd and AC Nielsen have built their multi-national operations on such audits.

Initiated as long ago as the 1930s, retail audits involve physically checking and analysing product stocks and sales in a sample of retail outlets selected to represent the national pattern. Such audits, carried out at regular monthly or two-monthly intervals in grocery and chemist outlets, for example, measure the volume of sales by product type, the average sales price, the volume of stocks, and the proportion of outlets with stock on display. The results collected in the sample of audited outlets are then used to project the estimated sales in the total number (universe) of outlets, from which the sample was selected. In travel and tourism, various agencies have audited holiday bookings and brochure display for tour operators using samples of travel agencies, although the technical problems are considerable and audit reliability has been much criticized. Hotels and other regular accommodation occupancy studies in samples of accommodation units, perform the same 'audit' function for the accommodation sector and have been used reliably for many years.

Consumer audits follow the same basic principles of regular reporting from nationally representative samples, based in this case on consumers who keep specially designed diaries, in which all purchases are recorded. Since the profile of the samples is known in detail, recorded purchases can be analysed by segmentation data. Experiments with diaries and samples of travellers have been tried in various sectors of the tourist industry in recent years, such as the English Tourist Board's study of day visitors, but no large scale systematic consumer audit of travel and tourism had been developed up to 1987.

A menu of marketing research methods

Drawing together the different categories of marketing research noted earlier and the types of approach which are commonly used, it is possible to present the wide range of methods available to any operator as a 'menu'. 'Menu' simply means a listing of research techniques which are available, and from which it is possible to make a selection according to need and circumstances. Each technique is available at a price. The menu, in a form relevant to producers of travel and tourism services, is shown in Figure 11.2. The menu concept is developed from papers originally presented in 1973 at a Market Research Society training course. It is important to stress that the 'menu' means prospective users can select items according to their needs and budget. Only the largest organizations, with research staff and budgets in excess of say £100,000 per annum, are likely to need or be able to use all of them over, say, twelve months.

Using the 'menu' – a Holiday Park operator

To explain the possible selective use of the menu in travel and tourism practice, consider a Holiday Park operator in England with eight parks comprising some 2000 caravans and chalets for let on a weekly or part weekly basis. A turnover of around £5 million would be realistic for such an operator, with a marketing budget of say £300,000 of which, say £20,000 is allocated for research (all in 1986 prices). Such a budget could be deployed as follows:

Menu
Item
A1   A computerized record system would show

A   Desk research (secondary sources)

1   Sales/bookings/reservations record; daily, weekly, etc. by type of customer, type of product, etc.
2   Visitor information records e.g. guest registration cards, booking form data.
3   Government publications/trade association data/national tourist office data/abstracts/libraries.
4   Commercial analyses available on subscription or purchase of reports.
5   Previous research studies conducted; internal data bank.
6   Press cuttings of competitor activities, market environment changes.

B   Qualitative or exploratory research

1   Organized marketing intelligence, such as sales force reports, attendance at exhibitions and trade shows.
2   Group discussions with targeted customers.
3   Observational studies of visitor behaviour using cameras or trained observers.
4   Marketing experiments with monitored results.

C   Quantitative research (syndicated)

1   Omnibus questions of targeted respondents.
2   Syndicated surveys, including audits.

D   Quantitative research (ad hoc and continuous)

1   Attitude, image, perception and awareness studies.
2   Studies of travel and tourism behaviour and usage patterns.
3   Advertising and other media response studies.
4   Customer satisfaction and product monitoring studies.
5   Distribution studies amongst retail outlets.

Figure 11.2   *The marketing research menu*

bookings for each park on a weekly basis, with analyses of areas from which bookings flow, type of caravan/chalet most or least in demand, size of party booking, etc. Many of these data would be required for constructing business accounts and customer invoices.

A2 On a continuous or a sample basis, customers checking in on arrival could complete a form establishing, for example, the incidence of repeat visits, how they heard of the park, whether the park brochure was seen, and distance travelled from home.

A3 Published results of tourist board surveys, e.g. BTS-M and BTS-Y, would throw useful light on overall trends for the self catering market nationally and by region. Occasional other inexpensive analyses of the market would be available from time to time (A4). There are several journals for the holiday parks and caravan industry, which provide valuable insights into current events and trends in the market (A6).

A5 Previous years records (as in A1 and A2) would provide valuable benchmarks against which to view current patterns.

B1 There are numerous trade shows and travel workshops available for the caravan/chalet park operator, as well as national conferences. All provide opportunities to see what others in the industry are doing, especially in terms of park design, accommodation unit design, product presentation in brochures and so on.

In terms of the foregoing uses of marketing research, assuming that management time is excluded from the cost and that business records are a by-product of essential accounting procedures, the total expenditure would be measured in hundreds, rather than thousands of pounds. To proceed beyond this point involves more significant expenditure to be set off against the expected value of results.

B2 Not affordable on an annual basis in this example, the decision to renew the main brochure could repay discussion of alternative covers, contents, and formats conducted with small groups of prospective clients. Such group discussions would also generate ideas and concepts for advertising. With 2,000 units to let, this operator might distribute 150,000 brochures per annum at a cost of say £70,000 (including distribution), so that up to £10,000 on group discussions could be productive over a three-year span, assessed against sales revenue achievable.

B3 If, for example, the capacity of washing and laundry facilities is open to review at one or more of the parks, cameras or simple observation of queues and their reactions would be a cheap but effective form of research.

B4 In terms of pricing, different advertising formats, and product developments (e.g. mini-breaks), this operator is perfectly placed to engage in systematic experimentation and monitoring (see later in this chapter) at low cost.

C2 In 1985 park owners of this type in Britain were able to purchase packs of printed, standardized, self completion questionnaires designed by a commercial market research agency. Owners were responsible for distributing and ensuring completion by samples of visitors, and collecting questionnaires; the price was just under £300 per thousand questionnaires. This price included a standard tabulation of all completed and returned forms. With a 50 per cent response rate of completed questionnaires, the cost per questionnaire was £0.60. This price was only available on the basis that several parks participated, to spread the costs of questionnaire design and printing.

D4 Of the 'D' options, D4 would be particularly important for this type of operator.

Administered as part of a syndicated (C2) survey, or as a separate entity during say six selected weeks of the operating year, measuring satisfaction would probably account for the largest portion of annual marketing research expenditure in this example. Analysed by type of product, type of customer, time of year, and in association with any marketing experiments, the value of this research in marketing planning would be considerable.

Using a market research agency

Whilst the great majority of marketing managers can expect to be more or less continuously involved in using marketing research data, relatively few will be directly involved in organizing and conducting surveys. Large organizations such as airlines, tourist boards and major hotel corporations have their own research departments but most survey work will be commissioned from specialist market research agencies, of which there were over 400 in the UK with an estimated turnover (1984) of £168 million. It is, therefore, important that marketing managers should be aware of what agencies do and how to get the best response from them.

In Britain, the Market Research Society (MRS) is the professional body for all individuals using survey techniques for market, social and economic research. With some 5000 members, the MRS claims to be the largest body of its kind in the world (MRS 1986) and it has developed sophisticated codes of professional conduct over many years. These codes are designed to protect and enhance the integrity with which research is practised, and to safeguard the interests of the general public and clients as well as of agencies offering research services. Similar codes exist in several other European countries.

In research, as in most of marketing practice, the best way to achieve cost effective work is to specify the problem with as much precision as possible, setting it in its wider marketing context. Unless a client and an agency have worked together on a regular basis, it is unlikely that agencies asked to quote for surveys will be experts on the client's business. Unless the budget is unusually large in travel and tourism terms, there will not be many hours available for the agency to absorb basic 'diagnosis' and 'prognosis' (see Chapter 13 on use of research data in marketing planning). Time spent learning about the business will be time not available for developing the research approach.

'Problems' in marketing are seldom clear cut. They are frequently matters of perception and judgement, and two managers may well see the same problem in different ways. It is for this reason that time spent systematically analysing the problem is seldom wasted. It focuses managers' minds and often changes the way the problem is perceived, or switches attention to a different problem area not at first sight apparent. Part of the process of thinking through the problem is a consideration of how survey results may be used. For example, if a survey of visitors to a tourist attraction is required to reveal ways to achieve higher spending in shops on site, the agency must be given details of current sales policies and trading results before they design their research methodology and the questions to be asked. The expected use of results also determines the nature of the questions to be asked, but surprisingly few research buyers recognize this basic truth when defining the 'problem'.

Problem specification, together with other information noted in Figure 11.3, should always be put in writing and filed for future reference. At this stage, with a clearly expressed 'Research Brief', clients can approach agencies and invite them to tender for the work. Where an agency's work is well known to a client, competitive tendering may be unnecessary. Where it is not, it is usual practice to invite three or four agencies to submit tenders, informing them that others are involved. The commercial market research world

The client brief
- Identifies the marketing context and perceived problem to be researched
- Specifies expected use of results
- Indicates time scale for completion
- States approximate budget limits

The agency tender
- Defines or redefines the problem in research terms
- Proposes a methodology relevant to the problem
- Specifies a realistic programme for completion including client liaison
- Recommends a reporting format and procedure
- Sets out terms and conditions of business, including costs and timing of payments
- Specifies personnel involved, their qualifications and experience, and their respective involvement in the proposed study
- Indicates agency experience relevant to the problem, including reference to previous studies and clients whose needs were broadly comparable.

Figure 11.3 *Basic requirements of client and agency in commissioning market research*

is highly competitive and tendering is the usual route to new business.

Preparing tenders is a costly process for agencies, involving several hours work even for small projects, and up to several days work on larger projects. Unless otherwise agreed, research agency tenders are not charged but absorbed as a business overhead. In preparing a tender, the agency would normally expect at least one meeting to clarify and interpret the way the problem is expressed in the client's brief. Through experience with similar problems, agencies may well be able to restate the problem or illuminate it in ways not obvious to the client. They may have access to secondary data not known to clients, which can reduce costs.

Tenders should cover all the points noted in Figure 11.3, and clients will often find broad similarity in the methods and costs proposed by competing agencies. Accordingly, selecting which agency to use will normally be based on the extent to which each agency demonstrates comprehension of the problem, and the effect-iveness and creativity of the proposed methods of tackling it within stipulated budget limits. Proven track record in travel and tourism research may be important, but more vital is the quality of the rapport between client and agency which will be evident from the first meeting and reflected in the tenders. It will always be wise for clients to meet the research executive directly responsible for their job, as well as the agency director or senior researcher who is more likely to produce and present the tender. If meetings are involved, visiting the agency's premises will often reveal much more about the nature and quality of its operation than the usual glossy brochure with its predictable claims of all-round excellence and expertise.

Successful research involves a relationship of trust between client and agency akin to that which develops between advertising agency and client (albeit on a smaller scale). Reputable agencies will normally reveal names of previous clients, and it is quite usual for prospective clients to talk in confidence to previous clients about their experiences with particular agencies.

Customer communication – priceless asset of service business

A commonly misunderstood advantage inherent in marketing most service products in travel and tourism, is the presence of customers on producers' premises.

Anyone who has owned, worked, or been brought up in a small business such as an hotel, travel agency, restaurant, pub or caravan park, will recognize the powerful immediacy of customer contact, and the ease with which it is possible to detect (or impossible to avoid) customer needs, behaviour and satisfactions. Such businesses hardly need market research surveys because in a very real way, their customer knowledge and 'feedback' are better, more natural and more continuous than any millboard-carrying researcher could ever provide.

However, once a business grows large enough to have multiple branches, or is run by managers with limited customer contact, direct customer – management communication is lost. The board directors of an airline or large hotel company may not speak at all to customers for months or years, and if they do, may so intimidate them as to negate any research value of the contact. In these management circumstances, systematic research is necessary but it can still be based on the inherent advantages of customer/product inseparability and the relative ease of communication on site or 'in house'.

By contrast, producers of most consumer goods typically have either no contact at all with their customers, who purchase anonymously in retail outlets, or at best have access to names and addresses provided for warranty or servicing purposes. But in travel and tourism, all hotel customers sign registers and/or enter details on an hotel registration card. Airline customers spend many hours waiting in terminals and in planes for their journeys to start or to end. Visitors to attractions stroll around reception areas and car parks; travel agencies have many opportunities to seek out and record customers' needs and interests, and so on. In the late 1980s it is quite extraordinary, that with the exception of some large tour operators, hotel companies, major attractions, airlines and other transport operators, these opportunities for research are for the most part overlooked and under-utilized.

Researching customer satisfaction

Large tour operators in Britain typically hand out self-completion customer satisfaction questionnaires to all travellers returning from holidays abroad, usually on the flight home. Such questionnaires request rating of all aspects of the holiday using scales, which can be communicated by words or sketches and calculated numerically. From this information, if plotted on a week by week basis, it is possible to detect comparative satisfaction with individual resorts and hotels, or check the performance of specific flights, or particular aspects of products such as food, excursions or the service provided by resort representatives (see also Chapter 24).

Because profile information is included in the questionnaire, it is possible to analyse satisfaction by age of respondent, region of origin, cost of package and so on. These questionnaires, mostly scanned and processed by computers, can provide a vast range of continuous management information, which is both a control tool for service operations and a fertile database for marketing decisions, such as product formulation and pricing. Airlines use in-flight survey questionnaires in the same way for the same purposes, usually on a sample basis. So do some hotel companies and major attractions.

Marketing experiments

Especially with multi-site operations, the possibility for managers to experiment with service products are endless. A hotel corporation might, for example, vary menus and prices, vary the formality of food service, offer new facilities for business or leisure customers, change room furniture and decor, or promote a particular type of inclusive weekend-break product. Provided always that the results in sales and satisfaction are monitored, there are many opportunities to carry out 'live' market research through conducting controlled marketing experiments or tests. Through a process crudely but accurately dubbed 'suck it and see', service producers can often test, learn and modify product developments prior to wider implementation in other sites or premises.

Tour operators can offer new destinations, or new product types, in the pages of an existing brochure. If the development is popular and sells well, it can often be extended quickly and modified as necessary by evidence gained from customer satisfaction questionnaires. The 'learning' opportunity available to producer organizations in services, who can set up and read the results of marketing experiments at low cost, is typically not available to manufacturers of physical goods, especially where powerful retailers control distribution outlets and the shelf space allocated to producers. Test marketing of physical goods is generally a far more costly and time consuming process.

There is ample evidence that most businesses in travel and tourism can create opportunities systematically to experiment and monitor. Above all they can build up their marketing knowledge of buyer behaviour by obtaining relatively inexpensive feedback from the customers using their premises.

Chapter summary

This chapter identifies the role of marketing research and its value as the information base for marketing decisions. It explains the six main types of marketing research that practitioners in travel and tourism are most likely to encounter, and describes ten of the commonly used technical terms applied to research methods. In particular, it draws a distinction between continuous and *ad hoc* research; 'continuous' implying the creation and use of a database for marketing purposes, a very important development, which is explained further in Chapter 19.

A market research menu is offered in Figure 11.2, which may serve with Figure 11.3 as a useful checklist for those involved in commissioning research to fulfil particular purposes. The section on using research agencies is also relevant in this connection.

Emphasis is put on the role of experimentation in the marketing mix which, combined with detailed monitoring of results, is a particular form of marketing research likely to be highly relevant to all organizations in travel and tourism. Carefully designed experiments may be used to exploit fully the advantages of having customers on premises or equipment owned or managed by producer organizations.

The chapter stresses that marketing research, both continuous and *ad hoc*, illuminates what is involved in marketing decisions, and reduces the level of risk and uncertainty associated with them. But it cannot be expected to provide simple answers or remove the essential quality of judgement from managers. The use of marketing research data is most obviously seen in practice in the process of marketing planning, which is discussed in detail in Chapter 13.

Further reading

Baker, M. J., *Marketing: An Introductory Text*, Macmillan, 1985, Chapter 11.

Kotler, P., *Marketing: Analysis, Planning and Control*, Prentice-Hall, 1984, Chapter 6.

12

Marketing planning: Strategy and operations

This chapter and the next focuses on the planning process by which organizations decide and communicate the goals and objectives they seek to pursue. The key word here is 'decision' because at any given time organizations are likely to be faced with a wide range of choices, of which the implications can never be fully clear. Ultimately the objectives which an organization sets and pursues are the most important decisions it makes because these determine all other operational decisions.

It is necessary to deal with objectives at two levels. The first level is a strategic level covering the whole business over the long term, and the second level is an operational or tactical level covering specific markets and products in the short term. In practice, as described in this chapter, a hierarchy of decisions exists within any organization, which the student of marketing must appreciate.

At the level of overall business strategy there are elements other than marketing which must be considered and these are illustrated in the chapter. Marketing strategy remains the dominant element because of its focus on sales revenue generation and the responsibility of marketing management for achieving it.

This chapter deals with marketing at the strategic level, while Chapter 13 develops a step-by-step approach to operational planning which is the basis of organizing effective marketing campaigns. As Hussey puts it 'the planning of marketing is really a divided activity. One portion falls squarely under the heading of strategic planning ... a second portion can easily be seen as the task of the operating manager in planning and developing existing markets ...' (1979: p. 159).

The need for planning

In order to provide an orderly and agreed basis on which to conduct its business in an ever changing competitive market environment, any business is obliged to plan its activities. The larger the business, and the more products and markets with which it is involved, the greater the importance of effective planning and the need for systematic procedures. The more volatile a market is in terms of annual fluctuations in customer demand, the more important it is to work within a framework of agreed objectives. Years of market growth tend to obscure and lessen the need for planning, whilst recession and market decline, with inevitable failures of some businesses, bring planning issues sharply into focus.

In essence, any plan comprises a statement of goals and objectives and programme of activity intended to achieve them. The statement of goals usually involves market research and analysis, and the programmes of activity have to be costed and monitored in some way to work out how well the objectives are actually achieved. All planning is conducted on the assumption that the effort in time and money will produce more profitable results over a period of years than the alternative of constant reaction to market conditions and the opportunist use of business hunch. This assumption is more likely to be valid for organizations run by committees of managers than those run by individual entrepreneurs. Managers will recognize how these simple truths tend to disappear in the compexities of planning analysis and techniques but students should hold on to this simple definition in understanding this chapter.

Strategic marketing planning

Stripped of its mystery and technique, overall strategic corporate planning for businesses attempts to answer the questions:

- where are we now?
- where do we want to be in five or more year's time?
- how do we get there?

The three questions help to explain three concepts in corporate planning (adapted from Davidson: 1975: p. 109):

- goals and objectives (chosen destinations)
- strategies (chosen routes for achieving goals)
- plans (action programmes for moving along the route)

In those simple terms, strategic planning is as relevant to small businesses as it is to large ones.

For marketing purposes, strategic planning may be defined as the process whereby an organization analyses the strengths and weaknesses of its current market, decides the position it seeks to attain, and defines strategies and costed programmes of activity to achieve its aims.

Strategic decisions are always focused on the longer run, usually defined as three or more years ahead. Included in the marketing planning process are:

Goals and objectives	The place in its markets which an organization seeks to occupy in a future period, usually defined broadly in terms of target segments, volume of sales, product range, market shares and profitability.
Images and positioning	Where the organization seeks to be in terms of customers' and retailers' perceptions of its products and its corporate image.
Budget	What resources are needed to achieve its goals.
Programmes	Broadly what actions, including development, are required to achieve the goals and objectives, expressed in terms of buildings, equipment or plant, personnel, administration, organization structure, and marketing.

Larger organizations with multiple products in multiple markets, such as an hotel chain or international car rental company, also require strategic planning to achieve effective relationships and allocation of resources between the component parts of the business. Strategy in this context is discussed later (see portfolio analysis).

Strategy is essentially pro-active in the sense that it defines and wills the future shape of the organization as well as responding to market conditions and perceived consumer needs.

Tactical marketing planning

Tactics are always associated with decisions focused on the short run, in which specific marketing campaigns are planned, implemented and evaluated. Short run may be a year or 18 months or only weeks. Tactics are inevitably responsive to market circumstances and particularly responsive to competitors' actions.

Tactical, or operational marketing plans, include:

Objectives	Specified, quantified, volume and sales revenue targets and other specific marketing objectives.
Mix and budget	Marketing mix and marketing budget decisions.
Action programmes	The implementation of marketing programmes and co-ordination of promotional activity.
Evaluation and control	Monitoring marketing results on a regular or continuous basis with regular evaluation.

A hierarchy of objectives

Figure 12.1 is a diagram of the two levels of business objectives, which serves also to put marketing strategy and objectives into the wider context of planning organizational goals and objectives. Overall, corporate planning specifies objectives and targets for all the elements in an organization, which combine to get it from where it is at the present time to the position it seeks to occupy at some future date.

In the first level of the hierarchy of objectives, and influenced by the external business environment, the diagram notes seven common elements, which are systematically planned and integrated in most overall corporate strategies. Marketing, as explained earlier, is one of the elements; it is shown in the centre of the diagram

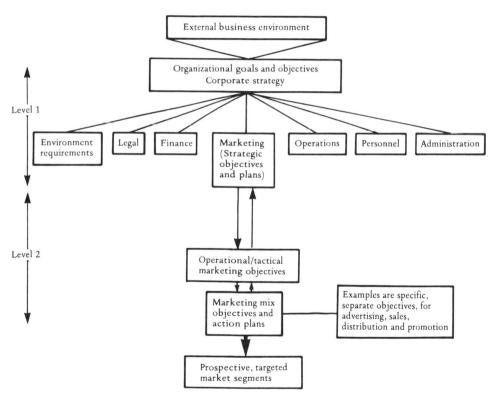

Figure 12.1 *Elements involved in a corporate business strategy, and hierarchy of objectives*

with a separate input below it to demonstrate the linkages with operational marketing planning shown as Level 2.

A brief description of six of the seven strategy elements is provided below, and explained in the context of a large international airline. All seven have specific implications for decisions at a tactical or operational level but, marketing strategy excepted, the other elements are not the subject of this chapter and are not referred to further.

Whilst hierarchies of objectives may not appear relevant to small proprietor-run businesses, the thought process and principles discussed in this chapter are fully appropriate to any size of operation. It is the failure to think strategically that causes many smaller businesses to decline and founder.

Corporate strategy in an airline context

In the context of a major scheduled airline with an international network of routes, the decisions to be brought together as a strategy can be explained briefly in the following questions:

Finance	What asset and loan structure is needed by the airline? What returns on capital are required to service the investment, meet the stake holders' interests and fund any new investment in aircraft and facilities?
Personnel	What numbers, remuneration levels, qualifications, organization, training and career structure are required for employees, to provide an effective service across the network?
Operations	What number, type and size of aircraft are required to cover what routes at what times? With what engineering and fleet servicing requirement? What passenger handling facilities across the network?
Legal	What agreements between countries are required to maintain and develop services on the agreed route network? How far and how fast might de-regulation proceed?
Environment	What aircraft developments must be completed to meet any new regulations concerning noise, emissions, night flights and energy consumption?
Administration	What facilities of management, buildings, equipment and general organization are needed to service the airlines' current operations and assist it to develop according to planned goals and objectives?

Marketing strategy

For any marketing-led organization, marketing strategy must be the most important single element in overall business strategy. It identifies, and largely determines future sales revenue generation by specifying the segments, products and associated action programmes required to achieve sales. Each of the other elements in the strategy involves expenditure out of projected revenue. However vital these elements are to the conduct of the business, they are ultimately conditioned by the organization's ability to persuade sufficient customers to buy enough of its products to secure a surplus of revenue over costs in the long run. Whilst it is obviously incorrect to conclude that business strategy is only about marketing, it is not difficult to establish that all strategy for commercial organizations has its bottom line in sales revenue, and that marketing managers are employed to achieve revenue targets through their specialist knowledge of market needs and circumstances.

To illustrate the point, the decision by an airline to purchase an additional aircraft, such as a Boeing 747, draws on each of the seven strategic elements. But, unless marketing managers can undertake on a daily basis to achieve adequate seat occupancy levels (load factors), at average prices which exceed average costs, the decision to purchase cannot be taken. In practice there is always an element of risk in the decision to buy new equipment, but the principal risk lies in projecting future customer demand and having the marketing will and competence to secure the demand against aggressive competition.

Three key concepts in strategy formulation

The subject of marketing strategy formulation has assumed greater significance since the 1970s for three important reasons. The first is the global uncertainty provoked by the major international energy crises of 1973 and 1979. These events, and the economic recessions which followed them, disrupted many of the long-range econometric forecasting models developed in the 1960s to plan long-term business goals.

The second is the development of information technology in the 1970s, which, amongst other contributions, facilitated the internationalization of exchange rates so that all currencies are now subject to hour-by-hour fluctuations and speculative pressures hitherto unknown. Consequently, exchange rates, which are so intimately connected to tourism prices, are highly volatile and cannot be forecast with precision.

The third is the growth of large organizations in travel and tourism, as in other industries during the 1970s, many with international links, and with wide ranges or products for a wide range of markets.

The three reasons affect all types of industries but they are especially powerful in price sensitive international travel and tourism markets. Without strategies to guide their responses to inevitable changes in the external business environment, organizations can lose sight of their goals in the time-consuming and urgent tactical decisions involved in the day-to-day management of demand, which all service industries require. Marketing strategy has to be flexible to cope with change and sufficiently sensitive to discriminate between different components of large businesses. Old concepts of centralized head office planning for large organizations are no longer seen as efficient in the 1980s, and new models of delegated planning for separate sectors of a business (known as strategic business units or SBUs) have emerged. These new approaches typically involve head office co-ordination and support but limited direct operational involvement (see also Chapter 10).

Within the limits of this book it is only possible to draw attention to the issues involved and the sources noted at the end of the chapter must be pursued to achieve further understanding. It is vital, however, that students of travel marketing should be able to distinguish clearly between strategy and operations or tactics. Three concepts in particular, drawn from the extensive literature on strategic planning, will assist in making the important distinctions. These are:

- Product-market portfolio analysis
- Alternative growth models
- Product positioning

Product-market portfolios

A very large business, such as Trusthouse Forte (ThF), comprises a range of businesses including fast food outlets (Little Chef), contract catering (Gardner Merchant) and Hotels (International and British in separate divisions such as Post-houses and Country Inns). In terms of their specific products and market segments, these are essentially quite separate businesses which share in common the strength of the corporate identity, the economies and advantages of bulk purchasing, and access to investment finance. ThF can thus be seen as a holding company with a *portfolio* of businesses or strategic business units (SBUs), each with its own management structure, profit and loss accounts and plans for the future.

The strategic planning process for a large international company, therefore, involves analysing its current portfolio of SBUs and deciding what changes are needed to secure future growth and profit in the light of international market conditions. Thus, 'the end product of the strategic planning process is a future best-yield portfolio ... taking into account risk and short-term versus long-term trade offs' (Boyd and Larreche: 1982: p. 9).

At a lower level of business size, the same concept of SBUs may be more narrowly interpreted in terms of the products and markets with which a business is involved. A large British tour operator may offer, for example:

Product	Market segments
1 *Winter sun*	Older, less active, budget conscious buyers – long stay.
2 *Winter skiing*	younger, active, more affluent buyers – short stay.
3 *Summer sun*	(a) Families, beach orientated, budget conscious (b) Young adults, activity and entertainment orientated, various price ranges.
4 *Exotic places*	Older, more affluent, experienced travellers.

In this example, the tour operator's product/market portfolio comprises at least four distinctive products, (each capable of subdivision by price and by destination or by accommodation variants), and at least four distinctive market segments, which could also be subdivided.

The tour operator may find it necessary to divide responsibility for marketing its four product groups between four management teams, and to operate each with its own budget and cost/revenue analysis. In this process the operator would effectively be managing a portfolio of products, following the same principles of SBUs noted above.

Within any portfolio of SBUs or product/markets it will usually be the case that some products are growing and some are declining. Some are more profitable than others. Portfolios can be analysed over time periods according to key variables of:

- share of market
- market growth
- cash flow generation
- return on investment
- strength of competition
- product life cycle

It will quickly become obvious from analysis that some products, or SBUs, in the portfolio have a relatively large share of expanding markets with good profitability. Such products are obviously candidates for strategic support if the general projections remain favourable. Other products, perhaps because the market sector is declining not because the product is inadequate, will be in decline and generating little profit, especially if prices are being reduced to maintain volume.

The ideal portfolio will comprise some new products with good shares of growth markets ('stars') and some profitable products with well established shares of stable markets ('cash cows'). In practice, portfolios will frequently also contain products with low shares of declining markets and poor profitability ('dogs'), which are candidates for liquidation. The labels (in brackets) are those created by the Boston Consulting Group in the USA, which developed one of the best known techniques for product/market portfolio analysis.

Alternative growth and development strategies

It is now commonplace in all sectors of business that no organization can afford to mark time, or rest on its past progress, and expect to maintain the structure of its existing product/market portfolio and profitability levels, even over a period as short as two years. Profitable product/market portfolios will usually be under constant competitive pressure, and it will be necessary to update and augment products continuously to match changing customer needs. Businesses will also have to respond to other pressures, such as unfavourable exchange rate movements, and to any changes in the regulatory or technology practices which are certain to occur over a five-year time span.

Accordingly, it is usual for marketing-led businesses continuously to review their portfolios, and search for ways to grow or develop in order to secure future profitability. The options for growth are wide but can be neatly summarized in an elegant model originally devised by Ansoff and much copied and developed since.

Product market growth strategies
(4 basic options)

	Present products	*new products*
Present markets	1 market penetration	2 product development
New markets	3 market development	4 diversification

Each strategy has radically different implications for marketing campaigns.
Source: Based on Ansoff, *Corporate Strategy*, 1968, p. 99.

The four numbered boxes in the model may be illustrated with typical travel and tourism examples as follows:

1 The case where an hotel group, already servicing the corporate meetings sector as its principal product, decides that it is well positioned to expand in this market. With its existing portfolio, any expansion above natural market growth would represent an increased market share, which is known as 'penetration'.

2 The case where a British tour operator, already operating a portfolio of European inclusive tours, decides to expand its operations by developing long-haul tours to the USA, aiming at the existing British IT market. This decision represents an addition to the portfolio and is known as product development.

3 The case where an international resort operator, such as Club Méditerranée with a largely European clientele, decides to market its European villages in the USA in order to extend its sales potential. This represents market development.

4 Finally, if an airline company decided to buy an hotel company, through an acquisition, it would be stepping completely outside its existing product/market portfolio and effectively diversifying its business activities with a completely new set of SBUs.

Each of these choices represents strategic considerations and normally would be undertaken only on the basis of a detailed analysis of potential revenues and advantages, as well as potential costs and disadvantages. The process for such an analysis is outlined in the next chapter.

Product positioning

Portfolio analysis and assessment of alternative growth strategies focus on securing long-term profitability. The third concept is about securing a long-term favourable image or perception among prospective customers, and other groups such as retailers, on which a business depends. While profit and image are related they are tackled by quite different marketing methods and must be separately planned.

The concept of product positioning was introduced in Chapter 8. A useful illustration in travel and tourism is that of British Airways (BA) which in 1981–82 was recording record annual losses in the wake of the international economic crisis provoked by rising oil prices. Whilst BA's losses were not unique, the management were well aware through research, that its customer contact staff were widely perceived as unfriendly and unhelpful, when compared with the staffs of other competitor airlines. BA was, in consequence, not highly rated in airline preference decisions by prospective travellers.

As a key aspect of its response, the airline developed a 'putting people first' campaign in which, over a period of two or three years, all members of staff were required to undertake participative courses designed to make them aware of customer feelings, and to develop social skills in customer handling. The airline's objective was to improve the position and image it held in customers' minds, through better service. The strategic aim was that more customers would choose, and fewer reject British Airways as an option, when purchasing air travel. The success of this effort is measurable in terms of changing customer attitudes and has been stimulated by promotional expenditure driving home the message that BA is the world's 'favourite airline'. The obvious success of the 'people first' programme created the perceptual climate in which BA could achieve profitable seat occupancies and contribute to its strategic goals for return on assets employed.

Goals down; plans up

A useful way to hold in mind the distinctions between strategy and tactics is encapsulated in the phrase 'goals down; plans up'. It means that the board of an organization will normally set goals, which its managers are expected to achieve. The goals will be based on the requirements noted earlier in this chapter, especially return on investment and long-term profit.

Boardroom goals are not always achievable in practice. It is the business of managers to plan and communicate upwards what is realistic within budgets, time, and market circumstances, both in strategic terms, and tactically for short-run periods of six months to a year ahead. Resolving the differences between desired goals and achievable objectives is a normal part of the management process of any organization. This process brings together and modifies strategic and operational decision processes. Since strategic goals are intended to motivate managers and always relate to desired future states, it is normal for there to be some tension and dispute between short-term and long-term planning requirements.

Chapter summary

This chapter introduces the basic concepts of systematic planning, which are central to the efficient conduct of marketing-led organizations in travel and tourism as in other industries. It distinguishes between strategic and operational or tactical levels of planning; it further distinguishes between corporate planning as it applies to the whole of an organization's business, and planning for the individual elements of a business, of which marketing strategy and tactics are only one, however important. 'Corporate planning decisions . . . are decisions that affect the whole structure of the company many years or decades into the future – huge decisions taken in conditions of extreme uncertainty about the future' (Argenti: 1980: p. 14).

The chapter focuses on the meaning of planning and strategy for marketing, as the management function most directly responsible for identifying and stimulating future customer demand and converting it into sales revenue. Drawing of an analysis of product/market portfolios (or SBUs), marketing strategy defines the future mix of products and segments, which best meet the organization's long-run goals, and the position such products are intended to occupy in the minds of prospective customers. The chapter defines a hierarchy of objectives found in most businesses, but stresses the need for flexibility and continuity in the planning process.

The 'goals down, plans up' dialogue is introduced at the end of the chapter to stress the way in which the different levels of planning are integrated in practice in larger organizations. It also provides a bridge into the next chapter, in which the main focus is on the process of planning and the tactical or operational level of marketing.

Further reading

Baker, M. J., *Marketing: An Introductory Text*, Macmillan, 1985, Chapter 21

Kotler, P., *Marketing Management: Analysis, Planning and Control*, Prentice-Hall, 1984, Chapters 2 and 12.

13

Planning marketing operations and tactics

The previous chapter stresses the differences between marketing strategy and tactics, and the relationship between them in the hierarchy of corporate objectives. This chapter focuses on the planning of marketing tactics or operations, which are implemented in the short run through action plans. Corporate objectives have been described earlier as 'destinations'; strategies as 'routes'; and plans as action programmes for moving along agreed routes. In other words, strategy sets the framework within which tactics are planned. Most of the work which goes on in marketing departments is concerned with drawing up, implementing and measuring the effects of action plans.

This chapter also focuses on the seven stages of the planning process which are common to marketing in any form of industry. It emphasizes that the planning process for strategy and tactics covers the same essential stages, usually drawing on the same research sources and often undertaken by the same people. For strategic purposes, the analysis and forecasting of trends in the external business environment is the most important part of planning, while for tactical purposes, the setting of precise objectives and action programmes is the main focus.

The chapter begins by stating why time and resources are devoted to the marketing planning process in most marketing-led organizations, and draws some contrasts with the alternatives of guesswork, hunch and feel for the market which

are characteristic of many smaller businesses in travel and tourism. It proceeds to explain the stages in the planning process, which are summarized in Figure 13.1. The chapter ends with a note on the role of objectives as an important part of internal communications within organizations.

The particular significance of marketing plans

In its principles marketing planning is no more than a logical thought process, in which all businesses have to engage to some extent. It is an application of common sense, as relevant to a small guest house or caravan park, as it is to an international airline. The scale of planning and its sophistication obviously vary according to the size of the organization concerned, but the essential principles remain the same.

Developing from the overall purposes of planning outlined in Chapter 12, it may be helpful to emphasize six main reasons why time and resources are allocated to marketing planning at the tactical or operational level:

1 To focus management attention on the current and targeted costs, revenues and profitability of an organization in the context of its own and its competitors' products and segments.

2 To focus decisions on the strategic objectives of an organization in its market context, and identify action plans relevant to the long-term future.

3 To set and to communicate specific business targets for managers to achieve in agreed time periods.

4 To schedule and co-ordinate promotional and other marketing action required to achieve targets and to allocate the resources required.

5 To achieve co-ordination and a sense of joint direction between the different departments of an organization, around agreed targets.

6 To monitor and evaluate the results of marketing expenditure and adjust the planned activity as required to meet unforeseen circumstances.

Are there alternatives to marketing planning?

The only alternatives to the systematic common-sense planning processes outlined in this chapter are guesswork, hunch, 'feel' for the market, simple intuition, or vision. Sometimes hunches and intuition are practised with brilliant success by highly energetic and determined business entrepreneurs, many of whom dismiss systematic planning as bureaucratic, rigid, time consuming, expensive, and often wrong. But hunch and guesswork also have their disadvantages, and the history of travel and tourism reveals many illustrations of brilliant entrepreneurs whose businesses grew rapidly and successfully for some years, only to crash spectacularly in the wake of unpredicted events. Clarksons Travel, Laker Airways, Braniff Airways, are just three illustrations which are widely known.

In principle, although systematic methodical planning procedures and entrepreneurial marketing flair are usually seen as opposites, they can be mutually supportive. Planning procedures must not be allowed to become inflexible or the cause of delays, but may be used to provide a framework of objectives and an information base, which supports and gives a sense of direction or roots for marketing judgement and flair. 'Entrepreneurial planning' may sound like a contradiction in terms but it is nevertheless a desirable goal to which most modern large

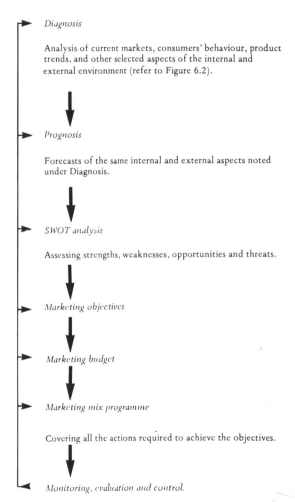

Diagnosis

Analysis of current markets, consumers' behaviour, product trends, and other selected aspects of the internal and external environment (refer to Figure 6.2).

Prognosis

Forecasts of the same internal and external aspects noted under Diagnosis.

SWOT analysis

Assessing strengths, weaknesses, opportunities and threats.

Marketing objectives

Marketing budget

Marketing mix programme

Covering all the actions required to achieve the objectives.

Monitoring, evaluation and control.

Figure 13.1 *The marketing planning process*

businesses aspire, and which they attempt to build into their internal management procedures. There is very clearly a balance to be struck in marketing management between analytical procedures and creative flair. Both are essential qualities for long-run survival and profitability. Creative flair will always be a vital quality in aggressive marketing action. Unbridled by agreed strategies and objectives such flair can also be self destructive.

Logical steps in the marketing planning process

There are seven logical steps in systematic marketing planning. Each step feeds into the next one, with feedback loops built into the process, which are noted with arrows in Figure 13.1 and explained in the text which follows.

Diagnosis

Described in some texts as part of a 'marketing audit', the first stage in the planning process is marketing research based, drawing on available published and unpublished data for analysis of trends under four main headings:

1 Sales volume and revenue trends over a five-year period at least, to identify total market movements and market shares for particular segments and for own and competitors' products. A tour operator would, for example, compare his own sales data with Civil Aviation Authority data for charter airline passengers, and with government and tourist authority survey data of travel and tourism movements.

2 Consumer profiles for own customers and competitors' customers, including detail of demographics, attitudes and behaviour, as outlined in Chapter 7. This information

typically comes from business records and through research surveys.

3 Product profiles and price trends for own and competitors' products, identifying product life-cycle movements and in particular noting growing and declining product types. Such information is typically drawn from analyzing internal business records and through trade press and trade research.

4 Trends in the external environment (as identified in Chapter 7) such as changing technology, changing regulatory requirements, exchange rate movements or changing distribution structure. This information also derives primarily from trade press and trade research sources although some aspects may justify undertaking marketing research studies.

Under the four headings above, *Diagnosis* represents a factual platform, which is the basis for all marketing plans at strategic and tactical level. Since the travel and tourism industry has access to data from many sources, the way in which data is selected, organized and presented for decision purposes, is an important management skill.

The level of detail involved in the diagnosis is a matter for each individual business, reflecting its size and the range of its operations. Diagnosis is likely to extend beyond the products and markets of immediate concern to a business, into adjacent markets. For example, a budget-priced hotel chain would expect to diagnose budget sector accommodation markets and products in full detail. It might also need to monitor trends in the de luxe end of the market in order to assess relative changes in the sectors which could have future strategic implications. A tour operator without a long-haul programme might monitor long-haul market trends, in case developments suggest an entry into that sector at some future point.

Prognosis

Described in many texts as 'marketing forecasting' the second stage in the planning process is also market research based but future orientated involving expectations, judgement and forecasting for each of the four headings already covered under Diagnosis. Because the future for travel and tourism products is subject to volatile, unpredictable factors, the prognosis is not expected to be highly accurate and must be updated regularly as new events alter expectations. The purpose of prognosis is not accuracy but careful and continuous assessment of probabilities and options, recognizing that most marketing mix expenditure is invested weeks, months or even years ahead of the revenue flows achieved. Since marketing planning is focused on future revenue achievement, it is necessarily dependent upon realistic prognosis.

As with the diagnosis stage, much skill exists in developing relevant predictions for key variables affecting an organization's business, and presenting them in ways to which marketing managers are able to respond in their strategic and operational decisions.

SWOT analysis

Equipped with relevant information through the process of diagnosis, and the best indications of developing trends through prognosis, the next stage is to access what the information means for marketing strategy and tactics. A useful framework for this assessment is contained in the acronym SWOT, which stands for strengths, weaknesses, opportunities and threats.

Strengths are normally expressed as inherent advantages, whether by design or historic good fortune, in the organization's market-product portfolio, and its operations in relation to competitors.

Products with increasing shares of growing markets are obviously strengths. Dominance of key market segments is another strength. For hotels, location may be a major strength. Strength may lie in historic artefacts or architectural style and it may reflect a particularly favourable consumer image. Strength may lie in the professional skills of a marketing team or a distribution system, or in customer service staff with an especially helpful and friendly approach.

It is impossible to indicate all the possible dimensions of an organization's strengths, but all such dimensions are identifiable elements, of which an organization has more, or does better, than its competitors. Once identified, strengths can be promoted to potential customers, and often enhanced through product augmentation, or developed within a strategic framework.

Weaknesses, ranging from ageing products in declining markets, for example, to surly customer contact staff, also must be clearly identified. Once identified they may be subject to management action designed to minimize their impact or to remove them where possible. Weaknesses and strengths are often matters of perception rather than 'fact', and may often be identified only through consumer research.

If, for example, an historic hotel in a market town is perceived by many of its customers as old-fashioned, noisy and inconvenient, it may be possible to highlight its strengths by repositioning it to stress old-world charm, convenience of location, and atmosphere. Such a representation may involve extensive refurbishment including double glazing and refurnishing, but it could provide a strategic route to turn a weakness into strength. If a modern competitor hotel were to be built on the outskirts of the market town, the historic hotel would probably lose some of its clients and might be forced to reposition its products and develop new markets in order to survive.

It is common practice in marketing-orientated businesses for managers to conduct regular *audits* of their current strengths and weaknesses, or to commission consultants to carry out such audits from an independent and unbiased viewpoint.

Opportunities, in their marketing sense, may arise from elements of the business which are under direct control, such as a particular product or process. They may also arise from shifts in the external environment, which a firm may exploit. Club Méditerranée, for example, strongly exploiting its island and enclosed resort destinations, and its concepts of freedom and activities, extended its operations throughout the world during the 1970s. It seized an opportunity to develop its particular holiday concepts with a powerful image in a way which no other operator matched at that time. A different type of opportunity arose for Australia when the USA was defeated in the America's Cup and it was agreed to stage the 1987 event at Fremantle, near Perth, Western Australia. With four year's notice, Perth did everything possible to use the opportunity to develop a modern tourist industry around this major event, which was the focus of the world's attention for several months. Perth was assured of film, TV, radio and press coverage beyond the dreams of any conceivable advertising budget.

Threats may also be presented by internal elements within the business's control, or by external events such as exchange rate changes, rising oil prices or acts of international terrorism. In Britain, the traditional British seaside resorts offering beach-based summer holidays are under heavy threat from seaside resorts along the Mediterranean coastline. The competition has severely eroded their customary markets and is forcing a strategic re-appraisal of their futures.

Although it is not easy to justify the point theoretically, practical experience of marketing proves that the time and effort spent in a systematic and creative SWOT analysis is invariably productive. There is much more involved than routine analysis of market statistics and ample scope for creative interpretation, judgement, and lateral thinking, both at the strategic and tactical levels of planning.

Marketing objectives and targets

Marketing objectives and targets derive logically from the previous stages of the planning process and state what managers believe can be achieved from a business over a specified time period.

To be actionable in operational practice, objectives must be:

- precise and quantified in terms of sales volume, sales revenue and, if possible, market share
- specific in terms of products and segments
- specific in terms of the time period in which they are to be achieved
- realistic in terms of market trends and in relation to budgets available
- agreed by and acceptable to the managers responsible for the programmes of activity designed to achieve results
- measurable directly or indirectly

If these six criteria are not fully observed, the objectives will be less than adequate in determining the success of the business and make the marketing programmes harder to specify and evaluate. The more thorough the diagnosis, prognosis, and SWOT, the easier the task of specifying precise objectives.

To give an example, consider the case of a medium-size British tour operator with a capacity of say 400,000 packages sold in the previous year. Assuming that favourable market circumstances are revealed by diagnosis and prognosis, and starting from a good competitive position, the operator might look for a 15 per cent increase in volume in the following year, e.g. *to sell 460,000 tours over the next year*.

Even if revenue and share were added to this statement it could not be considered fully actionable in marketing terms. To meet the six criteria previously noted, and drawing on a notional analysis of the operators' business for the sake of the example, the same objective would have to be explained as follows:

To sell 460,000 tours between April and September, at average 95% occupancy, to achieve a gross contribution of £14 million, with an overall market share of 6%;
by sales of 325,000 Summer sun tours (Europe)
(+ 12% on previous year).
by sales of 75,000 lakes & mountains tours (Europe)
(− 5% on previous year).
by sales of 30,000 coach tours (Europe)
(+ 50% on previous year).
by sales of 30,000 tours (Florida)
(+100% on previous year).

The figures in brackets represent target increase/decrease on previous years' sales, reflecting the prognosis stage of planning as well as a strategy, in this case to develop into the USA.

This level of precision would facilitate the task of planning weekly capacity for airports of origin, resort destinations, flight and bed capacity and contracting the necessary seats and rooms. In tour operating practice, the process of targeting numbers is built up on the basis of aircraft flight capacity and schedules, so that the operational implications of targeted increases for contracting purposes are immediately apparent to managers (see Chapter 24).

From these quantified capacity targets, the promotional and other marketing tasks involved in achieving the targeted volumes can be drawn up and costed for budget purposes. Subsequently the marketing effort can be evaluated in terms of bookings against target sales.

It should be apparent from this brief consideration of setting objectives, that precision cannot be achieved without prior analysis (diagnosis and prognosis). In every case, except for very small operators with one product and one segment, it will be found necessary to *disaggregate* the objectives into specific products and segments. Once this is achieved, the specification and costing of marketing mix tasks becomes easier.

Marketing budget

The marketing budget (discussed further in Chapter 14) determines the amount of money, which has to be spent *in advance* of bookings, reservations or immediate purchases, in order to secure targeted sales volume and revenue. In the tour operator example noted earlier, costs of brochure production, distribution, and of advertising, would be committed months before the full payments or even most of the deposits are received from customers.

The budget represents the sum of the costs of individual marketing mix elements judged necessary by marketing managers to achieve specified objectives and targets. There can never be total precision between costs and results for reasons discussed in Chapter 14, but this does not alter the principle of allocating money to specific tasks in order to achieve targeted results.

Because the budget is required to achieve objectives through expenditure on a marketing mix programme, there is a vital feedback loop between target setting and marketing management agreement on what can realistically be achieved with affordable budgets (see Figure 13.2).

Marketing mix programmes

The programme of marketing operations and tactics is the mix of promotion, distribution and other marketing activities, which are undertaken to influence and motivate buyers to choose targeted volumes of particular products. These include:

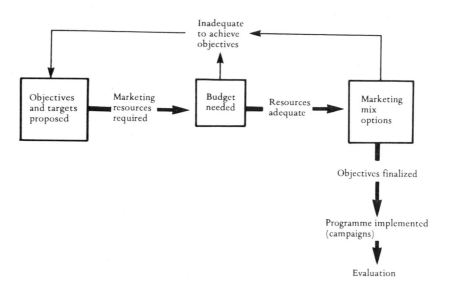

Figure 13.2 *Co-ordinating operational marketing objectives, budgets and programmes*

- *advertising*
- *sales promotion*
- *personal selling*
- *promotional literature*
- *public relations*
- *distribution*
- *price discounts*
- *commissions to retailers*

A marketing mix programme, which is also known as a *marketing campaign* expresses exactly what activities will take place in support of each identified product/market sub-group on a week by week basis. Since brochure production, distribution, advertising, and merchandizing in retail travel agencies have different time scales, there is a considerable management art involved in scheduling programmes of work which make best use of the marketing department's staff time.

Figure 13.2 demonstrates the essential dialogue or systematic interaction, which takes place in marketing planning between objectives, budgets and programmes.

The proposed objectives reflect overall business strategy and targets for managers to achieve, as previously described. The marketing resources include the numbers and skills of staff to undertake programmes. Also in resources are the size and structure of the distribution channels available to the business, its links with advertising agencies, etc. If an evaluation of objectives demonstrates that resources are inadequate, then additional budgets will be needed *or* the objectives must be amended.

For each marketing objective there will normally be a range of options as to how it will be achieved, involving more or less advertising, more or less price discounting and so on. Marketing managers are required to consider these options and the associated costs, using judgement, experience and analysis of previous results. If the preferred options cannot be met within budget, more money will be needed or the objectives must be modified again.

Over the space of several days or weeks, each of the three interlocking elements will be modified until agreement is reached and an agreed marketing mix programme is finalized for implementation. In describing targeting for the Thomas Cook Group, Davies comments, 'The essential features of targets are that they should be meaningful and that they should be acceptable to those responsible for their achievement' (Davies: 1981: p. 97).

Monitoring and evaluation

One of the important reasons for insisting on precision in setting objectives, is to make it possible to evaluate results. In the case of the tour-operator business discussed above under 'marketing objectives and targets', it would be possible to evaluate results for each market/product sector under at least six headings; e.g.:

1. Weekly flow of bookings against planned capacity.
2. Sales response related to any advertising activity.
3. Customer awareness of advertising messages measured by research surveys.
4. Sales response to any price discounts.
5. Sales response to any merchandising efforts by travel agents.
6. Customer satisfaction with product quality measured by research surveys.

Evaluation is a complex subject further discussed in Chapter 14. For this purpose it is sufficient to stress that efficient evaluation is vital to the diagnosis process, and that it is impossible to have efficient evaluation without first establishing precise targets, against which to measure results.

The communication role of operational objectives

Ways of involving as many staff as possible in contributing to the process of setting objectives and drawing up plans, is an important aspect of securing willing, enthusiastic participation in their implementation. It is a subject of increasing attention in many travel and tourism organizations, and is especially important in service businesses, in which so many staff have direct contact with customers on the premises. It is possible to arrange the stages in marketing planning, so that managers and as many staff as possible in all departments (or jobs), are involved in initiating and commenting on draft objectives and plans. It is common sense that those who have to carry out plans should identify with their success, and not see them as impositions laid down by senior managers who may not have recent practical experience of what can be achieved within the constraints which apply. Where target setting and evaluation are linked with some form of performance incentives, the motivation of staff may be easier to secure.

Many managers will be aware of the damaging effect on staff morale of working within an organization where the objectives appear to change according to management whim, or where directives are issued by planning departments with no opportunity to debate their practicality in operation. While marketing planning is conducted primarily to achieve more efficient business decisions, its secondary effect in providing a means of participation and communication can be vital in creating and sustaining a high level of organizational morale.

Marketing planning for strategy and tactics compared

Earlier in the chapter it was noted that the process of marketing planning is the same in principle for both strategy and tactics. Strategic planning usually focuses mainly on diagnosis, prognosis and the SWOT analysis, and is likely to look backwards over the trends of several years as well as forward to the extent that projections are sensible. Strategic planning is much broader in its approach than tactical planning, and strategic objectives are normally not expressed in precise, quantifiable terms. Strategic objectives typically state where an organization wishes to be with regard to its markets, expressed as goals which can be turned subsequently into short-term operational plans. Examples of strategic objectives for the Wales Tourist Board in 1987 illustrate the point:

- To shift existing [customer] perceptions of Wales towards that of a year-round destination . . .
- To place greater emphasis in promotional terms on higher quality products
- To extend and develop joint marketing activity with commercial operators and others willing to demonstrate new initiatives to promote their products, areas, festivals and events
- To assist the development and marketing of packages as inclusive offers, especially those for sale through travel agents, and those developed by marketing co-operatives

Strategic objectives may be expressed in terms of projected growth and profit, or organizational structure, or in relation to competitors. Strategies may be expressed in terms of the four Ps of the marketing mix, or any other aspect influenced by marketing managers and ultimately measurable in customer attitudes and purchase behaviour.

Marketing strategies usually require considerable organizational commitment and effort. 'Strong, offensive strategies do not come easily. They are usually the result of prolonged and painstaking analysis of the market, competitors and the trend of change' (Davidson: 1975: p. 115).

Operational marketing planning is a 'practical exercise in deciding what a business is to achieve through marketing activity in the year ahead. It is a logical thought process and an application of common sense. It provides a basis of objectives around which marketing tasks are set, budgets drawn up and results measured' (Middleton: 1980: p. 26). Operational plans express in precise, quantifiable terms, what an organization is seeking to achieve in relation to its portfolio of products and segments over a particular time period.

Chapter summary

In the late 1980s, most medium to large organizations in travel and tourism undertake some form of marketing planning; most smaller ones still rely on 'feel for the market' to guide their decisions on objectives and the routes by which they intend to get there. In this author's experience, only very large organizations have established systematic planning processes comparable to those in manufacturing industries. For most organizations there is great scope for significant improvement in the time, effort, and expertise which is employed to undertake what is arguably the most important single aspect of conducting any business.

Understood as the systematic process whereby objectives, strategies and plans are devised and adapted to changing circumstances, marketing planning – for strategy and tactics – is essential for effective marketing action. Planning does not replace flair and judgement, but provides a fertile base of information and broad strategic direction within which imagination, flair and vision can be harnessed to produce their best results.

Organizations vary as to the headings and labels used in their marketing plans; they may not be same as those used in this chapter. Readers should note that it is not the words that matter, but the logical thought processes which they describe.

In all cases, the current marketing plan represents the sum of the knowledge and judgement which an organization has built up over time about its products, markets, and competitive strengths and weaknesses.

Further reading

Kotler, P., *Marketing Management: Analysis, Planning and Control*, Prentice-Hall, 1984, Chapter 9.

14

Planning marketing campaigns: Budgeting and monitoring results

This chapter draws the other chapters of Part Three together in a practical focus on the meaning and nature of marketing campaigns. The broad, unifying concepts of campaigns is explained here, and developed subsequently throughout Part Four of this book. Campaign is not a term widely used in marketing texts, except in the specific contexts of advertising or public relations. For travel and tourism products, in which production operations, service delivery, and marketing are so closely interlinked, the campaign concept is considered to be especially valuable for the practical insights it provides into marketing tactics and operations, and it is strongly recommended to readers.

The word campaign, with its connotations of military action, is well suited to the activities of marketing managers aggressively promoting their organizations' interests against the competition. Marketing managers, or product managers responsible for undertaking campaigns, have been aptly described as the 'storm-troopers of marketing' (Davidson: 1975: p. 95).

The chapter begins with definitions, which are relevant to the whole of Part Four. It identifies the techniques marketing managers deploy in their campaigns to influence consumer demand. It proceeds with an outline of basic methods used for budgeting in marketing, and

explains them by working through typical campaign budgets. The final part of the chapter examines practical ways to monitor and control the budget.

Marketing campaigns are action programmes

'Campaign' describes any co-ordinated programme of marketing activities in the general field of promotion and distribution designed to influence and mould customers' behaviour. In marketing practice and in texts, the term is often used in a restricted sense of advertising, or sales promotion, or public relations. In fact the term is not used at all by Kotler (1984), and Baker (1979) refers to it only in the context of advertising. Stanton defines a campaign as 'a co-ordinated series of promotional efforts built around a single theme or idea and designed to reach a predetermined goal ... we should apply the campaign concept to the entire promotional programme' (Stanton: 1981: p. 391).

Without challenging Stanton's definition it makes sense to broaden it further and to tie it specifically into the implementation phase of the marketing planning process. Thus:

A marketing campaign is a planned, integrated action programme designed to achieve specific marketing objectives and targets through the development of a budget, on the promotion and distribution of products, over a specified time period . . .

Campaigns may be aimed at consumers directly, or indirectly through a distribution network, or both. The focus of a marketing campaign is operational and short run and several campaigns would normally be involved in achieving particular strategic objectives.

The 'menu' for marketing campaigns in travel and tourism

The full range of marketing techniques to be woven into campaigns is set out in Figure 14.1 as a 'menu'. Each of them has its own implications for action. The implications are mainly promotional, but price is included in its discounted sense; product augmentation is included where it overlaps with sales promotion; and distribution is both a target for campaigns and part of the promotional process. The menu represents choices, from which marketing managers will choose according to their particular targets and market circumstances.

Campaigns in travel and tourism have two dimensions:

(a) promotional techniques designed to motivate and move prospective customers towards a point of sale and also to provide incentives to purchase (includes promotion to distributors),

(b) facilitation techniques designed to make it as easy as possible for motivated people to achieve their intended purchase, especially at the point of sale.

Marketing texts, even when dealing with service products, generally exclude elements of customer facilitation from discussions of campaigns and focus only on aspects of promotion, especially advertising. But in the context of travel and tourism products this exclusion is not help-ful. Where products are frequently purchased ahead of consumption, as is the case for example in accommodation, transportation, tour operation or car rental, it makes sense to build and cost facilitation into the total campaign budget. Where distribution channels are highly diverse, as again is the case for much of travel and tourism, creation of consumer access for products is much closer to what is conventionally discussed as promotion than it is to what is conventionally described as distribution.

In other words campaigns include all four variables of the marketing mix (4 Ps), where their use is designed in the short term to manipulate buyer behaviour to achieve targeted campaign objectives.

The marketing campaign menu is shown in summary form in Figure 14.1. This summary is not intended to be a sufficient description of each technique but an indication of what it is within a spectrum of choice. The main techniques are discussed in some detail in Part IV of the book.

Marketing campaign budgets

The marketing budget may be defined as the sum of the costs of the campaign action programme judged necessary to achieve the specified objectives and targets set out in the marketing plan.

In practice, the most difficult decisions in a marketing manager's calendar lie in estimating and agreeing the budget. The budget, usually drawn up on an annual or campaign basis for each major product in an organization's portfolio, represents money which has to be spent 'up front', or ahead of the targeted volume and sales revenue it is expected to generate. Every £1,000 spent on campaign action programmes typically has to be paid for out of reserves, current cash flows, or by borrowing, and it is money which can only be recovered at some future point from the projected surplus of income over operating expenditure, which is operating profit. On the

Activity	Notes
Paid for media advertising	Includes TV, press, radio and outdoor. Also includes tourist board and other travel related guides, books and brochures which accept advertising.
Direct mail/door to door distribution	Including general sales literature or print items specifically designed for the purpose.
Public relations (PR)	All media exposure achieved as editorial matter, not paid for as advertising space. Also influence over target groups.
Sponsorship	An alternative form of media for specific target groups
Exhibitions/shows/ workshops	Important alternative forms of distribution and display for reaching retail, wholesale and consumer target groups.
Personal selling	Via meetings, telephone contact, workshops. Primarily aimed at distributors and intermediaries purchasing for groups of consumers.
Sales literature	Especially promotional brochures and other print used in a servicing role.
Sales promotion	Short-term incentives offered as inducements to purchase including temporary product augmentation. Covers sales force and distribution network as well as consumers.
Price discounting	A common form of sales promotion; includes extra commissions and bonuses for retailers.
Point of sale displays (merchandising)	Posters, window dressing, displays of brochures and other materials both of a regular and temporary incentive kind.
Familiarization and educational trips	Ways to motivate and facilitate distributor networks through product sampling.
Distribution networks and commission	Organized ways in which prospective customers achieve access to products, includes central reservation systems and computerized links between principals and distributors

Figure 14.1 *The principal marketing campaign techniques used in travel and tourism*

other hand, as marketing managers are expected to demonstrate, if the money is *not* spent, revenue targets will not be achieved. Perhaps the hardest decision to justify is that of borrowing thousands or millions of pounds to spend on promotional campaigns, not to secure a projected operating surplus, but to reduce the probable size of an expected loss. Such decisions have had to be taken by most airlines and many hotels over short-run crisis periods since the 1970s in various parts of the world.

In practice, setting campaign budgets involves finding answers to three fundamental questions:

Three fundamental budget questions

1 How much money must be spent *in total* on the marketing campaign, in order to achieve objectives?
2 How will the total be *split between the products and segments* included in the campaign?
3 How will the total be *divided between the component parts of the action programme*.

Budgeting methods

Kotler (1984: p. 621) notes four common

methods of setting both the total budget or any element within it:

- affordable method
- percentage of sales revenue method
- competitive parity method (matching competitors' spending)
- objective and task method

The first three of these methods are in fact quite closely related and rely primarily on historic information (previous budgeting levels), and marketing intelligence about competitors' actions. In essence, they are all 'rule of thumb' methods, which commence with some fairly broad notion of an appropriate marketing expenditure considered affordable, expressed as a proportion of sales revenue or turnover, such as 5 per cent. This aggregate percentage often becomes a norm which sets an expenditure ceiling not to be exceeded unless forced to do so to match or defeat the competition, or to respond to other unforseen events. Although they are widely used in practice, these are aggregate or top-downwards methods, and shed little or no light on *how* total expenditure should be allocated between product-market groupings or *divided* between campaign elements, two of the three basic questions posed earlier.

The objective and task method is quite different. It commences from a specification of what is to be achieved (objective) and proceeds by stating and costing the techniques (tasks) required to achieve it. This method, which is closely related to so-called zero-budgeting methods, is obviously the one most closely associated with the systematic marketing planning approaches discussed earlier in this book. Given precise objectives for each product-market grouping, the objective and task method can be used to construct a budget from the bottom upwards through specification of tasks, so that all three budget questions posed earlier, are answered. Objective and task methods are, however, time consuming and dependent on marketing judge-

ment. The tidy logic of the textbook is not often easily implemented in practice, especially for organizations with multiple objectives and several product-market groupings.

The next section explains and illustrates how these methods work in practice.

Affordable and percentage of sales revenue methods

An illustration of a notional British tour operator's budget is shown in Figure 14.2 to indicate how budgeting methods often operate in practice. The example assumes sales are achieved at targeted load factors (typically over 90 per cent) and the items, representing a typical trading, profit and loss account, have simplified headings for the sake of presentation. The budget is based on hypothetical figures but it broadly represents British tour operator cost structures of the early 1980s. See also the explanatory notes which accompany Figure 14.2.

While the percentages noted in the budget would fluctuate from year to year, the broad orders of magnitude hold good over time and the following points can be made:

1 Of the total sales revenue, some 72 per cent is absorbed in product component costs and a further 6 per cent in fixed costs of operation. Of the remainder, the brochure commitment is inescapable, and so also is the retail agency commission on the given volume of sales. In other words a total of nearly 90 per cent of sales revenue is, to all intents and purposes, committed in advance of any revenue received.

2 In Figure 14.2, advertising, sales promotion and other discretionary campaign costs to be decided by the marketing manager, represent just 1 per cent of total turnover. Since it is most unlikely that in practice such costs would be either halved or doubled in any one year, the real level of

Budget summary	Year (000's)	%
Total turnover @ £179 (arsp)[1] on 750,000 sales	£134,250	100%
Less cost of tour components,[2] say	−96,375	100%
= gross trading surplus	37,875	28%
Less targeted operating profit before tax @ say 9% of turnover	−12,000	9%
= maximum sum to cover all administration and marketing costs	£25,875	19%
Committed costs of operation (fixed)		
Reservation system and overheads[3]	3,000	
Non marketing administration costs[4]	2,025	
Marketing staff and overheads[5]	2,500	
	7,525	6%
Marketing campaign costs (fixed and variable)		
Advertising	500	0.4
Sales promotion	650	0.5
Brochure and distribution	3,000	2.2 } 12.1%
Other[6]	150	0.1
Sales commission to retail agencies (@ 10%)[7]	12,000	9.0
	16,300	
Contingency reserve[8]	2,050	
	£25,875	

Notes

1 arsp = average retail sales price, per tour sold,
2 accommodation, transport, transfers, resort staff,
3 includes computer systems, staff and all communication costs and depreciation,
4 office expenses, rates, staff equipment etc., including general administration,
5 includes any sales force costs, on-going market research costs, product development and all marketing department costs,
6 workshops, PR, familiarization visits etc.,
7 assumes 90 per cent of all sales commissionable, others booked direct,
8 held in reserve especially for tactical discounts to promote unsold capacity,

Figure 14.2 *Marketing budget calculations for a British tour operator*
Adapted from Middleton, V. T. C., 'The Marketing Implications of Direct Selling' in *International Tourism Quarterly*, 1980.

budget discretion is probably under 0.5 per cent of sales turnover.

3 In this example, the contingency reserve for tactical discounts at £2,050,000 is already almost as large as the itemized discretionary expenditure, although it represents only £1.50 per tour package. In practice, if bookings fell seriously below targeted levels, the contingency reserve would be increased by a factor of three or four but the money could only come from the £12 million targeted operating surplus. In the early 1980s, no large UK tour operator averaged anything near 9 per cent surplus on trading operations because of the need to spend contingency money on marketing, especially tactical price discounting.

4 There is no common agreement as to what items should be included or excluded from a marketing budget. There is a strong case for including retail commission since it is money paid out to ensure effective distribution of products, the fourth 'P' of the marketing mix.

From Figure 14.2, it should be clear that the so-called affordable, and percentage of turnover methods of budgeting are relevant and practical. Apart from establishing upper limits to expenditure, however, such methods do not provide any guidance whatever as to how best to apportion the affordable sums. For that, it is necessary to use the objective and task method discussed next.

The objective and task method

To illustrate this method, consider the hypothetical but realistic case of an hotel consortium comprising 100 individually owned hotels with a combined capacity of 6,000 rooms. Assume that, through careful diagnosis and prognosis, the consortium has set itself a marketing objective to sell one third of its aggregate capacity (2,000) rooms as weekend packages over 20 selected weekends between October and April. For ease

of calculation, assume that each package lasts for 2 nights and involves 2 people. The average price, published in the consortium's brochure, is £45 per person/package, which includes breakfast and dinner for the 2 nights.

The sales revenue target is, therefore:

2,000 (rooms) × 20 (weekends) × 2 persons
× £45 = gross sales revenue = £3,600,000
Plus additional spending in hotels
on meals, in bars, telephone etc.
@ say £5 per person per day =
2,000 × 20 × 2 × 2 (days) × £5 =

$$800,000$$

$$£4,400,000$$

Because the fixed costs of hotel operation are already committed, the hotel consortium stands to achieve a gross contribution (surplus of additional revenue over variable costs) of at least 70 per cent on this business, say £3 million.

The question to resolve is how much should the consortium spend on marketing in order to achieve the £3 million additional revenue? By applying conventional ratio methods, it is easy to calculate that:

5% of total sales revenue including additional spending is £220,000
10% of total sales revenue including additional spending is £440,000
20% of total sales revenue including additional spending is £880,000

Even beyond the 20 per cent level of expenditure on marketing, the consortium would be significantly better off than before – assuming that without marketing effort, the potential £3 million gross contribution would not be achieved.

With clear objectives set, which in practice would be split by area of the country and the projected profile of target buyers, the next step is to itemize and cost the tasks involved in an effective marketing campaign.

Task based campaign budget

The following costs are typical of what would be spent in practice (1986 prices) by the consortium to meet the objectives noted in the preceding section:

	£s
Cost of producing brochures (production run of 250,000), say	62,000
Direct mail (say 100,000 items identified by coupon response and via hotels' own lists)	25,000
Advertising, general consumer media and trade press	220,000
Advertising in tourist board guides	10,000
Point of sale material (retail agents and for hotels)	25,000
PR campaign	10,000
Retail travel agency commission (assuming 50 per cent of bookings via this route)	180,000
Other (includes distribution costs to retail agents)	50,000
	£582,000

The following points can be made:

1 Selecting the itemized tasks and estimating the expenditure required is based on a mixture of *fact* (postal costs, brochure costs, retail commission); *experience* (knowledge of which activities are most relevant for selling weekend packages and the costs and quantities of any previous campaigns); and *judgement* (especially in relation to media expenditure but drawing on advertising agency knowledge and expertise).

2 There can be no absolute certainty that £582,000 will produce 40,000 bookings for the consortium. There is, however, a systematic method and framework for making decisions, within which it is possible to focus facts, experience, and judge-ment. Given adequate evaluation of the campaign's results, the systematic framework would also serve as a learning mechanism to refine the decision process for any subsequent campaigns.

3 £582,000 happens to be 16 per cent of the product package price, 13 per cent of the total sales revenue and 19 per cent of the gross contribution. The advertising, (paid space in the media) is 5 per cent of the total sales revenue. In the end these ratios have little meaning except to establish that the pay-off is worth the investment. The cost of the campaign can be seen as the price for achieving the targeted business and at that point the ratios are only of interest for control and evaluation purposes – they were not used to determine the size of the marketing budget.

4 The functional relationship between marketing expenditure and targeted revenue should be clear.

Controlling the market expenditure

Accountants, both at financial year end and on a regular interim basis, generally exercise overall control of expenditure and revenue, and formally assess the profitability of business organizations. Marketing managers are usually directly responsible only for controlling expenditure out of agreed campaign budgets although the close relationship between campaign budgets and company profit and loss accounts has been emphasized. Marketing managers are also responsible for monitoring an organization's performance in its chosen markets.

Kotler (1984: p. 743) devotes an important chapter to the control function and distinguishes four types of marketing control:

- annual (campaign) plan control – tracking variance of actual results against targets
- profitability control – portfolio expenditure and revenue analysis

- efficiency control – analysis of campaign elements
- strategic control – overall audits of strategy

This chapter focuses on the first type and refers to the second. The third type is discussed in subsequent chapters which deal separately with the main elements of campaigns. Strategic controls are referred to in the travel and tourism examples discussed in Part Five of the book.

Campaign plan control – sales variance

The more that operational marketing objectives are made precise, in terms of volume targets, time periods, and specific products and segments (discussed in Chapter 13), the easier it is to measure results. Airlines, for example, forecast their passenger volume over a long-run period, by product type (e.g. first class, business class, or types of economy fare offered), and by route, with projections on at least a weekly basis. With modern computer facilities they are able to read sales results within hours of flight performance.

In Figure 14.3, projected sales represent weekly planning targets, based partly on previous years' operations and partly on diagnosis/ prognosis. Airline capacity and operations are scheduled on such projections and marketing campaigns are carried out ahead of sales. In weeks 4–6 actual sales dropped. It is at this point that marketing managers must establish the cause of the drop and consider action to generate more sales, employing contingency reserves if necessary. This type of control is known as variance analysis and, in forms suitable to the products involved, it is the cornerstone of most marketing control. A tourist attraction would target weekly sales by segments such as school groups, holiday visitors, day visitors, coach parties, and plot actual sales against those targets. The management would separately plot actual shop and catering sales against their targets, to measure variance.

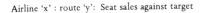

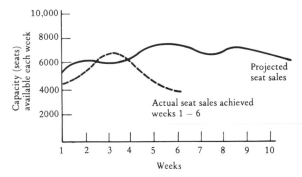

Figure 14.3 *Variance of sales against targets for an airline*

Sometimes, sales move far enough ahead of target to make it possible to reduce marketing budgets. British tour operators in early 1986, for example, drastically reduced consumer advertising expenditure partly because their pricing tactics generated massive unpaid publicity and produced booking levels well ahead of targets.

Market share variance

In consumer goods marketing, market share analysis and variance over time is a second basic aspect of marketing control. In travel and tourism, however, apart from transport operations which are legally required to register capacity and carryings, share data is generally either not known at all, or estimated months afterwards, too late to trigger a variance response. Own sales analysis, without knowledge other than general marketing intelligence of competitors' sales, can of course provide misleading information.

In using variance controls, as Kotler puts it, 'market-share analysis, like sales analysis, increases in value when the data is disaggregated along various dimensions. The company might watch the progress of its market share by product line, customer type, region, or other breakdowns' (1984: p. 748).

Customer satisfaction variance

The third principal element in variance analysis can be achieved by regularly monitoring satisfaction, both overall and by product components. As described in Chapter 11, providers of travel and tourism service products are particularly well placed to exploit opportunities to measure customer satisfaction on a regular basis and to read any departures from average scores. The figure below illustrates the point in the context of a tour operator monitoring the performance of one of the resort hotels included in its programme.

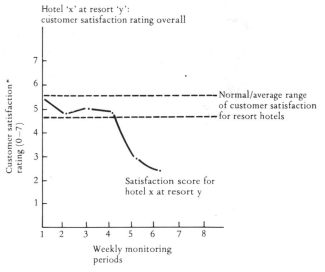

Figure 14.4 *Variance of satisfaction against targets for a tour operator*

In this illustration, based on data collected and analyzed over many months, normal customer satisfaction ratings of the product overall, typically vary between 4.8 and 5.5. In that band, hotels are generating acceptable satisfaction in the judgement of customers using them. In weeks 1 to 4 satisfaction is normal. In week 5 it

*The average rating obtained from all customers at hotel x replying to the question 'On a scale from 0 (very dissatisfied) to 7 (highly satisfied), phase indicate how well the hotel met your expectations overall'

plunges and stays down. Why? Analysis of other scores may reveal a particular problem of food or service, and management action can be taken to rectify the problem and return scores to the average band. To be useful, such variance must be known within days of its occurrence. Modern computer technology is of increasing value in making such rapid response possible. In this case marketing research methods to monitor satisfaction are also operational control mechanisms.

Ratio variance

Once the budget is agreed it is possible to calculate a series of financial comparisons between marketing expenditure and revenue targets, which can subsequently be reviewed against actual revenue achieved. Provided that an organization divides its total portfolio of product/markets into logical groupings or profit centres for management purposes, it is possible to establish the costs and revenues attributable to each grouping (see also Chapter 10) and then calculate for each:

- ratio of total marketing expenditure: total sales revenue
- ratio of total marketing expenditure: gross contribution
- ratio of total marketing expenditure: net profit
- ratio of total marketing expenditure: unit cost of production

By comparing current and historic ratios, and ratios between product/market groupings in the portfolio, valuable control data can be achieved. Total marketing expenditure can also be divided into its component parts to establish separate ratios for advertising, sales force, etc.

As with other variance controls, the purpose is to alert managers to any deviations from normal expectations which may require marketing action both within the campaign period and in the longer run.

Chapter summary

This chapter defines marketing campaigns as 'integrated action programmes designed to achieve specific marketing objectives . . . through the deployment of a budget . . . over a specified time period.' Within the deliberately broad definition adopted in this chapter, campaigns can be seen as the final stage in the hierarchy of business goals, strategies and plans, introduced in Chapter 12 (see Figure 12.1).

Action programmes have to be costed, and this involves marketing managers in finding answers to three vital questions concerning the budget needed to achieve marketing objectives. These are, how much to spend in total, how the total should be split between the products and segments in an organization's total product portfolio, and how it should be allocated among the wide range of promotional and other marketing mix techniques presented as a menu in Figure 14.1.

The chapter works through two different tourism related marketing budgets to explain the process and methods of budget setting, and especially to explain the important objective and task methods. This is the budgeting method which most closely meets the needs of modern marketing-led organizations. It is relevant in its principles to all sectors of the travel and tourism industry, both commercial and non-commercial. The method facilitates evaluation and control of the results of marketing activities, which are discussed at the end of the chapter.

Finally, this chapter serves as a bridge between Part Three, which explains the meaning and processes of planning, and the role of marketing managers who are responsible for it, and Part Four which reviews each of the main promotional techniques, and the way they are implemented effectively in practice. The marketing campaign is the co-ordinating framework, for all the marketing mix techniques included in action programmes.

Further reading

Kotler, P., *Marketing Analysis: Planning and Control*, Prentice-Hall, 1984, Chapter 24.

Part Four

Using the Principal Marketing Tools in Travel and Tourism

15
Advertising and public relations

In the various forms discussed in this chapter, advertising and public relations (PR) are two of the most important promotional tools, or *marketing functions*, used in the execution of marketing campaigns. As key elements of marketing communications, advertising and PR are considered together because they are primarily concerned to influence people away from the places of production, consumption and purchase of products. This influence is achieved through the use of press, television, and other mass media discussed in this chapter, making advertising and PR the most pervasive and visible elements of what the consumer sees of marketing efforts. But in common with Baker (1979: p. 254), it is sensible to interpret marketing communications broadly, to include the other promotional activities of personal selling and sales promotion, as well as advertising and PR. In travel and tourism, the special role of sales literature, which is partly advertising, partly sales promotion and partly distribution, (see Chapter 17), must also be included in marketing communications.

As a percentage of sales revenue spent on marketing, advertising and PR are less significant in travel and tourism than for many other consumer products. Even so, advertising is often the most costly element in campaign budgets, and has added importance where it is used in a supportive role to complement the other campaign elements, such as promotional print, tactical price cuts, and sales promotion. Advertising, and to a lesser extent PR also, are often required to make prospective customers aware of the existence of the other campaign elements.

The chapter begins by setting advertising and PR in the context of marketing communications. The barriers involved in the communication process are explained, using a tourism example, which also serves to introduce the main technical terms used in advertising practice. Advertising and PR definitions are discussed, and the objectives of PR and advertising are compared, followed by discussion of the creative role, media selection and costs, measuring results, and the use of advertising agencies. The different forms and usage of PR are outlined, and the chapter ends with a note on the reasons why advertising expenditure, as a proportion of sales revenue, is relatively low in the travel and tourism industry.

The scale of advertising and PR

The British Advertising Association estimates that over £3,000 million was spend in 1984 on display advertising, (as distinct from other spending on small, line entries in the press, known as classified advertising). This sum is equivalent to about 1.5 per cent of all British consumers' expenditure nationally. Expressed as a proportion of annual sales revenue, consumer advertising expenditure varies widely according to different types of product, from under 1 per cent to over 30 per cent. Approximately 5 per cent of all British advertising expenditure is accounted for by holidays, travel and transport, but very few advertisers in the tourist industry spend more than 3 per cent of their sales revenue on this form of communication.

PR expenditure in the UK is harder to define and measure than advertising. In terms of the overall turnover of PR agencies it is probably equivalent to well under 5 per cent of the total spent nationally on display advertising. Its total impact on consumers, however, is very much greater than this 5 per cent figure suggests and, for some sectors of travel and tourism, PR activity is at least as important as advertising. This point is developed later in the chapter.

The purpose of advertising and PR

Both advertising and public relations activity are part of the marketing communication process between producers and prospective consumers, the ultimate purpose of which is to influence buyer behaviour and manipulate demand. They are both highly technical subjects but their essential functions are easy to understand. Their principal purpose is to enable producers to *reach* people in their homes or other places away from where products are sold, and *communicate* to them *messages* intended to influence their purchasing behaviour.

The messages may range from subtly attractive visual images and symbols designed to appeal and stimulate travel desires and needs, to simple sales announcements drawing attention to specific product offers.

With over a century of continuous development, every aspect of creating and designing 'messages', and choosing how and where to show them, has been studied and analysed in depth. But the exact ways in which both advertising and PR work on buyers' minds, and influence their purchasing behaviour, are still not fully understood. In part, this is because most people are continuously exposed to so many advertising messages in their lives, that the actual effect of any single one of them is almost impossible to evaluate beyond the level of simple memory or 'recall'.

The communication process and its barriers

Provided an advertiser knows which market he seeks to influence, the 'reach' part of the process is relatively simple. It requires money to buy spaces in the press, TV, posters, and so on, and there is a great deal of expertise in the buying process, but reach is not the principal concern for advertisers. The main problem is to design and express chosen messages in a form that is most likely to communicate with a targeted audience. If there is no 'reach', there can be no communication. But even with maximum reach and wide exposure of an advertisement, no communication can occur unless the message is actually received, is understood, and is of interest to the receiver. Even then he may not take action in response to the message.

For reasons introduced in Chapter 5, all of us have barriers and filters in our minds, which influence the ways in which we perceive and understand the world around us generally, including messages beamed at us by advertisers. These filters are the product of our personalities, experience of, and attitudes to life; in many ways all of us are conditioned to see what we want to see. It is easy to demonstrate with group discussions conducted for marketing research purposes that, in any group of people, there will be several different perceptions of the same advertising message.

In other words, a vital skill in advertising communications lies in understanding at least the main filters at work in the minds of targeted buyers, and designing messages, symbols and images, which are most likely to be well received by them.

The 'reach and communicate' process is represented in the diagram shown in Figure 15.1. To understand the process, consider the example of an hotel group with around 10 per cent share of a residential sales conference market. The group uses its own sales team to motivate key

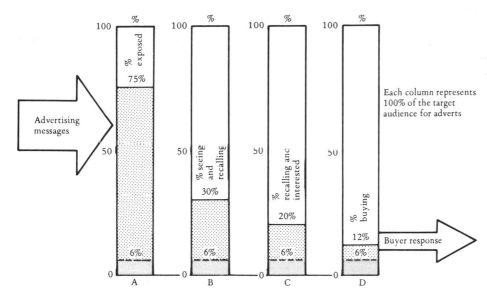

Figure 15.1 *Filters in the communication process*

conference buyers in client companies, but seeks also to communicate its advantages to the wide target audience of business people who have attended a residential conference at least once in the last three years. The hotel group has decided to use press advertising to reach its target audience. Figure 15.1 indicates how the original message works through several stages to the purchase decision. The explanation of the stages introduces some of the main terms used in advertising in a realistic context. These terms are further explained in the next section.

Figure 15.1 shows in percentage terms how the potential impact of advertising is reduced in practice. Column A represents 100 per cent of the target segment of people who attend sales conferences; their profiles as consumers would be identified in detail and quantified in the hotel group's marketing planning. With a realistic budget, the hotel group might hope to reach and expose its message to about 75 per cent of the total target group. This means buying space in magazines and press, which three-quarters of the

target are likely to buy and look at during the advertising campaign period.

Inevitably, not all who read the papers selected for the adverts read all pages, and many who glance at advertising pass on very quickly to other pages, and rapidly forget what they saw. Column B indicates that, in this case, 30 per cent of the target audience saw the hotel group's advertising, and would be able to remember at least seeing it, if they were asked to do so (a commonly used method of advertising evaluation). In practice, the proportion which B is of A, reflects partly the size of the adverts and the number of times they are shown, (frequency of insertion) and partly how memorable the adverts are to the target audience.

Column C represents the proportion of the target audience who not only remember something about the advertising they saw, but are sufficiently interested to consider the hotel group's product at some time.

Column D represents those who actually

participate in a sales conference at one of the group's hotels, in the twelve months during which the campaign runs. The dotted line drawn through all the columns represents the 6 per cent of existing regular or repeat buyers, who would have bought the product anyway, and are not converted by the advertising, although their interest may be reinforced by it.

In this example, therefore, an additional 6 per cent of target customers use the product as first-time buyers during the period of the marketing campaign. Of course, in that time, some previous buyers will have switched to competitors' products over the same period, so that advertising serves to maintain as well as increase shares of markets.

Simple though Figure 15.1 is, it makes it possible to appreciate that great expertise is required at each stage of the communication process, in order:

1 to purchase the spaces best calculated to reach the target (per cent of A),
2 to arrest and capture attention with appealing messages (per cent of B),
3 to keep attention through interesting information (also a per cent of B),
4 to communicate the key points that matter to buyers (per cent of C),
5 to turn interest into purchase (per cent of D).

At every stage there are losses in the communication process. Over time, consumers forget and have their attention drawn elsewhere by competitive offers, so that advertising messages suffer 'wear out', and have to be repeated at frequent intervals.

Modified to suit the circumstances of the other forms of marketing communication, the filters noted in this section are still applicable. Promotional print and direct selling, for example, are clearly subject to the same barriers of interest and recall.

Defining advertising and PR

Within the context of marketing communications, advertising is defined by the American Marketing Association as, 'any paid form of non-personal presentation and promotion of ideas, goods or services [to a targeted audience] by an identified sponsor'. The words in brackets are inserted by the author to stress that initial segmentation and targeting always precedes effective advertising. 'Non-personal', implies the use of media to reach a mass audience, as distinguished from face-to-face personal selling. An 'identified sponsor', means that the advertiser's name, or that of its product, is clearly evident in the communication.

For the price of chosen media space, the advertiser has full control over the message, its size, its appearance, its content, where and when it appears, and how frequently. 'Full control' is subject in most countries to legally imposed standards designed to protect the consumer from deception and fraud. 'Like any other aspect of business life, advertising is controlled, constrained and, where appropriate, punished by law' (White: 1980; p. 174). It is also subject to voluntary codes of practice, succinctly summarized in the British Code of Advertising Practice, in the requirement that all adverts 'should be legal, decent, honest and truthful'.

Most travel and tourism advertising is aimed either at consumers or the travel trade but large organizations, such as airlines and hotel groups, also buy media space to communicate with other target groups, such as shareholders, or politicians. Much of advertising specifically product related and part of marketing campaigns, but it can also be used more broadly to advertise the name and image of an organization as a whole.

Public relations activity typically has communication functions in the wider context of corporate goals, as well as in marketing, and its budget is normally allocated out of corporate rather than marketing funds. It is defined by the British Institute of Public Relations as, 'the

Message	What advertising aims to communicate, both visual and copy elements, including images and symbols.
Media	Newspapers, TV, radio and all other mass circulation means of communicating either paid or unpaid messages to prospective consumers. Advertising media are those which sell space to advertisers as a commercial transaction.
Editorial matter	The content of the media, other than advertising, which is controlled by editorial policies.
Scheduling	Choice of media to be used, and the timing and frequency of insertions of adverts.
Appropriation	Conventional name for the advertising budget, also known as 'above the line'.
Proposition	The single minded, clear message of an advert, usually focused on the reason to purchase a product.
USP	Unique Selling Proposition – a particular product or company characteristic that distinguishes it from competitors, and is a main reason to buy.
Creative execution	The choice of appealing concepts, themes, ideas, pictures, situations or words, chosen to communicate the decided objectives.
Copy	The words included in an advertisement, normally having three components: a 'headline' to attract attention; 'body copy' to convey information; 'strap line' to conclude or sign off.
Insertion	One appearance of an advertisement.
OTS	Opportunities (by the target group) to see any particular advert. OTS is a function of coverage and the frequency of insertions, and quantified for media buying purposes.
Coverage	The proportion of an identified audience which is reached. Coverage is related to frequency of insertions.
CPT	Cost per thousand of the target group to whom any advert is exposed. CPT is a basic cost figure used in buying media.
Threshold	The minimum level of expenditure necessary to achieve measurable impact with an advert.
Direct response	Advertising from which the intended customer response is a direct contact with the producer, by phone, letter, or coupon, without involving a distribution channel such as a travel agent.
Fees and commission	Advertising agencies earn their income through commission paid on media purchases, and/or fees usually charged for smaller accounts and below the line work.

Figure 15.2 *Advertising and PR terms in common use*

deliberate, planned and sustained effort to establish and maintain mutual understanding between an organization and the public'. PR may be personal or non-personal but it does not involve the purchase of media space and, therefore, the level of control over what appears in the media is limited. 'Public' has to be interpreted as comprising all the target groups an organization wishes to influence, from government ministers, to local politicians, and residents of an area in which a business is located. Although planned in its direction (like advertising), PR is more opportunist in its execution, exploiting events as they occur, and maintaining good links and goodwill with the media, which can be drawn on as circumstances require.

Both advertising and PR communications are designed to operate away from the places, in which the production, consumption, and purchase of service products takes place.

Terms commonly used in advertising practice

Advertising and PR are technical subjects, which have generated their own jargon terms. Sixteen commonly used terms are presented in annotated form in Figure 15.2. They are intended to serve as an aide memoire.

Above and below the line

Students of marketing always seem to have difficulty with the historic, unhelpful, but frequently used distinction between 'above and below the line'. For reasons which have no foundation in logic or relevance to current circumstances, commissionable expenditure on media advertising has traditionally been known as, 'above the line'. Expenditure on all other forms of communication and promotion are, therefore, 'below the line'. The distinction can be ignored for all practical purposes, especially in marketing travel and tourism products.

The role and objectives of advertising and PR

For the purposes of marketing campaigns, the role and objectives of both advertising and PR are summarized in tabular form in Figure 15.3. Both PR, and to a lesser extent advertising, also serve corporate purposes in influencing selected groups of people whose opinions and attitudes are relevant to an organization. As discussed in Chapter 12, marketing objectives invariably have a strategic dimension, to which the operational objectives of any campaign must be related. Both advertising and PR are used to achieve strategic objectives, especially product and corporate positioning. The role and objectives noted in Figure 15.3 therefore operate at both levels.

Most of the objectives in Figure 15.3 are self explanatory in terms of previous chapters in this book. 'Connections' refers to making links between a product and a target group, typically by creating visual or copy situations, and images with which customers can easily identify. 'Response' may be to fill in a coupon, use the telephone, or simply to feel motivated to make a visit (as for tourist attractions).

Stages in the advertising process

Decisions on advertising objectives are geared to marketing objectives and strategies, as defined in the marketing planning process. There are six basic stages in advertising, which are common ground, well covered in most marketing texts (see recommended companion chapters). Accordingly, this section is intended to be a summary of the six basic steps identified by Rodger (1968: p. 198) as:

1   identifying the audience to be reached (profiles of segments),
2   determining and creating . . . specific advertising messages . . . (to meet stated advertising objectives),

	Advertising	**Public relations**
Principal role	Targeted sales-related messages, aimed at influencing prospective customers, away from the point of sale	Targeted messages, aimed at general awareness and interest, away from the point of sale
Principal objectives	Controlled messages and symbols designed to: <ul><li>create awareness/remind</li><li>project images or 'positions'</li><li>impart specific sales messages</li><li>produce connections</li><li>reassure</li><li>alter perceptions</li><li>stimulate desires</li><li>generate action/response</li></ul>	Guided messages and symbols designed to goodwill and favourable attitudes: <ul><li>as for ads, from an 'editorial angle'</li><li>limited extent</li><li>very limited</li><li>as for adverts</li><li>limited extent</li><li>as for adverts</li><li>limited</li><li>very limited</li></ul>

Figure 15.3 *The role and objectives of advertising and PR*

3   selecting the most effective . . . media to reach the audience,
4   scheduling the chosen media . . . timing, frequency and impact,
5   determining the advertising budget,
6   measuring advertising results.

Rodger stresses the need to be specific in advertising messages and in media selection, and to draw up budgets around precisely identified target audiences. This common ground fits well with the task approach to budgeting covered in the previous chapter. Four of the stages need some further amplification here, 2, 3, 4 and 6. Stage 1 is covered in Chapters 7 and 11, Stage 5 is covered in Chapter 14.

Creating specific advertising messages

When the objectives which advertising is to fulfil are decided in relation to an identified segment of buyers, the crucial step in the advertising process is the creative one of producing memorable pictures and words. Creative execution captures attention, expresses the essence of a product in a few words which say it all, and provides key information. Creative quality cannot be defined but it can be recognized and measured in terms of recall. It is the factor most likely to push the message through the filters of the communication process previously described.

In travel and tourism good examples of creative executions are:

- 'That will do nicely' (American Express)
- 'We try harder' (Avis)
- 'We speak your language' (British Tourist Authority in the USA market)
- 'I love New York' (New York State)

At a different, less memorable, but very creative way in the early 1980s, Holiday Inns Inc. ran a series of advertisements in the USA with the headline:

'Only one hotel chain guarantees your room will be right'.

Subsequently extended to Europe, the advertising copy said, 'Everything in your Holiday

Inn room will be right. Or we will make it right. Or we will refund the cost of your room for that night'. The clever aspect of this is the concept of a 'guarantee', with all it communicates about assured quality standards. In fact, none of HI's competitors would be likely to refuse to make a room right, so the real product difference was only slight. But Holiday Inns created the proposition, claimed it first, and made it effectively their own concept since no other chain could say 'we guarantee our rooms too', without appearing to copy the original, and indirectly complimenting HI.

Doyle Dane Bernbach, the international advertising agency, quote Bill Bernbach on creativity as follows:

'. . . people can't believe you if they don't know what you're saying, and they can't know what you're saying if they don't listen to you, and they won't listen to you if you're not interesting.

And you won't be interesting unless you say things freshly, originally, imaginatively.'

Selecting the most effective media

As Joyce put it, 'Advertising in general can only work by being seen and heard by consumers and operating on their minds' (1967: 170). Finding effective, memorable ways to operate on consumer's minds is the creative aspect. Arranging to be seen and heard (reach), is the job of media selection and buying space.

The choice of media types is wide. Fifteen types commonly used in travel and tourism are noted below. Within each type, for example national press, there are multiple choices such as nine national daily papers in Britain, eight Sunday papers and so on. As always, it is the marketing manager's job, in this case usually employing an advertising agency, to consider the options and make the selection calculated to produce the best return for the available budget.

Media types

TV – national or regional,
Radio – local,
National press (daily/Sunday newspapers and magazine supplements),
Regional and local press,
Consumer magazines (quarterly, monthly, weeklies),
Cinema advertising,
Trade press and magazines (e.g. *Travel News* and *Travel Trade Gazette*),
Outdoor – transport sites (underground, airport, rail stations)
   – poster sites in general locations,
Tourist board brochures and guides (selling space to operators),
Commercial consumer guides (for hotels, campsites),
Directories and Yellow Pages,
Exhibitions (display space on stands),
In house magazines (e.g. airlines or hotel magazines, selling space to other operators),
Direct mail (using purchased address lists),
Door-to-door distribution (an alternative to direct mail).

The professional practice of media selection, buying and scheduling, requires extensive skills, plus experience and judgement. Since the 1970s, the use of computers to aid the selection process has become widespread. The principles of the media selection process are not difficult to grasp, however, and marketing managers have to be familiar with them. The process is marketing research based reflecting the facts that:

1   all market segments to be reached through media advertising must be precisely identified, in terms of numbers of people, key socio-economic variables, and psychographic aspects (see Chapter 7).

2   all media owners are able to identify their reader/viewer or listener numbers and profile with considerable precision. Each of the media has a particular style and characteristics of its own.

Given precision in 1 and 2 above, media selection and scheduling is essentially a matching process for the profiles of target buyers and media, having regard to the size of the budget available, which limits some options. For example, many travel and tourism organizations would prefer to use TV, but at around £30,000 (1986 prices) for minimal regional coverage, most cannot consider it.

Profiling of consumers was covered in Chapters 5 and 7, and establishing the reading and viewing habits of target segments is a normal part of the marketing research techniques covered in Chapter 11. Media profiles are provided mainly by the media owners themselves and have three main elements. First, to the owners of *The Times*, for example, the paper is a commercial product. To be successful in an editorial sense and attract readers, it must understand its customers' interests in considerable detail. To be successful in selling advertising space, *The Times* has to supply advertising agencies with a comprehensive profile of the readers it can reach. Since over two-thirds of press sales revenue in Britain comes from advertising revenue rather than readers' purchases, the media obviously have a vested interest in knowing their audiences in great detail.

Secondly, the physical characteristics of the media are important to advertisers, such as the size of pages, the quality of paper, the clarity of colour and the frequency of publication. Thirdly, media also have identifiable editorial styles, which reflect the interests of their typical readers. The *Daily Telegraph* and the *News of the World*, for example, are quite different in their style of presentation. There are some products which are better suited to advertising in so-called 'up-market' media, and others for which a 'down-market' appeal must be reflected in 'down-market' press.

Typically no single choice of media coincides exactly with an advertiser's target segments, and space has to be bought in several media to provide a balanced coverage.

Media costs

All commercial media publish their regular prices for advertising spaces, in rate cards. The prices reflect the size of an advert and the numbers of readers/viewers which the media reaches. The standard yardstick in the industry, for any given size (such as page, half page or so many column centimetres), is 'cost per thousand reached' (CPT). Thus, if a full page in the *Sunday Times* colour magazine is seen by 4 million adults, and costs £12,000, the CPT for that media is £3. The CPT for other media may be only £1.50, but there is no more to media buying than CPT. Some British media, such as *TV Times* and *Radio Times*, are known to be especially effective in travel and tourism around December/January time. Accordingly, their CPT rates are higher than average but may still represent good value for money calculated in responses per £1,000 spent. As with any other perishable product, the rate card prices are only indicative. Agencies are skilled at negotiating purchases at discounted rates and few advertisers pay anything like the nominal rate card prices.

Measuring the results of advertising and PR

Mainly because advertising and PR expenditure are only two of the ways used to influence sales through marketing campaigns, it is rarely possible to isolate the sales effect of such expenditure with any precision. As Rodger put it, 'the causal relationship between advertising and sales is, generally speaking, limited, and, as yet unmeasurable' (1968: p. 216). The effect of a price cut, or a competitor's actions, or even the weather, are all capable of distorting the relationship. A successful PR initiative, or an unforeseen change in exchange rates can easily outweigh advertising effects in the short run. Even so, marketing managers are required to assess the effectiveness of their spending, and the following ways are used in practice.

Response effect measurement

Where an advertisement is designed to create a request for information, or provides a phone number for bookings, it is possible to quantify response against the cost of each media used, with precision. It is common practice to code all advertising with letters or numbers, which identify each media used and the date of insertion, so that replies can be assessed against the original expenditure.

Market research measures of communication effect

For an important advertising or PR campaign, sample surveys or target customers can be interviewed before and after a campaign to assess levels of recall and any change in attitudes. For example, if 10 per cent of a target group can recollect advertising for an airline before a campaign, whilst 30 per cent can do so after it, there is clear evidence of increased awareness. If the percentage of those expressing a preference for using the airline rises from, say 8 per cent to 18 per cent, there is evidence of change in attitude. Neither of these measures correlates precisely with sales but they do indicate communication effects.

In travel and tourism, it is often possible to organize sample surveys of customers on a producer's premises. Visitors can be asked how they heard of the product and to state what advertising (if any) they had seen.

Pre-testing of communication effects

If a campaign is large enough to justify the cost, it is possible and normal for three or four alternative creative advertising executions to be tested on samples of the target audience, in order to assess their response. Many national campaigns are developed in this way, which helps advertisers to build on positive responses and remove images and messages with negative connotations.

Accurate targeting

In the end, because of the well known problem of isolating advertising and PR from other influences on sales, the best route to achieving more effective advertising and PR expenditure starts with marketing planning. Good advertising and PR require precision in stating target market numbers and profiles, clarity in deciding what messages should be communicated, and precision in assessing media audience profiles. With this precision, the prospect of achieving creative inspiration in devising memorable messages is more likely. Without it, both advertising and PR inevitably becomes a hit and miss affair, in which neither the successes nor the failures can be accurately understood.

The role of advertising and PR agencies

Only very small businesses, such as guest houses or small attractions, are likely to undertake their own advertising without professional help. Professional help varies from the design advice typically associated with printing firms, all the way up to comprehensive marketing services offered by larger advertising agencies to clients. By tradition, clients of agencies are always referred to as 'accounts'.

A large agency, on an account typically spending at least £250,000 at 1986 prices, would be involved in meetings and consultation on all aspects of marketing campaigns, often including direct involvement in marketing research. Once a campaign is agreed, the agency may be responsible for undertaking PR, sales promotion, direct mail and print, as well as traditional media advertising. Apart from participation in decisions, advertising agencies provide:

1 creative services, including original concepts and ideas, and the design of all visual and copy materials, using research as necessary,

2 media assessment, selection, purchasing services, and evaluation of response,
3 production services and implementation of agreed campaign elements and materials, as scheduled.

The agency person who works closely and in full confidence with a client's marketing managers, is known as an account executive, and is responsible for co-ordinating the three service elements noted above. Agencies are normally selected by competitive tender and, once engaged, may keep an account for several years, allowing a close personal relationship to develop with their clients.

Agencies are paid primarily by the commission (12–15 per cent) which they receive from media owners when they buy space. If commission is not adequate to cover the hours involved in working on an account, fees are payable in addition.

There is no advantage to clients in buying their own media space since, apart from negotiating skills, media owners pay commission only to recognized agencies. PR agencies usually operate on a fee plus costs basis.

Even small accounts with only about £10,000 to spend on campaigns, may find it advantageous to approach regional or local advertising agencies, which exist in most large towns and cities. Advertisers typically enjoy working on travel and tourism accounts as a welcome change from many less interesting products, and may put in some additional effort reflecting their interest.

Advertising plays a relatively small role in travel and tourism

Buttle notes that for hotels and restaurants 'hospitality advertising appropriations are very small compared to major fast moving consumer goods manufacturers who may budget over 30 per cent of turnover' (1986: p. 354). Certainly in terms of total sales revenue, the same is true for tour operators, travel agents and transport operators. In fact excluding breweries, only nine travel and tourism firms featured in the top 250 British advertisers spending league in 1984, and only three in the top 100 (TTG: 1985). The nine were mostly national transport operators or national tour operators, and for all of them advertising is well below the 3 per cent of turnover level. Typically advertising expenditure appears to average between 1 and 3 per cent of total turnover for most travel and tourism producers, although for specific campaigns and particular products, it may reach 20 per cent.

No reliance should be placed on these general industry averages by individual operators. Each operator must make his own decisions having regard to current demand and other communication options provided by:

1 distribution channels available,
2 the role of print,
3 the availability of links with other operators for co-operative promotion,
4 the scope for sales promotion,
5 merchandising.

These are all alternatives to expenditure on traditional media advertising, and they appear to be more effective in influencing demand for many travel and tourism products than they are for most manufactured products.

Tourist attractions appear to be the exception among travel and tourism producers, typically needing to spend up to 10 per cent of admissions revenue on advertising. The reasons for this are explained in a later chapter but reflect a relatively limited choice in terms of the alternative forms of communication noted above.

Types of PR in travel and tourism

Whilst all advertising is media based by definition, PR is not. The type of PR activity which aims to influence or 'lobby' small target groups of influential people, has no obvious connection with the media at all. In practice, however, much PR work in travel and tourism tends to be targeted at media exposure, and its typical forms are shown in Figure 15.4.

At the strategic level, PR may be used to enhance and sustain corporate and product images and positions, using a co-ordinated range of communications, especially printed materials of all kinds. In Britain, a good illustration of effective strategic PR can be seen in the use by the English Tourist Board, of a series of attractively produced publications dealing with aspects of tourism development. Each is carefully branded and themed with the ETB's name and image. These are designed to communicate targeted messages about positive prospects in English tourism, aimed especially at investors and developers potentially interested in the tourist industry. Most of the materials are also sent to the press and other media, achieving general as well as specific interests.

At the tactical level, PR may be used to create and exploit opportunities to communicate selected messages to the general public, or targeted groups. Such opportunities are reflected in Figure 15.4.

A typical opportunistic use of PR would occur, for example, with the opening of a significant new tourist attraction. If it were possible to arrange for a member of the Royal Family, or another leading personality to open it, the media would be interested to use the story in its editorial space. At the opening ceremony, journalists and other guests would typically be invited to a reception, and carefully prepared information packs would be available. Press releases designed to assist busy journalists and sub-editors would be prepared, with paragraphs of important copy ready for immediate use, together with supporting photographs. Pre-opening visits may also be arranged, with perhaps, spectacular events to generate interest. All the details of the launch would be pre-planned with great precision using every opportunity to secure good media coverage. In recent years, the use of PR surrounding the raising and restoration of the Mary Rose at Portsmouth Harbour has created hours of air time on TV and radio, and pages of press coverage over several years, which no advertising could achieve.

Another British illustration of opportunist PR work can be seen in the holding of one of the 1986 BBC TV 'Mastermind' programmes at the National Motor Museum at Beaulieu. The

Press releases	To draw attention to favourable news events (real or created for publicity purposes), or to combat unfavourable publicity arising from unexpected events such as food poisoning on cruise ships.
Press launches	To announce new products, changes or developments; also used for annual reports.
Receptions	To influence and 'lobby' targeted guests with particular messages about opportunities or problems perceived by an organizaton.
Personality appearances	To draw general attention to a product or an organization's name.
Staged events	For example ghost weekends at historic hotels, or mock battles by costumed soldiers at historic sites, which can be used to create media interest.
Product visits	Arranged for TV and radio holiday programmes, and travel journalists, especially to promote editorial comment.

Figure 15.4 *Types of PR activity used in travel and tourism*

programme makers were invited to the museum and offered full facilities for the necessary TV equipment. The programme audience were situated in the museum amongst the exhibits and as cameras panned across the audience area, they picked up posters and other unobtrusive but carefully placed materials designed to communicate Beaulieu messages – including a Beaulieu advertising poster strategically placed on a replica 1912 double decker bus. The presenter opened the show with a brief interview with Lord Montagu, the owner of Beaulieu, and on two Sunday evenings at prime TV watching time, attractive Beaulieu images were communicated to millions of homes. The invited audience included influential people in the area surrounding Beaulieu, whose goodwill the Museum values and seeks to sustain.

For most sectors of the travel and tourism industry, the range of subjects suitable for general PR coverage is wide, representing a powerful potential communication asset to be harnessed alongside advertising. As Melvyn Greene put it, writing about the hotel sector, 'Very few consumer industries are in quite such a position to obtain unpaid publicity as the hotel industry . . . In everyone's sales action plan it should be possible to set a specific feasible objective of, say, obtaining a free write-up in the local newspaper every month' (1982: p. 181).

Chapter summary

This chapter presents advertising and PR as two of the most important choices to be made by marketing managers when planning marketing campaigns. Both are part of marketing communications and are used primarily to influence targeted customers away from the places at which products are delivered and sold. Advertising is surrounded by its own professional jargon, and the main terms most frequently used

in practice are summarized in Figure 15.2.

Both advertising and PR are used by producers to reach prospective individual buyers and trading partners, such as retailers, and communicate messages intended to influence their attitudes and purchase behaviour. The communication process is complex and contains several filters between messages transmitted, and messages received and acted on. These are discussed, and summarized in Figure 15.1. The purposes for which advertising is used are often specific to achieving marketing objectives, and mainly sales related, whilst PR is used more in a supportive role, especially to maintain awareness and favourable attitudes. Both advertising and PR have strategic and tactical dimensions, reflecting the organizational needs outlined in Chapter 12, and play a vital role in communicating the positioning strategies adopted for products and organizations as a whole.

The main stages in producing cost effective advertising are noted and discussed, with emphasis on the creative aspects, media selection, and measuring results. The same stages are broadly relevant to planning PR and some specific examples of PR usage are provided.

For an identifiable cost, both advertising and PR provide opportunities for organizations to reach and communicate their chosen messages to selected audiences. It is worth noting that there are few willing advertisers in the commercial world, only producers who invest in advertising and PR because they do not know of any more economical way to achieve the sales targets they have set for their products.

Further reading

Baker, M. J., *Marketing: An Introductory Text*, Macmillan, 1985, Chapters 16 and 17.

Kotler, P., *Marketing: Analysis, Planning and Control*, Prentice-Hall, 1984, Chapters 19 and 20.

16

Sales promotion and merchandising

The previous chapter explained how advertising and PR messages are used to communicate with and influence prospective buyers, away from the place of production, consumption, and purchase of products. The main object of that communication is to move people towards purchase decisions at the point of sale, with good awareness of product offers, and with their attitudes favourably disposed.

This chapter explains how a different range of mainly tactical promotional techniques are used to provide special incentives to motivate prospective buyers, especially at the point of sale. The main object of this communication is to convert initial interest in products into actual sales.

The 'perishability' of tourism products means that marketing managers are constantly preoccupied with the necessity to manipulate demand in response to unforeseen events as well as the normal daily, weekly, or seasonal fluctuations. Sales promotion and merchandising methods are especially suitable for such short-run demand adjustments, and are vital aspects of marketing for most travel and tourism producers.

The chapter begins with the reasons for using sales promotion and merchandising. It proceeds with definitions, the meaning of 'point of sale', and the role of display. The three targets for sales promotion are identified, followed by marketing objectives attainable by sales promotion, explained in diagrammatic form, which is used also to indicate the range of techniques available. The chapter outlines the process of planning sales promotions, budgeting, and evaluating results. The last section compares and contrasts the roles of advertising and PR with sales promotion.

The reader will perceive that this chapter provides more details of the purposes and types of promotion, than the previous chapter on advertising and PR. This is because advertising and PR are extensively covered in standard texts, whereas sales promotion is not.

Reasons for using sales promotion and merchandising

At the stage when a tactical marketing campaign is planned, most of the elements of the marketing mix for established products are already largely determined by previous strategic decisions. For example, in the case of an hotel chain planning a marketing campaign for the next six months, its products exist, the price range is fixed, and the normal channels of distribution are established. In practice, even some key promotional elements, such as brochures, exhibitions, and sales force are largely committed, with limited scope for significant changes, unless a crisis in demand occurs.

Against this background, marketing managers are well aware that, for both predictable and unpredictable reasons, demand for their products will be subject to surges and fluctuations. Occasionally demand will exceed supply but more often it will not, and demand manipulation is a primary requirement of tactical marketing. Predictable short-falls in demand for city hotels, for example, occur from Friday to Sunday and at certain times of the year. Other short-falls in demand also occur, often as a result of unfavourable political, economic or social events, and especially in Britain, the weather. Such events affect demand and require rapid tactical promotional responses. Some events of course are positive, such as favourable exchange rate movements, and these represent opportunities to be exploited with equally rapid tactical responses.

Sales promotion and merchandising defined

Kotler (1984) offers no formal definition of sales promotion, (although the issues are fully covered) whilst Baker uses the American Marketing Association (AMA), definition, which is not best suited to travel and tourism. Adapting the AMA view the essential characteristics are:

> Sales promotion is part of marketing communications, other than advertising, PR, personal selling and sales literature. It is primarily designed to stimulate consumer purchasing, and dealer and sales force effectiveness in the short term, through temporary incentives and displays.

The definition stresses the short-term, non-regular, incentive nature of sales promotion, and the fact that it extends beyond consumers to distribution networks and the sales force. Much of sales promotion in practice takes place at points of sale and the term 'merchandising' is often used to describe that part of sales promotion, which takes place at the point of sale.

Rodger defined merchandising as the 'sum total of effort to move goods [products] at the point of sale . . .' (1968: p. 155).

While advertising is described as 'above the line' (see Chapter 15), Sales promotion and merchandising are usually referred to as 'below the line'.

Points of sale

Having stressed the important distinction between forms of marketing communication which take place away from the 'point of sale', and other forms which focus on it, it is necessary to consider what this means in practice. At its simplest, a point of sale (POS) is

> any location at which a purchase transaction takes place.

Chapter 18 deals with distribution networks created to provide access to products at places external to the producers' premises. But 'point of sale' in travel and tourism means much more than distribution networks. It covers three very different kinds of location with different marketing requirements:

External POS	e.g. retail travel agency (for most products), ticket/booking office or desk (for transport and car rental) or tourist information centre (TIC) (especially if bookings are taken).
Internal or 'in-house' POS	e.g. reception desk (hotels and attractions), reception desk may also operate a referral system linked with other outlets in the same organization. Locations within an operator's premises such as bars, restaurants, retail sales points (souvenirs and other items), duty free shops, etc.

Reservation system via customer's home as POS	enquiries or bookings, responding to direct mail and promotional offers by TV, radio, promotional mail, or telephone calls.

Most readers will be familiar with the external points of sale noted above, but because the production and consumption of service products on producers' premises are simultaneous, a considerable amount of internal sales promotion also occurs on site or 'in house'. Such promotion aims to persuade 'captive' customers to buy specific products, or more of them, or generally to spend more once they have arrived. Because producers have full control of their premises, within the law, 'in house' sales promotion and merchandising are vitally important to service producers in ways which manufacturers of most physical goods must envy. Banks, post offices, and retail outlets of motoring organizations provide other illustrations of growing awareness of the value of 'in house' promotion for service products.

In travel and tourism, many producers sell at least a half of their output direct to customers through guides and brochures, or in direct response to advertising. It is, therefore, necessary to recognize that direct booking systems, especially central reservation offices, also act as points of sale to customers in their own homes. In its way, a telephone response from a guest house, acts in exactly the same way as a sales person's response to a customer in a showroom used to sell physical goods.

All points of sale, external, in house, or via reservation systems, offer potential opportunities for effective sales promotion and merchandising initiatives.

Three targets for sales promotion

In practice, tactical responses designed to stimulate sales to customers involve three targets:

1　Consumers,

2　Distribution networks (points of sale) including 'in-house',
3　Sales force.

Consumers

All sales promotion is designed to achieve *additional* short-run purchases by customers, which producers have reason to believe would not occur without specific action. Aimed directly at customers, the objective is to provide specific incentives or inducements to buy particular products at particular times. Much of sales promotion is restricted to chosen segments to avoid the dilution of total sales revenue, which occurs if unnecessary incentives are offered to all customers, many of whom intended to purchase without the added incentive.

Distributor network

If an organization receives a large proportion of its sales revenue through third party distributors, achieving customer sales objectives is likely to require their active participation. Distributors, such as retail travel agents, are typically bombarded daily by operators wishing them to provide extra display space for their products and other forms of support. Any special effort, therefore, usually requires special incentives and if they are not provided, customer sales are unlikely to be achieved.

Sales force

For larger organizations, sales forces are required to service and motivate distributor networks. Being human, any additional effort on top of the continuous routine sales efforts which are made, often requires some additional forms of incentive or reward.

Thus sales promotions intended to influence individual buyers, often involve other forms of supporting promotion, the objectives of which are summarized in Figure 16.1.

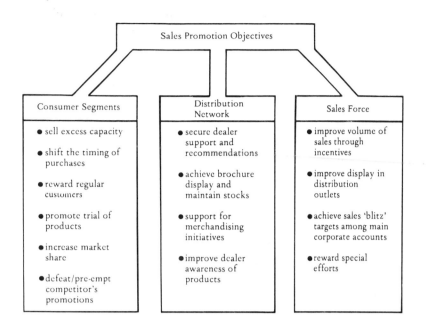

Figure 16.1 *Marketing objectives attainable by sales promotion*

Marketing objectives attainable by sales promotion

The types of tactical marketing objectives attainable through sales promotion efforts are noted in Figure 16.1. In practice, the objectives stem from response to a combination of factors, which may vary on a weekly basis, including:

- sales volume targets and variance analysis (see Chapter 14)
- problems of over or under capacity of production
- competitor threats
- other external environment factors representing threats or opportunities
- problems with the coverage, stocking, and/or display of brochures in distribution networks

Both for distributors and for sales forces, sales promotion objectives tend to focus on aspects of display space. 'Display' denotes the availability, visibility and accessibility of products in distribution outlets, or points-of-sale. Every metre of counter, shelf, or rack space performs a selling role for products in a retail travel agency or other outlet. Other things being equal, more space, in more accessible parts of a shop, will sell more product because more people's attention will be attracted by the higher visibility, in much the same way as a double-page spread advertisement in a magazine has more chance of being seen and read than a quarter-page advert, mixed with others. If eye catching window displays, video films and 'special offer' leaflets are added to a competitive product's display space, there is a high probability that more sales will result. In self service outlets where customers browse and select brochures, the amount and position of display is crucial to achieving sales volume.

Display space in retail outlets is always in short supply, and it is usually allocated, very roughly, according to a product's market share. In other words, if tour operator 'A' has 20 per cent of a market and tour operator 'B' has 10 per cent, A will normally be given around twice the available display space. One of the usual objects of sales promotion is to change these relative space allocations but it can only be achieved for short periods. At any one time, but especially in the main booking weeks, the competition to achieve prime display space is enormous, and the costs of sales promotion incentives to distributors rises proportionately.

The objectives noted under 'distribution network' relate to the broader issues of distribution discussed in Chapter 18.

Sales promotion techniques used in travel and tourism

Figure 16.2 summarizes the main promotional techniques on which marketing managers can draw. Advertising agencies and separate specialist sales promotion agencies are available to assist larger companies in the choice and design of techniques. Smaller firms will have no choice but to use their judgement, based on previous experience of the tools that are effective in their field, and by researching the range of promotions on offer by competitors. The travel trade press and marketing journals are all excellent sources of information about current promotional campaigns, operating in all sectors of travel and tourism.

It can be seen that the incentives noted for consumers and distribution networks in Figure 16.2, have three common elements, identified by Peterson (1978: p. 62) as:

- a featured offer (outside the normal terms of trade)
- a tangible advantage (not inherent in the normal product formulation)

- intention to achieve marketing objectives

These three elements fit precisely with the overall definition of sales promotion noted earlier.

Some examples of consumer sales promotion incentives

Price cuts for all categories of goods and services are commonly recognized as the most powerful of all consumer incentives. They are almost universally used by tour operators, for example to sell off unsold capacity on under-booked flights. 'Sale' boards have become a common feature in travel agents' windows, with offers of large discounts on specific flights notified by the operators.

Discount vouchers offering say 15 per cent off admission prices, or a money equivalent coupon such as '50p off', are commonly used by tourist attractions on the basis that most coupons are allowable on one adult admission only, and a typical party size is nearer three persons. '50p off', in the context of a high fixed price operation with spare capacity, still represents a very real gain in net profit terms, even before any additional on site spending occurs.

Disguised price cuts are a popular way to maintain the regular price structure, yet offer added value to customers and an incentive to buy. Hotels, with space to sell, often offer double room occupancy for single occupancy rack rates, but expect to generate added revenue through meals and bars. The rather coy 'spouse free' ads put out by Cunard in the early 1980s to promote transatlantic travel by business persons travelling alone are another example of disguised price cuts.

Extra product may be offered as an incentive, for example four nights for the price of three; free wine on certain dates; additional features offered 'free' by tourist attractions at times of the year when they are not crowded; additional sightseeing excursions may be added by tour operators.

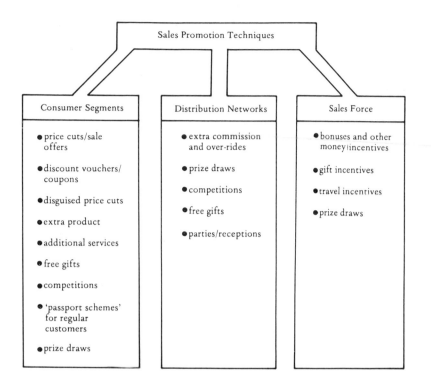

Figure 16.2 *Range of sales promotion techniques used in travel and tourism*

Additional services may include chauffeur cars from airport to town centre offered by airlines to first-class passengers, or the welcome receptions and vouchers for beauty salons offered in some hotels to weekend visitors.

Free gifts range from tour operators' travel bags and passport wallets, to badges or pens offered to children at some attractions.

Competitions are a common travel incentive, with the 1986 British Airways 'Go For it America' competition in the USA, and its Concorde competition in Britain, only two of the largest multi-million pound competitions provided by international operators in 1986.

Lastly *'passport'* schemes, of the type which Pan Am first made popular in the early 1980s, are powerful repeat purchase incentives to regular users. Each journey with an airline may count for points, with free or discounted travel subsequently available, according to the number of user points achieved over a stated period. Some hotels use similar schemes to reward regular customers, with equivalent free or discounted product awards graded according to the points achieved.

From this brief review, it will be clear that the range of possible incentives is both extremely wide, and very creative. There is constant rivalry between competitors to achieve a lead in incentives, and to gain market share. Sales promotions may also generate sufficient media interest to gain additional unpaid coverage, supported by skilful PR activity.

Examples of sales promotion incentives for distributors and sales force

Although separately designed to appeal to managers and (or) counter staff, many of the incentives used to motivate distributors are the same as those offered to customers, including gifts, prize draws, and competitions. In addition, to achieve the objectives of a major promotion, it is likely that additional commission will be paid on extra sales. As Holloway puts it, . . . 'incentive commissions of 2½ per cent or more [are] payable by tour operators for the achievement of pre-established targets' (1985: p. 147). Additional commission payments are often known in the trade as 'over-rides', although these may be paid also for all sales above an agreed level. Because of the nature of the product, it is normal in travel and tourism for distributor incentives to include free travel to sample the promoted items.

For sales forces, the incentives are also designed to appeal to the individuals concerned, and mostly they are available in the form of money bonuses and gifts available on achieving specified additional sales targets. There is, of course, a large sales incentive industry, especially in the USA, which specializes in designing and supplying incentives for sales forces and distributors in all sectors of industry. Within the range of incentives offered by specialist agencies, travel products are frequently found to be powerful motivators.

How long is 'temporary' for incentives?

By the definition of sales promotions, all these inducements, incentives and rewards, are tactical responses of a temporary, short-term nature. If they are sustained for too long they become perceived as part of the standard product, price, or terms of trade, and they lose their effectiveness

to secure vital, additional sales. Kotler suggests that 'probably there is risk in putting a well-known brand on promotion more than 30 per cent of the time' (1984: p. 662). He also draws attention to the dangers of subsidizing existing users by over-frequent promotions. There are no precise rules, but very few travel and tourism producers could afford to promote at anything like the 30 per cent level. Fortunately for service producers, they can usually be far more segment and product specific in their promotions, than manufacturers of physical goods. They also enjoy more influence over much of the distribution network in which most sales promotions occur.

Another reason for limiting the extent of sales promotion activity is that the cost, measured on a unit basis sold, (e.g. one seat or one bed-night), is usually high. It is justified on the grounds of recouping all or some of the high fixed costs of operation already committed, but could not be sustained without serious erosion of profitability.

Without contradicting the limit on how long any one promotion may be sustained, it should be noted that there are often strong reasons for linking individual promotions within a theme. Themes must be relevant to the organizations and products being promoted, and can be used strategically over time to create a sense of continuity in customers' minds. At the National Motor Museum at Beaulieu, for example, the theme of the motor car is used to 'brand' most of the visitor promotions, although the effect of each promotion is strictly temporary. McDonald's Restaurants use the character Ronald McDonald with many of their specific promotions, and so on. Sales promotions featuring collectable items, which together form sets of linked items, are another way to build themes and continuity into sales promotions. It is also possible to build a series of merchandising initiatives into recognizable themes, especially when they are used 'in house'.

Pricing down or packaging up?

Not confined to travel and tourism, there has been a debate in marketing for years as to which of two routes is the best to achieve targeted sales volume. One route is by promotional price discounting; the other is adding value to products (packaging up), to achieve targeted volume by promoting product enhancement. Packaging up means adding short-term value into one or more of the bundle of components, of which travel and tourism products are comprised. The marketing issues involved in this are covered in Chapter 8 under the heading 'Product Augmentation'.

There is no doubt that price cutting is easier to implement. It works faster and is popular with customers. But there is also no doubt that price cuts are easily matched and can degenerate quickly into price wars, which leave all producers worse off, and sometimes results in reduced product quality. To some extent, producers cannot stand aside if they are losing sales volume to a cheaper competitor. But, wherever possible, especially with key segments, the marketing advantages of packaging up are clear, and should always be explored and tested. Provided that a product is competitive and generating good satisfaction levels at existing prices, there is every reason to limit price cutting, unless it becomes essential for survival. A commitment to product enhancement, and knowledge of customer segments, offers the only long-term route out of price cutting wars, in which price becomes the primary reason for customer choice. Specific examples of packaging up are noted by Greene who concludes that '. . . the hotel and airline sector have tended too often to use price reductions as the first tactic for obtaining more business when other choices could be more profitably employed' (1982: pp. 62–67).

Planning effective sales promotions

The process of planning and executing successful sales promotions can be represented as six logical steps. The steps are based on the marketing planning process outlined in Chapter 13 and are undertaken in practice as part of planning campaigns (Chapter 14):

1 Calculate the volume targets and pattern of sales, which sales promotion activity is expected to achieve over the defined promotion period. For an hotel group, for example, this would be expressed in room nights per hotel, over specified periods of time. For airlines it would be seat sales by route, by period of time. For a tourist attraction it would be visitor numbers. The procedure is the same, whether the objective is to gain additional business above previously targeted levels, or reduce the level of an expected loss resulting from some unpredictable external event.

2 Calculate the potential revenue gain which would arise if the volume targets were achieved in full, (volume × average price of nights, seats or admission). This establishes the limits in which a budget must be set.

3 Specify the consumer profile of the segments to be targeted for sales promotion; business or leisure; drawing on details of place of origin and other profile data available from marketing research.

4 Choose the incentives best calculated to appeal to the target segments, and cost them in relation to budget limits.

5 Draw up and implement an action programme, in co-ordination with other promotional elements in the campaign, especially advertising, PR, personal selling, and distribution arrangements.

6 Evaluate the results achieved.

Budgeting and evaluating results

By their nature, sales promotion and merchandising are task-orientated techniques. The tasks relate to identified short-falls or opportunities, which can be expressed precisely in volume terms of bednights, seats, admissions etc., and in the amount of sales revenue which is at risk, or achievable. It follows that objective and task methods are the only realistic way to calculate sales promotion budgets (see Chapter 14).

Again, because sales promotion methods are so specifically targeted, results can be evaluated in sales or bookings achieved during the promotional period. Inevitably it will not be possible to separate out the effects of current advertising, or recent product enhancement, but short-run promotional efforts provide the best opportunity which marketing managers have to measure the results of marketing expenditure in sales terms.

Sales promotion or advertising and PR?

Theoretically, producers have a choice between spending most of their marketing communications budget on advertising and PR, or most of it on sales promotion. In fact, whilst the ultimate aim of all marketing communications is to influence buyer behaviour and generate sales, they perform essentially different tasks.

As Davidson expressed it:

> In general, the purpose of advertising is to improve attitudes towards a brand [product], while the objective of promotion is to translate favourable attitudes into actual purchase. Advertising cannot close a sale because its impact is too far from the point of purchase, but promotion can and does (1975: p. 190).

Advertising and PR have an essentially strategic role in developing and sustaining awareness, positive attitudes, images, product positions, favourable associations, and knowledge of product attributes. Sales promotion, by contrast, is essentially tactical in its short-run responses, and aimed at manipulating demand around the fixed capacity of service operations. It works by providing specific inducements, in association with displays and other ways of attracting customer attention at points of sale, at particular times.

Provided that a producer has achieved accessibility and display for customers through a distribution network, that of itself may be sufficient to create awareness of sales promotion offers. More often, especially if a purchase is made from the buyer's own home, promotional offers have to be advertised. This is the point of overlap between the two forms of communication, but their essentially different roles must not be confused.

Where opportunities for sales promotion occur on site or 'in house', there is generally no requirement for supportive media advertising because producers have full control over their own premises and a 'captive' audience to influence. The opportunity for 'in house' promotion is open to all producers of travel and tourism products because of the inseparability of production and consumption.

The conclusion is, therefore, that sales promotion and advertising are complementary techniques, not alternatives. For travel and tourism products they warrant equal attention in campaign planning.

Chapter summary

This chapter defines sales promotions and merchandising in their primary tactical role of managing short-run variations in customer demand for products. Both techniques are aspects of marketing communications and operate by providing additional incentives at the point of sale, which are strong enough to 'close' the sale for the products being promoted. Advertising and PR are used away from the point of sale and serve to bring in customers whose attitudes and interest in products is already favourably pre-conditioned.

Because of the perishable nature of travel and tourism products, and the operational implications of high fixed costs, the use of sales promotion and merchandising in managing demand is even more important in the travel industry than in industries marketing physical goods. Although very difficult to quantify, below the line techniques are more important than above the line for most producers. The existence of three different kinds of point of sale is noted, with particular stress on the merchandising opportunities conveyed by having customers 'in house', on the producer's premises.

The difference between the marketing objectives which advertising and PR achieve, and the objectives of sales promotion and merchandising are brought out, and the two forms of communication are normally planned together and co-ordinated to have maximum effect in integrated marketing campaigns.

Although the desired effect is on purchases by targeted customer segments, sales promotion techniques are aimed at consumers, distributors, and sales force in order to maximize the short run effects at chosen points of sale. The planning for sales promotion and merchandising follows systematic procedures which will be familiar by now to readers of this book, and which are integrated in the vital marketing and campaign planning stages discussed in Chapters 13 and 14.

Further reading

Baker, M. J., *Marketing: An Introductory Text*, Macmillan, 1985, Chapter 18.
Kotler, P., *Marketing Analysis, Planning and Control*, Prentice-Hall, 1984, Chapter 21.

17

Brochures and other printed materials

This chapter focuses on brochures, sales literature generally, and other forms of printed communications paid for out of marketing budgets. Known in the USA as 'collateral materials', print represents the third distinctive group of marketing communications to be planned in marketing campaigns, in addition to advertising and PR, sales promotion and merchandising.

The design, distribution, and use of printed items is one of the features that most distinguishes marketing in travel and tourism, from other forms of consumer marketing. Whereas all producers of consumer products use advertising and PR, sales promotion, merchandising, and personal selling, few producers of physical goods use print to anything like the extent found in tourism. The nature of service products, especially those which are relatively expensive and infrequently bought, confers a particular significance on printed communications as an integral part of the marketing process, which has no parallel in marketing physical goods.

Where a large proportion of sales turnover is achieved by direct sales between producer and consumer, not involving third party distributors, the role of sales literature is at its strongest. This of course, is the case for the bulk of all international and domestic travel and tourism products. While many tour operators are exceptions to the reliance on direct sales, they have other important marketing reasons for focusing their efforts on brochures. For some organi-

zations, especially tourist boards at national, regional and local level, the design, production and distribution of printed materials typically accounts for the major element of marketing budgets. In such organizations, the concern and involvement with print also takes up much of the time of marketing staff.

This chapter begins by explaining why printed materials are such an important part of marketing communications in travel and tourism, and provides a definition in the context of marketing campaigns. The types of printed materials used and their multiple roles in marketing travel and tourism are identified, followed by a step by step explanation of the process involved in producing effective print, both 'in house', and through external agencies. The key issue of achieving distribution to the user is discussed, followed by brief notes on evaluating the results of expenditure.

Print production and wastage – on a massive scale

The sheer volume of print associated with travel and tourism products is staggering. In 1974, a study by Booz, Allen and Hamilton for the American Society of Travel Agents (ASTA) estimated that 8,000 US travel agents received on average, 380 dispatches of printed communications per week, and that each dispatch contained some 30 items (leaflets or brochures)

(ASTA: 1974: p. 51). Over 52 weeks per annum, therefore, some 5 billion items were distributed in the USA through this one form of distribution alone. Most of the items were not requested, but sent out by producers hoping for display, and agency recommendations. The cost of those items was put at over $1 billion in 1974 prices. It was estimated that less than six out of every ten agents opened all the packs they received and that about a third of all packs were, 'automatically discarded'. Although the number of US travel agents has trebled since 1974. It is unlikely that the wastage implications of this research have changed. A later study carried out for the European Travel Commission in 1978 confirmed the same massive wastage of national tourist office materials.

Directly comparable figures are not available for Britain, but it is a strong probability that perhaps half all the literature packs received by the 6,000 British travel agency offices, never reach display racks, and that much is simply dumped. The concentration of travel retailers into fewer chains in the 1980s, means that retail display policies for brochures are more tightly controlled now than ever before, and likely to remain so. Major British tour operators in the 1980s typically produce between six to ten brochures per booking. Large brochures containing over 100 pages may cost around 75p each to produce. But, because one booking covers at least two people on average, the true ratio of brochures produced for each person booking is often in the range ten to twenty.

At £0.75p each, the brochure costs equate to say $15 \times £0.75p = £11.25$ per booking. In September 1986, *The Times* estimated that a typical seven-night summer holiday in Corfu costing £177 (brochure price), would earn for the tour operator only £8.00 (4.5 per cent of the brochure price), compared with the travel agent's commission of £18.00. Whilst one cannot put too much reliance on such examples, even at 50p and

only ten brochures per booking, the cost of print as a proportion of marketing expenditure, and as a major cost item to be paid for out of the tour operator's earnings, should be noted. The importance of achieving even marginal improvements in the effectiveness of brochures, and thus reducing print wastage, is obvious. It can only be achieved by systematic marketing and by refining the process involved in designing and distributing printed materials.

Defining printed materials

Print is part of marketing communications. It may be defined as comprising:

> Any form of printed materials paid for out of marketing budgets, designed to inform existing and prospective customers, and stimulate demand for specified products, or facilitate their use and enjoyment.

This definition covers not only the familiar promotional use of print, such as tour operator and hotel brochures, but also 'facilitation'. Facilitation is a useful word in travel and tourism marketing to describe the ways in which producers assist customers to decide between, and to purchase particular products, and achieve full benefit and enjoyment from using them. Leaflets provided on admission to tourist attractions, to inform and 'orientate' visitors to the experience they will receive, are one illustration of print designed to facilitate use and enjoyment.

Whilst travel and tourism are obvious spheres of interest to a wide range of commercial publishers, the definition above includes only print which is part of a communications mix intended to achieve marketing objectives. *Excluded* from the definition are all commercial publications, such as directories, maps, guide books, and timetables, which are sold through bookshops and other outlets, and for which the object of production is to achieve profit for the publisher through the cover price, and/or advertising revenue. Whilst maps, for example, may be elements of promotional print for tourist boards, the criterion for inclusion in the definition is whether or not their production is geared to marketing objectives. Occasionally, printed items within the definition may also be sold at a cover price. But if so, it is always seen as a contribution towards marketing costs and not a main reason for production.

The bulk of all printed items are aimed at consumers, but they are also produced to achieve promotional and facilitation objectives targeted at a distribution network. Printed materials may be designed for use in consumers' homes, at a point of sale, or 'in-house' on a producer's premises.

Types of printed materials used in marketing travel and tourism

From the previous discussion it will be obvious that the range of printed materials is wide. The lists below summarize typical items used in practice to influence travellers.

Promotional print

Tour operators' brochures.
Hotel, holiday centre, caravan park, campsite, and other accommodation brochures.
Conference centre brochures.
Specific product brochures (e.g. activity holidays, theatre weekends).
Attraction leaflets (theme parks, museums, amusement parks).
Car rental brochures.
Sales promotion leaflets (specific incentive offers).
Posters/show cards for window and other displays in distribution networks.
Tourist office brochures (general and product specific).
Printed letters/inserts for direct mail.

Facilitation and information print

Orientation leaflets/guides (attractions).
Maps (mostly provided free out of marketing budgets).
'In-House' guides and 'In-House' magazines (accommodation and transport).
Menus/tent cards/ show cards/ folders, used 'in house'.
Hotel group (and equivalent) directories.
'What's on' leaflets (such as those provided out of resort marketing budgets).

The marketing role of printed materials

Drawing on reasons outlined in Chapter 3, it is possible to summarize briefly the characteristics of travel and tourism products, which underlie the need for effective print and explain its importance in the conduct of marketing campaigns.

- Products are produced and consumed on producers' premises and cannot be inspected and assessed directly at points of sale away from the place of production. There are no physical stocks of tourist products as there are for manufactured goods, and brochures are used as product substitutes.

- Whilst service production and consumption are simultaneous, the production process is often separated by weeks or months from the act of purchase. Inevitably, products are ideas and expectations only, at the point of sale.

- Especially where infrequently purchased, expensive products such as holidays are involved, customers typically seek information and consider several options before making choices. Retailers of holidays are well aware that every minute spent answering questions costs money; they have a powerful incentive to distribute literature in order to reduce customer contact time.

- Producers' interests are best served by the widest possible distribution of their product offers. This means securing continuous communication at points of sale, which cannot be achieved through advertising alone.
- There are many marketing reasons for communicating with customers during the production/consumption process, partly to 'facilitate' the experience and inform, and partly to generate a greater level of 'in-house' expenditure.

To explain these points, consider two hypothetical examples which illustrate the role and use of promotional print. A prospective vacationer in Manchester in January may be contemplating a two-week holiday in Ibiza in July. Probably, it will be his most expensive purchase decision of the year; assume he has no previous experience of the Balearic Islands. A travel agent may suggest, friends may recommend, an advertisement or travel feature may arouse his interest, but in the cold gloom of a Manchester January, a choice must be made between, say, four alternatives. Tour operators' brochures are designed to make that sort of decision possible without promising more than can be delivered in July.

Consider another traveller who arrives for six nights at a resort hotel, in which his booking covers the room, breakfast, and one other main meal (Modified American Plan). On arrival, he will check in and receive a room number card. From that moment on he represents a spending opportunity not only for the hotel, but for many other tourist businesses accessible to the resort. The skill and tact with which a 'spending opportunity' is converted into sales, without at the same time damaging perceptions of enjoyment and good value for money, are reflected in the range of printed items the traveller will encounter during his stay, 'in-house', and in the resort.

The multiple purposes of printed materials

It is obvious from the definition and the range of items included, that marketing print performs a wide range of functions in travel and tourism. They are summarized below under seven headings:

- promotional (messages/symbols)
- promotional (display/merchandising)
- promotional (incentives/special offers)
- product substitute role
- access/purchasing mechanism
- 'proof' of purchase/reassurance
- facilitation of product use and information

Promotion

Brochures, such as those provided by tour operators, are designed to stimulate customers and motivate them to buy. They identify needs, demonstrate in pictures and words the image and positioning of products and organizations, and carry the key messages. In this role they act in the same way as advertising. They also perform a vital display function in the racks of distribution outlets, such as retail travel agents, where they serve in lieu of physical products. In the typical self-service shops run by most travel and tourism retailers, the display role, and the customer appeal of brochure covers in particular, are vital to marketing success. Supplementary brochures and purpose designed leaflets, are typically used to communicate and promote special offers, and the other sales promotion incentives discussed in Chapter 15.

Access/purchasing mechanism

Many product brochures contain booking forms to facilitate purchase, which contain the basis of the contract to provide services. Some of these forms may be over-stamped and filled in by travel agents, but all are designed to specify the purchase details. Carefully designed booking forms can also be used by operators as a source of basic marketing research data, providing valuable customer profile information about previous customers, their area of origin, party size and type. The addresses can be analyzed by ACORN methods to provide a detailed profile of typical buyers.

Product substitute role

Above all, for travel and tourism operators whose business depends on bookings made away from the place of production, brochures perform a product substitute role, the marketing importance of which it is impossible to over-emphasize. The brochure *is* the product at the point of purchase, especially for first-time customers, and it establishes expectations of quality, value for money, product image and status, which must be matched when the product is delivered.

Proof of purchase/reassurance

The brochure also substitutes for the product in the period between purchase and consumption which, in the case of vacations, may extend to several months. It becomes a document to be read several times as a reminder, to stimulate expectations, and to show friends and relatives. While not of itself 'proof of purchase' in any legal sense, producers' brochures do serve in that role in the buyer's mind.

Facilitation of product use/information

Once customers arrive 'in-house' or on the producer's premises, it is normal for them to be provided with a wide range of printed materials. Some may be found in rooms (hotels), or seat backs (airlines), at information desks (attractions), or on tables (restaurants and bars). The literature is designed to explain and promote what is available:

- either to promote awareness and use of ancillary services/products,

- or to assist customers to get the most value out of their purchase and enhance satisfaction,
- or to feature special offers (sales promotion),
- or to provide basic information which may be useful

Producers can, and do train staff to communicate with customers, in order to achieve all these things. But staff are usually busy and often forget. Printed items are the main way to provide standardized, 'user-friendly' messages to all travellers, in exactly the same way.

Carefully designed print can do much to create a sense of welcome by an establishment to its customers, and communicate that it understands and cares about their needs and interests. An illustration is the choice which tourist attractions have, either to provide a simple admission ticket, or a leaflet of welcome and user advice. At Beaulieu in Hampshire, at the National Motor Museum, admission is by tokens which are dropped into turnstiles and every visitor receives a leaflet and brief spoken information. The system is similar to that at Disneyland and other USA theme parks. Compare this approach with the bus or cloakroom style tickets used in so many attractions in the 1980s.

Stages in producing effective printed materials

The six stages noted below are presented in a logical decision sequence, which is relevant to all managers responsible for producing printed materials for marketing purposes. Although the distribution of printed materials has special considerations (see later in the chapter), the other stages are similar to those used for designing any form of marketing communication, and they are marketing research based for larger organizations. Print planning is normally carried out as one of the elements in the campaign plan, and it draws on data used for planning marketing strategy and objectives. The budget required for print production is best calculated using the 'objective and task' methods outlined in Chapter 14.

1 *Determining the size and profile of the target audience.* Information about target customers is derived through market segmentation; print volume is related to the quantified objectives in the marketing plan. The target profile for advertising (media selection) and for print production, will normally be identical.

2 *Marketing strategy and positioning.* Here also, advertising and print are likely to be planned together with co-ordinated messages, images and positioning. If print is the larger part of the budget, it may take the leading role in expressing product images. It will certainly take a leading role in communicating specific product messages to the target audience.

   Paper quality, choice of colours, density of copy, graphics, and the style and density of photography, are varied in practice to match chosen images to selected target audiences. Up-market target groups typically respond better to heavier quality paper, lower density per page, pastel colours, and thematic photographs. Down-market target groups are more influenced by bold colours, direct and straightforward copy, and are not put off by greater density per page.

3 *Specifying brochure objectives.* The essential task is to clarify and state concisely what the brochure is expected to achieve in the campaign, especially in terms of the specific products it covers. A list of specific messages, rank ordered according to perceived customer priorities, should be drawn up within the overall context of the agreed marketing objectives. These statements will be crucial in briefing designers.

4 *Deciding the method of distributing print.* The distribution of print to its intended recipients is arguably the most vital of the six stages, because communication can only work if sufficient numbers of prospective customers receive it. The cost of distribution per unit of print may easily exceed the unit cost of production, and most producers in travel and tourism will have to choose between several distribution options. This vital decision is discussed later in this chapter

5 *Creative execution.* As for advertising, the way in which product concepts and images are presented in print will strongly influence the way in which consumers receive and respond to messages. In particular, the appearance and appeal of the front cover, especially of items to be displayed in self-service racks, will be crucial in establishing eye contact and initial visual interest. Without the initial appeal, a leaflet or brochure is unlikely to be picked up and looked through. Maas notes that 'the cover of a brochure is just like the headline of a print advertisement: four out of five people never get beyond it. For these readers, you must get your selling message across on that page (or waste 80 per cent of your money)' (1980: p. 23). From research into the influence of pictures in advertising in Britain and the USA, Haines concluded that '. . . a majority of advertising pictures are not projecting their intended message; that some are so misconceived as to be counter-productive or even damaging to the advertiser's interest' (1984: p. 20).

   Whilst creative execution will usually be the business of designers (see below), marketing managers must accept full responsibility for the designer's brief and any marketing research associated with it.

6 *Timing.* Most travel and tourism print is required to fulfil its roles at particular times. Tour operators and other prod-

ucers, for example, must have their material available for distribution when customers are making their travel decisions, and print production and advertising normally require carefully coordinated phasing. Since it usually takes several weeks from an initial brief to final production of print, it is vital that print requirements are carefully programmed and that agreed timings are adhered to. If photographs are required, they have to be taken at the right time of the year. Many an hotel and tourist attraction has started to plan its brochure in September for production in January, only to find that the key photographs it needs should have been taken in July . . .

Whilst this may seem obvious, practice demonstrates repeatedly that the bulk of all print is commissioned too late; that most brochure work is rushed, often involving penalties of cost and mistakes; and that important deadlines are missed with consequent loss of revenue. Marketing managers have only limited influence over creative execution, but they should exercise total control over timing. The scope for marginal improvements in better timing alone, may have a considerable impact on revenue. This is one of the few ways in marketing to achieve marginal revenue gains and marginal budget savings at the same time.

Using agencies to product print

In large organizations the creative aspects of print design are often handled within the organization itself, and through advertising agencies. Print production is invariably handled by specialist firms. Smaller organizations typically obtain quotes from two or three printing firms, many of whom have access to designers, photographers, and copy writers.

Printing agencies will normally undertake whatever aspects of the total print design and production process clients specify, and some may only work to specific instructions. Many printers will, however, be willing to provide professional and technical assistance with all or most of the following decisions:

Creative execution of the client's product concepts
- most effective structure, layout, and content
- design theme, and image presentation, especially of the front cover
- use of colours and 'atmosphere'
- artwork and use of photographs
- captions, copy, and choice of typefaces

Print production and distribution
- choice of paper weight (affects costs and indicates quality)
- packing (bulk and individual copies)
- distribution

To achieve good work from any agency, especially to get the best assistance in aspects of design and layout, it is essential for the client to supply a detailed written brief. The brief should refer to all the stages in producing effective print noted in the previous section, and include extracts of the marketing plan, and details of the print budget. Whilst printers are not always involved in distributing materials, the distribution considerations (see later in this chapter) must be clearly explained, since they will heavily influence the creative execution.

In practice, many smaller organizations fail to produce adequate briefs for print, and worse, they change their minds after the initial design, layout, and artwork has been produced. Such changes are certain to add to cost, cause delays and produce a less than satisfactory result. Where external agencies are used, the process of agreeing print production usually involves detailed liaison at the following points:

- agreement and interpretation of initial design brief, production schedule and costs
- preliminary ('rough') artwork sketches,

headlines, format and content, colours and typeface
- photography (if necessary), finished artwork, copy
- printer's proofs for correction

Distributing printed materials to target audiences

In the enthusiasm for creating an attractive leaflet or brochure, it is easy to focus all attention on the design, photographs, images and copy. In practice, a most important consideration for any printed material is how it will reach its intended target readers. If the answer is direct mail, there is an immediate design concern related to the cost of postage. It is not unusual for unit distribution costs of literature to exceed unit print costs. If the intention is to distribute through travel agencies, it must first be ascertained how many travel agents are willing to handle the item. For every brochure currently displayed in a British travel agent's racks, there are probably at least fifty others seeking space. Again, if travel agents are an agreed distribution source, the size of their standard display spaces will tend to dictate brochure size and page layout. These may appear obvious considerations, but experience suggests that distribution problems often come last and not first in the print decision process.

In practice, the distribution options for getting printed items into prospective buyers' hands, is very wide. Where brochures or leaflets are displayed and given out 'in house' or on site, the distribution process can be fully controlled by the producer on his own premises. Where a larger producer, such as an airline, hotel group or car rental company controls multi-site outlets, the literature distribution process is also easily controlled.

To distribute materials away from owned premises, there are at least ten main options for getting print into the hands of prospective buyers. These are summarized below:

- advertisements carrying coupons to be completed by those requiring information
- cards or other inserts into press and magazine media, which are an alternative form of media space
- direct mail to previous customers, or others, using names and addresses bought for the purpose from a list broker
- direct distribution on a door-to-door basis in targeted residential areas
- direct distribution at exhibitions and shows open to the public (e.g. camping and caravan exhibitions, World Travel Market)
- distribution via retail travel agencies
- distribution via tourist information centres and public libraries
- distribution via relevant third parties. For example, American Express, Access and many clubs and societies will, for a fee, include printed leaflets with their regular mailings to members, or, via hotel reception desks and similar relevant outlets (suitable for attractions, entertainments, car rental)
- distribution via consortia (this is considered a variation of distribution via multi-site operation under one owner)
- distribution via counter sales (if a cover price is charged)

Beyond these common choices, there will usually be other places such as airports, railway station concourses, or bus station waiting rooms, at which relevant opportunities to distribute literature may occur. Any controlled place which attracts a sufficient number of targeted prospects past a central point, may be used for literature distribution purposes. The scope is very wide indeed.

In practice, the choice of distribution outlets will be based mainly on experience of what has worked in previous years for the same or similar products. The scope for experimentation with new forms of distribution is, however, wide. It is strongly recommended as an essential method of learning how to improve the effectiveness of distribution at the margin.

Evaluating the results of print

Generally, it will be impossible to separate with any precision, the effectiveness of expenditure on printed communications from other elements of the marketing campaign, such as advertising and sales promotion. Bookings and sales revenue result from the marketing mix as a whole. Through marketing research, however, it is possible to reach some conclusions and studies may be carried out:

1   to choose between alternative cover designs and content, using evidence of qualitative discussions with target groups of potential customers (see Chapter 11),
2   to measure the results of 'split runs', in which two different brochure formats are distributed to matched samples of target recipients, and bookings compared. Using direct mail to distribute print makes this a relatively easy option for all producers,
3   to measure customer reaction through *ad hoc* telephone or postal surveys of brochure recipients; selected, for example, from coupons included in adverts.

Tour operators and tourist boards typically use all three of these measures, although the costs involved in 1 and 3 are unlikely to be affordable by any organization with a sales turnover much under £1 million (1986 prices).

In every case where printed materials are part of the marketing mix, it is common sense to identify all items with code numbers or letters which identify, as appropriate:

1   through what media the print was requested (if any),
2   by what distribution methods print reached the customer (assuming more than one method).

Provided that consumer responses are analyzed by the codes assigned, the use of printed materials and its distribution methods normally provide many opportunities for experimentation and testing responses.

Alternative brochure formats

Recent technology, including radio cassettes, video films, video-text, and on-line communications between a principal's stock of products and a consumer's home TV set could, in theory, replace the role of the brochure. But the *physical* value of attractively produced print, and its ability to inspire images and dreams, appears to be critical in travel and tourism. This author, at least, does not believe that print is likely to be replaced by other forms of visual communication in the foreseeable future, although alternative forms have a complementary role to play and might be used to reduce existing levels of wastage.

Chapter summary

This chapter identifies the vital part that printed materials play in marketing travel and tourism products, within the context of communications paid for out of marketing budgets. It notes the massive volume of items produced in the industry and the range of functions they perform, distinguishing between promotional and facilitation uses.

The different purposes for which print is used in marketing are discussed and the six main stages involved in producing effective print are explained, with reference to the part to be played by printing and other agencies.

The chapter emphasizes a particular need for organizations to analyze the problems of securing effective distribution for printed materials to targeted readers, and notes the choices available to producers. The objective and task method of costing print requirements (introduced in Chapter 14) is recommended, and makes it easier in practice for managers to measure the results of their expenditure.

In summary, it is interesting to reflect that, at least for commercial producers in the travel and tourism industry, their printed materials frequently embody all aspects of the marketing mix to the extent that they:

- state and physically represent the product in consumer terms

- state the price in full detail as the basis of a legally enforceable contract
- are a principal medium of promotion
- have a distribution process which represents 'place' for customers

Given the nature of service products in general, and travel and tourism products in particular, printed communications are often the most important single element within co-ordinated marketing campaigns.

18

Distribution channels in travel and tourism: Creating access

This chapter considers the last of the four Ps in the marketing mix; distribution or 'access' as it was introduced in Chapter 6. In defining access, it is important to note two points. First, that the nature of distribution systems and processes is one of the principal ways in which the marketing of services differs from the marketing of goods. Second, that distribution processes vary considerably between sectors of the travel and tourism industry. Whereas there are many similarities in the methods of product formulation, pricing, and promotion for all types of travel and tourism products, this is not the case for distribution and the provision of access.

Up to the present time, a widespread myth persists, that because services cannot be inventoried on shelves and in warehouses, distribution systems or 'channels' are less important in service industries than in others. Paradoxically, the inability in travel and tourism to create physical stocks of products, adds to rather than reduces the importance of the distribution process. In marketing practice, creating and manipulating access for consumers is one of the principal ways to manage demand for highly perishable products. Producers are willing to pay relatively high costs for the advantages of extending their points of sale.

This chapter recognizes the importance of location for businesses in travel and tourism, but stresses the need to provide points of sale away from the place of service production, for all but

the smallest of businesses. Definitions of distribution channels and of 'pipelines' are discussed, and key terms defined. The marketing functions performed by different kinds of distribution outlets are noted, and reservation systems discussed. The chapter ends with a discussion of distribution costs.

The importance of location and access

For most small businesses with only one 'production unit', such as proprietor-owned restaurants, guest houses, taxi firms, small tourist attractions or independent travel agents, the choice of location is the most important business decision. A well located small business can often be sure of an adequate flow of customers to its area and past its doors.

In such circumstances, consumers come to the producer, and the concept of distribution channels has little relevance, other than a telephone for reservations. Product formulation, promotion, and above all pricing, remain vital marketing considerations for small businesses, but not distribution. Thus: Location = place of production = point of sale = front office.

For smaller businesses then, the well known industry cliché about the three golden rules for running a successful business – location, location, location – is true. But increasingly, the circumstances of very small single-unit

184

businesses do not provide useful marketing guidelines for the travel and tourism industry, and a wider focus is needed to understand access and distribution.

Location inadequate as sole point of sale

As businesses expand in size and volume of sales, the fundamental attraction of well located sites does not diminish. The more or less continuous search in the 1980s by international hotel companies seeking suitable hotel sites in major European cities, provides some illustration of the power of location. But location of production units ceases to be a *sufficient* source of sales volume for bigger businesses, and supplementary points of sale *away* from the locations of service production and consumption, are required. The factors which focus attention on supplementary points of sale are:

1 growing size of business (production capacity),
2 increasing number of units within a group or chain (under one ownership, or linked in marketing co-operatives),
3 greater distances which customers travel to reach a unit – especially where international travel is involved,
4 the greater importance of drawing in first time rather than repeat visitors, in order to grow,
5 growing competition for shares of markets, for which there is excess capacity in a location.
6 the need to reduce dependence on day-to-day sales, by selling capacity ahead of production, through a reservation system.

These six factors, separately or combined, tend to force the obvious marketing response, which is to generate more demand. One logical route to this is by creating additional points of sale or, in other words, moving the purchase decision away from the location of production, towards other places, which prospective customers find more convenient. These additional points of sale make up what is known collectively as a 'distribution system'. As this chapter will indicate, there are other good marketing reasons for developing distribution or access systems, but the overriding reason is to generate sales revenue additional to that which may be sustained solely by a good location. Whilst, to some extent, additional expenditure on advertising or other communications are alternatives to creating more points of sale, in practice there is usually a balance to be achieved between promotion and place. A massive demand generated by advertising could be lost, for example, if convenient points of access were not available to turn demand into sales. Sales promotion and merchandising, which take place at points of sale, are of course vital activities in travel and tourism marketing, and the possibilities and requirements of such promotion, both reflect and influence the choice of distribution systems.

Defining distribution or access systems

'The concept of marketing channels is not limited to the distribution of physical goods. Producers of services . . . also face the problem of making their output *available* and *accessible* to target populations' (Kotler: 1984: p. 545). Kotler adopts Bucklin's 1966 definition of distribution channels as comprising . . . 'a set of institutions which performs all of the activities (functions) utilized to move a product and its title from production to consumption'. Whilst Bucklin's definition is clearly based on physical goods, which move from a place of production, it nevertheless contains key elements for an adequate definition for services. Drawing on these ideas the following definition is proposed for distribution in travel and tourism:

A distribution channel is any organized and serviced system, created or utilized to provide convenient points of sale and/or access to consumers, away from the location of production and consumption, and paid for out of marketing budgets.

The essence of this definition is that channels are not in any way left to chance, but carefully planned by producers and serviced regularly by them with sales visits, literature, computer links, and in other ways. Each channel, once organized and serviced at a cost to be paid out of marketing budgets, becomes in effect a 'pipeline'. Through this pipeline flows a targeted volume of sales over a marketing campaign period. This definition is deliberately wider than that proposed by either Bucklin, or a decade later by Donelly, in a seminal article on channels of distribution for services, which has been much quoted. His definition states:

'Any extra corporate entity between the producer of a service and prospective users that is utilized to make the service available and/or more convenient is a marketing intermediary for that purpose (1976: p. 57).'

Experience with travel and tourism services suggests that pipelines should not be restricted to 'extra-corporate entities', and that several of the vital pipelines do not use intermediaries. This chapter suggests, therefore, that a more fertile approach is to define the functions served by distribution systems, and then use functional criteria to identify the pipelines.

All the definitions noted above exclude the activities of sales representatives, who negotiate contracts with corporate clients to deliver a specified number of products, over a specified period of time, at a specified price. The essence of any pipeline is that it is set up in advance, to facilitate targeted sales volume, but the actual flow of sales achieved over the period of a campaign, cannot be known in advance. The rate of flow may be influenced by marketing activities in the pipeline, or external to it, such as advertising.

Key words in services distribution

Because of the special nature of distribution in travel and tourism, many people experience confusion over the way in which terms are used. Rathmell suggested that: 'To facilitate integration with conventional thought, location and distribution, and channel and delivery are used interchangeably' (1974: p. 104). If readers attempt to use these terms interchangeably, confusion is certain. The following terms are defined, therefore, to limit semantic difficulties; they draw on the views of the principal American and British contributors to the subject and appear to represent common ground:

Distribution process	the process of creating access for the consumer in one or more places convenient for him, but away from the place and time of delivery of products being bought.
Location	the geographical location of a site or sites, at which service products are delivered to customers on the premises.
Delivery	the physical process of producing or performing the service product simultaneously with consumption.
Distribution channel or pipeline	any organized and serviced system, created or utilized to provide convenient points of sale and/or access to consumers, away from the location of delivery.
Intermediary	any third party or organization between producer and consumer, which facilitates purchases,

the transfer of title to the buyer, and sales revenue to the producer.

Principals, customers and intermediaries

In the terms used to discuss distribution in travel and tourism, a 'principal' is any producer who has products to sell. Principals have a basic choice whether to sell direct to the customer or to achieve sales through one or more third parties, known as intermediaries. Drawing on the definitions used by Kotler (1984: p. 542) the five main choices open to any principal are presented in Figure 18.1.

From the examples provided, it will be clear that distribution channels vary according to size and types of organization, and that larger principals use several forms of distribution. Thus, a car rental business may establish desks at airports to service travellers by air; provide direct pipelines to frequent users; offer commissions on sales by travel agents, and provide allocations of cars to tour operators who include car rental in their holiday packages. A guest house or a small tourist attraction typically deals only directly with customers, many of whom will purchase at the location of the business. Holiday caravan parks may offer allocations to an operator such as Hoseasons, which incorporates the products of many parks into one brochure distributed direct and to travel agents.

Zero level channel	Principal ──────────────→ Customer (on producer's premises). Typical of attractions, cafes, museums, guest houses, taxis.	Principal is retailer at own location.
Zero level channel	Principal ──────────────→ Customer (at home). All forms of direct response marketing practised by hotels, some tour operators.	Principal is retailer via reservation system.
Zero level channel	Principal ───────────→Owned retail → Customer (on producer's outlets/ premises). multiple units. Typical of car rental companies, railways, airlines (in part), and hotels with multiple units acting as referral system.	Principal owns the distribution system.
One level channel	Principal ───────────→Independent → Customer (on retailer's retail premises). outlets. Typical of many tour operators, holiday centres, airlines (in part), hotels.	Principal pays commission to retailers.
Two level channel	Principal → Tour operator/ ───────→Independent → Customer (on retailer's Wholesaler retail premises). outlets. Typical of resort hotels, some camping and caravan sites, charter airlines.	Principal negotiates bulk sale or allocation of production to another principal.

Figure 18.1 *Distribution channels in travel and tourism marketing*
Adapted from Kotler: 1984: p. 542

Two main roles of a distribution system

As previously indicated, the main function of a distribution system is to extend the number of points of sale or access, away from the location at which services are performed or delivered. In this sense at least, the function of distribution is the same for tourism products as it is for physical goods.

An important secondary function of services distribution is to facilitate the purchase of products in advance of their production. 'Advance' could be anything from two to three hours (for transportation products), up to two or three years or even longer (for major conventions or exhibition venues). It is a basic law of services production that the greater the volatility of daily demand, the greater the imperative to sell forward if possible. Obviously, for an airline running shuttle routes for business commuters, daily and hourly demand is closely predictable to within a very few percentage points. For a resort hotel, contemplating July's profits in January, the daily or weekly demand is open to very wide fluctuation. The logical marketing response is to reduce risks by selling summer holidays throughout, say January to April, so as to achieve 100 per cent room occupancy, weeks if possible, before the July tourists arrive.

Advertising, print, and sales promotion are, of course, geared to this pattern of advance sales, but will be of little value unless pipelines are organized and an efficient reservation or advance booking system is continuously in operation to receive the flow of sales.

Advance purchase through reservations

To modern students brought up in the computer age, it must seem strange that well into the 1970s, most travel reservation systems were manual, even in the USA. Teams of clerks using tele-phones toiled like ants around massive peg-boards, blackboards, or charts which filled the whole wall space of large offices. Such charts physically represented production capacity for several months ahead. The systems were slow, inflexible, liable to failure through human error, and very costly in labour employed. By the early 1980s most manual systems had disappeared from large and medium-sized producers, to be replaced by on-line, electronic information systems, operating on each principal's main computer, through as many peripheral terminals as the flow of business could justify. Such systems handle not only reservations, but also searches for alternative products. The systems may be linked with automatic printers which produce travel documents, confirmations, and invoices, and can also be used to generate continuous marketing research data. Through the use of satellites, modern systems operate internationally and in the future, when different main computers can merge their data bases and communicate better with each other, the implications for improved efficiency in travel and tourism distribution systems are expected to be very significant.

Paradoxically, the inability to transfer and store products physically, which was once thought to be such a disadvantage in travel and tourism marketing, has now become a powerful asset in that product capacity can be accessed across continents and across months or years, at the touch of a button. Electronic information technology conveys enormous flexibility to producers, the full scope of which has yet to be fully developed.

An important split between reserved and non-reserved services

Before explaining the specific functions of a distribution system, an important distinction between reserved and non-reserved products in travel and tourism must be noted. Distribution pipelines may be a relevant consideration with or without reservations, but their full functions are best understood in the context of products capable of reservations or advance booking. Burkart noted that products in travel and tourism split between those, for which a large excess of supply over demand typically exists at most times, and others, for which an excess of demand over supply typically exists for much of the time (Burkart: 1976: p. 240). In the first category are museums, other managed attractions, seats in most trains, touring camp sites, much of car rental, pubs, popular catering, country parks, and so on. Where reservations are not made, the point of sale typically is the front desk at the producer's location. Pipelines may still be needed to secure particular customer segments and as points of information and display (such as tourism information centres). In the second category are most hotels, most airlines, inclusive tours, car ferries, theatres, and shows. In those cases, advance bookings are normal and the point of sale typically is a distribution outlet away from the producer's location.

Ten functions of a full service distribution system

Figure 18.2 notes ten functions typically carried out by distribution outlets offering the full range of services to tourist industry producers. Other than the lack of physical stocks to move about and maintain, these functions are identical to those carried out by the distributors of physical goods, with only one other important exception. Travel and tourism distributors do not purchase products in bulk and do not share with principals, therefore, in the financial risks of production. By contrast, distributors of physical goods typically purchase their stocks and take responsibility for selling them to customers and risk losing money on unsold stocks. This process of sharing risk has led to buying in bulk and has

been part of the impetus to growth of large, multi-site retail chains for physical goods in the last three decades, which has given them great power over manufacturers. It has also led to the larger retail outlets, such as supermarkets, using their 'own labels' to sell products which they have bought in bulk at factory prices. Some distributors have integrated their operations backwards by buying producer organizations to service their needs.

In travel and tourism, the responsibility for generating and managing demand has rested mainly with the principals. It is they who have controlled product design in the industry, borne the bulk of the marketing costs, fixed prices, and generally been responsible for the volume of sales which their products achieved. At the time of writing, the rapid growth of large multiple retail chains of travel agents has caused significant changes to travel distribution in Britain over the last five years. Some of the large multiples are now able to secure more commission from principals, and some are beginning to produce their 'own label' products by taking allocations of capacity, as tour operators do, from producers.

Full service distributors in travel include retail travel agents, airport, rail, or coach terminal booking offices, hotel reservation companies, and tourist information offices (TICs) if they include booking facilities. All of them provide the range of functions noted in Figure 18.2.

Where large producers, such as hotels and airlines, have their own multiple units, each unit acts as a retailer for the others and also fulfils all ten distribution functions.

Six functions of limited service distribution systems

As discussed in Chapter 17, the product substitution role of print in travel and tourism means that access, if not always points of sale, can be

1	Provide points-of-sale and convenient customer access, either for immediate purchase or for booking in advance.
2	Distribute product information such as brochures and leaflets.
3	Provide display and merchandising opportunities.
4	Provide advice and purchase assistance (e.g. itinerary planning).
5	Arrange transfer of title to a product through ticketing and travel documentation.
6	Receive and transmit sales revenue to principals.
7	May provide ancillary services (e.g. insurance, advice on innoculations, passport assistance).
8	May serve as a source of marketing intelligence for principals.
9	May supplement principal's promotional activities.
10	Receive and assist with complaints from customers.

Figure 18.2   *Ten functions provided by full service distribution outlets*

created wherever sufficient numbers of prospective customers gather.

Limited services are those listed in Figure 18.3. Although limited, these services are nevertheless of great value to many smaller producers for whom they provide opportunities to merchandise their products, achieve display, and distribute their sales literature (including sales promotion offers) to prospective customers, away from their location of production.

Limited service distributors in travel and tourism include most TICs, hotel porter's desks, reception areas of holiday centres and holiday parks, and reception areas of tourist attractions. Many of these limited service outlets are to be found in tourist destinations.

There is wide scope for extending limited service distribution outlets, using petrol stations, roadside restaurants, newsagents' shops, and post offices, all of which offer potentially valuable ways to reach prospective customers.

For small producers, who are most unlikely ever to achieve display in retail travel agents, the flexibility of these limited service outlets is attractive.

The functions performed by these limited channels in distributing information, and promotional print, to some extent overlap with the functions performed by advertising media. All of the channels in this section are, however, permanent locations, to be serviced by producers and maintained in much the same way as full service distribution outlets.

Other forms of travel and tourism distribution

Reflecting the flexibility conveyed by the non-physical nature of travel and tourism products, there is a third group of pipelines, which are increasingly used by airlines, hotels, car rentals, restaurants and some attractions. The channels

1	Provide customer advice and assistance.
2	May provide supporting services (e.g. bed reservation schemes).
3	May receive and assist in following up customer complaints.
4	Distribute product information, such as brochures, leaflets, and sales promotion offers.
5	Provide space for display and other merchandising activities.
6	May act as a source of marketing intelligence for producers.

Figure 18.3   *Six functions provided by limited service access points*

noted below are not normally referred to as pipelines, yet they can be used to fulfil all the distribution functions noted in Figure 18.2. They also meet the essential criteria included in the definitions noted earlier in this chapter. It should be noted also that the pipelines below are strongly associated with sales promotion, and some forms of direct response marketing. This association with other marketing functions is significant and requires careful co-ordination in planning marketing campaigns. Each of the pipelines below is relevant to a specific user or segment group and is not accessible to customers as a whole. Provided that any such system is structured in advance to generate a targeted, but unknown volume of business over a campaign period, it meets the pipeline criteria previously noted. In an era of increasing market segmentation, these types of pipeline are likely to be increasingly used:

- VIP/Privileged User cards and membership clubs for frequent customers (provided by hotels, airlines and some visitor attractions).
- Secretaries' Clubs (maintained by some hotels and airlines).
- Special links with other bodies such as schools, clubs, societies; (maintained by attractions and hotels).
- Allocations of product capacity to credit card companies acting, for this purpose, as tour operators.

Fixed and variable costs of distribution

Some of the costs of maintaining and supporting distribution systems or pipelines, are fixed for the duration of any marketing campaign in the sense that outlets must be organized, and serviced in advance of any business which is expected to flow. Fixed costs in this sense include:

1. The costs of installing reservation systems, computers and programmes, and staff capable of dealing with enquiries and bookings through each pipeline.
2. The costs of brochure production, distribution and maintaining supplies to the points of sale.
3. Costs of sales promotion incentives aimed at motivating retailers and other points of sale.
4. The costs of support visits to intermediaries, including any costs of merchandising efforts and display materials, which may be used at points of sale.
5. The costs of maintaining and motivating a sales force (if any) to negotiate agreements with intermediaries, in order to secure literature distribution and display.
6. Costs of any *educationals* and workshops organized in support of distributor systems, and staff training.

The variable costs are measured in commission, which is typically paid only when sales are achieved, and any phone calls connected with bookings or enquiries and paid for by principals.

Calculating the costs of distribution channels

Because no physical transfer of goods is involved, it is the experience of most producers in travel and tourism that distribution or access channels are relatively flexible and may be increased at relatively low cost, according to opportunities available. At least in theory, the only limit to creating additional channels is the marginal point at which unit costs of access exceed unit profits. Up to that limit, more profit is achieved by creating more access.

In practice, producers tend to balance and monitor the costs of distribution as the following example shows. Assume a small hotel group, with 3 hotels and 500 double occupancy rooms, for which it targets 25 per cent sleeper nights to be distributed over twelve months through three channels *other* than referral between units, and direct bookings arising from locations and repeat customers. For the sake of simplicity it is assumed that all bookings have the same unit value (e.g. £25 per person night):

- 500 rooms × 2 persons × 365 nights × 25% distribution via channels = 91,250 sleeper nights.
- Channel A costs £25,000 to service and generates 50,000 sleeper nights
  average unit cost of distribution per night = £0.50p.
- Channel B costs £10,000 to service and generates 25,000 sleeper nights
  average unit cost of distribution per night = £0.40p.
- Channel C costs £19,500 to service and generates 16,250 sleeper nights
  average unit cost of distribution per night = £1.20.

'Cost to Service' is the calculated cost of staff, and equipment overheads, which have to be spent to sustain a channel at the targeted level of business turnover, plus brochure costs and expenditure on incentives required to secure distributor support.

It does not include the cost of commission on sales (say 10 per cent) which is assumed to be standard for all three channels. If commission levels were variable in practice, it would be sensible to include them in the cost to service since it would alter the average unit cost of distribution.

Of course, in practice the value of bookings may be greater in one channel, or more useful in creating low season bookings in another, but these complications should not obscure the basic need to assess and compare the unit costs of providing customer access in each pipeline. Such calculations are inputs to decisions about which existing channels to develop, and valuable in assessing the potential value of any new channels which might be opened up.

Provided that an hotel group, or other principal is willing to apportion the costs of servicing and commission for each channel, the costs of creating pipelines for customer access can be budgeted with precision using the objective and task methods described in Chapter 14.

Chapter summary

This chapter explains why distribution or access systems are important considerations in the marketing of travel and tourism products, excepting only very small businesses where location remains all important. Within the context that distribution or access is a generic difference in the marketing of goods and services, the key differences between location, points of sale, and place of delivery, are identified and discussed. The definition of principals and intermediaries in the distribution process makes clear the potential flexibility of pipelines in travel and tourism, reinforced in recent years by the growing use of advanced information technology, especially for products involving advanced bookings. Many principals use several different distribution channels simultaneously to create additional points of sale for their products, and the marketing tasks associated with different types of channel are outlined, distinguishing between full service and limited service distribution.

Whilst the distribution of travel products is flexible and multiple pipelines are commonly used, there are significant costs in providing access to customers and a need to balance the costs of the different channels used. Throughout the chapter, the linkages between providing access, and the other elements of the marketing mix are noted. Access typically acts in a supportive role by providing convenient points of sale to customers already motivated through advertising and PR, but it is also the focus for many forms of sales promotion, especially those designed to stimulate last minute purchases.

Overall, flexibility in the distribution of travel and tourism products, and the absence of physical stocks are presented as powerful potential marketing assets, and not as the disadvantage suggested in some texts.

Further reading

Baker, M. J., *Marketing: An Introductory Text*, Macmillan, 1985, Chapters 10 and 15.

Kotler, P., *Marketing: Analysis, Planning and Control*, Prentice-Hall, 1984, Chapter 17.

For those interested in the particular characteristics of British travel retailing, see Holloway, *The Business of Tourism*, Chapter 18.

19

Direct response marketing in travel and tourism versus retail distribution

As Americans express it, the 'bottom line' of all marketing is achieving sales volume and revenue targets. Within the integrating framework of the marketing mix, Chapter 15 to 18 review the individual functions of advertising and PR, sales promotion, printed materials, and distribution, all of them key techniques in the implementation of marketing campaigns in travel and tourism, all of them obviously sales related.

This chapter discusses the strategic choice to be made between planning the marketing mix to generate sales on a *direct* response basis, in which the producer promotes to and deals directly with the customer, or an *indirect response* basis. Indirect means that sales are achieved through third party distribution channels created and maintained for that purpose, as described in Chapter 18. In practice the choice is seldom clear-cut and a combination of both strategies for achieving sales response is common in the travel and tourism industry.

Because of the choice and flexibility of distribution channels in service products generally, the strategic choice between direct or indirect response marketing has always been much more important for selling travel and tourism products than for selling most manufactured products based on physical goods. New computerized data base technology, available only in very recent years for identifying individual customers by their addresses, profiles and purchasing behaviour, is altering the strategic choices facing many operators at the end of the 1980s. On current evidence, this new technology looks likely to shift the emphasis in marketing toward direct response strategies for all types of product, whether physical goods or services.

This chapter begins by identifying the nature of travel and tourism sales from the customer's standpoint and placing sales in their practical context of enquiries, reservations, and bookings. This is followed by key definitions, and a review of the strategic options for generating sales open to operators, using a diagram representing the marketing flows in the producer, distributor, customer triangle (Figure 19.1). The same diagram provides a framework for reviewing the tactical options in the marketing mix, once the nature of the product portfolio and prices have been decided. The chapter proceeds to review the methods available to direct response marketers and summarizes the potential benefits achievable by those who use such methods in conjunction with new forms of computerized data bases. The chapter concludes with a discussion of the balance to be achieved in travel and tourism between direct and indirect marketing response methods.

The nature of sales in travel and tourism

At its simplest, a sale is made when a customer parts with money in exchange for a promise to deliver a product. That is the bottom line. In practice there is a complex decision process at work between a customer's initial awareness and review of what is available, consideration of the options which best meet his or her needs, and the final selection and purchase. The decision process, introduced in Chapter 5, is especially complex in much of travel and tourism because of the relatively high cost of many products and the relatively high level of customers' psychological involvement with the product. Holidays are good examples of what are described in marketing texts as 'shopping' or 'speciality products' in the purchase of which most buyers are willing to invest considerable time and effort. (For a discussion of this issue, see Middleton: 1983.)

Because of the nature of the product, buyers will typically make enquiries of several producers, and evaluate the choices according to their perceptions of what is offered, their interests and needs, and their ability to pay. The way in which travel brochures are laid out is an obvious illustration of producers' response to this purchasing behaviour. Accordingly, much of the marketing is aimed first at generating enquiries, and secondly at motivating and converting interest into sales through the provision of packages of printed promotional materials.

It is axiomatic in commercial marketing that there is no sale without customer interest, and no interest without awareness. All producers are, therefore, interested in creating greater awareness of their products and converting it into sales. Their basic choice in creating awareness is to approach customers directly, or to do so indirectly through distribution channels, or some combination of the two.

Defining marketing methods of achieving sales

This section sets out the key definitions relevant to this chapter. It deserves careful reading because the loose usage in practice of terms such as 'sales', 'selling', 'personal selling', 'direct selling', 'direct marketing', 'direct response marketing', and 'data base marketing', is the source of great confusion among students of marketing. To some extent, this confusion reflects changes which are occurring in the travel and tourism industry, and it is worth the effort to use the main terms with some precision. Three important clarifications can be made at the outset:

1   distinguishing reservations or bookings from in-house sales,
2   distinguishing bookings by the general public from bulk or group sales,
3   distinguishing marketing methods from those which are sales orientated.

The first clarification is to stress that this chapter is concerned only with product sales which are bookings or reservations made by the general public in the places where they live or work. It is *not* concerned with any aspects of in-house or on-site selling, which were described in Chapter 16. The focus on reservations means that the chapter is more relevant to all forms of accommodation suppliers, transport operators, and tour operators than to attractions, although the principles are applicable to all sectors.

The second clarification is to distinguish between individual sales to the general public, and sales which are group bookings or bulk purchases negotiated between a sales force or a head office staff, and buyers who represent a group. This chapter is about the sales methods used to generate bookings from the general public and is not concerned with the techniques involved in using a sales force. The use of a sales team to generate group bookings is, of course, very important in the travel and tourism industry, especially for hotels (see for example Taylor: 1979). The techniques used to achieve such sales are widely known as personal selling because they typically involve a form of face-to-face negotiation between buyer and seller which may take hours, or weeks in the case of a large contract such as a major conference. Important as personal selling skills and managing a sales force are, however, the techniques involved have been practised and developed over many years and they are fully covered in general marketing literature. New techniques for generating sales directly from the general public in travel and tourism are not well covered and for this reason they are the focus of this chapter.

The third clarification is to draw a distinction between traditional selling methods aimed at the general public, which have also been practised for decades, and modern sales techniques integrated within a marketing system. In the former case, selling is the dominant element in achieving revenue targets, typically within a sales orientated business philosophy of selling the products that are designed by production and accounting led organizations. In the latter case, selling is no more than one element in an integrated marketing mix employed by organizations which put knowledge of customers needs at the centre of their business philosophy. Hotels and holiday centres, for example, have for many years used cut-out coupons with their advertising in order to generate enquiries. The regular mailing of brochures and leaflets directly to previous customers to encourage repeat purchases, is another technique of considerable vintage. While modern direct response marketing employs many of the traditional techniques, fundamental differences lie in the way they are used, especially the data-based learning process about customers which is involved, and the continuous adaptation of the product around identified needs.

Direct sell or direct response marketing?

It follows from the three clarifications noted above that the focus of this chapter is on direct sales links between producers and the general public, which always involve two-way direct communication links. In its traditional form it was usually known under the generic title of direct selling, defined as 'selling without the use of a retail outlet, distributor, broker or wholesaler or any other form of middleman' (Hart & Stapleton: 1977: p. 52). In the 1960s and 1970s, direct selling techniques were typically practised by producers using direct mail colour catalogues of consumer goods, often targeted at housewives. Names and addresses of prospective buyers were obtained by advertising, which incorporated coupons to complete or telephone numbers to ring, and were added to lists of previous customers. This form of selling is much more significant in the USA than in Britain, although it has increased its share of total consumer sales in both countries over recent years.

The shift from direct selling to direct response marketing in travel and tourism, which is taking place in the 1980s, reflects two important changes in the overall business environment:

1 The growing need to know more about customers' profiles and needs, in line with any form of modern marketing.
2 The growing ability to research, store, retrieve, and analyze data on hundreds of thousands of individuals, made possible at relatively low cost by new forms of computerized data base technology.

In Britain, the ACORN system, and its derivatives available since the early 1980s, have revolutionized the ability of producers to obtain and exploit their detailed knowledge of customer segments. As this chapter explains, this new technology opens routes to more cost effective generation of enquiries, and better design of materials sent to convert enquiries into bookings, which appear especially well suited to the requirements of producers in travel and tourism.

The essence of a marketing approach to achieving sales by direct response is expressed succinctly by Gater; he uses the term 'data base marketing', which he defines as 'the building of a continuous relationship' between principal and customer. That means not always selling when a communication is made and not always demanding a response . . . it means . . . obtaining loyalty through customer service and care, by building a relationship centred around the customer rather than the product (Gater: 1986: p. 41).

What distinguishes the marketing approach from traditional direct selling is a detailed and evolving knowledge of the customer, and of the effectiveness of the response packages used to convert awareness into sales. As a highly cost effective tool for market research, segmentation, and market experimentation of all types, the new direct response methods offer possibilities for improving marketing efficiency, which are only just being realized at the end of the 1980s. In Britain, expenditure on this form of marketing is growing faster than on the other ways of communicating with customers.

Key definitions

Four important, frequently used terms are defined below, and recommended to readers to avoid communication problems based solely on semantics. In a developing topic such as this, readers will certainly encounter other usage of terms and will have to make their own interpretations of what is meant. The following explanations should be useful:

Personal selling (Group sales)	Achieving group or bulk sales through direct negotiation, normally face to face with group buyers. Telephone selling to the general public, or tele-marketing as it is known in the USA, is *not* included in this definition. Door to door sales (not common in travel and tourism) are also excluded from this definition of personal selling focused on group buyers.
Direct selling	Any form of selling to the general public which involves direct communication between producer and customers. Direct mail, and telephone selling are included in this definition. Direct selling is characteristic of sales orientated businesses.
Direct response marketing	Two-way communications, linking producers and their targeted individual customers in continuing contact. The producer's aim is to achieve more cost effective product awareness and promotion, and better conversion of awareness into first-time sales and repeat bookings. The producer's sales effort is integrated within a promotional mix developed through the use of an interactive data base. By definition, data-based marketing involves a continuous learning and development process focused around target markets and their responses to the producer's marketing initiatives. The techniques are only found in marketing orientated organizations.
Response fulfilment package	Marketing jargon for the promotional package of envelope, letters, leaflets, brochures and any other printed

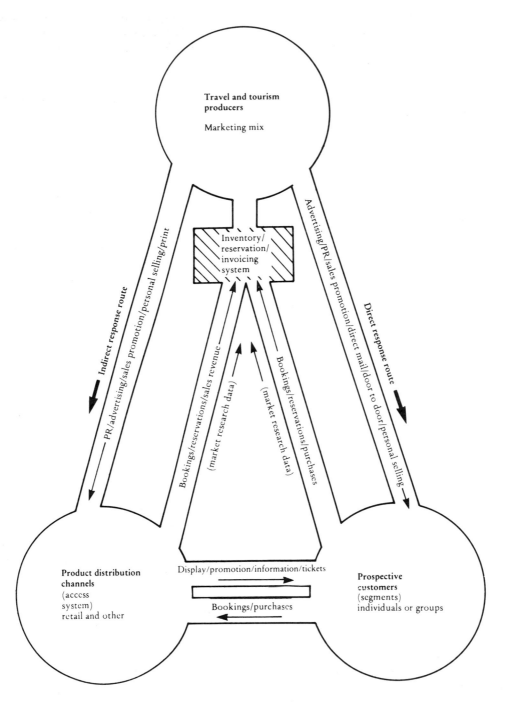

Figure 19.1 *The producer, distributor, customer, triangle*

materials, such as prize draw announcements, which are sent out in response to enquiries generated by direct marketing methods.

The producer: distributor: customer triangle

Figure 19.1 is used to represent the main flows, which take place in any marketing operation between producers, or 'principals' as they are often termed, distributors, and customers. The diagram is valid for the marketing operations of all types of travel and tourism principals, whether they are involved for example in accommodation, transport, attractions, or tour operation.

The shape of the triangle reveals the two basic options:

- two-way direct response between producer and prospective customer, and
- indirect response involving distribution channels as third parties.

Within the triangle, there are two types of flow:

1 outwards from the producer covering all the forms of promotion and sales support paid for out of marketing budgets, whether these are aimed at the travel trade, the final customer, or both. Also outwards is the flow of tickets, information, and other documentation which is provided to customers who have books and/or paid.
2 inwards to the producer are flows measured in the volume of enquiries, reservations, bookings, and sales revenue.

Because of the nature of travel and tourism operations, it will be appreciated that all inward flows of reservations and revenue are typically managed within an inventory or reservation system. Such systems are increasingly computerized for all medium-sized and large organizations, and are typically set up to handle the provision of options if the customer's first choice is not available, as well as confirmations, ticketing, and invoicing.

The inward flows in the diagram, which convey information about customers, may also be incorporated into a data base for recording and processing vital data for market research purposes, such as address and purchasing behaviour (party size, date of booking, repeat bookings and so on). Depending on the recording system operated, the data base may be used to identify responses from different forms of promotional techniques, such as bookings from advertising in different media. Such data are by-products of modern service product reservation systems and, as pointed out in a previous chapter, they cost very little to collect once the inventory/data base system has been set up to record and analyze the flows or routine information.

In Figure 19.1, *prospective customers* may be one or more segments of the general public, or targeted individual buyers such as corporate clients who purchase on behalf of groups or numbers of individuals. The pattern of flows remains the same. The *product distribution* channels are travel retailers or other pipelines, which offer display space for products and pass title on behalf of principals. The diagram is still relevant as an explanation if the distributor performs only part of the function, such as a tourist information centre acting as a display and distribution point for an attraction's leaflets, but not selling tickets (see Chapter 18).

To market direct or via a distribution system?

The triangular concept of flows makes it easier to understand a most important strategic marketing choice which has to be made by producers; whether, and to what extent, they should distribute and promote their products directly to the customer, or aim to achieve sales through third party channels of distribution. With few exceptions, there is rarely a simple answer to this question, and the answer may vary for different products within the same principal's portfolio at different times. Thus, it may be advantageous for an hotelier to market most of his business travel on a direct response basis to corporate clients, but to market the bulk of his weekend packages through retail travel agents.

At any point in time, according to the ever shifting circumstances imposed by external and internal constraints, a principal has to take a judgement on the marginal revenue and the marginal costs implied by the balance between direct response sales and indirect sales through distribution channels. The decision is mainly a financial one, reflecting the fact that any use of retailers will normally cost a minimum of 10 per cent of the sales revenue generated, usually deducted at source. Commission may be as high as 15 per cent, and there are additional costs of servicing retailers with brochures, promoting to them, and possibly employing a sales force to maintain product awareness and levels of display. On the other hand, commission is a variable cost, which is not paid until sales are made and the principal's cash flow is not affected ahead of the sale.

By contrast, there is every prospect in many cases of achieving the bulk of advance sales at a lower average cost per unit sold than 10 per cent, by using direct response methods. But to do this, the operator has to invest large sums ahead of bookings in direct response techniques (see Figure 19.2). Cash flow is obviously affected and there is no guarantee that the investment will succeed. If the initial investment does not produce all the required sales, further investment will be needed and, as the date of production approaches, direct response costs rise steeply;

the techniques are not cost efficient in generating vital last-minute sales.

Although the direct/indirect choice is mainly one of cost and revenue equations there are other implications, such as being seen to be supportive or not of the retail system. Where retail distribution chains command significant shares of product sales, it may not be possible for a principal to exercise his direct response options without risking the good will of distributors he may need for other parts of his business. Many caravan park operators, for example, would be glad to use travel agents to sell their spare capacity in April, May, and October, whilst marketing the easier and more profitable peak season weeks direct. But this is not a practical option as the majority of retailers would refuse to handle the off peak weeks unless they had a main season allocation, which is easier to sell and generates more revenue and commission through higher prices.

For small businesses there may be no alternative to direct response marketing, because the amount of revenue they can generate is too small to interest retailers and too costly to handle. Their telephone response systems are often too slow and inefficient and their brochures would take up too much valuable display space. Smaller firms, which group together to form co-operatives with a single joint brochure and one reservation system and telephone number, are a different proposition. Achieving exposure in retail distribution systems through collective representation is, in practice, one of the main reasons why small businesses join co-operative marketing groups, and it helps to explain the expansion of such groups in recent years.

Direct response marketing methods

Figure 19.2 shows the range of direct response marketing methods available to producers aiming at target segments of prospective customers. The techniques were introduced as

Direct mail	• to previous customers • to purchased lists of targeted prospects • via lists owned by third parties • in response to enquiries • via joint mailing with relevant partners
Telephone/tele-marketing	• to targeted customer lists • in response to enquiries
Door-to-door distribution	• to targeted blocks of residential streets/roads
Travel related exhibitions	• to enquirers at stands; e.g. boat shows, travel exhibitions, and caravan and camping shows
Media advertising	• with coupons • with response telephone numbers, or 0800 lines
Interactive TV	• on-line TV terminals in customers' homes, used to make bookings direct

Figure 19.2   *Direct response marketing methods to reach individual consumers*

elements in the marketing campaign planning process covered in Chapter 14 and need only brief additional comments noted below. Any direct response marketing campaign is likely to involve a combination of these methods rather than any individual one.

In terms of direct mail, the use which many hoteliers and airlines make, for example, of American Express or Access member lists, illustrates the value of third party address lists. Such lists can be accessed at a standard cost per thousand names and, although the names are not released to producers, their leaflets are distributed with routine mailings to members. An example of a joint mailing with a partner would be a country hotel group joining with, say, a manufacturer of conservatories, so that two non competing leaflets, appealing to the same group of prospective customers, could share the cost of postage.

Telephone marketing is known as tele-marketing in the USA. As indicated in Figure 19.2, it may be reactive to enquiries, or proactive to target customers. Its use for selling to the general public has undergone important changes in the last five years and it may play a

much larger role in travel and tourism markets in the future.

Door to door distribution costs of printed materials are typically much cheaper per household than postal costs, but its value depends on the ability to target appropriate neighbourhoods, for example using the ACORN analysis.

Media advertising covers the whole spectrum of choice noted in Chapter 15. Interactive TV for use by the general public in their own homes is in its infancy in the 1980s and it is impossible to predict the rate of growth in ownership of adapted TV sets and their use in travel marketing. The technology exists and the possibilities are clear. Producers will watch the developments with interest, and the larger ones are likely to experiment to see if the use of interactive TV can gain a share of direct response business. On a small scale in the 1980s, some interactive terminals are already in use in tourist information centres to display information, such as available capacity in a range of hotels. Some of these are already capable of two-way communication between customer and principal.

The potential benefits of direct response marketing

Given the high costs of personal selling in the traditional sense, and the inevitable limitations as well as high cost of commissions involved in achieving access through third party distribution channels, the scope for utilizing modern direct response marketing techniques should be most carefully considered by all producers in travel and tourism.

The benefits discussed below are *potential* in the sense that they cannot be achieved without considerable effort in marketing planning. Use of the available data base for accurate segmentation and area targeting, followed by detailed attention to product presentation in advertising and print, are all involved in carrying out effective direct response campaigns. Detailed prior programming of the data base to receive, monitor, and analyse customer response, is essential to achieve the benefits. But, if the systematic marketing procedures set out in this book are followed, the following benefits are achievable by any size of business willing to invest in a personal computer:

1 Detailed knowledge of the customer (using the data base for research), not only name and address, but neighbourhood type (ACORN), and purchasing behaviour.

  Both telephone and coupon response mechanisms provide limited but valuable opportunities for market research questions, such as identifying new or previous customers, frequent users, and how they heard of the product.

2 Ability to assess the cost and effectiveness of generating enquiries, including response by type of media, type of advertisement, type of leaflet, or timing of advertisements. Such responses can be analysed by market segments, market areas, and product variations offered. Cost per enquiry can be monitored with precision and the cost per booking can be quantified, if the data base is programmed to match bookings with enquiries.

3 Ability to measure the effectiveness of alternative response packages sent out to enquirers in terms of conversion enquiries into sales.

4 A framework for marketing developments, whereby relatively small scale experiments with new or adapted products, new segments, or alternative forms of media, or response packages, can be systematically tested and evaluated at low cost.

These four groups of marketing benefits, stemming from the two-way communication process, are profound in their implications for more cost effective marketing. They are especially useful to smaller businesses in travel and tourism, which are too small to engage in large scale advertising, and too small to achieve cost effective access through retail distribution channels. Once again it is worth stressing that these benefits derive from the use of new information technology, not previously available to marketing managers. The new technology apears very likely to shift the balance of advantage in marketing towards those smaller businesses willing to make the modest effort of time and cost involved. Many are already involved in the new technology; others will be forced to follow as a response to the new competition.

The cost of harnessing the potential power of computers for small businesses has dropped significantly over recent years. Gater notes, 'While a computer cost the equivalent of 20 people in 1970, by 1990 one person will cost the same as 20 computers of the same size (Gater: 1986: p. 41). Whilst that view may be exaggerated, not to purchase the marketing capabilities of a personal computer at, say, one-fifth of the annual cost of a competent secretary, must be short-sighted for any but the smallest of businesses in travel and tourism.

The flexibility conferred by the range of direct

response marketing mechanisms is also important. Distribution networks require careful planning and organization, and continuous motivation and servicing with supplies of print (Chapter 18). By contrast, the use of direct response techniques can be set up or changed in a matter of days as the need arises, although the time taken to generate responses and convert them into bookings will normally be measured in weeks rather than days.

And a disadvantage

The biggest disadvantage of direct response mechanisms appears to lie in their limited capacity to secure last-minute bookings. For tour operators in particular, a national distribution system of retailers provides the best available mechanism for notifying and promoting their unsold capacity in the vital four weeks before the departure dates in their programmes. In that period, all sales are likely to be marginal and their effect on profitability is high. Using on-line links with an operator's inventory, agents can provide a top-up bookings service with a speed and flexibility, which direct response marketing cannot match.

By contrast, in generating advance bookings in the period up to the last four weeks before delivery, direct response marketing can provide a service at a cost which retailers cannot match. In addition direct response also creates a detailed knowledge of customers which retailers do not provide for operators. Achieving the best balance between the two advantages is discussed in the next section.

Balancing direct and indirect response marketing in travel and tourism

Traditionally, as this author noted in 1980 in the first systematic analysis of direct response marketing in British travel and tourism, most businesses before the 1960s developed through direct communication with their clients. Direct selling, as it was usually known, was the industry norm for all but a few principals, such as scheduled shipping lines (Middleton: 1980). The rapid expansion in the numbers of retail travel agents, mainly to service airline passengers, inclusive tour customers, and business travellers in the 1960s and 1970s, created a national network of some 6,000 outlets by the mid 1980s in Britain. Similar trends in the USA, biased more towards domestic business travel and the USA internal airline and car rental markets, produced over 28,000 retail outlets. As a result, a retail travel outlet is conveniently situated to provide easy access for the bulk of the urban populations in both countries. Parallel developments have produced similar situations in most European countries too.

It was entirely logical, if they were large enough to secure display space for their brochures, and able to give retailers efficient access to their reservation systems, that tour operators should adapt to and use these large networks to sell inclusive tours to destinations abroad. In Britain, traditional direct response organizations, such as Butlins, Ladbrokes and Hoseasons, have made great efforts in the 1980s to adapt their marketing to travel retailers and achieve a greater proportion of their sales indirectly. Other domestic producers have followed this lead, notably hotel groups seeking maximum distribution for their weekend breaks and, in particular, to achieve vital marginal revenue.

By the early 1980s, in a process of acquisition and new development colourfully known as the 'march of the multiples', six large multi-site retail chains had emerged in Britain, with over a third of the total market between them, and able to dominate the trends in travel retailing. With the support of principals investing in on-line computer systems, they were able to achieve economies of scale and much greater operational efficiency by the rapid introduction of newly available computer technology. Their largely automated offices are now able to handle very large volumes of bookings, cancellations, surcharges and invoicing, and their computer networks are interfaced with direct 'on-line' access to the larger principals' systems, which reduces the costly time spent in satisfying their customers' requirements. As a result, the balance of advantage in producing the most cost effective sales was seen to shift in favour the indirect or retail outlet system of travel distribution. Many medium and smaller principals in the industry became involved in efforts to secure a share of the limited display space and selling effort available through the powerful new outlets. For their part, the sophisticated new multiples were anxious to rationalize the product lines they offered and maximize revenue generated per metre of display space; techniques practised for many years in the retailing of groceries in supermarket chains.

Some tour operators, such as Tjaereborg, Portland, Martin Rooks, and the older established operators such as SAGA, retained their single minded focus on direct response marketing. Interestingly, the developments in information technology which enabled retailers to achieve greater operational efficiency in the early 1980s, are now assisting the direct response marketing groups to improve the efficiency of their own marketing efforts. In the mid 1980s it is impossible to be certain whether the future of travel and tourism sales lies more with direct, or indirect response mechanisms. In the end it will probably lie in a combination of the two, with the balance of advantage constantly shifting in a competitive struggle to achieve marginal sales at least cost.

Where, as for hotels and scheduled airlines, principals have a large proportion of frequent repeat customers such as regular business travellers, the balance of advantage must lie with direct response marketing. It is no accident that hotel groups and airlines have been competing strenuously in the 1980s to bind their customers to them with a wide variety of membership or club schemes, frequent traveller awards, and special arrangements for their key accounts. Holiday Inns, for example, claim that over a million members joined their 'Priority Club' within months of it being introduced in the USA in 1983. The operation of the Club, only possible on the basis of Holiday Inns' fully automated international reservation system, has since changed its basis of operation but it is an interesting example of modern direct response marketing, which is still in its early stages of development (TTRA: 1986: p. 52).

In the mid 1980s it appears probable to this author that, for most travel and tourism businesses, especially for smaller and medium sized operators, direct response marketing will often yield better overall sales results per thousand pounds spent, than the alternative indirect response routes. For most operators, the payment of commission on sales produces a minimum marketing/sales revenue ratio of 10 per cent for the indirect approach, and an average ratio, allowing for all the associated costs of promotion and additional incentives to third parties, of between 12 and 15 per cent. Of course, if allocations are made to tour operators by hoteliers and other principals, the cost of achieving sales by that method may be closer to 30 per cent (see Chapter 23). Each operator has to decide the balance of advantage for his own product portfolio at any particular time, but the direct route provides advantages of customer knowledge and communication, which cannot be matched by the indirect route.

Chapter summary

This chapter deals with a fundamental strategic choice concerning the method of distributing and selling products, which has to be made by all sizes and types of business. It is a choice which vitally affects the cost effectiveness of travel and tourism marketing, and it is a matter for surprise that it is so inadequately covered in the books and journals which deal with the industry. This author advocates the use of direct response marketing techniques wherever possible, because they are especially suited to the common travel marketing tasks of generating enquiries, converting them into bookings, and securing repeat business. They are vital too for the majority of businesses which are too small to use retail distribution channels, and the many others, which market themselves partly direct and partly indirect. In all countries, the number of organizations which sell *only* through retail distribution channels is very small indeed and, although powerful in the industry, they appear to be a special case which provides no guidance for the majority.

The balance to be struck between direct and indirect marketing is based, first and foremost, on the financial argument of unit costs required to achieve unit sales. It is secondly a matter of rapidly changing information technology, which alters the relative costs of achieving distribution and appears certain to shift the current ratios of direct/indirect sales over the next decade in all sectors of travel and tourism. The balance is thirdly an issue of travel trade politics reflecting the relative power of principals and retailers within the distribution channels. Because travel retailers do not take risks by purchasing the products they sell, it appears unlikely that they will dominate travel producers in the way that supermarkets have been able to do with the manufacturers of many fast-moving consumer goods. Even so, concerted action by retailers against a producer of inclusive tours would be very effective, and few in the British travel trade will have forgotten the months of outcry and threats which accompanied Thomson Holidays' decision to establish Portland as a direct marketing organization in 1980. Thomson, as market leaders in the sale of inclusive tours, proved they had the power to overcome the retailers' reaction on that occasion. But that was before the recent rapid growth of the large multi-site retailers, and no other tour operator has the same amount of market influence.

Finally, this chapter stresses that the choice of direct and indirect marketing methods has great implications for the knowledge which producers have of their customers, and in this aspect the advantage of the direct response methods is very clear.

Part Five

Applying Marketing in the Travel and Tourism Industry

20

Marketing countries as tourist destinations

This chapter is about the marketing role of National Tourist Organizations, Boards or Offices, commonly known as NTOs, which are responsible for marketing countries as tourist destinations. It shifts the focus of the book away from the marketing practice of individual companies and other organizations concerned with their own products, to what are commonly public sector or government funded organizations, marketing destinations and overall travel and tourism products, as defined in Chapter 8. The majority of NTOs are not producers or operators; they generally do not sell products directly to visitors; they are not directly responsible for the quality of services delivered; and they mostly represent only a small proportion, however important it may be, of all the travel and tourism marketing activity carried out on behalf of their country. The principles and practice of an NTO's approach to marketing are essentially the same as those adopted by regional, state, or local tourist offices, although the scale of operations is often very different.

Historically, the principal marketing role of NTOs has been seen in fairly narrow promotional terms of creating and communicating overall appealing destination images and messages to prospective visitors, mainly through advertising, PR and print, as a necessary basis for the product specific marketing activities of operators. The traditional image

creation role is, however, beginning to look less credible in the remaining years of the twentieth century, especially for developed tourist destinations, such as Britain, the USA, and Spain. Attention is increasingly focusing on targeting specific segments and products and on the indirect or 'facilitating' roles of marketing outlined in this chapter.

The chapter begins with a definition of NTOs and their marketing operations internationally. The factors influencing NTO marketing are summarized and the nature of marketing strategy is discussed, distinguishing between what NTOs can achieve by spending their budgets mainly on promotion, and what they can achieve through various forms of facilitation, by assisting the component sectors of the travel and tourism industry in their country. Because the marketing process for NTOs is different from that for providers of accommodation, transport or attractions, the process is outlined in some detail, using two figures, and the meaning of 'facilitation' is explained. The chapter concludes with an example of a modern approach to marketing undertaken by an NTO.

NTOs defined: some international dimensions

A tourist organization, as Burkart and Medlik explain it, 'is defined by reference to the interests of a geographical area as a tourist destination, which may be a country, region, or an individual town' (1981: p. 255). Within this context, 'the term NTO is used to designate the organization entrusted by the state with responsibility for tourism matters at the national level. It may be a fully fledged ministry or a directorate general or a department or corporation or board'. (A definition adopted by McIntosh: 1972: p. 86.) There are many different forms of organization which an NTO may take, although the principle of government support through official recognition and funding is normal even in cases where the NTO is not part of the state administration. The scope of an NTO's marketing function is usually two-fold:

> 'In the first place the tourist organization can formulate and develop the tourist product or products of the destination; secondly it can promote them in appropriate markets. It can base its approach to development and promotion on market research and thus achieve a close match between the products and the markets. In doing this the tourist organization is acting on behalf of all interests in tourism and on behalf of the whole destination and is complementary to the development and promotion activities of individual providers of tourist services . . .' (Burkart & Medlik: 1981: p. 256).

In Britain, established by the Development of Tourism Act of 1969, there are four statutory bodies, each of which meets the definition of NTOs. They are the British Tourist Authority (BTA), the English Tourist Board (ETB), the Scottish Tourist Board (STB), and the Wales Tourist Board (WTB). BTA is primarily a marketing organization responsible for marketing Britain overseas, whilst the tourist boards for England, Scotland and Wales are each responsible for the development and promotion of tourism in their areas. There are separate boards under different legislation for Northern Ireland, the Channel Islands and the Isle of Man. In the USA, at Federal level, the NTO is the United States Travel and Tourism Administration (USTTA) which is responsible mainly for the promotion of tourism into the USA. Most of the US State governments have formed their own tourist offices, mostly for the promotion of US domestic tourism into their areas. All of these national and state TOs act as policy advisers to their respective Governments. All have established formal and informal links for consultation and joint action with the tourist industry in their countries or regions as appropriate.

Around the world there are well over 100 NTOs of different sizes and organizational patterns. Nearly all of them are engaged in one or more aspects of destination promotion, although relatively few are practising the systematic approach to marketing developed in this book. Most of the promotional effort organized by these NTOs is aimed at international markets, but in recent years many have been also spending considerable sums on the promotion of 'domestic tourism', by residents within their own countries. On the international side, a recent report by the Economist Intelligence Unit (EIU: 1983), commenting that 'there exist no definitive statistics covering this topic', estimated that NTOs supported some 500 to 700 branch offices around the world in 1983. Larger networks, such as those supported by Britain or Greece, comprise over 20 offices in the main countries from which they draw their tourists, but most developing countries maintain only a few offices in key markets.

The best, although still limited source of data about the activities of NTOs, is the World Tourism Organization (WTO) based in Madrid. WTO is an inter-governmental organization to which most, but not all countries belong. Using data for 1980, based on the returns made by a larger number of countries, it appears that a broad average of around three to four US dollars per tourist arrival were being spent in promoting international tourism at that time. Given the constant fluctuation of exchange rates against the dollar, the figure is obviously very crude; it is obtained by dividing reported promotional expenditure by the estimated number of international tourist arrivals. With more than 300 million international tourist arrivals reported for the mid-1980s, the current total marketing expenditure by NTOs may realistically be estimated to exceed one billion (1,000 million) US dollars. Expenditure aimed at domestic tourists is additional to this figure, but it is quite impossible to estimate it at the present time.

It is informative to relate the expenditure on marketing to the tourism revenue achieved by individual countries. In the early 1980s, for example, BTA were spending on promotion, excluding staff costs, in the region of 0.5 per cent of the total expenditure spent in Britain by overseas visitors. Board Failte, the NTO for the Republic of Ireland, for whom tourism is identified as a key sector of the economy, have traditionally spent proportionally more, at around 3 per cent of international revenue. Although the figures are not exactly comparable, the equivalent percentages for Japan, Spain and Yugoslavia were around 3, 1, and 1 per cent, respectively. Another useful measure is the evidence, also from WTO data, that expenditure on marketing accounts for between one half and two thirds of the total budgets of NTOs. If full allowance is made for the overhead costs of marketing, including staff and premises, the proportion would be much higher.

It appears reasonable to conclude for all practical purposes, therefore, although the figures provide no guidance as to what should be spent, that an annual expenditure on marketing international tourism, which lies between 0.5 and 5 per cent of tourist expenditure, covers the range represented by current budgets of most NTOs around the world. The larger proportions will have to be spent by governments in developing destinations, which do not have a well established tourist industry sector to participate in the cost of reaching and persuading international travellers to visit their destination.

In practice, apart from being dated, the average NTO marketing expenditure of three to four dollars per arrival is misleading. Much of the travel between countries is for business and other non-leisure purposes, which are not significantly influenced by the promotional expenditure of NTOs. Also, because the average party size is generally more than two persons, it would be more realistic to relate expenditure to bookings rather than to individual arrivals. Thirdly, especially for developed destinations, it is obvious that a high proportion of leisure visits would continue to be made without NTO expenditure, influenced for example, by previous visits, recommendations of friends, and of course the marketing efforts of the tourist industry as a whole. With such allowances, the true average expenditure by NTOs per booking actually influenced in the mid 1980s, may be much closer to an average of 20 US dollars, and in some cases much higher.

In common with many other sectors of the expanding tourist industry, the development of professionalism in marketing is relatively recent in NTOs, but it appears certain to become more important over the next decade as competition between countries for shares of tourist markets increases. On the broad evidence of the data above, notwithstanding the lack of precision in the available statistics, it is reasonable to expect that the application of systematic marketing techniques by NTOs could make a major contribution to cost effectiveness measured in dollars spent per tourist arrival.

NTO marketing has influence, but limited control

The introduction to this chapter drew attention to some of the reasons why marketing for NTOs differs from marketing as practised by commercial operators. As a result, it is always difficult to evaluate the results of NTO marketing, especially the results of international tourism marketing.

Ideally, all governments would like their NTOs to prove that for every thousand pounds or dollars spent on marketing in their targeted markets of visitor origin, there is a response which can be measured in the number of visits and expenditure achieved over a given period of time. If such proof were possible, governments would be able accurately to allocate larger or smaller budgets to travel and tourism, according to their policies for growth, maintenance, or other priorities discussed later. For all countries, however, apart from the size of their marketing budgets and the quality of the marketing activities in which NTOs engage, there are three main underlying factors continuously at work in determining the actual volume and expenditure of tourism generated over any period of twelve months, between markets of origin and countries of destination. These factors distort the measurement of expenditure and response, as discussed below:

1 expenditure on marketing is only one of the influences which determine tourism volumes and expenditure to any country,
2 the marketing effort of NTOs in most countries is only a part of the total tourism marketing effort made on behalf of that country,
3 Very few NTOs are directly involved in selling products to prospective visitors. Even where they take responsibility for operating some elements of the product, such as hotels or transport, it is typically only a part of the total product supply.

Marketing is only one of the influences
Chapters 4 and 5 set out the economic, social, and behavioural factors at work in societies, which collectively determine the volume and types of travel and tourism generated by any

particular country. These so-called 'determinants and motivations' of tourism, include disposable income per capita, amount of leisure time available, personal mobility, availability of transport systems, the price of travel, and exchange rates. The importance of understanding the external business environment as the basis for marketing strategy has been stressed throughout this book and needs no further emphasis here.

NTO marketing must respond to, but cannot influence the external factors directly. For example, Britain derives about a quarter of its international tourism revenue from American travellers, who are its most important market. But neither the British Government, nor the BTA, can influence in any way the level of US incomes, the international value of the dollar, or the US overseas deficit on trade, which in the mid 1980s was the major influence on that country's economy. Effective NTO marketing begins with an understanding of the determinants influencing its main markets, and aims to work with the opportunities created by favourable events, while limiting the impact of unfavourable ones. For example, if an NTO in the Pacific region had its marketing budget increased by 400 per cent in a year in which, say, the level of air fares with its main markets doubled, the number of tourist arrivals would almost certainly fall. By contrast, no increase in a marketing budget in a year of favourable changes in external factors could be associated with a very large increase in the volume of travel. This point in no way denies the value of NTO marketing, but does set it in the context of national and international events over which it has no control.

NTO marketing is only part of the total effort
Heneghan, in attempting to trace the effectiveness of marketing for the Irish Tourist Board (Bord Failte) in the mid 1970s, calculated that the marketing expenditure by the Board amounted to about 15 per cent of all tourism marketing

expenditure for the Republic of Ireland in the USA (Heneghan: 1976). It is difficult to estimate such figures because records do not exist, but the proportion looks realistic having regard to what is spent by airlines, tour operators, accommodation interests and others based in Ireland, and the travel trade in the USA. For developing destinations, the proportion which NTOs represent of all expenditure on marketing is likely to be higher, but rarely as much as a half. If the bulk of all tourism marketing expenditure is not controlled by an NTO but by independent third parties, it is impossible for an NTO to claim all the credit, or be blamed for failure in the fluctuations in tourist arrivals which occur over any given period of time.

Limited influence over the supply of products
In developed tourist destination countries, such as the USA or Britain, there are tens of thousands of commercial firms, and many public sector organizations involved in providing tourist products and services. Of these, only a small minority have any formal relationship with an NTO through membership of state, regional, or area tourist boards. Thus a large number of businesses generates a very wide range of tourist products, most of which are beyond the marketing influence of an NTO with regard to volume, design, price, and promotion decisions.

Thus, one may conclude that the marketing effort of an NTO, especially in developed destination countries, will always be *partial* or even marginal in terms of the range of products it influences; *submerged* to a large extent in the greater impact of the determinants and motivations affecting markets of origin; and *outweighed* by the marketing effort of commercial interests in tourism. Although NTOs of developing tourist destination countries have a far greater potential influence over their countries' tourism, and are potentially better able to evaluate the success of their marketing efforts, in practice they often lack the profess-

ional management skills to exploit their advantages.

These conclusions do not imply that NTO marketing expenditure is necessarily ineffective or wasted. They do mean that most NTOs are not in direct control of the products they promote or the results which are achieved, as measured in annual visitor numbers and expenditure. It is, therefore, helpful to explain the role of NTO marketing from a perspective of *influence* rather than control; a very different perspective from that used to explain commercial practice.

Destination promotion role for NTOs or marketing facilitation?

From the previous discussion it can be concluded that there are two levels involved in marketing for any destination. The first level, concerned with the destination as a whole and the total tourist product, is the focus of what NTOs do. The second level involves the marketing activity of the mainly commercial operators promoting their individual products. Within the first level of marketing, NTOs have to choose between two alternative strategies; one of which involves reaching prospective visitors through expenditure on a promotional mix intended to promote destination awareness and influence prospective customers' attitudes; the other is concerned with exercising influence over the tourist industry.

The *promotional strategy* means spending budgets to project destination images and key messages to targeted segments of potential visitors, and encourage them to send for product brochures, or call into travel agents in their area. Using a metaphor which has been widely quoted, Burkart and Medlik summarize this strategic choice as creating an 'umbrella campaign', under which, at the second level, the various individual providers of tourist services can market their own components of the total tourist product.

The second level of marketing thus covers the

full range of mainly commercial marketing initiatives in which, 'Airlines and other transport operators, hotel groups, and tour operators can market their individual services to a market of potential buyers already aware of and predisposed to the destination...' (Burkart and Medlik: p. 197).

The decision to invest the greater part of their budgets in promoting destination awareness and images appears to be an obvious and convincing strategy, and it is chosen by most NTOs and regional tourist offices around the world in the mid 1980s. Following the logic of the strategy, the bulk of NTO marketing expenditure and its organization structure should, of course, reflect overall promotional campaign priorities. In selecting this strategy, however, it has to be assumed that the budget which an NTO has to spend is large enough to implement effectively the promotional campaigns which its market segmentation studies identify as necessary. To be effective, such campaigns must be of sufficient weight and impact to create the necessary numbers of potential buyers who are aware of and predisposed to the destination. But, if budgets are not adequate for the task, expenditure on an image creating strategy may in practice be a waste of money on desirable objectives which cannot be achieved. Having regard to the size of the budgets discussed earlier for most NTOs operating internationally or in domestic tourism markets, one must question the effectiveness in practice of much of their promotional expenditure.

To illustrate the point about budget size in relation to the task, in the mid 1980s the Wales Tourist Board has a total budget for advertising, promotions and print of around £1½ million. Expenditure by tourists in Wales was estimated at £500 million over twelve months. In terms of promotion, therefore, the budget represented only a small fraction of one per cent of total tourism revenue; a sum with which it was impossible to make a major impact on national

images and attitudes. The budgets for England and Scotland were proportionally similar.

Fortunately there is an alternative strategy, increasingly employed in Wales and in other destinations, which is relevant to all NTOs. This is the strategy of *marketing facilitation*, as it is termed in this chapter. This strategy creates marketing bridges between an NTO and the individual operators in the travel and tourism industry; and a bridge between the first and second levels of distination marketing discussed above. The case for marketing facilitation is based on three considerations, commonly found around the world:

- First, that a destination country has specific government policy objectives for wishing to promote tourism, which may be expressed in economic, social, or environmental terms as well as marketing goals.
- Second, that the destination country possesses a range of tourist areas, products, and segments, some growing and some declining, to which it attaches differing priorities, and which have different implications for achieving government policy objectives.
- Third that budgets granted to NTOs will, in almost every case, be less than adequate to undertake all the marketing tasks identified, so that selection of priorities is required.

If these three considerations apply, the most effective marketing role for an NTO lies in establishing promotional priorities for specific markets and segments; co-ordinating the elements of overall tourist products; liaising with the tourist industry; providing support for new or growth products relevant to policy; and creating co-operative marketing campaigns accessible especially for the hundreds of small businesses, which would otherwise be unable to participate in marketing on a national or international scale.

These processes amount to a facilitation strategy, which normally involves extensive voluntary co-operation; has implications for marketing organization and personnel; and brings the NTO and its commercial sector together in joint operations which are quite different from traditional concepts of spending money on image campaigns. It brings into sharp focus the very difficult task which all NTOs face, of allocating available budgets between competing marketing priorities.

The strategy which an NTO adopts in practice, should vary according to the stage of development which its tourism and tourist industry have reached. Where destinations are largely unknown in the markets they seek to promote; where existing tourism flows are small; and where the tourist industry within the country is mainly weak and fragmented; the NTO will have no choice but to take the leading role in putting its destination on the international map and playing a major role in promoting its destination's products. Even in these circumstances the available budgets will normally not be adequate to engage *effectively* in image campaigns in several markets, and the marketing support of international operators such as airlines, hotel chains and tour operators will be essential for success. For better known, well established destinations such as Britain and the USA, where the tourist industry has forged many of its own international links, it should increasingly be possible for the NTO to focus more of its expenditure on the strategy of support and facilitation and less on buying media space for general image advertising.

Destination positioning themes, images, and concepts

Not to be confused with the expenditure of money on purchasing advertising space and sales promotion, NTOs always have a vital function to perform for their destinations in choosing the unique, single minded communication propositions (messages and symbols), which may serve to identify and position their countries in the minds of prospective visitors, and differentiate them from all others.

BTA's Heritage themes, Scotland's Rainbow and 'Scotland's for me', Wales' Dragon, or 'I love New York', and Birmingham's 'Big Heart of England', all serve to brand and identify their destinations with unique destination relevant labels. To be successful in practice, such labels must be incorporated into the overall promotional efforts of a country's regions, resorts, and the marketing of the tourist industry; sustained over several years if they are to overcome the communication barriers referred to in Chapter 16; and systematically exploited in a range of sales promotion and customer servicing techniques designed to reach existing visitors at the destination as well as prospective visitors in countries of origin.

Planning successful images and implementing them effectively involves detailed consumer research and creative flair in relation to a destination's intrinsic visitor attractions. This is usually a role which only the NTO can fulfil, and only the NTO can take on the task of communicating the chosen positioning to the tourist industry. But it should not find it necessary to spend the bulk of its own scarce resources in promoting the image to the general public in markets of origin.

It will often be possible for NTOs to develop co-operative promotional efforts arising out of the facilitation strategy, and draw on the financial support of the travel and tourism industry in mounting any overall advertising and publicity campaigns judged necessary to support or enhance the overall destination image. Working within an overall strategy of facilitation, there will often be a tactical role for NTO publicity campaigns, for example to correct the short run effects of negative attitudes in markets of origin, arising from news stories about prices, or

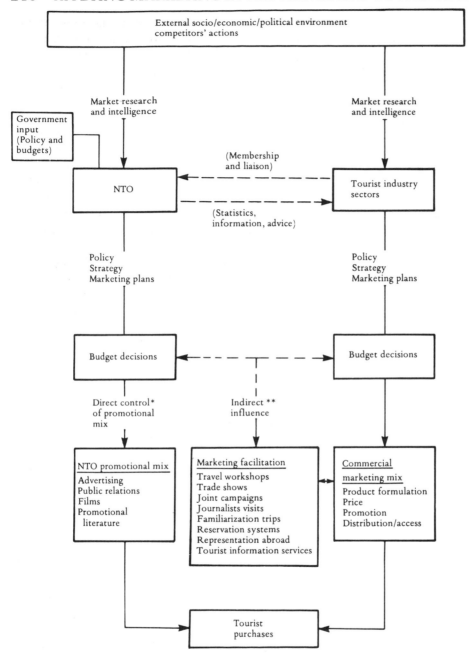

* expenditure mainly in the countries of origin from which international
  tourists are drawn
** expenditure in countries of origin and the destination

Figure 20.1 *The destination marketing process for NTOs*

personal security. These tactical efforts should not be confused with highly expensive attempts to use NTO budgets to create overall tourist motivations and attitudes through expenditure on image campaigns.

The marketing process for NTOs

Figure 20.1 illustrates the marketing process for NTOs (on the left of the diagram), side by side with the same process for individual operators in the travel and tourism industry (on the right). The figure reveals both the similarities in marketing, and the important differences which exist. Readers may wish to refer back to Figure 2.1 included in Chapter 2, with which Figure 20.1 is fully compatible. The main difference occurs at the budget decision stage, where NTOs have the choice of apportioning funds between the two routes shown as direct control of the promotional mix on the left, and marketing facilitation in the middle of the diagram. Facilitation forms the important bridge between NTO and the component sectors of the industry, whilst the promotion strategy reflects the more traditional approach to destination marketing.

Important liaison and co-ordination links between NTO and individual operators are shown in the diagram at the policy level; at the budget decision level (industry financial participation in NTO schemes and vice versa); and between marketing facilitation and the individual marketing decisions of operators in the tourist industry. Each of the main stages in Figure 20.1 is discussed briefly below, followed by a more detailed explanation of the less familiar methods of marketing facilitation.

Researching the external environment

As in all marketing, the process begins with researching the external environment. Since only larger operators, such as airlines and hotel chains, will have the resources to undertake large-scale marketing research, especially into international markets, an NTO has a unique role to play in the travel and tourism industry in gathering and communicating market analysis and trend data, not only for its own marketing purposes, but for the industry as a whole. Most NTOs publish research facts; few appear to perform the task in a way which is easily accessible and understandable to the majority of operators in the travel and tourism industry in most countries. Provision of usable market information is an important basis for effective facilitation; failure to communicate data effectively means that a potentially valuable method of influencing the decisions of suppliers is lost.

Government policy and tourism strategy

Where NTOs are financed by governments, there is usually a requirement that marketing objectives serve government policy. Most governments do not normally involve themselves with tourism marketing objectives in any detail, but lay down the broader strategic goals, which NTOs are required to pursue. These goals, in principle, are much the same all over the world, typically requiring that tourism revenue should generate foreign exchange earnings and secure employment, in accordance with national economic policy.

Government policies relevant to tourism marketing strategy may be summarized as:

- to generate increased tourism revenue,
- to channel demand by season, and by area of the country,
- to protect consumers' interests and enhance the quality of the product.

The first two of these policies tend to be common to most countries; the third, discussed later under facilitation, is less well understood.

The representation of commercial and other organizations on various committees and boards of NTOs, is also a common feature of NTO operation. It is intended to create a productive dialogue between the main organizations in the travel and tourism industry, and the direction of government and NTO policy. Marketing strategy is only one important aspect of this dialogue, and the liaison stages are noted in Figure 20.1.

Marketing planning

It follows from earlier comments about the limitations of an NTO's budget and its influence on markets, that selecting priorities and turning these into strategies and specific targets for products and segments is a vitally important exercise. In practice, marketing planning for an NTO has two separate functions to discharge. The first is in relation to any promotional campaigns it intends to carry out in its main markets of origin, and the second is in relation to guidelines, facilitation and marketing support for the industry as a whole.

For reasons explained in Chapters 11 and 13, effective planning for marketing strategy and tactics is impossible without an adequate information base. The marketing planning process for an NTO is no different in principle from any other application of standard techniques. Regrettably, the travel and tourism industry in most countries is still notorious for the paucity of its research information base compared with what is commonly available for most other manufacturing and service industries. It is a criticism of most NTOs that they have spent millions of dollars over recent years on advertising campaigns, while expenditure on basic marketing research into tourist interests, behaviour and attitudes, necessary to achieve the most effective use of the money, has been very limited.

Marketing objectives and targets

The most important output of the marketing planning process for an NTO is the identification of product market strategies to match market trends and the resource base, and the selection of specific, broadly quantified targets for allocating budgets. Figure 20.2, sets out in a format adapt-able for use in any destination, a simple model of a market/product planning matrix, comprising a number of cells, each of which represents the volume and value of target segments and products.

The segments and products to be included in the model are decided by marketing analysis and planning, and liaison with the travel and tourism industry. The same procedure is used to estimate the volume and revenue figures to be inserted, and the matrix may be used for historic data or as a framework for forecasting. With appropriate supporting statements, the model may also play a useful part in summarizing strategy and communicating it to the tourist industry.

Budget decisions

It was stressed in Chapter 14 that marketing tasks must relate to objectives, and that the size and cost of undertaking specified tasks acts as a constraint on the choice of objectives. In terms of budgeting principles, exactly the same considerations apply to NTOs. Possibilities of joint funding of marketing tasks exist and these are noted later. Very few countries have successfully developed a systematic method of relating the size of budget required to the achievement of specific objectives. Precedent (what was done last year) and broad comparisons with other precedent based budgets for public expenditure, are still the general rule in budget allocation for NTOs, adjusted more or less, by annual levels of inflation in the country's economy.

As noted earlier, the basic strategic choice of NTOs in allocating available budgets, lies in the apportionment they must make between involving themselves directly in promotional tasks, or choosing to engage in facilitation tasks.

Marketing facilitation strategies for an NTO

This section discusses facilitation strategy, neatly summarized by Jeffries (1973), who noted that

Market areas → ↓ Product types	Country/ Segment A	Country/ Segment B	Country/ Segment C	Country/ Segment D → Other market areas/ segments
Resort based holidays	volume: value	volume: value	volume: value	volume: value
Touring holidays by car				
Capital city holidays				
Business and conferences ↓ Other products				

Notes:
1 A developed destination country with tourism from several countries of origin may identify as many as fifty or more relevant segments.
2 The products in the matrix are those identified by marketing research, or by analysis of supply. A developed destination country may easily identify over 25 principal products allowing for regional area, and seasonal variations.
3 Where research is available, it will obviously be used to complete the cells of the matrix; where it is not, the matrix model may still be useful as a tool for summarizing managers' judgements. The process of completing the model may also serve to identify aspects of products and markets requiring new, or additional market research.

Figure 20.2 *Market/product matrix model for NTO marketing planning*

an NTO '. . . can hardly run the whole of tourism, even in countries where it actually owns hotels and transportation. Its major role everywhere is to provide leadership and guidance: to indicate marketing opportunities and to produce a climate where all concerned will be prepared to exploit them. Having reached this point its role will be to encourage and assist'.

To assist British producers in travel and tourism to develop their overseas visitor markets, for example, the British Tourist Authority (BTA) has developed an extensive range of marketing facilitation techniques over recent years. It distributes regularly a booklet, 'Promoting Tourism to Britain: How the BTA can help' which extended to 18 pages in 1986. It summarizes the assistance available under 16 headings ranging from advertising and print, to travel workshops, with most headings containing more than one option. Most of these marketing services are not free, but they can be obtained at costs which few individual medium-sized or small operators acting on their own could match. For BTA, the income derived from these services achieves funding additional to that available from government sources.

Twelve of the most important facilitation processes used by NTOs are discussed below.

1 Flow of research data

By providing a regular, user friendly flow of research data to the tourist industry, through digests of statistics, short reports on market trends, and help with research enquiries, an NTO may make valuable inputs to the marketing planning processes of individual businesses in all sectors. Co-operative and syndicated research surveys also provide cost effective ways in which an NTO can stimulate the flow of relevant data. The regular distribution of research summaries is a practical way of maintaining contacts with the industry and exercising influence at the same time.

2 Representation in markets of origin

By establishing a network of offices in foreign countries generating the bulk of its international visitor flows, an NTO can create and maintain vital travel trade contacts, and act as a point of distribution for the destination's range of tourist products. By manipulating the choice of contacts and its distribution priorities, the NTO can exercise an important influence over the producers it helps, in relation to its chosen marketing objectives. The network of offices may also generate flows of vital marketing intelligence, to be fed into the NTO's information system, and used in the marketing planning process.

3 Organization of workshops and trade shows

Since the 1960s NTOs have been making arrangements whereby groups of suppliers of tourist products may meet with groups of prospective buyers, such as tour operators, travel agents, and other travel organizers, at relatively low cost. Either in the market of origin or at the destination, individual hoteliers, attractions, suppliers of conference facilities, or businesses offering youth products, for example, may be able to make contact and discuss business in one or two days of intensive meetings, which on an individual basis, could take weeks to organize. By choosing the theme of workshops, such as self catering, coach tours or attractions, issuing the invitations, and possibly subsidizing the costs of accommodation and travel, an NTO can make a powerful contribution to its objectives. It may, of course, use the workshops as an opportunity to convey information and other messages designed to promote its aims.

4 Familiarization trips

By arranging for parties of selected foreign travel agents, journalists and tour operators to visit the destination and sample the products available, NTOs can influence the effectiveness with which the travel trade in markets of origin acts in support of the destination and its products. Such trips are part of the sales promotion process discussed in Chapter 16, and are one method of improving the advice and information available to customers at key retail outlets and gaining better display space at points of sale. The trips also serve an important PR role and offer many opportunities for communicating key messages to influential people in distribution and media channels.

5 Travel trade manuals

With a wide variety of products available in many destinations in a country and a large number of producers, it is usually impossible for foreign travel agents and tour operators to be serviced individually by an NTO. It is, therefore, customary for NTOs to produce one or more trade manuals, which serve as references and guides for use by the travel trade. A conference users' manual, for example, lists the details of all the operators and their facilities, probably classified by area, particular facilities available, and prices, including commission available and how to make bookings. A different manual would be required for activity holidays, and so on. For smaller suppliers who cannot afford to establish access arrangements with the distribution system, these manuals provide an opportunity to gain some access to foreign markets at low cost. Of course, they also make the busy distributor's job easier, and they are more inclined to recommend the products which are easier to deal with.

6 Support with literature production and distribution

Because printed materials are so vital an element in travel and tourism marketing (see Chapter 17), some NTOs produce brochure 'shells' for use by small businesses. These are normally full colour leaflets containing themed but general photography and areas of blank space, which may be overprinted by an operator's logo and product messages. Quantities of shells suitable for a range of purposes, such as activity holidays or weekend breaks, may be bought at standard prices per thousand as required, and then over-printed in one colour to produce a professional leaflet at a cost well below the price of commissioning a purpose-designed colour brochure in small numbers from a printer.

Many NTOs sell advertising space in their range of brochures, which they promote and distribute overseas. Indeed, often the main purpose of NTO brochures is to provide advertising opportunities to the tourist industry; many produce a surplus of revenue over costs. Assuming the NTO's own literature distribution processes are efficient, these brochures may be very cost effective media, through which small and medium sized businesses can reach otherwise inaccessible international markets. NTOs may also offer direct mail distribution services for the operator's own printed material.

7 Participation in joint marketing schemes or ventures

Joint schemes or ventures are names commonly given to specific forms of financial and promotional support offered by an NTO to its commercial and public sector operators. Schemes normally involve formal application procedures and scrutiny, and criteria are applied, such as whether or not the products concerned are judged likely to proceed without some financial support for their marketing; whether they potentially contribute to stated national marketing objectives; and whether they have adequate backing from their originators and appear likely to succeed. Successful applicants may be granted up to half the cost of their scheme, although many receive less. Equally important, an adopted scheme can draw on the professional expertise of an NTO's marketing department, and the other facilities available for production of print, overseas representation, research advice, and so on.

According to the way in which the criteria for support are drawn up, an NTO can use schemes to influence operators in the tourist industry along lines indicated through its strategic planning process. By monitoring the success of schemes, it also develops its research knowledge of particular products, segments and markets.

8 Information and reservation systems

By using new computerized information technology, such as Prestel, NTOs may assist sectors of their tourist industry by establishing central reservation systems in support of the brochures of product offers they distribute. Although primarily designed to facilitate commissionable bookings by retail travel agents, access to the system may also be made available separately to individual customers. Travel agents who can access products rapidly, through one central reservation operation, are likely to find this a much quicker process than dealing individually with small businesses.

9 Support for new products

Through selective pro-active marketing support, using criteria established through marketing planning. NTOs can help new products to emerge and establish themselves in their markets in the initial two to three years after their launch. Smaller businesses are usually unable to afford the costs of national and international marketing, and 'pump priming', as this form of support is often known, is a well established technique, by which NTOs may contribute to their long-term policy goals. In Britain, the 'commended hotels' scheme, supported over a number of years is an example. The development of farm tourism is another example likely to require considerable support to establish itself successfully. This form of assistance overlaps with the investment and development support programmes which many NTOs also operate, increasingly using market-ing orientated criteria.

10 Trade consortia

An interesting illustration of the facilitation role for an NTO exists in the support they may offer for consortia of small businesses, formed for the purposes of more efficient marketing. Aided by NTO marketing expertise and some funding of promotional activities, groups of hire boat owners, museums, caravan parks, hotels and other facilities may be assisted. The support given in Wales to caravan parks meeting high standards (Dragon Award Parks) is an example of this type of support.

11 Consumer assistance and protection

It is well recognized that the marketing task does not end with the sale of a product. For service products it extends into a concern for customer satisfaction with the service delivery. In tourism, this task includes information services, which are provided to enable visitors to become aware of and gain access to the full range of available products, about which many would otherwise have no knowledge. By creating and subsidizing a network of information offices in destination areas, an NTO can extend its influence and communicate messages directly to a wide 'audience' of its visitors; in practice this may be a wider audience than many can hope to reach with available budgets through their promotional efforts in countries of origin. By their choice of emphasis in the information provided, an NTO can expect to exert considerable promotional influence over visitor movement in destinations, and their expenditure patterns. Market research indicates that many visitors to tourist desti-nations, especially foreign and first-time visitors, are open to suggestion and persuasion from all sources of information, but especially those which have the official endorsement and authority of the NTO and its regional bodies.

Associated with this concern for customer satisfaction are forms of consumer protection, such as the requirement that tourist prices should be clearly notified, and the operation of tourist complaint procedures, supplemented in some countries with tourist police. Finally there is a growing concern in many countries to protect and enhance the quality of tourist products through schemes of accommodation classifi-cation and grading designed to increase customer satisfaction with their overall experience. Not normally considered a part of NTO marketing, such schemes make no sense unless they are firmly marketing led, and designed around the identified needs of the customers the NTO seeks to promote.

12 General advisory services for the industry

Although the provision of advice to businesses is a time consuming process and it cannot reach more than a fraction of the tourist industry as a whole, its availability can make a very important contribution to the marketing decisions of suppliers with limited market contacts, and budgets too small to commit more than a minimum sum to market research. There are many ways in which expensive person to person advice can be extended. An NTO may, for example, organize seminars and conferences on marketing topics and disseminate the contributions as widely as possible through its publications. An example is Wales Tourist Board's launch of a distance learning course in 1987, in conjunction with the national education system, which is designed to give farmers in Wales an opportunity to learn how best to provide, manage, and market farm tourism.

The destination image strategy

Earlier in this chapter it was explained that many NTOs fund and organize overall destination awareness and image campaigns, in the form of 'umbrella' promotions, under which the specific products of operators may be marketed. This is a strategic choice, which may be implemented instead of or in addition to the alternative of marketing facilitation. As noted in Figure 20.1, an image campaign involves planning and executing a promotional mix typically comprising advertising, public relations, films, sales promotion, and marketing literature. The requirements of these techniques are the same in principle for NTOs as they are for any other marketing organization, and they are covered in the principles outlined in the chapter on each subject earlier in this book.

If the budget resources are not sufficient to implement an effective image campaign, there remains a vital role for NTOs in identifying and communicating to the tourist industry, the integrated promotional themes, images and 'positions', a destination should aim to create in the minds of prospective customers. The choice of themes is a matter for marketing research among visitors, but it must also be relevant to any inherent qualities and particular distinctions of the resources a destination offers. This is a creative process, likely to emerge out of an assessment of resource strengths and weaknesses in the marketing planning process. One of the best known examples of this is 'I love New York' campaign of the late 1970s; another example is described below.

A campaign illustration – 'Heritage 84'

The following example is drawn from the work of Britain's British Tourist Authority (BTA) in the mid 1980s. It indicates how both the promotional and facilitation strategies can work together to produce co-ordinated results. It also shows how creative theming can influence the tourist industry, regardless of the size of the financial resources to be put into advertising by the NTO.

Background

As the overall focus for its 1984 world wide marketing campaigns, BTA selected the integrating theme of Britain's heritage. Britain is particularly well endowed with historic sites, buildings, towns, events, and festival, and there is ample evidence from marketing research to prove that history is one of the principal motivations for many overseas visitors to Britain. Heritage attractions are widely dispersed throughout England, Scotland, and Wales and, because much of their appeal is relatively weatherproof, the heritage theme is relevant to the two important national goals of spreading visitor demand by seasons, and by areas of the country.

Marketing research

In this case, the principal research role lay in analysing and interpreting the extensive range of existing data about tourist motivations and behaviour patterns; new studies were not needed. On the supply side, additional research was involved in obtaining and listing full details of the available heritage resources and events planned for 1984. It involved a process of liaison and collaboration with site owners and many other bodies involved, such as local government and, of course, the tourist boards for Scotland and Wales, and the regional tourist boards throughout Britain. By focusing the industry's attention on the range of possibilities the promotions offered, and the scope for creative product formulation, heritage interests in many destinations in Britain were stimulated to provide additional, enhanced products and to stage more events.

Marketing planning and scope of the campaign

The planning process identified target markets for heritage products and formed the basis for budget allocation. After selecting target markets, the main decision to be made was the split between putting resources into promoting the theme to the final customer, and facilitation. In this case, reflecting the fragmented nature of the products, the facilitation strategy featured strongly. Suppliers and travel organizers were brought together through brochures of product offers distributed overseas. Shell folders were produced in large volume and made available for purchase by suppliers requesting them, using a standard format to achieve economies of scale.

A regular newsletter was introduced to communicate with the British tourist industry, entitled 'Heritage Herald'. Using direct mail and all the usual channels of communication, it was a useful medium for reaching the thousands of potential contributors to the theme. In its first issue it claimed 'All sections of the British tourist industry are enthusiastically backing a co-operative and creative effort to make 1984 an event starred year for visitors ... Co-ordinated by the BTA, it may prove to be one of the most integrated marketing campaigns ever mounted to attract visitors to Britain.' A public relations and marketing co-ordinator was appointed for the duration of the campaign. BTA commissioned a special logo for use in all publicity material.

NTO promotional mix

The BTA used heritage as an overall image and message for its worldwide advertising and promotional print. As a theme, the subject is rich in general interest and offered many opportunities for creative, cost effective, PR activity. Trade shows and sales missions also focused on the theme. Much of the advertising was supported by commercial partners, serving to extend the original BTA budget considerably. As a result, and as the overseas markets saw it, the theme of 'Heritage 84' had consistency and an integrity, giving it an impact beyond what could have been achieved by more generalized destination images and messages. This integrity extended through the heritage product range, reflecting the level of co-operation which had been achieved in Britain in preparation for the promotional effort. The BTA felt that the level of support for this campaign was sufficient to justify its extension for a further year, and made the decision well ahead of the results. It is impossible to say what proportion of extra business the campaign generated. It happened to coincide with favourable trends in the external environment and the volume of overseas tourism to Britain in 1985 was the highest on record.

The tourist

Apart from its initial motivating influence, one of the important effects of the heritage campaign was that visitors to Britain in 1984–5 were able to find and experience more heritage products and events, better presented and delivered, than would otherwise have been possible. Such products were also better promoted and made more accessible through information networks within Britain, so that the level of visitor usage of the available products tended to increase, bringing more revenue to operators and greater satisfaction to visitors.

Chapter summary

This chapter explains the scope and extent of NTO marketing world wide, drawing attention to the large sums of money which are spent annually on persuading international visitors to choose particular destinations. It discusses three principal reasons why NTOs, especially in developed destination countries, are not likely to achieve more than a marginal influence over tourist movements, and outlines two levels of destination marketing, distinguishing between the role of NTOs, and of suppliers of particular products. The strategic choices facing an NTO in deciding how best to deploy its available, usually limited, budget are discussed in some detail.

The chapter outlines the stages in the marketing process for NTOs, paying particular attention to the facilitation strategy. Facilitation is defined as the unique marketing role for an NTO; unique in the sense that if the NTO does not fulfil it, it is unlikely that obviously important tasks will be undertaken at all. Twelve of these tasks are described and they serve to co-ordinate the tourist industry as a whole, recognizing and strengthening industry linkages in the overall products which destinations provide, and devising themes and images to integrate promotional efforts. By its nature, facilitation is task

orientated and, in terms of securing value for money from promotional expenditure, it is usually easier to prove success through this strategy than through expenditure on image campaigns. The links between marketing and product formulation, which emerge naturally through the facilitation process, help to ensure that tourism development in a country is market led.

The individual activities described as facilitation are not new in the 1980s. But the balance in the use of NTO resources, and the co-ordinated use of the range of techniques to achieve targeted objectives is new, and results from more professional marketing in the sector. The allocation of resources is likely to be most cost effective if it is integrated around creative images and themes, which are relevant to the interests of prospective customers and the special characteristics of the destination's resources.

The principles set out in this chapter are broadly applicable to regional and area tourist boards, who have much the same co-ordinating role and strategic choices in using their resources as NTOs do. The smaller bodies work mainly on domestic tourism and deal with smaller, mainly local operators, but they are in many ways microcosms of their larger national organizations.

21

Marketing tourist attractions

Most managed tourist attractions in Britain and in many other countries are typically small operations in terms of their annual visitor volume and revenue, based on a single location, and not operated as businesses with a view to profit. There are exceptions to this general view and the number of large commercial operations increased rapidly since the 1970s. Nevertheless the sector as a whole presents a strong contrast to the large, multi-site commercial corporations, which so strongly influence tourism markets for transport and accommodation. This chapter aims to show that the principles of marketing still apply, even in a sector of the tourist industry not distinguished by its business management skills.

As initially outlined in Chapter 8, all forms of tourist attractions are important 'elements within the destination's environment, which largely determine consumers' choice and influence prospective buyers' motivation.' This chapter is concerned only with *managed attractions* based on a wide range of natural or man-made resources, which either naturally or after development, have the power to draw or motivate visitors to their locations. There is ample international evidence to prove that the power of resources to motivate visitors is not an absolute but a relative quality. It may be enhanced and developed with the use of management techniques generally, and of marketing techniques in particular. Although the point should not be overstated, it is easy to agree that 'tourism is a resource industry . . .' (Murphy: 1985: p. 12).

This chapter focuses only on attractions which are the responsibility of managers or owners for whom the use of marketing techniques is both possible and relevant in terms of their objectives and budgets. The term 'visitor attractions' rather than 'tourist attractions' is used, partly to reflect industry practice, and partly because many attractions are visited as much by the residents of an area, as by its tourists. The chapter commences with a brief explanation of what the term *managed* attractions means, and proceeds to define and categorize the types of attraction to which systematic marketing techniques may be applied. Common characteristics of attractions are reviewed, followed by a discussion of the product which attractions offer and the standard customer segments on which they draw. Aspects of the external environment and of internal operating constraints are outlined, and management responses are summarized under the headings of strategic and tactical marketing. The chapter concludes with two examples drawn from recent marketing practice.

Modern concepts of attractions management and marketing

Increasingly since the 1960s, with the extension of travel and tourism on a large scale, the original notion of permitting uncontrolled visits to natural resources in their unmanaged state has given way to concepts of resource control and visitor management using one or more forms of management techniques. The widely used cliché that visitors tend to destroy the things they travel to see has its applications in most countries and management of natural and built resources stemmed originally from a desire to protect attractive places from the damage inflicted by too many visitors. Where management techniques are employed, marketing is increasingly fundamental to success, but it can only be practised effectively for natural resources when focused on specific areas of land or water which are enclosed or have controlled access. For example, visitor management and marketing are commonly practiced in areas of national parks, or in country parks or lakes which are used as reservoirs. Other attractions based on built resources such as castles, museums or cathedrals have typically been subject to some form of management for decades, although here too the new forms of marketing are very different from tradit nal forms of information and promotion.

What distinguishes the last part of the twentieth century is the scale of visitation by mass markets, which increasingly involves the exercise of sophisticated management techniques at attractions. The techniques may be used simultaneously to protect the resource, to enhance the visitor experience, and to promote a site in an increasingly competitive market. Associated with this new emphasis on management is a growing understanding of the ways in which new visitor attractions can be developed out of resources and structures not originally associated with such uses, or created where none existed previously. The construction of Disney World and EPCOT in Florida involved the purchase of some 27,400 acres of low-lying swamp and agricultural land of no obvious visitor attraction in the mid 1960s. The development of canal basin warehouses at Wigan Pier in the North of England in the mid 1980s is an example of industrial dereliction turned into an attraction.

Within this context of modern professional management, marketing techniques are emerging as the best way to develop and sustain satisfying products, create value for money, influence the volume and seasonality patterns of site visits, and generate sufficient revenue to cover the costs of operation and maintenance of the resource base.

The concept of applying systematic modern business management techniques at visitor attractions as diverse as museums and national parks, is not yet fully accepted in all countries. The idea of charging for access to the primary assets of national heritage is even less widely accepted, although charging is now commonplace in most new purpose designed attractions. The evidence suggests, however, that the rate of change in management and marketing awareness at visitor attractions has been rapid in the 1980s. This change is supported by the expanding educational provision for travel, tourism and recreation, especially in North America and Europe, and one may confidently predict a far wider extension of modern management techniques by the end of the century.

The development of marketing thinking is of course stimulated by the pressures of competition. It is noteworthy in England that approximately half of all the visitor attractions available in the mid 1980s, were developed in the previous two decades. New attractions, often dependent on admission income for their survival, tend to be commercially orientated from the outset in contrast with more traditional sites. In the mid 1980s, in preparation for their bi-centennial celebrations, Australians were travelling the world to study the latest management techniques for use in some of their major new visitor attractions in Sydney, an interesting illustration of the extent to which modern visitor management techniques, are now international.

The nature of managed visitor attractions

Managed visitor attractions as discussed in this chapter may now be defined as:

designated permanent resources which are controlled and managed for the enjoyment, amusement, entertainment and education of the visiting public.

Designated means that the resource has been formally committed to the types of use and activity outlined in the definition. Designation may be either a commercial decision within the normal statutory planning regulations which apply to land and structures, or a decision by a public sector body acting on behalf of community interests, or the decision of a Trust acting on behalf of Trust objectives. In all cases the boundaries of a managed attraction must be clearly specified – even for wilderness areas such as the upper slopes of mountains – and normally attractions are enclosed or controlled to reduce or prevent public access except at established points of admission.

Permanent is used to exclude from the definition, travelling fairs, shows, temporary entertainments and any other form of visitor attractions not based on a fixed site or building. Temporary attractions have their own different forms of marketing which are not discussed in this chapter.

The definition is not restricted to attractions

1 Ancient monuments	Typically excavated and preserved sites such as fortifications, burial mounds and buildings dating up to the end of the Roman Empire
2 Historic buildings	Castles, houses, palaces, cathedrals, churches, town centres, villages, commonly termed heritage sites
3 Parks and gardens	National parks, country parks, long distance paths, gardens (excluding urban recreation spaces), includes sites of particular scenic quality
4 Theme parks	Mostly engineered as artefacts, such as Disney World, but may be associated with historic sites such as Colonial Williamsburg in the USA, or with Gardens as at Alton Towers in Britain
5 Wildlife attractions	Zoos, aquaria, aviaries, wildfowl parks safari parks, butterfly farms
6 Museums	The range is enormous; it includes *subject* specific museums, such as science, transport, farms, ships; *site* specific museums such as Colonial Williamsburg (USA) or Ironbridge Gorge (Great Britain); or *area* based museums, either national, regional or local collections
7 Art galleries	Mostly traditional galleries with collections built up over many decades
8 Industrial archeology sites	Mostly sites and structures identified with specific industrial and manufacturing processes such as mining, textiles, railways, docks or canals, and mostly relevant to the period post 1750
9 Themed retail sites	Mostly former commercial premises such as covered market halls, commodity exchanges or warehouses, used as speciality retail shopping malls, often themed
10 Amusement and leisure parks	Parks designated primarily for permanent thrill rides, such as roller coasters, log flumes, dodgem cars and associated stalls and amusements

Figure 21.1 *Ten main types of managed attractions for visitors*

which have an admission price, although the attractions listed in Figure 21.1 mostly do charge, and the trend is in this direction rather than for free provision. The charge for using the attraction may be made at a ticket office, barrier or a car park, or for the use of parts of the site, and it may be obligatory or operated on a voluntary basis. Prices may be intended to cover the full resource cost of operating an attraction, or just to cover its current (not capital) expenditure, or simply to make some contribution to costs which are otherwise paid from some other source.

Within the definition it will be obvious that there is a wide range of different types of attraction. To illustrate the range, ten different categories of permanent managed attractions are listed in Figure 21.1. The marketing principles put forward in this chapter will be found applicable to all of them.

Common characteristics of the visitor attractions shown in Figure 21.1 are that they are typically small in terms of the number of visitors and the revenue they receive; many are product rather than market orientated; most have very limited marketing knowledge and marketing budgets so small as to limit what they can achieve in practice to improve their revenue performance.

The English Tourist Board (ETB) estimate that there were in England just under 3,000 tourist attractions open to the public in 1985, and they attracted an estimated 206 million visits over the year. Compared with a population of just over 47 million in England (plus overseas visitors), the importance of attractions is clear. But only 33 sites making an admission charge exceeded half a million visits in the year, many of those being in London and drawing on the large number of overseas visitors. The 3,000 attractions sustained an estimated 23,000 full time job equivalents, but it is clear that only a few, probably no more than about 150 attractions, have the staff resources to employ their own professional marketing

managers, although most are engaged in marketing activities to some extent. For the rest, compared with the larger operators which dominate transport and hotels, most are still in the cottage industry stage.

There are some obvious and important well managed exceptions to the generalizations above, such as Disney World and Disneyland, and the other major operators in the USA; Madame Tussauds, Alton Towers, the National Trust, English Heritage, and Beaulieu for example in the UK. But the management philosophies at the bulk of all visitor attractions around the world are typically not strongly orientated towards marketing concepts.

In the 1980s it seems true to say that the attractions sector of the tourist industry is dividing into a few which practise modern management techniques, and others which are still far from the philosophies of customer orientation advocated in this book. In the first group are most of the larger operators achieving at least 100,000 visits per annum, plus some of the smaller attractions, especially where they have managed to forge links with others to operate as members of consortia for marketing purposes.

Historically, many attractions, especially those based on collections, were formed and are directed by dedicated enthusiasts and scholars. Typically these enthusiasts have always been short of funds and had to overcome great difficulties in defeating the forces of inertia to establish their collections. As a result many attractions are located in structures and sites which are barely adequate for the purpose, having only limited facilities for display and interpretation to the general public. At the same time, the management structure of individuals, trusts, local authority recreation departments and government agencies which control many attractions, is not noted for its marketing expertise.

On this evidence, certainly in Britain, the typical site manager is responsible for one site location only; has very limited links with other sites; has never undertaken any form of market research; has had no marketing training and has a marketing budget of under £5,000 per annum. Such a manager is likely to be more concerned with the daily problems of financial survival than with expansion and development through marketing initiatives.

Whilst there are very few multiples established in the attractions field in Britain offering unified product standards, the National Trust and English Heritage (with their equivalents in Scotland and Wales) provide the closest equivalent to large multi-site chains, marketed with a common image and under central management control. These large groups have some smaller voluntary equivalents among the independent attractions including, for example, The Magnificent Seven (historic properties – see later in the chapter), Great Little Trains of Wales (steam railways), and several area co-operatives. These groupings are a logical development in the marketing of attractions, both for promotion and distribution purposes, and they are believed to point to a future in which such linkages will become increasingly common.

The attractions product

Both transport and accommodation products are defined in this part of the book as performing an enabling rather than a motivating role within the overall tourism product. It is also stressed that much of transport revenue still derives from various forms of business and other non-leisure travel, and from the carriage of freight. Similarly, for hotels and other forms of accommodation, a significant proportion of total sales revenue derives from non-leisure travel and from bars, catering, and functions which are geared to a local community rather than to visitors.

By contrast, managed visitor attractions are almost exclusively concerned with leisure travel segments and motivations, with the possible exception of school and other educational visits, although even these fit more into a type of leisure rather than business travel. In other words, attractions constitute part of the primary motivation for the destination choices of leisure travellers, and as such, lie at the core of the overall travel and tourism product.

As noted earlier in this chapter, managed attractions are based on resources which may be natural or built. They often involve collections of scarce objects as the basis of their appeal. But it is not resources or collections which are the product. It is the *visitor experience* which the resources provide. The attractions product cannot be effectively marketed unless this key point is understood. The visitor experience in each case reflects the resource which the site provides. It ranges from simple aesthetic pleasure and interest, as in gardens; through 'white knuckle' thrills and excitement of amusement parks; fantasy as at some of the Tussauds exhibitions; to serious learning and awareness associated with new techniques for museum display and presentation, such as those found at modern folk museums. The range of experiences is very wide. What a particular experience provides to targeted market segments can usually be established only through consumer research among key market segments rather than through management guesswork. But at all managed sites, the *experience* is a matter of product formulation which can be influenced or controlled by management decisions.

Product formulation

The visitor experience at attractions begins with anticipation. It may be stimulated by effective promotion, especially printed materials, and by personal recommendation. It begins in earnest at the entrance to the site. From the moment of arrival, well exemplified by the sense of scale and quality conveyed by Disney World's astonishing motorway style entrance route and the row of parking toll booths spread across the traffic lanes, every aspect of the experience which visitors undergo is potentially under management control. To some extent this is also true of transport and accommodation operations, but more so for attractions since the purpose of being on site is not usually functional, but to derive satisfaction in an awareness and enjoyment of the surroundings. In some historic buildings and sites, the degree of management control is governed by planning and policy restrictions but the essential components of the product may be summarized as follows:

- appearance of the entrance and initial orientation provided to visitors, including information provided at the admission point
- visitor circulation patterns on the site, managed through the logical lay out of the resource elements, paths, signposting, and in other ways
- displays, presentation, and interpretation of the main elements of the resource, including audio visual materials and any events or activities provided
- location and layout of any subsidiary attractions on the site
- location and layout of facilities such as toilets, cafes, and shops

It is helpful to view each of these product elements within the overall experience as part of a 'bundle' or package of components which may be varied by management decisions. Because one of the prime objects of attractions marketing is to generate motivation, customer satisfaction, and value for money, marketing inputs into product formulation will be crucial to success.

Market segments for visitor attractions

Experience with researching attractions both in Britain and in other countries indicates that, in varying proportions, all attractions draw their customers from the same basic range of segments. Any differences between sites in the segments they attract are likely to be explained, either by the motivating power of the attraction, or by locational factors such as proximity to a holiday destination.

Some attractions, such as Disney World in Florida or Shakespeare's birthplace in Stratford-on-Avon, are strong enough and sufficiently well known to break through the normal locational influences which govern visitor flows. But for most attractions, the influence of locational factors will be at least as strong as the resource base. The reason is that, apart from specialist visitors with knowledge of the subjects covered by the resource, most visitors to tourist attractions will typically have little or no knowledge of the resource at the point of entry to the site. For example, visitors to parks and gardens may well include botanists with a deep knowledge of plants and horticulture. They will, however, typically comprise no more than a very small proportion of all visitors.

Practical segmentation of the general visitor public begins with user types and only then proceeds to demographic and other segmentation factors which are covered in Chapter 7. Within Britain, the following segments will normally apply:

1 Local residents living within approximately half an hour's drive from the site.
2 Regional residents making day visits away from home and drawn, depending on the motivating power of the site, from a distance of up to two hours' driving, or more in the case of sites of national significance.
3 Visitors staying with friends and relatives within about an hour's drive from the site.
4 Visitors on holiday staying in hotels, caravan parks, and other forms of commercial accommodation within about an hour's drive from the site.

5 Group visits, typically arranged in association with coach companies, or through direct marketing contact with groups made by the attractions management.

6 School visits and other educational groups.

Foreign visitors may be separated from groups 3 and 4 and treated as separate segments for marketing purposes.

Because of the nature of attractions, their fixed location, spare capacity on most days, and need to draw as many visitors as possible, it is very rarely sensible to approach the marketing task by concentrating only on one or two of the possible segments. Where attractions charge for admission, the need to generate revenue will make it even more important to appeal to as many visitor groups as possible.

For the accommodation and transport sectors of travel and tourism, segmentation is normally an essential step in product design and adaptation. Segmentation for attractions, however, is more important for targeting promotion and distribution than for product formulation. For example, if it appears for a particular attraction that holiday visitors will be especially important in its visitor mix, the implication is not so much to design the product for holiday visitors, but to focus most promotional and distribution efforts on them. The marketing approach to local residents will be quite different from that aimed at tourists. Although the length of time holiday visitors spend on the site could be important in terms of a sensible day which perhaps starts in their accommodation at 10 a.m. and ends back there around 5 p.m., the product they enjoy is not necessarily affected by their being on holiday.

Factors in the external environment

Because they mostly operate on a small scale, single site attractions are normally less affected by the constant changes in the external environment which preoccupy the marketing managers of large-scale transport and accommodation suppliers. Four long-term factors may be stressed. These are actions of competitors, growing customer sophistication, application of new technology, and the effects of other destination organizations' decisions upon specific attractions.

So far as competitors are concerned, the most important characteristic is the growing supply and capacity of attractions which compete, often in the same locality, for the same market segments. In Britain the growth in the number of sites competing for a fairly static market demand has meant that individual sites have to work much harder in the 1980s to sustain their visitor numbers. As more and more localities look to tourism to generate employment lost from primary and manufacturing industry, this competition will increase. Much of the new competition will be purpose designed or adapted to attract and satisfy visitors and some of it may be substantially subsidized by government and its agencies and Trusts. In this more competitive environment, some older attractions are likely to disappear, no longer able to attract sufficient customers or adequate funding from other sources to cover their operating expenses.

Customer sophistication reflects the increasing exposure which visitors have to international standards, partly through their own travel, partly through television, and partly because the leading attractions in any country are continuously developing new standards of excellence against which all other sites will be judged.

New technology has opened up new opportunities which museum and other site designers can utilize in the display and interpretation of the resources with which they are concerned. Lighting, sound, film, lasers, IMAX (very wide screen effects for film displays), and new materials such as plastic and carbon fibre, are all involved in modern displays. Even the traditional roller coasters are giving way to new corkscrew and looping tracks, employing the flexibility of tubular steel. Computer operated simulators, to create realistic sensations of movement, and visual and aural effects, are becoming less expensive and are likely to be more popular in the attractions of the future. At a more mundane level, attractions which are not employing electronic cash tills as part of their management control systems are losing valuable market research data about their customer profile.

The external effects of decisions made by other suppliers at destinations must be mentioned, because managed attractions are usually only a minor element in the total travel and tourism products on which the future of destinations depends. Whilst the decisions of the Disney Organization were highly instrumental in what happened around Orlando in Florida, this is quite exceptional. Normally the overall demand for attractions varies with the fortunes of the host destination. In the case of London or Paris, for example, the visitor revenues of the major attractions fluctuate with the number of foreign visitors. But the attractions themselves have only a very minor role in such market fluctuations.

The net effect of all these external factors is to focus increasing attention on marketing aspects. The point made by Cossons, a leading British pioneer in the marketing of museums, can equally be applied to other forms of managed attraction:

> 'Museums will stand or fall not only by their competence to care for collections, but by their ability to care for people. In other words, they need to be market-orientated if they are to survive . . .' (Cossons: 1985: p. 44).

Operating constraints on marketing

As noted earlier in the chapter, attraction managers tend, by the nature of their occupations and backgrounds, to be more inwardly concerned with their resource base than outwardly concerned with customer interests. Fortunately, product formulation interpreted as managing experiences leaves ample scope for developing customer benefits without damaging the intrinsic quality of the resources. In practice, there are fewer constraints on product formulation than might appear at first sight. There are however, three other constraints influencing the marketing of attractions which require brief discussion.

The first reflects the by now familiar concern with the effects of high fixed costs and low variable costs of operation. This affects attractions just as it affects transport and accommodation suppliers. For example, a busy Summer day at the National Motor Museum at Beaulieu, Hampshire, sees over 5,000 visitors through the turnstiles. By contrast, a Winter day in February may produce only 150 people. Yet, if the quality of the visitor experience is to be maintained, the fixed costs of operating in February are much the same as in July. Any savings in the numbers of part time staff are offset by the increased costs of heating and lighting. Obviously, on a simple *pro rata* basis, the museum operates at a loss in February and at other times of the year, so that the role of marketing in generating marginal extra admission income is exactly the same in principle for attractions as for transport operators. In practice large attractions have fixed costs to cover around the year, and the contribution of the February visits has to be seen as a revenue gain which would be lost if the attraction were to be closed.

The second constraint, made worse by the fact of high fixed costs, is the effect of seasonality. A rule of thumb relevant to British attractions is that maximum capacity or volume of demand will be experienced on only about 20 days in the year. On each of those 20 days an average of about one per cent of the year's total volume will be received. Where the site is located near a holiday resort, it is not unusual for over 45 per cent of the year's volume to be achieved over about eight weeks. The role of marketing is to contribute to the generation of demand, outside the limited number of peak days.

A third constraint affecting many attractions is the extent to which repeat visits to any one site in any one year are usually a minority of all visits. Some attractions have the kind of resource which encourages repeat visits, whilst many are designed for one visit only. But, with the competition now facing most attractions, it is probable that people making more than one visit within a 12-month span will be in the minority. Finding promotional ways to encourage new, first time visits is, therefore, a primary concern for most attractions. This fact helps to explain why the successful large attractions find it necessary to spend 10 per cent or more of their admissions revenue on promotion and distribution. It might be less if there were more repeat visitors. Smaller attractions typically spend far lower proportions, but many will be unable to grow unless they accept the logic of gearing marketing budgets to revenue targets as explained in Chapter 14 (marketing campaigns).

The marketing task for attractions

It is logical to distinguish between the strategic and tactical levels of marketing decisions.

Strategic tasks

The main task of strategy for attractions on which all marketing will be based, involves segmenting the total market and targeting the potential volume demand from each group. This becomes the base for forecasting maximum achievable revenue flows. Such forecasts will be essential inputs to site management, affecting both capital and operating revenue decisions. This strategic task will be also the basis for creating effective campaigns for promotion and distribution targeted on the specified groups of prospective customers.

The second, related task of strategy, is to identify the nature of the experience which the resource base is capable of sustaining, either as it is, or as it might be if enhanced. Enhancement is possible through affordable development and improved presentation, display, and information techniques. Because of the obvious dangers of product orientation in managing attractions, the only effective way to ascertain the *experience*, is through consumer research with targeted segments of customers.

Following logically from the first two aspects of strategy, the third task lies in product formulation and augmentation to provide and enhance customer satisfaction with the quality of the experience which the resource base affords. School parties for example, will often require specific materials and facilities, both to attract them and to help them derive maximum satisfaction and perceived value for money.

Mostly, it will be possible for promotional and product formulation purposes, to identify one principal underlying theme, or idea, which encapsulates the resource base and the experiences it sustains. This theme will be the basis for positioning the attraction and the benefits it offers, in all marketing communications aimed at prospective visitors.

Fifth, strategy will also involve the search for productive promotional and distribution linkages between the attraction and other sites of the same type, or of different types in the same location. Such links may be achieved with the support of tourist boards, or directly between co-operating producers. Another aspect of this search for linkages may be the arrangements for promotion and distribution which can be made with transport and accommodation interests seeking to provide extra interest and motivation in their own product offers. The obvious link is with coach tour operators, but hotels offering weekend breaks are increasingly interested to feature admission to attractions as part of an inclusive price. In this context, attractions become a part of the augmentation of an accommodation product, which in turn serves as a form of distribution for the attraction.

Tactical marketing

Working within the strategic framework, marketing tactics will draw on the wide range of promotion and distribution techniques discussed in Part Four of the book. As with other forms of travel and tourism marketing, the main focus will be to mould demand around the fixed supply, especially to secure the vital additional admissions which represent pure revenue gain once the high fixed costs of operation have been committed. The latter point obviously applies only in circumstances where revenues have to be earned rather than provided as grants or subsidies.

The most productive promotional tools will normally be forms of targeted advertising aimed at creating and maintaining awareness and interest in the site, especially among prospective first time users; supported by PR exploiting whatever public interest may lie in the resource base. In addition, many attractions have discovered that staging special events, such as craft fairs, demonstrations, displays and temporary exhibitions, creates interest and achieves media space other than that which has to be paid for. Events may also bring in first time visitors who may be persuaded to return on a 'normal' day.

On the distribution side, the prime task in respect of prospective tourist visitors is ensuring that leaflets, posters and show cards are continuously available in all forms of accommodation in the identified catchment area; at tourist information centres; and through any other links which may be formed with other attractions or producers.

There is little evidence to show that last minute price discounting is a relevant tactic for attracting new visitors to attractions, although this is a common practice for transport and accommodation sectors. This is partly because of the difficulty of communicating temporary price changes, and also because of the relatively low level of repeat visits. Once people have made the effort to visit an attraction, provided the normal prices are realistic as measured by research into value for money, they are unlikely to have their minds changed by discount offers at the point of admission. Of all tourist products, the motivation to visit an attraction is one of the least likely to be based on a price discount.

Experience suggests that allocating around 10 per cent of admissions revenue for marketing purposes, is a realistic guideline for most visitor attractions. There may well be a convincing argument for spending more than this, especially to promote awareness of new facilities, and if the evidence achieved through visitor monitoring indicates that the promotional efforts are paying off in admission revenue. Objective and task approaches to budgeting, outlined in Chapter 14, are particularly appropriate for visitor attractions.

Marketing illustrations

Two examples of good practice in attractions marketing are provided to illustrate some of the main principles outlined in this chapter. The first is a joint marketing operation, and the second is a membership campaign designed to increase loyalty and intensity of usage of National Trust properties.

Magnificent seven – the treasure houses of England

The seven are a group of attractions in England which come under the broad category of historic houses, although some of them also feature other major visitor attractions and exhibitions in their grounds. Known until 1986 as the 'Magnificent Seven', the group was first formed in 1975 as a voluntary co-operative of fully independent owners who saw advantages in joint promotion to the overseas visitor market. The Seven, who had extended their joint marketing operations to include UK domestic visitors, changed their name to 'The Treasure Houses of England' in 1987 when they were joined by Chatsworth House. The eight are now, Beaulieu, Broadlands, Blenheim Palace, Castle Howard, Chatsworth, Harewood House, Warwick Castle, and Woburn Abbey.

At the upper end of the visitor numbers scale, these are all large attractions which draw in over 3 million visits per annum between them and employ professional management and marketing staff. Each property has always had, and still retains, its own identity, image, name, and marketing budget. Each is responsible on an individual basis for a marketing programme which generates the bulk of its visitor business. Spread around England, the eight are hardly in direct competition, even for foreign visitors, and they see strong advantages in joint marketing activity which included, for 1986:

- advertising themselves in guides and other media, as a group
- production of a joint leaflet, incorporating privilege voucher discounts, primarily for distribution overseas, but also available in the UK; with each property acting as a referral system
- production of showcards and posters for use in support of the leaflet, and at exhibitions
- use of joint stands at major workshops and travel exhibitions
- production of a travel trade manual to facilitate the way in which tour operators, coach tour firms and others in the travel trade can build the properties into their programmes
- joint PR, as the opportunity presents or can be created.

The group does not publish its financial arrangements, but it is understood that members contribute on an equal basis so that their group subscriptions probably amount to between 5 and 20 per cent of their individual marketing budgets. For that outlay, they achieve valuable coverage, especially in guides and through distribution of leaflets, which they could not achieve on their own for the equivalent sum. They also generate marginal admission revenue through the working of the privilege voucher scheme included in the group leaflet, which incorporates a competition for visitors who get to at least four of the houses. The size of the group's activities and, of course, the intrinsic quality of the product, has made it possible to draw in sponsors to supplement the group budget. Lastly, the process of meetings necessary to agree the scope of each year's activities, provides lines of management communication between the properties which are used to exchange information on market trends and other aspects of mutual interest, which adds value to the more tangible forms of co-operation noted above.

National trust membership scheme

The National Trust in Britain, established in the late nineteenth century, is a charity whose interests extend throughout England, Wales, and Northern Ireland. There is a separate Trust for Scotland formed in the 1930s. The principal object of the Trust is to preserve and manage historic and beautiful properties and areas for the benefit of the public, and for posterity. Over the years, the Trust's portfolio of properties has grown and, in 1985, its ownership and management responsibilities extended to 24 castles, 184 houses, 108 gardens, 21 wind and water mills, half a million acres of countryside and 440 miles of coastline.

Within the definitions of this chapter, the National Trust is by far the largest non-government sponsored owner of managed attractions in Britain. It is very much a large multi-site operator which merits comparison with other large marketing organizations in travel and tourism. Nearly 20 of the properties have annual visitor numbers in excess of 100,000, whilst uncounted millions more each year take advantage of access to the areas of countryside and coastline which the Trust owns and manages. As a charity, the Trust is financially self-supporting. It relies heavily on visitor revenue at the properties for which it charges admission, to cover its annual operating costs and to contribute to the heavy cost of conservation.

To help it achieve its annual revenue targets, the Trust has adopted the logical marketing response of any multi-site service product operator; it has promoted repeat business and rewarded loyal customers through a membership scheme open to the general public. The marketing director of the Trust revealed some of the details of this scheme in a recent paper to the International Conference of National Trusts from which the following facts are taken (Beaumont: 1986).

Through a carefully targeted promotional campaign, the Trust has increased its membership from half a million people in the mid 1970s to nearly one and a half million in the mid 1980s. The subscriptions which these members pay generated some 20 per cent of the Trust's annual revenue in 1985. A further fifth of revenue came from the gifts and legacies of donors, a large proportion of whom are also members and were doubtless influenced by membership benefits and communications.

Logically exploiting its multi-site merchandising opportunities, the National Trust was able to obtain four fifths of its new members through on-site recruitment efforts at its properties. The annual membership fee in the mid 1980s was £12.50 for adults and £25.00 for a family ticket. The principal benefit to members is free admission to any Trust owned property during the year. While to many of its members the Trust offers just an attractive season ticket, the operation is much more important in marketing terms than that. The management of the Trust have:

- a list of over 1.4 million members to whom they mail a magazine three times a year, promotional offers, and a mail order catalogue of gifts, the sales of which are an important additional contribution to Trust revenue. The value of such a list for targeted marketing is obvious
- a potential pool of volunteers who may be approached for support in some of the work of the Trust to which volunteers can make a contribution
- powerful word-of-mouth recommendation by committed members to their friends, relatives and acquaintances
- an ideal list of contacts for launching appeals for donations and gifts which are important to the Trust's work
- a list of great potential value for market research purposes, not least in the profile of customers revealed by addresses.

Although not strictly related to the membership initiative, the National Trust has used the national image and impact it has created to establish some 150 retail shops around the country, most of which are not based at Trust sites. These gift shops generate a sales turnover of specific, mostly Trust branded items, which contributes both to the Trust's revenue, and also enhances its national image.

The National Trust Membership scheme can thus be seen as a highly effective use of modern marketing principles. It is not of course achieved without cost, and the fact that the organization puts some £3 million a year into membership administration, recruitment, literature and PR gives some idea of the commitment. Even so, this is only 10 per cent of the Trust's annual expenditure and is obviously seen in the context of the benefits it generates.

Chapter summary

Stressing the important motivating role which attractions as a whole play as one of the core elements in the total tourism product for leisure travellers, this chapter identifies the common operating characteristics which determine how managed attractions may be marketed. Ten categories of managed attractions are set out, all of which are controlled and managed for the enjoyment, amusement, entertainment and education of visitors. Mostly, these attractions charge admission prices and increasingly the larger ones are professionally managed and marketed. The bulk of all attractions, however, are mostly small in visitor numbers and revenue, are inherently product or resource orientated, and have a low level of visitor management and marketing skills. The profile of this latter group, many of which provide their facilities free or at low admission charges, is obviously not conducive to the development and application of the systematic marketing procedures recommended in this book. For reasons discussed, the pressures of competition and the need to generate revenue, are forcing changes in professional management throughout the sector.

The definition of *products as experiences*, and the way to assess the components of the experience for product formulation, are important to successful marketing. Product formulation is always relevant to identified segments and this emphasizes the importance of market research among visitors. Owners of attractions, in common with other producers of travel and tourism services, always have a 'captive audience' on their premises, providing opportunities for cost effective research which should be exploited as the first step in the marketing process.

The *strategic marketing* tasks for attractions reflect the high fixed costs of operation, the seasonality of visitor flows, and the constant need to motivate first-time visits. Marketing strategy focuses on segmentation, product formulation, and positioning, and the need to ensure that the benefits offered by the attraction are clearly understood by targeted prospective visitors. As a recent British Tourist Authority report expressed it, reflecting on lessons learned from studying museums in the USA, 'Marketing is a positive analytical matching of a product to its market. For a museum this is the presentation of its collection or theme in a way which best communicates this to its audience or potential visitors' (BTA: 1983: p. 21).

In their essential need for marketing, managed attractions are not different in principle from other travel and tourism producers. Their needs at *tactical level* to achieve extra, marginal admissions, through maximum awareness and distribution of products, are common to all sectors.

22

Marketing transport operations

Transport is one of the five integral elements of the overall travel and tourism product defined in Chapter 8. Importantly, the forms of transport available at any period of time, and the ways in which they are marketed, have a massive influence on tourist behaviour and on the types of product which travellers purchase.

It has to be understood, however, that the development of transport systems by road, rail, inland water, sea, or air, has not usually been associated with travel for leisure purposes. Historically, transport design and development owe their impetus to the need to move goods and mail; the need to administer countries and empires; the need to move armies and military equipment; the development of new weapons of war; and the need to move people more efficiently in the conduct of their day-to-day lives. Most transport systems are still primarily geared to business, administrative and military interests, but increasingly in the latter part of the twentieth century, they are extending their original orientation towards leisure and recreation travel. The reasons for this shift in emphasis reflect the operators' need to develop into new and growing markets for transport products, and to utilize surplus capacity, both overall and especially at times of otherwise slack demand. Typically, this means creating new products, especially those which contribute to economies of scale, as part of an integrated portfolio of transport operations.

This chapter traces briefly the historical links between transport supply and tourism demand, and the increasing orientation of transport systems to travel for leisure and recreation purposes. It proceeds by defining the nature of transport systems and products, the constraints on their marketing, both internal and external, and the nature of strategic and tactical marketing tasks for passenger transport. The chapter ends with examples selected to illustrate recent practice.

Historical links between transport supply and tourism demand

Transport represents the physical means of access whereby travellers can reach their chosen destinations. As such, it is not difficult to trace the ways in which the growth of tourism around the world has been geared to developments in transport. In their unpublished work, Burkart and Medlik identify three main phases of development. The first covers the pre-industrial period and takes the story to the early nineteenth century. The second spans the next hundred years or so to the Second World War. The third covers the post-war period of mass tourism since 1945.

Until well into the nineteenth century the bulk of journeys were undertaken for business, vocational, and military purposes, by people travelling mainly in their own countries. The volume of travel was small and confined to only a fraction of the population in any country. From the 1840s onwards, as the industrial revolution in Europe and North America gathered pace, the growth of pleasure travel on an increasing scale can be identified with the development of railway systems and early steamships on inland and coastal waterways. For over a century the rail-

239

way and steamships dominated passenger travel, both facilitating and stimulating travel between countries and continents.

In this century both motor transport by road and air transport emerged but their full impact was not felt until after the Second World War when, in the 1950s, tourism became a mass phenomenon. By the 1980s car ownership had grown to approaching two thirds or more of the population in Europe, with higher levels in North America. Aircraft development received a massive impetus through the war and planes quickly took over from ships as the main means of long-distance transportation. A growing volume of travel became international and on many routes vacation traffic came to match and often greatly exceed other forms of travel. Tour operation emerged on a large scale and supported the development of charter airlines, which now carry more traffic than scheduled airlines on many European routes.

While the dates notes above are not precise, the ways in which tourist destinations developed are obviously closely linked to changes in the means of transport. For example, in the nineteenth century, seaside resorts in Northern Europe could not have developed as they did without the building of railway links which provided access for the markets emerging in the growing industrial cities and towns. Across the Atlantic, the State of Florida could not have developed as a major vacation destination in the 1970s for domestic and international tourists, without its national and international air links and the corresponding development of the State road system for cars and buses.

The nature of transport systems

Figure 22.1 summarizes the wide range of modern transport systems, the marketing of which affects all tourist destinations to some extent, and vice versa. Most destinations are simultaneously influenced by several of these systems. At first sight it is easy to suppose that each of the forms of transport is so different in kind, that comparisons and the development of common principles for marketing are impossible. In fact, all the systems share some common characteristics which have important implications for marketing practice. As Burkart and Medlik expressed it: 'A transport system can be analyzed in three parts: the track, the vehicle, and the terminal' (1981: p. 111).

Tracks: controlled air routes, sea routes, canals, permanent ways (railways), roads, trunk routes and motorways.

Vehicles: aircraft, ships, trains, buses and coaches, private vehicles.

Terminals: airports, seaports, stations, garages, and off-street parking.

In considering the external threats and opportunities in the environment influencing marketing managers' product responses in transport, it should be noted that, railways excepted, the three basic elements outlined above are typically owned and controlled by different parties. For example, in the case of air transport, the vehicles are owned and operated by airlines; the routes are effectively owned by governments who allocate and control air space; and the terminals are owned for the most part by national, regional or local governments and their appointed agencies. Without permission to fly to a country, or with permission to fly only a specified capacity of certain types of product (such as scheduled rather than charter flights), marketing managers do not enjoy full scope for responding to the market forces they perceive. Similarly, if the external agencies controlling the routes or the terminal facilities cannot cope with the added volume, marketing decisions to develop new routes or products have a very restricted meaning.

In the case of private transport, the vehicles, and to some extent the off-street parking, are owned and controlled by individuals; routes are typically developed, owned and controlled by

Air transport	**Long-haul scheduled airlines** operate networks which carry most long-haul travellers, for all purposes, around the world, and offer an extensive range of promotional fares for economy class leisure travel.
	Medium/short-haul scheduled airlines operate networks which serve mostly business and non-leisure forms of travel.
	Charter airlines – long or short haul operate networks which serve mainly leisure travel of all kinds, are sometimes subsidiary companies of scheduled airlines, or part of tour operator groups; they dominate European short-haul air travel for holiday purposes.
Sea transport	**Ferries** operate scheduled networks on short sea routes, serving as extension of road network: carry passengers for all purposes; mainly roll-on, roll-off design to suit cars, coaches and trucks; have increasing links into the inclusive tour business.
	Charter cruise ships serve as floating resorts; important market in USA, but smaller elsewhere.
Rail	**Scheduled rail services** – tourism use is restricted mainly to scheduled inter-city services for all forms of travel; extensive range or promotional fares for leisure; links with conference and accommodation; important for day excursions.
Bus and coach	**Scheduled bus** tourism use is restricted mainly to inter-city services, serving mainly non-business forms of travel.
	Charter or private hire includes coach tours and long-distance coach transport to resorts, and are a significant element of inclusive tour holidays; coaches are also an important form of intra-resort travel for transfers and excursions.
Private transport	**Private cars and car rental** are the dominant forms of travel in domestic tourism, leisure day visits and recreation, and in international travel in continental Europe; car rental fulfils a substitute private transport role and has close links with other transport operators, tour operators and accommodation providers.

Figure 22.1 *Principal passenger transport systems used in tourism*

government and its agencies; while at destinations, the bulk of the terminal or parking facilities available for private transport are often provided, and mostly regulated by local government.

So far as destination interests are concerned, such as national or regional tourist offices or attractions, marketing strategies which are not related to the changing capacity, routes and terminals of both public and private transport, are very unlikely to be successful.

In summarizing the common characteristics of transport systems influencing marketing decisions, it should be noted that:

1 All passenger transport systems involve more or less closely controlled and regulated vehicle movements along networks, which link points of origin and destination.

2 The operation of all such systems involves continuous concern with the utilization of available capacity, whether of vehicles, routes or terminals.

3 All systems display typical characteristics of peaks and troughs in demand, whether by month, week, day or hour.

4 Most systems involve massive investment in infrastructure, vehicles, track, and control systems, requiring efficient

marketing both to justify and to pay back the expenditure.

5 Most systems involve the movement of freight as well as passengers and freight requirements may take precedence.
6 Most systems are only partly involved with leisure travel.
7 All systems put some pressure on the physical environment, especially that of host communities.

Supply increasingly leads demand for transport products

Although, historically, transport services have generally developed in response to economic and other demands, it is increasingly difficult to be sure to what extent demand creates supply, or supply generates demand. As Shaw puts it; '... demand analysis in any transport industry poses problems because it cannot be viewed in isolation. Rather, it has inextricable links with supply. When an airline introduces service on a route, notable developments may follow' (1982: p. 13). The ability of supply to generate demand is clearly also true of roads and bridges as well. The channel tunnel between England and France, for example, is clearly expected to be an important generator of new traffic when it is opened.

The supply effect can be seen in all types of travel, but it appears to be especially true of modern forms of leisure travel, which can be persuaded through effective marketing and promotion, to switch its choices to alternative destinations. According to consumer surveys there is in Britain, for example, a huge potential demand for holidays in the USA. Whenever the dollar/pound exchange rate has been favourable to the British, the traffic has surged. The greatest obstacle to growth is the cost of travel across the Atlantic, despite the range of promotional fares available. If the cost of transport could be significantly reduced through new economies of scale, or through some technological, cost saving breakthrough, there can be little doubt that demand could be led by the supply of cheaper transport.

The powerful effect of the supply leading role of transport in tourism markets is especially obvious in the case of islands, such as those in the Pacific area, where the development of new routes acts almost like a tap for new demand. The important point in travel and tourism is that supply and demand are essentially interactive. It is an interaction which can be exploited to good effect by transport marketing managers.

Functional role of transport in the overall tourist product

Although it is one of the five integral elements of travel and tourism products, modern transport is not normally a part of the motivation or attraction of a destination visit. There are some exceptions to this, such as steam railways, the Orient Express, or cruise ships, although the latter are better viewed as floating hotels or resorts, than as forms of transport. The transport element, as Holloway described it (1985: p. 23), is only an 'enabling condition'; that is to say, a functional element which is essential to the existence and growth of tourism, but not of itself a sufficient reason for travel.

The role of transport in leisure travel was not always so functional. In the pioneering days of both public and private transport, journeys of all kinds, especially those by air and sea, could be presented as exciting, glamorous, and romantic. In those circumstances, the journey was an adventure and an important part of travel motivation. By the 1970s, however, except possibly for first time travellers by air and sea, the journey had lost most if not all of its earlier magic. Experienced travellers, especially those on business trips, increasingly see the journey element as a necessary but often unpleasant part of the overall trip. Journeys by public transport have to be paid for not only in money terms, but also in the stress and strain of heavily congested access routes, queuing in crowded terminals, and increasing risk to personal safety. When using private transport, the strain of driving along congested trunk routes and of finding parking space at the destination, has removed most of what was once the glamour of the open road.

This changing attitude towards one element of the overall travel and tourism product, is most clearly evident among frequent business travellers. But it has many implications for the marketing of transport and especially for the way in which product 'benefits' are presented to prospective customers. In particular it encourages transport operators to move closer to destination interests, which provide the principal motivation for journeys, and this important point is explored later in the chapter.

The transport product

For charter airlines and touring coaches the transport element is no more than one component within the overall tourist product, and the marketing of such products is not normally the responsibility of the transport operators. By contrast, whatever links they form with other elements of the overall product, all scheduled transport operators have to compete for shares of their passenger markets with specific products based on their services and route networks. It is in this latter context that most transport marketing takes place.

As defined in Chapter 8, any specific service product offered to customers, represents a combination or 'bundle' of components available at a specified price. The main components in the transport bundle are service availability and convenience (reflecting routes, schedules and capacity); the design and performance of the vehicle; comfort, and any services offered in transit; passenger handling at terminals; and convenience of booking and ticketing arrangements.

Viewed from the customer's standpoint, the products offered by operators of the same type of transport, such as airlines or sea ferries, tend to be remarkably undifferentiated in comparison with the products offered in other sectors of the tourist industry. Perceived 'sameness' of product is an obvious problem for marketing managers and it is interesting to note the reasons for it. In a closely regulated transport environment (explained on page 215), formal and informal agreements between governments, other regulatory bodies, and other transport operators, serve to produce virtual uniformity in the basic components of the *formal product* (see Chapter 8). In the case of international air transport, until the early 1970s almost every aspect of the product, from price down to the smallest detail of in-flight services, was covered by agreements. The products were commonly offered in identical aircraft with the same cabin layouts.

In a more liberated or de-regulated climate, the use of the same equipment, shared terminals, and fierce price competition still produce virtual uniformity in the formal product. As a result, most airline advertising has tended to focus on corporate images and the quality of service, rather than on promoting specific products. Apart from obvious distinctions between, first class, business class, and economy class products, and with limited but important exceptions such as Concorde, the traditional approach to product formulation based on analysis of the components of supply, now appears rather sterile. As Shaw put it, 'the airline product is intangible, amorphous, and difficult to analyse . . .' (1982: p. 114).

A more fertile approach to understanding transport products appears to lie in the analysis of demand. This is a customer segmentation approach working from the profiles, attitudes, and behaviour of the identified groups in the total market, with which the transport operator is concerned. While the main components of supply remain the same as before, it is in the area of customer orientated *product augmentation* (Chapter 8) that there is real room for manoeuvre and differentiation in the formulation of transport products. From this standpoint, an operator's portfolio of products, is best approached as a portfolio of customer segments. The knowledge which the operator has of the profile and needs of his segments, is the logical basis for effective marketing strategy and tactics. Such knowledge requires a massive commitment to customer research of the type discussed in Chapter 11, but the same research serves also to identify the relevant links with other elements of the overall tourist product, which can be exploited for marketing purposes.

The dominance of the external environment

Part One of the book emphasizes the ways in which the external environment surrounding all kinds of businesses, dominates the marketing decisions of producers. In particular the marketing decisions of transport operators are influenced by their response to six specific external factors, over most of which they have only very limited control. These factors are listed and briefly discussed below:

- vehicle technology (major innovations)
- information technology
- regulatory environment
- price of fuel
- economic growth or decline (national and international economy)
- exchange rate fluctuations

Vehicle technology

From private cars, through cruise ships, to aircraft, competition among manufacturers is constantly developing the capabilities of vehicles in terms of their size, seat capacity, speed, range,

fuel efficiency, noise, and passenger comfort. Such changes affect the profitability of operations, and can also influence customer choice. Over time, as noted earlier, the changes also determine which destinations can be reached within acceptable time and cost constraints. The development of wide-bodied long-haul jets, for example, made possible the rapid expansion of tourism during the 1970s to the Pacific region and other parts of the world.

Whilst the implications of developing vehicle technology for tourism markets are most obviously seen in public transport, the extension of car ownership and the increasing comfort, reliability, and efficiency of the vehicles, is equally vital to the market growth of many forms of tourism. Short week-end breaks, self-catering accommodation, and day visits to attractions are all highly dependent on car travel.

Information technology

The development of computers in the 1960s and the widespread application of the technology during the 1970s, has made it possible for passenger transport operators to deal efficiently with the increasing volume of their business. Led by airlines, reservations, cancellations, ticketing, invoicing, options on routes and fares, are now handled by computers, which simultaneously generate a wealth of research data on the characteristics of the business, of great value in the marketing planning process. Information technology (IT) has also transformed the distribution process for travel and tourism generally. Many of the developments have been led by transport operators in search of greater cost efficiency in the conduct of routine operations, and, equally important, in the conduct and control of their marketing operations. New marketing linkages between product elements are greatly facilitated by the creation of interactive, on-line computer networks, bringing together, for example, the reservation systems of airlines, hotels, and car rental organizations.

Regulatory environment

For most of the twentieth century, the operations of international and national passenger transport systems have been closely controlled and regulated in all countries, both for domestic and international movements. In air transport, permissions to fly between countries and through national air spaces involve treaty agreements between governments, typically covering which airlines will be permitted, over what routes, with what capacity, and with what price ranges and options. The government agencies which control these decisions, such as the Civil Aviation Authority (CAA) in Britain, or the Civil Aeronautics Board (CAB) in the USA, are in effect, participating directly in crucial areas of marketing decisions and acting in lieu of market forces. Whichever agency controls product capacity (supply of seats), and determines or influences price, obviously has a very powerful influence over demand.

Requiring non-commercial agencies to act in lieu of market forces is not necessarily efficient and, originating with legislation in 1978 covering USA domestic airlines, there has been a widespread international shift towards removing regulatory controls. There are strong arguments that the forces of supply and demand, and unfettered competition between operators, are a better way to determine air transport markets than regulation. The same arguments have been applied to other forms of transport. The full effects of deregulation in the USA are still far from clear at the time of writing, and by early 1986, of 72 new entrants to the airline industry, 33 had failed and the evidence pointed to market dominance by five very large corporations. The process of dismantling regulation is currently under active discussion in Europe, with some routes already partially deregulated. But many governments around the world are not convinced by the free market arguments and it is not clear how the issues will be resolved by politicians. The further removal of parts of the international regulatory framework, and the encouragement of further competition in the remaining years of this century, appears very probable. Such changes will have the effect of further stimulating marketing efforts.

Other external factors

External economic factors generally are discussed in Part I of this book and in Chapter 9 on pricing. Economic growth or recession obviously has a major influence on the market volume carried by transport operators for business and leisure purposes, with the latter especially susceptible to fluctuations in exchange rates. The influence on transport costs of rapidly rising fuel oil prices also affected most forms of transport in the last decade.

Operational constraints on public transport operations

The previous section considered the influence of factors in the external environment on marketing decisions. This section focuses on the internal constraints that arise from the nature of operating a passenger transport system.

Capital investment and fixed costs

A principal characteristic of any modern transport operation is the high level of capital investment and fixed costs which are required in terms of purchasing and maintaining vehicles and equipment, setting up and maintaining route networks, and employing staff to operate the system. Whilst the level of investment is especially high for airlines, with modern long-haul 'jumbo jets' costing up to £100 million each at 1987 prices, the same characteristic, relative to the size of their revenues, applies equally to shipping lines, railway systems, or to bus and coach operations. In each case, expensive new equipment, often associated with increased seating capacity, is usually justified on the grounds that through more efficient operation it will lower the operating cost per passenger seat mile and thus permit potentially lower fares to be charged, or more profit to be made at the existing prices. A vital proviso in this argument is that the potentially lower costs can only produce real savings, *if*, enough of the seats on offer are sold.

A second dominant characteristic which acts as a constraint on marketing decisions is that the committed, or 'fixed' costs as they are known, of operating any service are typically high, and the variable costs are typically low. Accountants and economists have different conventions for deciding which aspects of costs are fixed and which are variable. Strictly, for airlines, fuel costs and landing charges are variable costs since they are not incurred if a flight does not take place. In practical terms, once the decision is taken to fly a particular route at a particular time, all the main costs become effectively 'fixed' since they have to be paid regardless of the number of seats sold. Whilst full aircraft use more fuel than empty ones, the difference measured on a per seat mile basis is very small. From a marketing standpoint, it concentrates the mind to recognize that any seat sales achieved after the decision is made to operate a service, which may be weeks before it is performed, represent pure revenue gain. This revenue gain goes either to cover committed fixed costs or, once the break-even load factor is reached, it represents gross profit.

Load factors and fleet utilization

Because of the investment and high fixed cost implications of passenger transport operations, there are two key measures of operational efficiency which are especially relevant to marketing managers. The most critical measure is the seat occupancy which is known technically as the *load factor*. The other key measure is fleet utilization. As in any form of production based on expensive plant, the more intensively a piece of equipment is used, the better the performance in terms of revenue achieved against the fixed costs incurred. If, for example, an expensive aircraft (on long haul routes) can be kept in the air

and flying with more than a break-even load of passengers, for an average of some 12 hours in every 24 around the year (including allowance for routine inspections and servicing), it can obviously generate more revenue to cover its fixed costs, than the same aircraft flying for an average of only 10 hours a day. Utilization is partly a function of efficient maintenance and scheduling the network to achieve the shortest possible turnround of vehicles, but it is much more a function of generating sufficient demand to justify the flight frequency.

The role of marketing in passenger transport is not confined solely to achieving higher load factors and increased utilization at the margin. Nevertheless, the necessity of maintaining the level of seat occupancy on each service performed, and at the same time supporting economically high utilization rates throughout the year, underlies all transport marketing thinking. The significance of this point can be realized from the estimate that the world airline industry suffered 'five straight years of losses totalling $6.2 billion' between 1980 and 1984. Yet 'airlines will need to invest between $150 billion and $200 billion in aircraft and other fixed assets over the next ten years'. (*The Times*, March 28, 1986). The absolute importance of achieving marginal revenue can be seen in the break-even load factors of scheduled European air transport carriers, which varied in the years between 1978 and 1984, from 50 per cent to 53 per cent. Actual load factors achieved in the same years, varied from 50.7 per cent to 55.4 per cent (Wheatcroft and Lipman: 1986: p. 35). Only in two of those years did the load factor exceed the break-even level by more than 2 percentage points; in none of them did the carriers involved generate sufficient revenue for their investment needs.

The nature of the marketing task for passenger transport operators

The overall marketing process summarized in

Figure 2.1 (Chapter 2), and explained in Parts II and III of this book, is as applicable to transport operators as to any other producer of consumer products. The marketing tasks in passenger transport derive logically from the characteristics of operations, and the internal and external environment in which they are conducted, as explained in the preceding two sections. The main tasks may now be summarized under the headings of strategic and tactical marketing, which apply to all forms of public transport operators, whether by rail, road, air, or sea.

Strategic marketing

The strategic marketing task has four main elements. The first, through extensive use of marketing research techniques and continuous passenger monitoring, is to provide forecasts of market potential, on the basis of which future operational networks, schedules, and the associated investment can be planned. Because fleet purchases along with other investment needs are geared to revenue forecasts (volume of customers × the average price they will pay), the ability of marketing managers to provide realistic inputs to demand forecasting, is crucial to the profitable development of any transport business. Estimates of traffic flows have to be built up route by route, separately for each main market segment. In practice, while forecasting models are normally the responsibility of transport economists and statisticians, the quality of the marketing research inputs relating to segments, products, customer satisfaction and market developments, is vital. The decision of most airlines in Europe in the 1980s to follow the lead of British Airways, and to develop the business for club class sections now common on most scheduled flights, is one example of an important strategic marketing decision with far-reaching operational implications. That decision relied heavily on available marketing research data, when the crucial estimates of business volume and revenue were made.

Inevitably, estimates of network traffic flows will always be surrounded by risk because of the unpredictable nature of the business environment. But the better the operator's knowledge of customer behaviour, the better the chance of reducing the risk. Marketing strategy can be seen, in this context, as contributing to the balance which every operator seeks to achieve between his portfolio of products and markets.

As part of the process of converting the estimated market potential into real revenue, the second element in marketing strategy lies in the way in which operators match, and seek to lead their competitors, in the continuous struggle for market shares. In an increasingly de-regulated environment, strategy tends to focus on identifying operators' strengths from a customer standpoint, in terms of which images or 'positions' of products can be communicated through advertising to targeted segments. At the highly sensitive margin of business, either side of the break-even load factor, uncommitted potential customers may have their choice influenced by positive or negative images of different operators. Recognition of the power of such images explains the considerable commitment of operators to both corporate and product advertising.

The third common element in strategic marketing lies in the effort which all operators tend to put into creating and retaining regular, repeat buyers of their services. Mostly business travellers, a small number of frequent users may typically provide a high proportion of total revenue. For example, 20 per cent of customers could easily generate 50 per cent of all revenue on some routes, because of the fares they pay, and the frequency with which they travel. Such customers are worth careful cultivation and one of the strategies used is to create schemes to reward people who make repeat purchases with the same operator. Traditional season tickets have been available for many years on rail and road commuter routes, but competition between airlines is generating new forms of loyalty schemes, which are likely to develop further in the rest of this century. Identifying the small number of customers who are very important to the business is not restricted to transport operators; it is now also common in accommodation marketing, again mainly for business travellers.

The fourth element in marketing strategy lies in the way in which some transport operators are increasingly shifting their focus outwards, away from the performance of their traditional roles as operators of vehicles, routes and terminals, towards linkages with other elements of the overall travel and tourism product. In other words, the extent to which providers of transport seek strategic marketing links with destination interests and with the distribution network for travel products. The scope for these links is already wide, and ranges from relatively limited links with accommodation providers and attractions, all the way up to full integration with marketing organizations such as tour operators or wholesalers. From the earliest days of railways, links with terminal hotels were seen as necessary to the efficient development of transport businesses. A century later, some airlines formed similar links with hotel groups for exactly the same reasons. In leisure travel, the logical extreme of the linkage strategy is seen most clearly in the charter airlines which are integrated with tour operators, such as Britannia (Thomson Holidays) and Air Europe (International Leisure Group) in Britain. In this latter context, the charter fleets provide a vital but essentially functional role within a wider product, of which the marketing is undertaken by the principal and not by the transport operator.

Closer linkages between transport and the other elements of the total product, especially with destination interests, appear highly probable in the rest of the twentieth century. The case for creating totally integrated travel and tourism

corporations under one ownership is not yet proven, as may be seen in the ill fated merger in 1986 between United Airlines of America, Westin Hotels, Hilton International and Hertz Car Rentals. More probably, the need for links will lead to strategic marketing and operational agreements and deals, which make sense for a period of time to the businesses involved in them.

Tactical marketing

Tactical marketing in passenger transport takes many forms, reflecting the wide range of promotional tools discussed in Chapter 16. The tools are used with one principal focus; that is to secure on a daily basis throughout the operating year, the vital marginal increment in customer purchases, which can make such a major difference to profit or loss in the typically high fixed cost operations of passenger transport systems. Of course, some routes at some times of the year are likely to be fully booked, but for the bulk of any transport operator's planned services, extra demand at the margin makes a great difference to annual profitability. Especially around the break-even level of seat occupancy, or in achieving additional hours of profitable utilization for expensive vehicles, the contribution of tactical marketing is to mould demand, or manipulate customer behaviour to buy more of the available supply or capacity of products, than would occur without such expenditure.

On first consideration this role for tactical marketing could be confused with a production or sales orientated business philosophy. On reflection, it should be clear that there is nothing necessarily product orientated about demand manipulation. The success of promotion is measured in revenue achieved in relation to the size of the marketing budget deployed, and this in turn is directly related to the knowledge which marketing managers have built up of the profile, needs and the probable behaviour of the customer segments with which they deal. Chapter 14 stressed that commitment to knowing the customer, is a necessary pre-requisite for the planning and execution of all forms of effective promotion. The more that promotion is segment and product specific, the greater the need for a detailed understanding of target customers.

For transport operators, most tactical marketing will tend to be segment specific, whether the object is to seize and exploit a marketing opportunity resulting from some unexpected event in the external environment, or to defend a position from the threats posed by less favourable circumstances, or by the actions of competitors. For example, railways usually do not need to reduce the fares paid by commuters, because their services are typically overcrowded at commuter times. Similarly, they do not seek to reduce the fares paid by first class travellers, because most of them are travelling on business and their demand is known to be relatively inelastic to changes in price. On the other hand, operators have every incentive to use price to promote use of the network outside peak periods, and a common response is to devise specific fares with conditions designed to prevent the 'dilution of revenue', as it is known by passengers switching from higher fares, which they otherwise would have paid.

The whole concept of segment specific fares, often accompanied with the presentation of services as special products, is found internationally under a multitude of different names. Advanced Purchase Excursion Fares (APEX), which are widely used in Europe and North America, are examples of the same concept of segment specific fares and products. They usually involve minimum lengths of stay at a destination, and restricted times of travel to reduce the possibility of revenue dilution. The object is to generate the marginal revenue on specific operations that would otherwise be performed with many empty seats. Where it is possible to provide group fares for pre-booked parties, operators will invariably allow a very

significant price reduction; in this context, groups are just another illustration of segment specific promotional activity.

Reflecting the many unpredictable variations in the external environment, there is always a strong element of contingency planning involved in marketing tactics for transport operators. Each year brings its own examples. In the early months of 1986, following record carryings in 1985, transatlantic airlines were confidently planning for a similar volume or some increment on the previous year. They had organized their network planning and capacity on that basis, and most were committed to investment in fleet replacement based on revenue forecasts. Over the period May to July, the impact of three events produced a slump in passenger volumes of crisis proportions. The US dollar weakened against European currencies compared with 1985; the American reprisal raid on Libya, following terrorist attacks on European airports, had a considerable psychological effect on prospective US travellers; and the nuclear pollution threat from the leak at Chernobyl power station added to travellers' worries. These events combined to cause an abrupt drop in holiday travel out of the USA to Europe, which is estimated in some places to have fallen in volume by some 40 per cent against forecast. At one point, British Airways was estimated to be losing up to half a million dollars a day in actual revenue compared with their target.

Crisis conditions of this magnitude required a massive promotional response, far in excess of any planned budget. A series of promotions and competitions designed to restore confidence and promote American visits to Europe, added to the planned marketing costs by many millions of dollars. But such costs must be compared with the size of the daily losses. By the end of the Summer, transatlantic traffic was beginning to return to the levels forecast, but it was too late to recover the volume lost over the peak summer period. In marketing terms, the tactics employed were clearly the only way to limit the damage, which could not have been foreseen. Whilst this example is an extreme case of responding to crisis, the perishability of service products, and the need to cover the high fixed costs of operation, will always oblige marketing managers to devise contingency plans and be able to implement them at great speed.

Marketing illustrations

Within the space constraints of this chapter, two illustrations of recent marketing practice are included. The first is a specific example drawn from airline marketing, and the second is a general illustration of marketing for sea ferries. In each case, the examples indicate the principles of both strategy and tactics noted earlier in this chapter.

Marketing an airline

Qantas, the international scheduled airline of Australia, is heavily involved in Australia's aim to increase its international tourism over the next decade. In particular, in the mid-1980s Australia sought to exploit the opportunities associated with the staging of the America's Cup yacht racing in 1987 and the Bicentenary celebrations of 1988. Responding to the perceived opportunities, the airline developed 'Jetabout', a tour operator subsidiary described as its Holiday Wing. Launched in Britain in 1986, the intention behind Jetabout was to promote the attractions of the destination and to facilitate the way in which prospective visitors could get access to a range of products. Because brochures showing packaged products can achieve far wider distribution and display through travel agents than the mere availability of its scheduled services and fares, the effect of promoting the destination goes much wider than the simple marketing linkage with destination interests may suggest. With Jetabout, Qantas also has better access to joint promotion schemes with the Australian

Tourist Commission and various product suppliers, than would otherwise be the case.

Also launched in the UK in 1986, after some three years of developing the scheme in Australia, was 'Qantas Connections'. Connections is a form of membership club aimed mainly at independent travellers for holidays, business, and visits to friends and relatives who are the bulk of British visitors to Australia. In return for an annual membership fee of 28 Australian dollars, the full club benefits provided discount entitlement at a range of over 3000 hotels in Australia, 3500 car rental locations, and a very wide range of destination attractions and retail outlets across the country. Members are issued with a plastic membership card and a 700-page planning kit which is designed to assist them to plan their itinerary to best effect, and to gain maximum use of the discount opportunities. The card is distributed through travel agents and commissionable, which again reinforces Qantas awareness and links with the travel trade. It also provides a good reason for choosing the airline, which is properly exploiting its national image advantages that competitors on Australian routes cannot match directly. There is a second card, Qantas International, designed to provide similar discount opportunities in countries other than Australia which the airline serves. The cards were offered with the attractive consumer proposition that, 'if you don't save 4 TIMES your membership on your next overseas trip, we'll refund the A$28'.

While the bulk of Qantas operating revenue will continue to be from its ticket sales, rather than from tour operating or from membership fees, the example illustrates most of the points outlined earlier in this chapter under the heading of strategic and tactical marketing. It shows one way in which destination links can be made; it represents both product formulation and product augmentation; and it demonstrates ways to link with the distributors of travel products. From the customer's viewpoint an added benefit is provided, and both Jetabout and Connections provide an excellent focus for promotional messages and materials designed to stimulate demand. The example also illustrates how one national carrier exploited its natural advantages and sought to position itself in a way which the competitors on its routes could not match directly.

Marketing sea ferries

Linking Britain with Continental Europe, and carrying some 40 per cent of UK outbound travellers a year in the 1980s, plus a comparable number of inbound visitors to the UK, are a number of sea ferry companies. Their business involves year-round high frequency operation of services on short sea route networks, including both roll-on and roll-off cargo as well as passengers and their cars. Since the early 1980s, and recently heightened by the need to secure competitive positions before the planned Channel Tunnel is built and becomes a major competitor for the East Channel routes, the companies were locked in an aggressive battle for market shares. The competition included massive investment in new 'vehicles' (ships), and terminals (harbour facilities). In a relatively static market volume between 1983 and 1985, the inevitable result of such competition was a price war which diluted revenue for all and lowered profitability.

More productively, the operators have forged destination links as the principal motivation for choosing their services. They have been so successful that it could be claimed in 1986, 'most ferry companies are now not only concerned with transportation but are also in the holiday business . . . For example, over 50 per cent of Brittany Ferries business [operating routes in the South-West sector of the Channel] now comes from holidays' (Travel Trade Gazette: 1986). Brittany Ferries, acting as a tour operator and distributing three holiday brochures in 1986, has developed an important self catering holiday business targeted at travellers with private cars, especially families, and exploited the natural geographical advantages of its route structure to good effect. The company has close links with accommodation and destination interests in both France and Spain, and with the motoring organizations which service their customers.

On the sea routes between the East Coast of England and Scandinavia, exactly the same development has occurred. Norway Line could claim in 1986, that 'the increasing trend towards ferry based inclusive tour holidays has been the basis of Norway Line's success'. On the very short route between Dover and Calais and the adjacent routes, there is less scope for marketing holidays. Nevertheless, through links with coach operators in particular, the companies on those routes have been very successful in marketing short excursions for a day, or up to two nights, both for shopping and for short-break trips.

The examples above demonstrate the operation of the strategic and tactical marketing principles outlined in this chapter, in the context of sea transport. In particular they indicate how creative product formulation, targeted to provide benefits tailored to the needs of identified market segments, together with systematic linkages with destination interests, can help to break the traditional trap of price wars, by engaging in non-price competition.

Chapter summary

This chapter stresses the functional links which exist between the availability and capacity of transport operations, and the demand for travel and tourism products in their overall sense. Although transport is only one of the five elements of the total product, and typically performs an enabling rather than a motivating role, accessibility is a fundamental condition for the development and growth of any destination. The extent to which transport marketing is constrained by constantly changing factors in the external environment, and the pressures of operating constraints is explained, and the continuous preoccupation with achieving revenue above the break-even level is emphasized. The contrast between the total tourist products which ultimately determine travel flows, and the specific transport products which are the focus of transport marketing campaigns, is discussed and the route to product augmentation through a detailed and carefully researched knowledge of consumer segments is stressed.

Throughout, this chapter seeks to define and illuminate the characteristics of marketing strategy and tactics, which are practised in all forms of transport, rather than focus on the specifics of either airline, rail, or other forms of surface travel. Undoubtedly there are aspects of marketing which are particular to individual forms of transport, but they are derived from the general principles outlined here and they do not alter the conclusions drawn.

The chapter does not deal specifically with charter airlines because these are referred to later in Chapter 24. In practice, most charter airlines adopt a form of *industrial marketing* in which they negotiate their routes, products, and capacity, with a relatively small number of major clients. Major charter operators are owned or linked financially with tour operating companies, and typically they do not market their products directly to individual customers. In these circumstances charter airlines provide a vital operational function for tour operators but it is the latter who take on the responsibility for marketing to the public.

23
Marketing accommodation

Apart from day trips, all other forms of tourism involve stays away from home for periods of one or more nights, and thus require overnight accommodation. Accommodation is, therefore, described as one of the five integral components of the total travel and tourism product as defined in Chapter 8. The many different forms of tourist accommodation and the ways in which they are marketed have a massive influence on tourist choices, behaviour, and the types of product which they buy. In terms of influence over demand, there are strong similarities between accommodation and transport marketing, and the two forms of marketing are increasingly being brought together with the interests of destinations, to achieve maximum impact through co-ordinated activities.

As with transport, the early development of accommodation was not concerned with leisure travel. Historically, inns and hotels were developed primarily to meet the needs of those required to travel in the conduct of commerce and industry, and in the administration of countries and empires. Since the eighteenth century, the development of accommodation for travellers has been inextricably bound up with servicing the growing and changing needs of transport systems. Inns and the forerunners of modern hotels were located naturally in cities and ports and along the routes which linked them, for much the same reasons that modern hotels are located in areas served by airports and road systems.

Chapter 22 noted that transport systems are still vitally concerned with non-tourism products, such as journeys to work and the carriage of goods. Accommodation services also have important dimensions unconnected with travel and tourism, such as institutional and welfare provision, accommodation and the related provision of catering in fields as diverse as schools, prisons, hospitals, the armed services, and the care of the elderly. In all these areas of the hospitality industry the influence of marketing is being felt but this chapter is, of course, only concerned with tourism products.

Thus, when considering the meaning of marketing for transport and accommodation operations, it must be recognized that travel and tourism contribute only part of the overall turnover in each industry. In the case of hotels, depending obviously on their locations, many are also involved in the provision of food and drink for residents in their surrounding local communities, who are not tourists.

In the latter part of the twentieth century, while most of the major national and international hotel groups are still very much orientated to the needs of business travellers, the provision of accommodation designed for leisure needs in tourist destinations has become a major area of market-led development. In the sunshine resorts of the USA, Europe, and the Pacific area, thousands of resort hotels have been built specifically to cater for the needs of vacationers, while similar developments in ski resorts also owe their origins solely to leisure travel. In all such cases developments have exploited the market potential made possible by modern transport systems.

This chapter commences by defining the constituent parts of the serviced and non-serviced sectors of accommodation and their role in the total travel and tourism product. It considers accommodation products as experiences and discusses business characteristics which are common to all forms of commercial accommodation operations. The marketing tasks for accommodation suppliers are considered under the headings of strategy and tactics, and the implications of these for the size of marketing budgets in the sector are reviewed. The chapter concludes with two illustrations of marketing practice, one from the serviced sector, which works through the product/segment mix of a particular hotel, and the other from the non-serviced self-catering sector.

Defining tourist accommodation

For the purposes of this chapter, tourist accommodation is deemed to include all establishments offering overnight accommodation on a commercial or quasi commercial basis to all categories of tourist. The marketing of catering is, therefore, excluded from the discussion. Also excluded are all forms of privately owned accommodation used for holidays, such as second homes, static caravans or chalets in private ownership, boats, and time share apartments.

'Quasi commercial' refers to the many tourist accommodation products outside the commercial sector for which a charge is made to contribute to costs (even if a subsidy is involved). For example, the British Youth Hostels Association (YHA) is a membership organization which provides a national network of hostels in the UK, mostly for young people willing to use inexpensive dormitory and shared accommodation. YHA is a non-profit-making body but, in the context of its corporate objectives, it operates increasingly on commercial principles to secure the revenue needed for its refurbishment and development programmes. Other

forms of quasi commercial accommodation products may be found in colleges and universities, many of which have begun in recent years to market their accommodation capacity for conferences and for holidays, at times when students are not in residence. Such operations are increasingly required to cover their operating costs and sometimes to make a contribution towards the overhead costs of their parent institutions.

An important distinction in accommodation for tourists is the split between serviced and non-serviced types. Serviced means that staff are available on the premises to provide some services such as meals and bars and room service. The availability of such services, even if they are not in fact used, is included in the price charged. Non-serviced means that the sleeping accommodation is provided furnished on a rental basis, normally for a unit comprising several beds, such as an apartment, villa, cottage or caravan. While services for the provision of meals, bars and shops may be available on a separate commercial basis, as in a holiday village, they are not included in the price charged for the accommodation.

The serviced sector ranges from the many first class and luxury hotels, which provide full service on a 24 hours a day basis at relatively high cost, all the way down to homely bed and breakfast establishments, which may only operate informally for a few weeks in the year. In the non-serviced sector, which is known in Britain under the unattractive product label of 'self-catering accommodation', lies a wide range of different units comprising villas, apartments, chalets, cottages and caravans, the bulk of which are rented equipped but with no personal services included in the published price. Some of these units, for example in converted historic buildings, are furnished with antiques and may cost more per person night than four star serviced accommodation. The bulk of self-catering units, however, still cater for a budget priced market and the cost per person night is very much less than could be obtained in the serviced sector.

In the late twentieth century there are so many variations of serviced and non-serviced accommodation products that the distinction is often blurred in practice, although it remains useful for the purposes of analysis and discussion of marketing implications. For example, the accommodation in many holiday villages and condominia is marketed as 'self catering' units. But within the village or complex there is often extensive provision of bars, restaurants, coffee shops and a wide range of other services available for purchase, although not paid for in the initial holiday price. In these circumstances, the real difference to the operator between serviced and non-serviced accommodation looks increasingly irrelevant in practice. In the customer's perception and from a marketing standpoint, however, there may be all the difference in the world. The endeavour by accommodation interests and tour operators to keep down holiday prices explains much of the growth in non-serviced tourist accommodation in recent years.

Using the serviced/non-serviced split, discussed above, the types of accommodation referred to in this chapter are summarized in Figure 23.1. The boxes in the diagram divide each of the two accommodation sectors by destination and by route, because this fundamentally influences the nature of the accommodation products that are offered. It further distinguishes segments of users for business and other non-leisure purposes, from users for leisure and holidays. Non leisure purposes includes stay away from home on family business such as school visits, funerals, or stays in an area while seeking a new house or apartment, and so on.

Functional role of accommodation in the overall tourist product

When the purpose of a visit to a destination or an overnight stay en route is for business and non-

Sector Market segment	Serviced sector		Non-serviced sector (self catering)	
	Destination	Routes	Destination	Routes
Business and other non-leisure	City/town hotels (Monday–Friday) Resort hotels for conferences, exhibitions Educational establishments	Motels Inns Airport hotels	Apartments	Not applicable
Leisure and holiday	Resort hotels Guest house/pensions Farm houses City/town hotels (Friday–Sunday) Some educational establishments	Motels Bed and breakfast Inns	Apart hotels Condominia Holiday villages Holiday centres/camps Caravan/chalet parks Gîtes Cottages Villas Apartments/flats Some motels	Touring pitches for caravans, tents, recreation vehicles YHA Some motels

Figure 23.1 *Principal serviced and non-serviced types of accommodation used in tourism, by market segment*

leisure purposes, it is obvious that accommodation is not normally a part of the trip motivation or any part of the destination's attraction. Rooms, serviced or otherwise, provide a necessary facility which makes it possible, convenient, and comfortable to engage in the primary reason for travel. In marketing terms, factors of locational convenience and high standards of comfort and efficiency are, therefore, the primary elements to be built into accommodation products. Within their price band, the extent to which the primary elements are believed to be delivered is the basis for customer choice and the platform for communicating product benefits through promotional means.

For holiday and leisure purposes, accommodation plays a very different role in the total tourist product. While a destination's attractions are likely to remain the dominant motivation for most tourists, customers' destination choices are also influenced by their perceptions and expectations of the accommodation available. Sometimes, as with repeat trips to stay at the same hotel or caravan park, the image and quality of the accommodation may be strong enough to make it a primary rather than a secondary aspect of destination choice. More often, however, the destination's appeal is the more important element in motivation and choice of destination for leisure stays.

Leisure visitors are likely to spend many hours of a stay in their accommodation, especially if the weather is poor. Serviced or non-serviced, their overall trip and destination enjoyment will be highly geared to perceived value provided, and satisfaction experienced with the bedrooms, bathrooms, and any other rooms and facilities provided. This holds good for tented pitches in camping sites as well as for bedrooms in five star resort hotel accommodation offering high standards of service.

In other words, for leisure purposes, accommodation is integrally related to the attractions of a destination as well as part of the facilities.

Whilst transport in the late twentieth century appears to be losing much of its former glamour and appeal as part of the attractions of a trip, it appears probable that accommodation is moving in the opposite direction and enhancing its appeal. Current marketing trends to shorter stays suggest that destination and accommodation marketing are likely to come even closer together in a logical partnership of mutual interests.

The accommodation product as an experience

It is worth restating that accommodation products of all types are perceived by customers as experiences. The experience is organized by suppliers to meet the identified needs and benefits sought by customer segments, as described in chapters 7 and 8, and it comprises a series of service operations. For larger organizations these operations correspond with operating departments, of which the most important are:

- *booking services* — from letters to advanced computerized central reservation services
- *reception/ checkout services* — to register arrivals and departures, check bookings and allocate rooms, possibly associated with support services, such as baggage handling
- *rooms/site services* — to deliver rooms or self catering units cleaned, checked, ready to occupy
- *food and beverage* — (if provided) including restaurants, bars and coffee shops
- *other services* — *(if provided) including shops, leisure facilities, secretarial services, dry cleaning, and all other services.*

Product experiences are complex and involve physical elements (such as food and drink); sensual benefits (experienced through sight, sound, touch, smell, and conveyed by the quality of buildings and their furnishings); and psychological benefits experienced as mental states of well being, status, comfort and satisfaction (see for example, Sasser et al.: 1978: p. 10). For holiday visitors the psychological benefits of the accommodation product are likely to be closely associated with the benefits provided by the destination's attractions.

In Chapter 8 an accommodation example was used to explain recommended product formulation methods for tourism, organized around an analysis of target customer segment's needs and benefits sought. The basic components of *core*, *formal* and *augmented* products were described and are not repeated here although they are completely relevant to this discussion of the product.

The nature of the accommodation business

This section focuses on five particular characteristics of any accommodation business, serviced or non-serviced, which strongly influence the way in which marketing is conducted at the strategic and tactical level. The commercial accommodation sector displays of course, the special characteristics common to service producers which were defined and discussed in some depth in Chapter 3, and which underlie the management of the marketing functions discussed throughout Part Five of the book. They are generally assumed in this chapter but not repeated in any detail. Of particular relevance here are:

- choice of location
- existence of peaks and troughs in demand
- influence of room sales on profits
- focus on bookers, not occupancy levels
- low variable costs of operation, especially at the margin.

Location

Location tends to dominate all accommodation operations. It determines the customer mix which the business can achieve and, therefore, the direction of marketing strategy and tactics. Location also largely determines the profitability of an operation. Where feasibility studies are undertaken to investigate the value of alternative sites prior to investment in new facilities, the inherent demand potential for each location under investigation is always the primary consideration. Of course, once an accommodation unit is established, location of operations becomes fixed for the lifetime of the asset. Whereas an airline can move its fleet around the world to serve alternative destinations as its markets justify, an hotel is an immovable fixture. It has to use its skills in marketing to overcome any difficulties which may emerge after the initial location is decided.

Many of the difficulties experienced in accommodation marketing are in fact difficulties which stem from external changes affecting the market potential of the locations in which they are established. For example, seaside resort hotels in Britain, which relied on the traditional summer holiday market, were in considerable difficulty in the 1980s because their locations are no longer able to attract the volume of holiday demand for which they were originally built. For very different reasons, associated with over-investment, hotels in Singapore faced very difficult times in the late 1980s because too much capacity was built to accommodate a demand which did not grow at the rate anticipated by such limited feasibility studies as were undertaken. Greater commitment to sales and marketing was the inevitable response of the Singapore hotels in an attempt to influence demand. Marketing, of course, cannot cure all problems. In the not uncommon circumstances faced in Singapore, many hotels are forced to operate at a loss for as long as their resources allow or until the market expands. The only alternative is to sell properties, which in a buyer's market, usually means a massive capital loss. Such forced sales are a common phenomenon in the industry, especially amongst smaller businesses with limited financial resources.

Less obviously, the type and style of accommodation provision influences many destinations no less than they are influenced by it. In vacation destinations certainly, the buildings and sites which accommodation occupies become part of the image as well as of the physical environment of a destination. The attractions of the new island destinations on the Great Barrier Reef in Australia, are in fact identified with the physical appearance of the accommodation structures built upon them; the image and attractions of Austrian ski resorts are highly dependent on the traditional wooden chalet style of hotel building which gives them a distinctive appeal and position in prospective customers' minds. In Britain, Brighton's image and appeal is strongly associated with the fine Victorian architecture of its promenade hotels, while in Singapore the appeal of Raffles Hotel is an important element in the destination's image.

Business peaks and troughs

By weeks in the year and days in the week, nearly all forms of the accommodation business are vulnerable to highly variable demand patterns, reflecting the nature of the market demand which the location sustains. Thus, hotels in many towns and cities in Northern Europe can normally expect high occupancy from business travellers from Mondays to Thursdays, and the peak of their occupancy in the Autumn and Spring, with a typical drop at weekends and in the July/August period. Most self-catering units by the seaside can anticipate full demand in a period of little over 12 weeks, and many still close completely for around 5 months of the year. Accommodation is not unique in this existence of peaks and troughs but it is a matter of common concern with which marketing managers are continuously engaged.

Marketing efforts cannot reverse these natural locational rhythms of demand, but campaigns can be targeted around identified segments to lessen the impact and to generate increased business at the margin.

Profit is linked to room night sales

While sales of room nights, especially in the serviced hotels sector, are often not more than around 50 per cent of total sales revenue, the average contribution of room sales to overall profitability is very much greater. According to Horwath and Horwath, in London in 1985 the gross profit on room sales averaged over 75 per cent (defined as room sales less room operating costs), while the gross profit on food and beverage sales was in the region of 20 per cent. The effect of high fixed costs means that the profitability of additional or marginal room sales is often even greater than 75 per cent, while the marginal profitability of food and beverage sales tends to remain fairly constant.

Of course, the sale of room nights also affects the sale of food and beverages within the hotel and such other services as the hotel provides. Effective merchandising to customers once they are 'in house' is a logical, associated marketing approach to increase total turnover. Accordingly, by the nature of the accommodation business, the main focus and effort of marketing has to be on room night sales. In practice, because nine out of ten people typically make reservations as distinct from impulse purchases by walking in off the street, this means focusing on bookings which are made in advance of the customers' arrival. The only exception to this natural focus on room nights and bookings occurs, for example, where hotels develop functions for banqueting business which does not involve overnight accommodation. The focus on accommodation sales and on advance bookings is even more important for self-catering operators.

Targeting bookers, not room or bed occupancy

Following on from the previous section on room night sales, it is important to clarify a common misunderstanding about the nature of the accommodation business – that marketing focuses on room or bed occupancy. The preoccupation with occupancy is certainly understandable for reasons already discussed, but marketing targets cannot sensibly be expressed as occupancy levels. Occupancy levels represent the *results* of marketing effort and they are a statistical measure of marketing success or failure. Marketing targets are always *prospective customers* and, to use an unattractive but useful word, not just customers but *bookers*.

A *booker* is a customer, or an agent of the customer, who makes a reservation for one or more persons, for one or more nights, in any form of accommodation. Thus, a person making a family booking for two rooms over 7 nights for 4 people (14 room nights and 28 bed nights), is a proper target for marketing strategy and tactics. A secretary who makes hotel reservations for one or more members of a company, may never see a hotel or meet its staff, but he or she is a 'booker'. The secretary of a national association, responsible for organizing an annual conference for members, may be seeking several hundred room nights in more than one hotel, but is also a booker, and so on. Medlik uses the term 'Buying agent' to distinguish those who book on behalf of customers, from the customers themselves (Medlik: 1980: p. 21).

In the holiday parks sector of accommodation, covering caravans and chalets for rent, marketing is traditionally considered in terms of unit sales or 'static' unit rentals. These terms are no more than trade jargon and logically the marketing task in this sector, as in the others, is to identify, persuade, sell to, and satisfy targeted groups of bookers and buying agents.

High fixed costs of operation

The marketing implications for service businesses operating with high fixed costs and low variable costs, is discussed in several parts of this book and requires little further comment here. Suffice to note that, once the fixed costs of operation have been covered at the break-even level of occupancy, the marginal costs of operating an additional, otherwise empty room, are negligible in all sectors of accommodation. Beyond the break-even level the contribution to gross profit of additional room sales is typically very high. This is especially so for self-catering operations where the marginal costs are even lower than in the serviced sector.

Because the marginal cost of supplying an additional product is low, accommodation suppliers are often tempted to reduce prices in an attempt to achieve sales, especially last-minute sales before unsold capacity is lost forever. As Kotas put it, 'the higher the proportion of fixed costs to total costs, the wider the range of price discretion' (Kotas: 1975: p. 32).

The nature of the marketing task for accommodation businesses

To introduce the nature of the marketing task for accommodation suppliers, one can hardly quote a better authority than the President of Holiday Corporation, which includes Holiday Inns as part of the world's largest international accommodation organization.

'All segments of our travel and tourism business have become more competitive. A growing number of competitors offer their products to the same customer groups . . . travellers have a wider range of choices than ever before for matching a hotel to their particular travel needs. Those needs change according to the travel purpose. Unless a company can understand those changing needs and deliver a quality product and services appropriately targeted to specific customers' needs, wants and expectations, that business cannot survive' (Goeglein: 1986: p. 1).

Strategic marketing tasks

There are four main elements in the strategic marketing response which accommodation suppliers make to their external business environment, and the operational characteristics previously noted. These are:

1 Planning the most profitable business mix of segments and products.
2 Deciding the position or image which each accommodation unit (or chain of units) should occupy.
3 Encouraging and rewarding frequent users.
4 Developing marketing integration between units in common ownership (chains) or units in individual ownership (voluntary co-operatives).

Planning the business mix

In the context of the demand potential inherent in each location, the basic strategic decision for accommodation businesses is to determine the optimum, or most profitable, mix of segments for whose needs specific products are to be created and promoted. For example, a city centre hotel will obviously target clients travelling for a range of business purposes, a resort will draw different categories of leisure visitors and so on. Figure 23.2 provides a fairly typical illustration of a customer mix which has important implications for the conduct of marketing. The same figure, with additional calculations, is used later in the chapter to illustrate an important point about marketing budgets; it is based on a resort hotel in the South of England with a location which supports a significant element of business visits within its chosen mix of segments. The hotel has two basic customer types (business and leisure), which permit of six segments, each representing a strategic choice, and requiring

separate marketing treatment in any marketing campaigns. For convenience of illustration, the business/leisure ratio in figure 23.2 is 50:50, but it could vary from say 70:30 to 30:70 according to the strategy of the hotel's owners, reflecting their judgement of marketing potential and what they seek to achieve for the hotel.

The optimum customer mix for most businesses will usually comprise several segments, which combine to maximize achievable revenue and minimize the effects of seasonality and other normal business fluctuations.

Whilst hotels and the rest of the serviced sector may appear to have more scope to plan a co-ordinated customer mix, exactly the same principle operates for self-catering operators in the non-serviced sector. For example, holiday park owners, marketing static units such as caravans and chalets for holiday lets, may plan a segmentation strategy which separately targets adults aged over 50 travelling in pairs, from families with children of school age who are largely tied to school holiday periods; they can differentiate between visitors who purchase traditional one or two weeks stay, and others who are interested in weekends and shorter stays.

Devising the optimum mix for any accommodation business usually involves some form of marketing research to analyse the volume and revenue potential of current and prospective customers in each location. There are very few operators in the commercial accommodation sector who cannot achieve at least a four way customer split, or business mix, as the basis for a more efficient marketing strategy.

Deciding the position or image

Relevant always to selected target segments, the next, and obviously related strategic consideration for accommodation suppliers, is to determine the 'position' which each unit or group of units should aim to occupy in the minds of its targeted customers. Increasingly, where competitors offer closely similar products to the same

Resort hotel located near to a business centre generating visitors for conferences, general commercial purposes as well as holiday visitors.
120 twin rooms, with 65 percent annual room occupancy = 28,470 room nights capacity over a year (120 × 365 × 65 percent)
Rack rate £70 (twin/double) per *room*night including breakfast; £45 (single occupancy)

Customer mix	% of room sales (per annum)	Volume of rooms sales (per annum)	tariff type
1 Business (individuals)	30	8,540	rack rate
2 Business (corporate clients)	20	5,695	corporate rate
3 Vacation (individuals)	10	2,847	weekly rate
4 Coach tour clients	10	2,848	inclusive group
5 Holiday breaks (i)	15	4,270	inclusive price
6 Holiday breaks (ii)	15	4,270	wholesale rate
Totals	100	28,470	

(i)   sold directly by the hotel to customers
(ii)   rooms allocated to tour operators; and packaged and marketed by the operator

Figure 23.2   *A typical product/market mix for a resort hotel*

group of customers at very similar prices, it becomes necessary for operators to differentiate and brand their products with particular identities which can be communicated. Identities, known in marketing jargon as 'positions', are perceptions in the minds of customers, which may be based on the strengths of a building and its location, the specifics of products on offer, the quality of service provided, the design and quality of rooms and furnishings, or any combination of these product characteristics.

To illustrate the point, in developed countries all around the world, hoteliers have for many years recognized the value of their regular business visitors. Yet the systematic marketing battle for the favourable opinions of these all important customers in Britain can be dated to around 1984, when a regular, syndicated survey of frequent business travellers, was launched by NOP Market Research Ltd. Frequent business travellers, defined by NOP as people who stay at least twenty-one nights a year in hotels, are

estimated (by NOP) to contribute some two thirds of all nights stayed in British hotels. The survey measures awareness of advertising, ranks preferences for different hotel companies in terms of users and non users, and quantifies customer perceptions of the wide range of attributes on which such hotels are positioned. The survey provides a sophisticated measuring tool, with which competing hotels can trace the success or failure of their positioning strategies over time. It puts marketing for the larger hotel groups on much the same footing as the marketing of fast moving consumer goods, most of which have had the benefit of this type of research monitoring for at least twenty years.

Encouraging and rewarding frequent customers
The third element in strategic marketing responses for accommodation suppliers is to find ways to encourage and reward regular customers. Not surprisingly, for the same strategic

reason as airlines, most hotel groups created membership clubs and other schemes, during the 1980s, often involving privileged user cards designed to appeal to their regular customers. Some of these schemes offered credit facilities in addition to the normal range of benefits such as rapid check in and check out. Some also offered awards through which frequent travellers could earn points for each stay, leading to attractive prizes according to the number of points collected over a given period. In most cases the frequent or 'loyal' customer schemes involved the building up of name and address lists into data bases suitable for direct response marketing initiatives, as discussed in Chapter 19.

Whilst the strategic objective of rewarding repeat visitors is clear, not all of the schemes currently in use are immediately or fully successful. In part this is because they are difficult and often expensive to administer, and partly because they may also serve, unintentionally, to reduce the average room rate to some customers who were prepared to pay the full price. Horwath and Horwath estimate the level of repeat customers in larger hotels in Britain in 1985, at between 30 and 40 per cent. Many smaller accommodation businesses, both serviced and non-serviced, may achieve over 70 per cent repeat visits, and a customer loyalty generating strategy appears generally valid for all suppliers offering tourist accommodation.

Regular customers represent an important strategic marketing asset, not only in terms of their own decisions, but because they provide a very cost effective route through which it is possible to reach their friends and others like them, using carefully designed and targeted direct response promotions.

Integrating marketing across several units
The fourth strategic consideration for accommodation businesses reflects a relatively new and rapidly growing dimension in accommodation marketing, which is relevant to the other three elements and focuses on the level of co-ordination which individual units can achieve in marketing their products. The strategic advantages of *marketing co-ordination* may be summarized as:

distribution | referals of business between units
central reservations service
better access to distribution networks

promotion | corporate positioning and branding
joint advertising opportunities
use of professional marketing teams
access to group brochures and leaflets
group representation at trade fairs and shows
product and price harmonization in group quality assurance schemes to build up customer satisfaction.

Obviously, co-ordination is most easily secured through ownership and is part of the process whereby large, multi unit accommodation chains have emerged over the last twenty years and expanded the scale of their operations. Multi unit chains are now found in all parts of the world; many of the chains are international in their scope, and there is no indication that this level of growth has reached any natural limits at the end of the 1980s.

The process of growth and the economic and marketing reasons for it are a vast topic, explored for example by Housden (1984), and lead into issues of franchising, leasing, turn-key operations and the separation of management from the ownership of accommodation properties. It helps to explain the reasons for the emergence of voluntary co-operatives of independent hoteliers such as Best Western and Consort in Britain. Most recently, the search for the marketing advantages of co-operation are spreading into the small businesses sector of both serviced and non-serviced units.

Tactical marketing

Strategic decisions are expected to generate a profitable mix of bookings and room occupancy through the production and distribution of appropriately priced, distinctive products, which match the needs of identified customer segments. In other words, for accommodation operators in all sectors, three of the four Ps of the marketing mix are strategic decisions, and even the fourth, promotion, is planned within boundaries set by the positioning strategy.

Tactically, as for passenger transport marketing, the main contribution of marketing is to secure additional marginal sales from targeted buyers at times when rooms are predictably likely to be operating at less than optimum occupancy, typically reflecting normal seasonal variations. Its other contribution is to cope with sudden and often dramatic losses of anticipated business, which happens all too often as a result of unpredictable economic or political events.

Occasionally, in certain destinations at certain times, room occupancies in hotels may exceed 80 per cent on an annual basis, as they did in London in 1985. At this level, most hotels are full for most of the time and the inevitable result is a rise in prices and profitability. Such circumstances are exceptional and usually are not achieved by marketing alone but by a combination of favourable circumstances in the external environment. It is more common for accommodation businesses to operate somewhere between 55–65 per cent of room occupancy over the months in which they are open for business.

As in other sectors of travel and tourism, reflecting the highly perishable nature of the products, marketing managers are required to manage demand by stimulating additional bookings on a daily and weekly basis. The high fixed costs and low variable costs of operating accommodation provides extensive scope for providing short term incentives to buyers. Tactical marketing for accommodation businesses involves choosing from the range of sales promotion tools discussed in some detail in Chapter 16, those best calculated to motivate the short run purchasing decisions of target buyers. See, for example, Figure 16.2.

Specifically, sales promotion tactics for accommodation businesses include:

1 Short-term price discounting, used especially to sell unsold capacity in unanticipated circumstances. (See also Chapter 9)
2 Sales promotions, typically involving value added aspects to products in order to attract targeted customer segments, often used to attract business at times of predicted seasonal troughs in demand.
3 Sales promotions, often using commission incentives, designed to motivate a retail distribution system (where applicable) and achieve added influence at points of sale, including improved display for brochures.
4 Sales promotions, invariably using deep price discounts, designed to motivate and conclude deals with third parties such as tour operators, coach tour operators and other agents making bulk contracts for the supply of accommodation. (This form of selling capacity may have strategic as well as tactical implications.)
5 Use of sales force (where applicable) to generate additional sales both from the range of normal buyers, and from others targeted for short run sales initiatives.
6 Tactical use of advertising, usually in association with items 1, 2, and 3, in order to achieve better communication of promotional offers.

Whilst the use of these tactical techniques is clearly sales orientated, their efficient use depends on the detailed knowledge marketing managers have of the profile, needs, and probable behaviour of target segments in responding to promotional incentives. Because, like transport companies, the accommodation sector is so often subject to unpredictable external factors, it is always necessary for operators to allocate contingency funds to be held in reserve for use in influencing short run demand, if the need arises.

The size of accommodation marketing budgets

With an understanding of the size of the task involved in implementing strategy and tactics in accommodation marketing, it is appropriate to consider the implications for the size of budgets. The cost of achieving marketing objectives is typically a relatively high proportion of sales revenue, and the budget allocation is rightly seen as a high risk decision. A systematic procedure for allocating money to marketing campaigns in order to achieve planned volume and revenue targets is set out in Chapter 14; the principles in that chapter apply fully to all sectors of commercial accommodation.

This section sets out to challenge what appears to be a widespread belief in the industry in a norm, or rule of thumb, that it is appropriate to spend between 2–5 per cent of total sales revenue on marketing. Thus, commenting on the annual surveys of hotel accounts undertaken by Horwath and Horwath, Medlik notes, 'In most regions and countries hotels spend between 3–4 per cent of their total sales on marketing activities as defined [in the *Uniform System of Accounts for Hotels*]' (Medlik: 1980: p. 114). The Horwath and Horwath percentages have remained fairly constant over time in many countries and have become part of the received wisdom in the industry.

Of course, the percentage depends on the definition of what the marketing budget should include, but this author believes that the real proportion of sales revenue devoted to marketing by most successful organizations in the accommodation business is very much greater than 2–5 per cent. Properly calculated, and based on the view of marketing expressed in this book, the real average proportion of sales revenue devoted to marketing activities by accommodation businesses of all types is probably over 20 per cent in most countries, with many firms spending more to secure their business turnover. This is obviously a highly contentious statement and it is justified as follows. Supporting calculations for the argument will be found in Figure 23.3.

1 In analysing the accounts of a business providing tourist accommodation, rooms sales revenue should always be calculated in two ways. First as the sum of actual receipts for a year from accommodation sales (this figure, divided by the number of room nights sold, provides the average room rate achieved over a year). Second, room sales revenue should be calculated as the sum of theoretical sales revenue achievable if rooms were sold at the published rack rates.

2 Marketing expenditure should then be calculated as the sum of the costs of *all* the decisions marketing managers take to secure the business they actually achieve (not just the expenditure on advertising and sales promotion). The total expenditure may be expressed as a percentage of sales revenue achieved over a campaign period.

Although hotel accounts are not normally drawn up as suggested above, highly valuable marketing insights can be gained if the calculations are undertaken by marketing managers for their own purposes. It is interesting to note that during 1986 in Britain, Kleinwort Grieveson Securities in association with Huddersfield Polytechnic, developed a 'Hotel Companies Performance Index', designed to compare companies in terms of actual against potential room rates achievable.

The closer a company gets to its theoretical room rate (based on published tariffs) the more efficient it is.

In an ideal world, an hotel with an excellent product range and a good location, will set its rack rates for the year ahead and complete the trading period without unpredicted events preventing it from achieving the targeted mix of bookings which best matches its capacity. No one in this ideal position accepts group bookings at a discount if they are confident of filling their rooms with rack rate business, which raises their turnover towards the theoretical maximum. No one offers special rates for leisure break business if they can fill their rooms at higher rates.

In the real world, hoteliers and operators of other forms of accommodation are daily forced to tackle the realities of regular payment of contracted fixed costs out of cash flow, while contemplating unsold rooms and beds and consequent loss of potential revenue. In these circumstances, they typically discount their rack rates in order to manipulate short-run demand. Putting the point bluntly, they reduce prices in order to 'buy' business from whatever sources they can find at whatever price they think is better than the certain alternative of lost sales. The high fixed cost nature of accommodation operations makes business at almost any price appear worthwhile in the short run. Of course, over time, price discounting may be counter productive because it damages regular customers' good will, but businesses in serious cash flow crises may not have a long run, and they will aim to survive by any possible means.

The foregoing explanation is designed to make the point that marketing expenditure should always be calculated as the full cost of all the expenditure which managers decide to incur to achieve their actual turnover. Marketing costs, therefore, includes expenditure defined as marketing in the Uniform System of Accounts for Hotels, on:

- advertising, PR, and other media
- sales promotion and merchandising
- print production and distribution (including direct mail)
- marketing research
- consortia fees (marketing proportion only) or Group marketing levy imposed by chains

it should also include the costs incurred in:

- staff costs, expenses and share of overheads for all undertaking marketing work
- negotiating with, maintaining and paying commission to travel agents, wholesalers and any other distributors who receive commission
- negotiating and agreeing discounts for tour operators, coach tour companies and any other bulk sales
- agreeing discounts for other forms of group business such as conferences, or airlines
- share of costs of central reservations systems, since this is a vital tool of efficient marketing operations which must be organized around marketing requirements

It has to be stressed that several cost elements noted above, which account for the bulk of all the costs of securing business otherwise judged to be at risk or lost (the only valid reason for incurring the costs), are not in practice included as marketing costs in the Uniform System of Accounts for Hotels. This is not a criticism of the uniform system because it was not conceived around marketing principles but in order to make industry comparisons possible using standard definitions. If an accommodation supplier wishes to understand costs and revenues and make his marketing more efficient, however, it will be necessary to count all the costs noted above.

Because revenues and the costs of marketing accommodation are in practice related to segments, it is obviously sensible that an accommodation business should budget for marketing, not as a percentage of total sales revenue, but separately according to the costs of securing sales in each product/segment with which the business is concerned.

Marketing illustrations

Two illustrations of marketing practice are included in this chapter. The first shows a method for analysing an hotel's revenue by segments/products and the way in which the full cost of achieving the revenue may be calculated; the second describes changing marketing practice by small self catering businesses in response to changes in their external environment.

Marketing a resort hotel

The example chosen is a medium sized, four star hotel, part of a national chain, in a seaside resort in Britain with a location which generates a mix of business, and justifies an average bed and breakfast rack rate per room night of £70.00 (assuming double occupancy). The hotel has 120 twin rooms and is targeted to achieve 65 per cent room occupancy over twelve months.

Originally built for holiday customers fifty years ago, changing markets have caused the hotel to shift its focus and upgrade its facilities to appeal to a business market. The hotel does not have its own conference facilities but it is located near to a resort conference centre from which it draws a significant part of its total visitors for business purposes. Short-break holiday business, to fill the weekends when business visits are not available, is now its principal involvement in the leisure market.

The business mix and tariff types

Following standard marketing logic, the total annual business is divided into the segments for which it is considered necessary to organize different products, prices, promotion, and distribution, and to conduct different marketing activities. As set out in Figure 23.3, there are two types of customers (business and vacation visitors) but they generate six viable segments. All other types of customer are excluded from the figure to avoid complicating the example. The rationale for the segmentation strategy is simple. The location does not generate an acceptable level of rack rate business, and the hotel has to organize marketing initiatives (in this case with its parent company) to secure the targeted level of sales.

Of the six visitor segments shown in Figure 23.3, only the first group pay the full rack rate. They comprise only 30 per cent by volume of the hotel's business. The second segment comprises business visitors paying a corporate rate which is 15 per cent below rack rate; some of them are conference visitors who also receive an average discount of 15 per cent off the rack rate.

Of the vacationer groups, it would not be possible to achieve targeted levels of business at the full rack rate, and most hotels offer a special rate for these customers, usually built into a product with a minimum length of stay and perhaps meals and other services to reduce the possibility that such rates will be used by business visitors. If the individual vacation business is projected on the evidence of recent years to leave many rooms unoccupied, the hotelier will normally approach tour operators, in this case coach operators (segment 4 in Figure 23.3). Such operators will, if the hotel suits their own product range, take allocations of rooms. If they do, it will normally be at a large discount in order to cover their own costs of administration and marketing, including distribution. The discount, which must also cover the tour operator's profit, will be set on the hotel's published tariff for that type of business (in this case an average per room night of £45).

The two final vacation segments are short breaks of two to three nights offered as an inclusive product. For segment 5, the product is sold from a brochure put together by hotel marketing executives at group level and there is

Resort hotel located near to a business centre generating visitors for conferences, general commercial purposes as well as holiday visitors.

120 twin rooms, with 65 percent annual room occupancy = 28,470 room nights capacity over a year (120 × 365 × 65 percent)

Rack rate £70 (twin/double) per *room* night including breakfast; £45 (single occupancy)

Customer mix	(a) % of room sales (per annum)	Volume of rooms sales (per annum)	tariff type	(b) Published room rates (in brochure)	(c)* Actual room rate achieved*	(d) Theoretical revenue	(e) Actual room revenue achieved (a × c)
1 Business (individuals)	30	8,540	rack rate	£70	£55	597,800	£469,700
2 Business (corporate clients)	20	5,695	corporate rate	£70	£55	398,650	313,225
3 Vacation (individuals)	10	2,847	weekly rate	£45	£45	199,290	128,115
4 Coach tour clients	10	2,848	inclusive group rate	£45	£32	199,360	91,136
5 Holiday breaks (i)	15	4,270	inclusive price	£50	£45	298,900	192,150
6 Holiday breaks (ii)	15	4,270	wholesale rate	£50	£35	298,900	149,450
Totals	100	28,470				£1,992,900	£1,343,776

*Includes allowance for single occupancy of rooms and retailer commissions for segments 4 and 6 of the customer mix
(i)   sold directly by the hotel to customers
(ii) rooms allocated to tour operators; and packaged and marketed by the operator

actual revenue (e) as per cent of (d) = 67%

Figure 23.3   *Calculating the full impact of discounts and sales commission on potential hotel revenue*

no discount from the target tariff of £50 per room night. Because this hotel still has spare capacity at weekends, it also makes an allocation of rooms to another wholesaler or tour operator who includes the hotel in a brochure comprising a range of products marketed under a brand name. In Britain, several such brochures are currently branded and marketed under labels such as Superbreaks, Stardust, and Rainbow. As with the coach tour operators, marketing through a group has to be paid for and discounts of around 30 per cent are common, to cover wholesaler costs, marketing, and profit margins.

Revenue calculations in Figure 23.3
Column (a) shows the volume of room night sales per annum for each segment, as targeted at

the beginning of the year in the hotel's marketing plan. The total of 28,470 is the sum of 120 rooms × 365 days × 65% occupancy, (as noted earlier). Column (b) lists the published room rates per night designed to attract each of the segments and column (c) converts these into actual room rates achieved. The column (c) figures would in practice be calculated by the hotel accountants, and they allow for the fact that some of the rooms are let to only one person at less than double occupancy rack rate; that group discount must be deducted from some segments, and that travel agency commission is payable on some sales.

Column (d) shows the maximum revenue potentially achievable if all rooms could be sold at full rack rate of £70 per night. The only reason for making this calculation is to demonstrate that there is always a cost, represented as potential revenue foregone, of accepting business at less than rack rate.

Column (e) shows actual revenue received over the year (a × c). By comparing the actual and theoretical revenue totals it can be seen that the sum of column (e) is 67 per cent of column (d). By dividing the total revenue (e) by total room sales (28,470), the average room rate achieved can be calculated at £47.20 over the year.

To summarize, almost every accommodation business will operate in practice at average room rates significantly below its theoretical maximum. The difference between actual and potential reflects the composition of its segment/product mix and the level of discounting and commission required to achieve business in each segment. Measured over periods of time and between different hotels in a group, the size of the gap between theoretical and actual revenue provides a measure of a hotel's marketing efficiency.

Cost of marketing

In Figure 23.3, part of the costs of achieving sales in some segments is reflected in the discounts and commission payable. In addition are the costs of advertising, sales promotion, print, and any other expenditure on marketing judged necessary to secure the targeted 65 per cent occupancy. In the example discussed, part of this marketing expenditure will be paid by the hotel directly, and part through the Group to which it belongs, typically through a group marketing levy amounting to around 3 per cent of the hotel's annual turnover. Whichever way the marketing budget is calculated, it is obvious that the true cost of marketing reflected in Figure 23.3, will be a very far cry from the comfortable industry 'norm' of 2–5 per cent usually quoted.

Marketing holiday parks

The second illustration relates to the thousands of mostly small businesses offering self catering holiday accommodation in Britain based on caravans and chalets for holiday lets, and touring pitch facilities for people owning their own caravans and tents.

Throughout Britain in the 1960s and early 1970s, a major expansion occurred in the number of parks (or sites as they are generally known) offering caravan based holiday lets and touring pitches; with site owners able to respond to and profit from a significant growth in market demand. They were also able to benefit from the decline in demand for traditional serviced accommodation offered by boarding houses in seaside resorts. By the mid 1980s, three times as many domestic holiday nights were spent in caravans and tents in Britain, as were spent in hotels, motels and guest houses put together.

Caravan and touring parks have always had a short season, with maximum occupancy occurring in little over ten weeks in the main Summer holiday months. Inevitably in a growth market with a limited season, the temptation to pack sites to the maximum density and a disregard for environmental impact, led to severe image problems among prospective customers by the end of the 1970s. As a result, caravan sites offering holiday lets suffered from a widespread image of overcrowding, low quality, and cheap and ugly facilities suitable mainly for those who could not afford better alternatives. The belief that British touring sites could not match the quality of those of Continental Europe was equally widespread.

Most of the parks are managed by their owners, many of whom have no marketing background or experience, and entered the industry by investing their life savings in their sites, more to secure an alternative life-style than to engage in a competitive struggle for business growth and share in a rapidly changing tourist industry. The parks, taking the sector as a whole, represent a classic illustration of a production orientated industry comprising thousands of individual small businesses, which expanded naturally and largely unplanned to supply a seemingly endless growth in demand. The individuals lacked (and did not originally need) the systematic marketing concepts of analysis and orientation of business around customers discussed in this book.

Times change. By the early 1980s, it had become obvious to many in the industry that the total domestic holiday market in Britain was in decline, especially the family market for summer sun products. It was inevitable that the accommodation sector offering most such products would suffer. The effects of holiday competition from tour operators taking the British abroad, combined with demographic changes and increasing customer affluence, meant that the market for holiday caravans declined. By the misfortune of timing, other factors in the external business environment for parks, especially less favourable treatment of capital allowances for equipment, increased the financial difficulties of operators and reduced their ability to refurbish their parks.

Since 1951, many of the more professional site owners belonged to a trade body known, until 1986, as the National Federation of Site Operators (NFSO), which included sites for holiday and residential purposes. Disturbed by the evidence of market decline in the holiday sector and seeking to find an effective response, NFSO commissioned in 1985 a detailed marketing investigation of their industry. The study discovered that, for the most part, site owners made no systematic analysis of customer records, undertook no research into customer needs and satisfactions, typically spent under 3 per cent of turnover on marketing their products, and revealed little understanding of consumer orientation in their product presentation as revealed in an investigation of their brochures and booking procedures.

Following recommendations made by the study, NFSO changed its name at the end of 1986 to British Holiday and Home Parks Association (BH&HPA); commissioned a new corporate holiday logo designed to communicate the key concepts of freedom, independence and attractive countryside/coastal scenery, which research identified as principal customer benefits of park style holidays; and relaunched its corporate image around a newly introduced product quality assurance scheme to which all members agreed to adhere. Through this process, BH&HPA was able to persuade the national tourist boards for England, Scotland and Wales to share in the cost of its national promotion and publicity efforts. For its members, BH&HPA introduced a marketing manual produced specifically for the industry (VCL:1986) and supported a distance learning training package in business management available through one of the colleges of further education in England.

Chapter summary

This chapter is concerned with the provision of overnight accommodation to tourists by commercial, and what are defined as quasi commercial, operators. Categorized according to serviced and non-serviced provision, accommodation is one of the five integral elements of the total tourism product, with a strong influence on the overall volume and patterns of tourism flows to destinations. Being fixed in location and part of the destination environment, accommodation is normally strongly associated with the attractions of a destination. For leisure segments, accommodation and destinations are often closely linked in the customer's mind. In many cases accommodation products may be as strong as attractions, and constitute the principle motivation for a tourist visit.

The chapter seeks to define and illuminate the characteristics of accommodation operations and marketing practice which are common to all sectors of serviced and non-serviced sectors, and not restricted to a particular sector or only to large operators in the industry. As with transport, there are aspects of marketing which are peculiar to individual sectors but the common aspects are more important than the differences. The principles outlined are broadly relevant to all the sectors.

As in other chapters dealing with key elements of the total tourist product, this chapter stresses the importance of linkages between sectors in the tourist industry for marketing in the future. Other important marketing linkages are current-ly occurring *within* sectors, such as those found in accommodation consortia formed by serviced and non-serviced operators. Individual pro-ducers, especially those owning small units, see consortia as a logical route to achieving econo-mies of scale in marketing. Such economies are vital to successful competition against the grow-ing power of the larger organizations, with their multi-site networks of units operating to com-mon standards within corporate identities.

24

Marketing inclusive tours and product packages

This chapter focuses on the mainly commercial operators who assemble the components of tourist products and market them as packages to the final consumer. Defined in the first part of this chapter, a package is essentially a selected combination of individual elements of the total travel and tourism product, marketed under a particular product or brand label, and sold at an inclusive price. Most such products are aimed at leisure and holiday markets.

Although the activities of national tour operators, such as Thomson Holidays and Intasun in Britain, who between them take millions of Britons abroad every year, are the best known and most obvious illustrations of modern tour operation, they are by no means the only businesses marketing travel packages.

The history of tour operation goes back to the nineteenth century in Britain, although in its modern form it can be traced to the 1950s. At that time, the availability and technology of air transport, and the growing level of affluence of the holiday market in Britain and other countries, coincided with the needs of both customers and component suppliers to facilitate a mass market for packages, or inclusive tours (ITs) as they are known in the trade. This is now a major market for domestic as well as international tourism; it includes surface transport; and there appears to be much scope for further growth in the rest of this century.

This chapter commences with a brief

historical review of the development of travel organization and tour operation, followed by definitions presenting a broad view of packages. It proceeds to consider the role of tour operators in the overall travel and tourism product and the nature of the tour operating business which determines the marketing response. This is followed by an assessment of the marketing task for tour operators, and the implications for strategy and tactics. The chapter concludes with two illustrations, one of which outlines a new product development aimed at a targeted market sector for ITs to destinations abroad; the other dealing with tour operation in the British domestic market for short breaks in hotels.

Historical development of tour operating

The origins of travel organization and tour operation are usually traced back to 1841 when Thomas Cook, founder of the internationally famous company which bears his name, took on the personal responsibility of organizing one of the earliest whole train charters, for a day excursion to a temperance meeting. The excursion was a sell-out, achieving 100 per cent seat load factor! By 1845 Cook was operating longer, overnight tours in Britain on a commercial basis and in 1871, he organized the first round the world tour (Swinglehurst: 1982: p. 9).

Over the century to the Second World War,

tour operating developed internationally through railway companies and liners, and there were well patronized circuits around Europe, especially to Switzerland and the South of France. Skiing tours owed their origins and early popularity to another Briton, Sir Henry Lunn, in the 1880s. After the First World War the first coach tour operators established themselves, and became involved in excursions and longer tours in the 1930s, adding a new dimension to the possibilities for packaging.

Coming up to date, the Second World War left another large surplus of transport equipment, especially of air transport, which was put to early tourism uses by the forerunners of modern international tour operators. In fact, Thomas Cook claim to have pioneered the first air inclusive charter holiday to the South of France in 1939, but war put back the development of air ITs to 1950, when Vladimir Raitz of Horizon chartered 300 seats in his first year's operation to Corsica. Out of such modest beginnings the modern European tour operating industry developed. The British market for ITs abroad (air and sea), still the largest in Europe, was measured at just over one million packages in 1962 when formal measurement began, and sales exceeded ten million by 1986. Over that time, from a tiny minority of the British that had ever travelled abroad, the mid-1980s estimates are that over two in three British adults have travelled abroad at some time in their lives, higher among the more affluent socio-economic groups. Whilst Britain's island situation has been particularly conducive to the growth of packages, similar trends may be observed throughout Northern Europe.

Although appearing much later than the packages to destinations abroad, the production of domestic holiday packages has also enjoyed remarkable growth over the last decade. Depending on definitions used, for there are no accurate statistics in this sector, the volume of British domestic holiday packages is probably about the same size as the volume of holiday packages abroad, although much smaller in value.

Thus modern, risk-taking tour operators, and others with interests in packaging aspects of transport, accommodation and attractions, have origins going back over a century.

Role of packaging in the overall tourist product

In Chapter 8, the overall tourist product was introduced as a package and defined in terms of five main components comprising destination attractions, destination facilities and services, accessibility of the destination, images and perceptions, and price to the customer.

Drawing on Burkart and Medlik's succinct view, an inclusive tour operator can be said to be 'the manufacturer of a true tourist product; he buys the components of the package, the inclusive tour (transport, accommodation, etc.) from the suppliers of the individual tourist services and packages and brands them into a single entity' (Burkart & Medlik: 1981: p. 216).

Although the manufacturer concept most accurately describes independent tour operators, who contract with suppliers for all the components they build into the products offered in their brochures, the same principle holds good for packages which are put together by owners of one of more of the components, such as an airline, sea ferry company, or an hotel group.

From the customer's viewpoint, packages generally appear similar in kind when presented in brochures, and the extent of owning or contracting for the components is neither evident nor relevant to the buyer. For example, Club Méditerranée own their villages, which are a combination of destination, attractions, accommodation, and supporting facilities, and they usually also control access and act as a tour operator. Yet in the eyes of prospective customers, the brochures they put together and the process of promotion and distribution is no different from other competing tour operators, except in so far as there are intrinsic or perceived differences in product quality. Club Med is not normally described as a tour operator, yet the company is most certainly 'manufacturing' products for its target customers.

In other words, the packages which operators assemble, are drawn from the five basic elements of the total tourist product, plus whatever added value of their own operations is built in, such as price guarantees, convenience, accessibility to the customer, image, reputation for high standards and sense of security in dealing with a reputable operator.

Defining inclusive tours and product packages

This chapter takes a deliberately broad view of packages and includes two distinctive types of operator. The first type always includes transport in the package, mostly chartered air transport. These are the traditional tour operators, of whom the two biggest in Britain are structurally integrated with charter airlines, from which much of their profit is derived. The second type always includes accommodation in the package, and may or may not include transport; most of these operators are primarily involved in accommodation, although many are now independent package operators in their own right.

Thus, it makes most sense to define operators of packages according to the products they offer to the public. So many commercial and non-commercial organizations in the travel and tourism industry are now marketing packages of every kind, that it is important to be precise. There are three main considerations in a broad definition of packages, reflecting:

1 the nature of the product itself, which is always a package,
2 the business relationship between operator, and main product elements,

3 the dominant method of distribution to the customer.

The nature of the product
Product packages are:

Standardized repeatable offers comprising two or more elements of transport, accommodation, food, destination attractions, other facilities, and services (such as travel insurance). Product packages are marketed to the general public, described in print or other media, and offered for sale to prospective customers at a published, inclusive price, in which the costs of the product components cannot be separately identified.

This definition *includes* a wide range of tour operators and producer organizations marketing standardized packages, such as air inclusive tours, coach tours, short holiday breaks, weekend breaks, activity packages of all kinds, and sea cruises. Most modes of accommodation and transport are increasingly involved with packages. The definition *excludes* special packages put together for a particular purpose or for a closed group of users. For example, many conference products in hotels have standard elements and are often referred to as packages, but they are typically put together to meet the needs of specified members of particular organizations, and are 'one off' events adapted for each group purchaser. Whilst important, such packages are not marketed according to the principles outlined in this chapter.

Business relationship between operator and product elements
The second consideration is to distinguish between a category of operators who conduct their business as independent contractors, free to purchase whatever components of a package may make best commercial sense, and a second category who are owned by or closely linked

with producers of one of the package components such as hotels or airlines.

In the first category are the major British contracting operators of packages such as Thomson Holidays, Intasun, Superbreak, Hoseasons, and Rainbow. In the second category are producers marketing packages, such as Trusthouse Forte Hotels (Leisure Breaks), British Airways (Sovereign Holidays), British Rail (Golden Rail), Wallace Arnold, and Haven Holidays. Although no figures are available, it seems probable that the second category of operators generate at least as many packages which conform to this chapter's definition, as the better known first category. The key point to note is that there are strong similarities in the ways in which both categories approach their strategic and tactical marketing. From the customer's viewpoint, the packages produced by each category are essentially in direct competition.

Distribution method

The third consideration relates to the form of marketing used to sell the packages. Organizations marketing packages have a basic choice between a strategy based on direct response approaches to the customer, or the alternative strategy of marketing through third party distribution networks (see Chapter 19). Some operators, especially those in the producer rather than the contractor category, have a split strategy of part direct response marketing and part distribution through retail outlets.

The function of tour operators

As explained earlier, large tour operators are mostly independent contractors, who bring together the products of individual suppliers, and market them as packages to the final customer. As such they would not survive unless the services they provide were firmly rooted in the needs of both parties. It is possible to identify three sets of reasons, which explain the development of independent tour operating businesses.

First, with a few exceptions at certain periods and in certain locations, the matching of tourism supply with demand is a remarkably inefficient process, especially in leisure markets. On the supply side, producers of accommodation and attractions are mostly small businesses dealing with a single fixed location, aiming to attract infrequent buyers, many of them buying for the first time and on a once only basis. Moreover, prospective buyers are typically drawn from a very wide catchment area. For example, over the space of three months in the Summer, an hotel in Wales may draw its customers from up to six overseas countries and up to half of all the counties in England and Wales. A resort hotel in Cyprus may draw most of its customers from only four or five countries, yet their addresses may be geographically spread across half the land mass of Europe and the Middle East.

Effective marketing on a national and international basis, to secure exposure and promotion of their product offers to target customers, is not an option for independent suppliers. While advertising in national tourist office guides will be as sensible for the Cyprus hotelier, as for the one in Wales, it will hardly be a certain or sufficient process to secure the sale of otherwise unsold capacity on a daily basis. Both will tend to look to other sources, to supply business which they are not able to achieve through their own direct marketing efforts. Other sources usually mean tour operators looking for room allocations, which explains the prime function of tour operators for suppliers, and why they are able to secure such favourable bulk prices from individual producers.

The contrast between this and the operations of most small service businesses is extreme. For example a small local retailer will typically derive most of his sales from a small group of frequent repeat buyers, drawn from a local catchment area within a small radius of his shop's location. Most cafes, pubs, restaurants and fast food outlets will similarly draw on a small catchment area and rely on repeat customers for much of their turnover. Their marketing problems are quite different to those faced in travel and tourism.

Second, from the customer's point of view, purchasing the elements of a total product separately, especially for the first time in an unknown destination, is often a very hit and miss process, fraught with the risk of making an expensive mistake. Where large sums of money are involved as well as a personal sense of achievement or failure, as is normally the case with purchasing annual holidays, the sense of risk may be acute. For travel abroad, with its added complications of language, currency, and distance from home, the problems for inexperienced travellers acting on their own account, may be too daunting and too time consuming, even if the cost is not a problem. Providing customer convenience, protection, and the confidence of product assurance, are the vital benefits which tour operators offer to prospective buyers.

Third, the prices charged to individuals putting together the components of their chosen packages on an individual basis will typically be relatively high, because individuals cannot obtain the volume discounts available to any large buyer in competitive conditions. Tour operators, from the time of Thomas Cook onward, have been able to achieve volume discounts large enough to cover all their own costs and still pass on (in almost all cases) a price which is significantly less than the customer could achieve for himself. In the highly price-elastic leisure market, this is often seen to be the tour operator's most important function.

To summarize, the tour operator's essential function is to solve producers' needs to sell their spare capacity, and customers' needs for convenience and security at advantageous, affordable prices. At a profit to themselves, tour operators solve the natural inefficiency which is inherent in matching demand and supply in most leisure sectors of travel and tourism. That is their role and the reason for their importance in the industry.

Two dimensions of the tour operator market

Figure 24.1 is provided to act as a summary for the definitions covered in this section. It indicates *approximately* where some of the better known British operators lie in the mid-1980s on the two structural dimensions of ownership and distribution. The vertical axis ranges from the independent operators in the top half of the diagram to the wholly owned subsidiaries of producer organizations in the bottom half. The horizontal axis represents the choice between wholly direct marketing methods on the left, to full commitment to the retail distribution system on the right.

Some operators, such as Hoseasons, change their strategic position over time. The company started out as the marketing arm of a Norfolk hire boat owner, using only direct selling methods, and developed by offering its services to other owners in Norfolk and other parts of Britain. It expanded further in the 1970s as an independent contractor for self-catering holidays of all types and by the 1980s the company was targeting its main marketing effort through retail travel agencies.

The process of constructing an inclusive tour programme

All involved in marketing packages assemble product elements into what are known as programmes. A programme is normally expressed in a brochure, which typically contains a range of product choices in several destinations. To explain how programmes are constructed, this section focuses on air inclusive tours as the most developed sector of packaging, but the principles

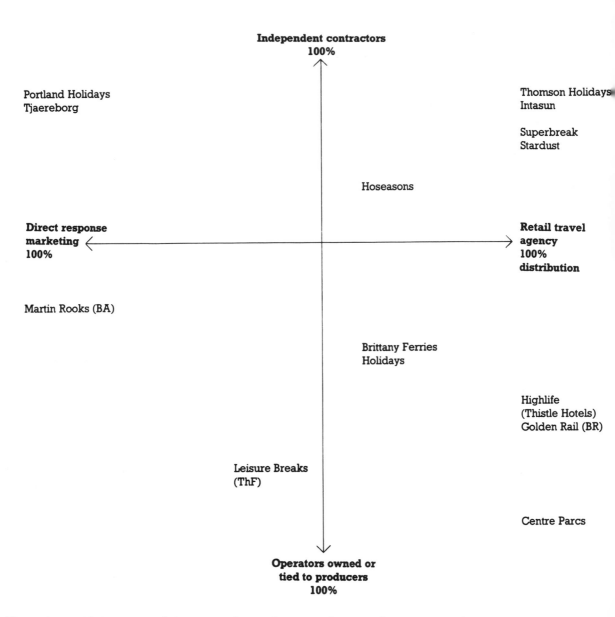

Figure 24.1 *Main structural dimensions for producers marketing inclusive tours and other product packages*

are the same in constructing any programme (see the example at the end of the chapter).

A tour operator offering ITs by air has a choice of using reduced fares (known as ITX) on scheduled airlines, or bulk fares available from charter airlines. The cost per seat on charter airlines naturally varies according to whether the operator charters the whole flight, or only a number of seats, and the volume involved. The largest international tour operators have their own subsidiary airlines to transport the bulk of their programmes, and are thus able to secure the lowest possible seat cost available. For example, Britannia Airways, owned by the International Thomson Organization, carried over five million passengers in 1986, and is a bigger and more cost efficient airline than many of the scheduled carriers in Europe.

An air IT programme out of Britain in the 1980s typically comprises ten or more airports of departure, fifty or more resorts in a dozen countries, and a range of products based on accommodation types, such as luxury hotels to simple self-catering apartments. Putting a large programme such as this together, involves translating estimates of market demand into production capacity; and matching aircraft seats with beds; in batches adding up to full aeroplanes flying between pairs of airports. The skill lies in matching potential demand with contracted supply, to achieve optimum average load factors for flights, and maximum occupancy of available beds. It is an instructive exercise for students to take a current IT brochure and identify the products, destinations and airports of origins involved.

The process of putting a programme together is shown in Figure 24.2, in a diagram adapted by the author from an original version produced by Roger Heape, when he was Director of Marketing for Thomson Holidays. The diagram reflects the initial planning dialogue common in all marketing, between marketing research and forecasting, corporate strategy, and marketing implementation. A key element in this for programme planning purposes will be deciding what volume of products is to be offered in the year ahead. Planning will start at least 18 months before the first customers travel, and product volume has to be turned into numbers of seats and beds in order to see how flight schedules and bed capacity in resorts can best be matched. This process identifies capacity objectives for the staff, who negotiate for beds and seats. In the 1980s, optimizing flight schedules and blocks of beds to achieve the most cost efficient utilization of aircraft and hotels, is carried out by computer.

With a draft programme worked out to meet projected demand, the next stage is to draft the all-important price and departure panels, which will appear in the brochure, stating the price of each product according to the date of departure and number of nights. (See Chapter 9 for a discussion of pricing.) Normally included on each product page of the brochure, below the description of the accommodation, price and departure panels are sometimes produced separately in loose-leaf format, to facilitate tactical price changes without reprinting the whole brochure. Up to this stage, there is ample room for change in all aspects of the programme, and there are numerous feedback loops in the process, although not all are shown in the diagram to avoid clutter. Product prices and capacity are not in practice finalized until the last possible moment, about 10 weeks before the brochure is distributed and customer purchases begin. Even then, as noted later under tactics, both may have to be changed again after publication.

As soon as the programme is on sale, the available capacity is put into a computerized reservation system. In the case of the larger tour operators, direct on-line access to capacity is provided for distributors through the installation of desk-top terminals in travel retailers' offices. These terminals provide continuous information

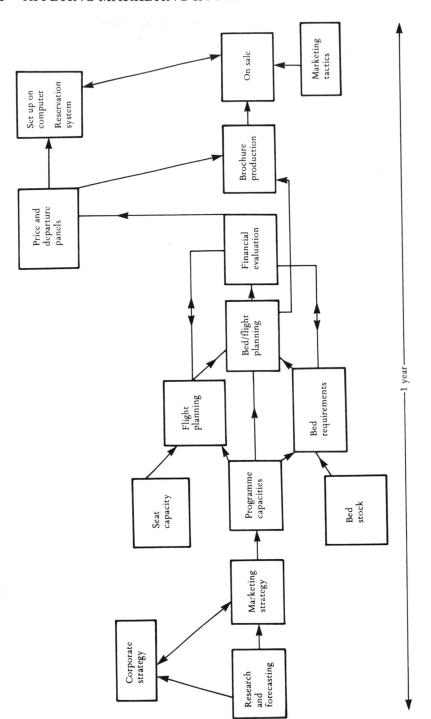

Figure 24.2 *The logical sequence of constructing and marketing an air inclusive tour programme*

about products for sale through view-data systems, and their value, both for cost efficiency in handling bookings and in providing vital information for tactical marketing purposes, is noted later.

In order to put together a credible programme and sell it through the process noted above, it is essential that each product should, so far as humanly possible, be carefully controlled to deliver consistent quality which varies only by season. Customers who read and select between the various brochures on offer, have to make the assumption that the operators can achieve consistency, or they have no effective basis for making their decisions. In this, tour operators are acting exactly as the manufacturers of cars or TV sets do. All manufacturers are involved in quality control procedures. Modern marketing cannot be undertaken on any other basis.

The nature of the marketing task for tour operators

For tour operators, as for other producers in the travel and tourism industry, it is appropriate to divide the discussion of the marketing task between strategic and tactical considerations. In practice, as any reading of the travel trade press will confirm, the nature of tour operation with its daily fluctuations and seemingly continuous atmosphere of 'boom and bust', puts great emphasis on the short-run tactical considerations required to survive in a fiercely competitive market place. The strategic dimensions are nevertheless very important and are likely to become more so as markets which have grown for some thirty years with only a few minor setbacks, approach saturation and maturity during the next decade.

Tour operators are first and foremost marketing organizations with a strong commitment to customers and products. Nevertheless they do have strategic considerations which are wider than marketing; many are concerned with ver-

tical integration between themselves and product elements and distribution, especially charter airlines and travel retailers; and with issues of ownership and other forms of linkage with organizations in travel and tourism. This chapter is not concerned with these broader elements of corporate strategy but only with the primary issues in marketing packages.

Strategic marketing

Four elements are noted in this section:

1 interpreting the strength and direction of change in the external environment,
2 choice of product/customer portfolio including segmentation and pricing,
3 positioning and image,
4 choice and maintenance of distribution systems/preferred marketing method.

The external environment

This book has stressed that effective marketing begins with a detailed appreciation of the effects on demand of the external business environment. External influences are especially powerful in their implications for tour operation, reflecting both the non-essential character of leisure products, and the international nature of much of the business. The total British market for inclusive tours demonstrates strong underlying growth in the 1980s but also large annual fluctuations triggered by economic events affecting employment, levels of wages and real income, and the impact of international exchange movements on prices. The role in marketing of travel retailers has been very much influenced by the rapid introduction of new information technology for reservations and bookings, without which the growth of multiple chains now dominating travel retailing in Britain could not have occurred. Above all the operator's external environment reflects the actions of competitors whose intense rivalry dominates the responses of all operators in the market. The susceptibility of operators to the external environment is of course heightened by the relatively long lead times involved in putting a programme together (about 18 months), from the start of the assembly process to delivery of products to the first customers.

Two key strategic decisions have to be made from the assessment of external factors; what prices are likely to be, based on cost calculations of estimated contract prices; and what volume of products should be offered in twelve to eighteen months time. The two considerations are obviously inter-related with other estimates of what prices the market will bear. Both price and volume decisions have to be based on judgement rather than statistical projections, and successful managers need strong entrepreneurial flair to get the answers about right. They also need a very strong nerve to hold onto their judgements, or change them as unpredictable events emerge.

Product/market portfolios

The second, and related strategic consideration for operators is concerned with the content and balance of the product portfolio, as represented in their programmes. The volume and price aspects noted earlier are not independent variables, but functions of specific product types. A product portfolio is a mix of destinations, accommodation types, and range of elements to be included in the product such as excursions. To give two examples, there was a massive switch to self-catering apartments and villas abroad offered to the British holiday market in the early 1980s, reflecting a strategic portfolio change. From a small base, the demand for self-catering holidays trebled between 1981 and 1985, while the demand for tours based on hotel accommodation increased by less than a half. In terms of markets, inclusive tours to Italy from Britain fell by 14 per cent between 1980 and 1985, whilst ITs to Greece grew by 70 per cent over the same period. Where profit or loss is balanced on just a few marginal percentage points above break-even load factors,

it becomes vital to offer the range of products most in demand.

While segmentation of tour operator products is still at the development stage in the 1980s, it is already reflected in the way in which brochures, the main marketing tool for operators, are put together. There is a strategic balance to be struck between the need for separate brochures to appeal to different market segments, and the even more powerful current need to reduce the number of brochures because of the limitations of rack space in retail outlets. There is an uneasy balance at present in which segmentation occurs within the brochure, but this is not a very cost effective or consumer appealing procedure, and strategic changes may be expected in the next few years.

Positioning and image

Competition between tour operators has tended in the last decade to focus primarily on price and on product portfolio. Image and positioning, although not ignored, have very clearly taken second place to price competition. This probably reflects the strong growth trends which price has stimulated in a highly price elastic growth market. As the market reaches maturity, however, competition seems certain to switch from price to branding and images. Hotels in developed countries already operate in mature markets in the late 1980s, and it is interesting to observe the extent to which positioning has become a major element in their marketing strategies.

Distribution

The fourth strategic issue to be noted in this section is that of distribution, or providing access for customers. For all operators the cost of distribution is normally the largest item of their total marketing expenditure. Apart from the basic variable costs of commission paid on sales, there are heavy, essentially fixed costs incurred in distribution, including the printing and distribution of brochures, installing and maintaining computer links with retail outlets, regular sales promotion and merchandising efforts to maintain display space, and educationals. The use of a sales force may also be involved as part of the continuous process of motivating distributors in competitive conditions.

For all operators there is a strategic choice to be made between marketing directly to customers or achieving sales through travel retailers. Most operators of ITs in Britain are members of the same trade association as the retail agents, the Association of British Travel Agents (ABTA). The USA equivalent is the American Society of Travel Agents (ASTA), although tour operators are far less important in the American market than in the British market. Some tour operators, such as Portland Holidays, Martin Rooks and Tjaereborg have chosen to pursue a straight direct-sell policy with no retail agency involvement. The major operators in Britain are Thomson Holidays, Intasun and Horizon and they sell almost exclusively through retailers. In the mid-1980s it seems probable than some 80 per cent of all ITs to destinations abroad are sold through agency outlets.

Apart from the basic choice, direct or retail sales, there are many nuances which are strategic matters. For example should particular retailers get extra support? Should extra commission be paid in some circumstances but not in others? Is there scope for some retailers to put their own labels onto some tours? Above all, because general travel retailing of holidays is not a very skilled business given modern technology, and carries few risks or capital start-up costs, is there scope for creating completely new retail travel outlets by exploiting the earning capacity of space in high street outlets such as national banks, post offices, and supermarkets, which may be currently under-utilized?

In the late 1980s these important issues are not addressed openly since they call into question the whole business relationship between retailers

and operators, as well as their 'political' relationship within ABTA. Such issues are beyond the scope of this book but strategically, because operators carry the main risk and control prices, operators are in a stronger position in distribution channels than manufacturers of consumer goods dealing for example with supermarkets which do take risks. At the time of writing there is an uneasy status quo between operator and retailer in which both are more or less satisfied. Again, as markets mature, these issues seem certain to emerge and will require careful strategic response.

Tactical marketing

As noted in the previous section, strategic decisions will determine the product/market portfolio, the product images and positioning, the capacity of the programme to be offered, the price range in the brochures, and the structure of the distribution system to be used. In other words, all the four Ps are essentially strategic decisions, and the principal role for marketing tactics is to secure a continuous flow of bookings for the programme from the day it is offered for sale. The flow of bookings is, of course, related to the target load factors for seats and beds, on which the profitability of the operator depends. The rate at which bookings and deposits are achieved, also determines the weekly cash flow of both operators and retailers, and is required to meet ongoing commitments to fixed costs and contractual obligations, especially deposits to air charter operators.

Because of the long lead times involved in getting a programme from initial planning to the point of sale, and especially because competitors' prices and the capacity of their programmes cannot be known in advance, it is almost inevitable that every year operators will find themselves with too much, or too little capacity, in relation to the available demand. This is not incompetence, it is the nature of the business described earlier in the chapter. In this tactical context it is easy to support the view of Alan Sugar (entrepreneurial boss of the highly successful Amstrad corporation) who informed an astonished audience at the City University Business School of London in 1987, that 'in a way, marketing is just like a stall in Petticoat Lane.... Frankly it is no different'. Tour operators have products as perishable as any on a market stall and they have a fixed amount of product which they have to sell in the time available to them. If sales are slow (see below) customers will have to be stimulated through the range of available tactical methods.

Figures 24.3 and 24.4 illustrate the key point that tactical responses are a function of the rate at which bookings are achieved over the selling period for each programme. Any programme which has been on the market for a year or more will have established a sales pattern, which can be represented as a graph with percentage load factor on the vertical axis, and weeks during which the product is on sale, on the horizontal axis. For new products, the pattern will have to be estimated based on any previous experience

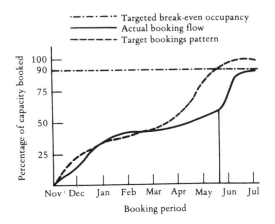

Figure 24.4 *Targeted and actual bookings achieved – problem year*

with comparable products. With modern computer technology linked to reservation systems, it is easy to plot actual bookings against target on a weekly, or daily basis if necessary.

If bookings follow the predicted path, the operators' strategy is working and tactical promotional intervention will be minimal, with no need to commit contingency funds. Some last-minute intervention may still be necessary in the four weeks before departure, but otherwise Figure 24.3 represents the implementation of a successful strategy. If bookings move significantly ahead of prediction and are sustained at high level over some weeks, provided that the market indications remain favourable, the tactical response will be to look for additional product capacity and to reduce promotional spending. If, on the other hand, bookings fall below the targeted level, as they do over the months of April and May in Figure 24.4, decisive, aggressive tactical action becomes essential to reach the targeted break-even occupancy level represented in the figure at around the 90 per cent load factor level. For every booking

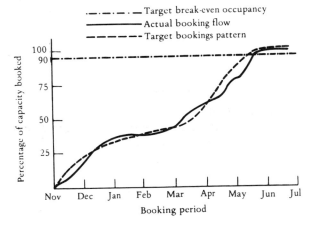

Figure 24.3 *Targeted and actual bookings achieved – normal year*

below the 90 per cent level the operator loses money; for every booking above it up to maximum occupancy, he generates a significant addition to profit. The incentive to engage in active tactical promotion will be obvious.

It is, of course, very much a matter of judgement as to when any additional promotion starts, and to what extent it occurs. Assuming that operators' prices and products are broadly competitive, if one operator sees the trend noted in Figure 24.4, it is probable that all operators in the same product field will experience similar weaknesses in their rate of bookings, at about the same time. They will all have to react, but how quickly, and by how much, will be closely guarded commercial secrets reflecting their view of the influences at work in the external environment.

For tour operators, the choices for tactical promotion are:

1 increased advertising weight,
2 sales promotions aimed at consumers, such as competitions, free childrens' places (assuming these are not part of the original product), special discounts for bookings received by a certain date,
3 sales promotion aimed at retailers,
4 price cutting to stimulate sales for targeted weeks.

In Figure 24.4 the tactical action is shown to push the rate of bookings back up towards target, although only to the break-even level. If such tactical effort did not succeed, the operator would have no choice but to consolidate his programme in order to avoid a heavy loss. Consolidation is the technical term used in charter airlines to denote the cancellation of specified flights which would be uneconomic to operate at the load factors available. Passengers are typically offered other flights in the expectation that, say, two flights could operate profitably, where three may all operate at a loss. Consolidated flights lead to cancelled accommo-dation allocations, and are understandably un-popular among customers as well as hoteliers. Since tour operators depend heavily on the goodwill of clients and suppliers, there is every reason to stimulate demand before taking the superficially less costly option of consolidation. The powerful interest of the mass media in stories about badly treated holiday makers is an ever present concern for operators, as are investigations by consumer associations seeking to expose unreasonable business practices.

The operators' links with retailers, especially where on-line computers and view-data systems can be used to communicate the late availability of products and handle bookings, are enormously helpful in the tactical process of notifying and selling last-minute discounted offers. The merchandising power of a national retailer distribution system to secure last-minute sales, often just days before departure, is perhaps the retailers most powerful advantage to operators. No other form of marketing in the industry works as fast and cost effectively as the combined operator and retailer promotion focused on price. It is widely recognized in the industry that the first 60 per cent of bookings are easy to achieve on a well-designed programme. The next 30 per cent, and especially the last 10 per cent, on which so much of the profit depends, are very much more difficult; these sales at the margin are the main target of tactical marketing.

Marketing illustrations

Thomson freestyle

The International Thomson Organization originally entered the sphere of tour operation in Britain in the 1960s by acquisition of several small holiday operators whose names were soon merged into that of Thomson Holidays. Britannia Airways, a charter airline, was acquired in 1965, and in 1968 they purchased the first Boeing 737s to be used in Europe to operate pure jet inclusive tours using the latest aircraft technology. From the outset Thomson Holidays made it clear that they intended to dominate and lead all the main categories of the British IT market which they have done with great success over the last decade. Also from the outset, albeit with highly entrepreneurial senior management, Thomson have adopted and developed the style of systematic marketing dealt with in this book, on which their continued success and market leadership has been based. The extent to which they have met the challenges of a series of brilliant entrepreneurs including Tom Gullick (Clarksons), and Harry Goodman (International Leisure Group) is some measure of the effectiveness of their marketing systems over the last twenty years.

Their approach to marketing is evident in the launch of 'Freestyle', a strategic new product carefully researched, positioned, and targeted at a particular segment of young adults taking inclusive tours. The product is aimed at people aged around 20 to 35 whose holiday needs and interests are defined more by particular lifestyle attitudes than by traditional segmentation variables of age, income, or social class.

In Britain, the number of people in the 20–35 age bracket will increase over the period 1985 to 1995 as the baby 'bulge' of the 1960s reaches maturity. The majority of them in employment will be relatively affluent, mostly in the pre-family stage, and typically couples with two incomes, whether married or not. In the mid-1980s some two million such people were buying ITs to destinations abroad, but less than one in ten were buying purpose designed products, apparently preferring to buy standard products available in general brochures. Thomson research confirmed the widely held marketing proposition that many young adults are strongly interested in certain types of lifestyle and status, and so called 'designer' products. The research also confirmed that many young people do not mix easily on holiday with families with young children, or with older people whose needs and

aspirations do not extend to their concept of enjoyment and style.

Thus, on the grounds of taking advantage of potential represented by market volume and spending power, and apparently unsatisfied customer needs, Thomsons recognized a convincing case for the introduction of a segmented, purpose designed product for young adults. In the early 1980s the main competitor in the British market was provided by Club 18-30, part of the International Leisure Group, and Thomson Holidays' major rival. For a variety of reasons, some of them no doubt unfair and unfounded, Club 18–30 was the focus of widespread media attention in the mid-1980s and suffered from a national reputation of attracting many under-20s, often motivated by alcohol and the opposite sex, and given to indulging in loutish behaviour; the very antithesis of 'style'. Club 18–30 holidays were also preceived to be highly organized, with pressure to join in frequent noisy parties and group activities.

Into this seemingly promising potential market, Thomson launched its carefully researched new product in the Autumn of 1984, under its own brand name 'Freestyle'. It adopted a revolutionary brochure format to represent its concepts of style, with a glossy magazine type cover and advertisements for stylish products inside. This was a radical departure from conventional brochures which had changed relatively little in their presentation for over a decade. Freestyle offers its readers, in its opening page, 'a new look, new style of quality holiday for young people . . .' The copy goes on:

'With Freestyle there are no age limits; the only restrictions we make are that we are not about family holidays – most of our hotels are exclusive to Freestyle – and if your idea of a great holiday is a gang of fellas getting mindlessly drunk or a bunch of idiots singing and chanting at the tops of their voices at five in the morning then look elsewhere, Freestyle is definitely not for you ... so, if Freestyle sounds like your style read on' (Freestyle brochure: Summer 1986).

Whatever else, the Freestyle product benefits and its image and positioning, supported by careful photography and copy, are made perfectly clear to its intended purchasers.

To support the product launch, Thomson invested no less than £1.2 million in advertising support in the first year and printed one million brochures for national distribution through retail travel agents. The target capacity for the first year was around 30,000 holidays. Assuming a turnover on 30,000 of around £7.5 million, the marketing costs must have been over £75 per holiday sold, including agents' commission, and share of Thomson's overheads, as well as advertising and brochure costs. This level of support can only be justified as a strategic investment intended to establish a national brand image for a product expected to grow rapidly over a five-year period to 1990.

By the middle of 1987, the new brand was still in its early stages. It had launched, and then taken off the market, a ski programme intended to give it year-round presence and, at the time of writing, it is not possible to be certain of the brand's future. In the Freestyle launch one can see all the four Ps of the marketing mix in their strategic context and, whatever the outcome, all the original strategic rationale holds true. Thomson have gathered much vital research information about its target customers through its continuous programme of evaluating customer reaction and satisfaction with their holidays.

Superbreak mini holidays

This illustration focuses on the development of one of Britain's largest independent domestic packaged product operators, Superbreak Mini Holidays, which specializes in the short-breaks market for serviced hotels in Britain. The product range was extended to the whole of Ireland in 1986. Short breaks have varying definitions; most are of two to four nights duration, although Superbreak also includes one-night offers and longer stays for seven nights.

The Superbreak brand was originally developed to sell short weekend breaks in Autumn and Spring by British Transport Hotels (BTH), the hotel subsidiary of British Rail. Before the hotels were sold and the units split up in the early 1980s, BTH owned some 28 properties throughout Britain, including Gleneagles and Turnberry Hotels in Scotland, and famous city hotels in London, Edinburgh, York, and other places. At the time of sale, the marketing director and the sales and marketing manager negotiated to buy out the Superbreak name, and the operation thus became an independent contracting tour operator, with strong links with many of the former BTH hotels but no commitment through ownership.

From its initial base, Superbreak Mini Holidays, perceiving itself to be in a growth market, expanded rapidly and claimed a fourfold increase in business in 1986 compared with their first independent year in 1983. Its operations focused primarily on hotels in cities with strong tourist connections, and the growth strategy was based on hotels in the three, four and five star categories. In 1986, the brochure included over 200 hotels in some 150 locations, 38 of them in London accounting for around half of the total business turnover. By 1986 mini holidays were a year-round product operating over 365 days in the year, including special packages for Christmas and Easter.

The product range offered in 1987 included optional packaged transport arrangements available through British Rail, airlines and car hire companies. It ranged from traditional London sight-seeing stays, to theatre and cabaret options, activity holidays, romantic weekends, and Go-As-You-Please vouchers covering countries in mainland Europe as well as the UK and Ireland.

In analysing this operator's success, it is clear that the positioning of Superbreak Mini Holidays owes less to its product formulation strategy, which is not very different from that of its competitors and includes many hotels which also feature in other brochures, and more to its chosen distribution strategy. Influenced no doubt by the fact that as independent contractors they could not achieve in-house sales through a multi-site network, Superbreak single-mindedly pursued a strategy of sales through retail travel agencies ahead of most of their competitors. As a result, at a time when there was awakening interest among travel agents in the growth prospects for selling British travel products, Superbreak have been able to secure and often dominate shelf space allocated to domestic products. With active competition from some 60 UK operators in the domestic market, most of them seeking display space in retail outlets, leadership in the distribution channel is not only a marketing advantage for Superbreak but also a basis on which their services are sought by hoteliers seeking retail agency distribution.

With their strongly coloured, distinctive brochures, and advanced reservation system technology, they have achieved preferred operator status amongst the main large multiple chains which now dominate British travel retailing. To sustain this valuable position they produce and regularly distribute some two million brochures to support current sales of around 150,000 packages and claim 85 per cent sales through retailers. They also claim racking in 80 per cent of the 4,000 agencies they deal with, and to be the brand leader within the retail market.

Retail prominence is a big marketing advantage to Superbreak, since about half of all short breaks are bought on impulse rather than planned, and within days rather than weeks of departure. To be able to maintain continuous exposure and customer awareness through brochures displayed in a national network of retail outlets, is especially productive in these booking circumstances. The alternative would be continuous heavy investment in advertising to sustain product awareness, which is certainly beyond the budget limits of most hotels, even those in groups. Up to 1987 Superbreak have not found it necessary to engage in consumer advertising, and the current distribution strategy is obviously effective. Interestingly, their brochure includes many hotels from hotel groups which also operate their own mini-break programmes.

From an initial position of seeking contracts with producers to expand their brochure, the operator is now able to turn away some of those who seek their support, and to insist on conditions of entry to their brochure. In return, in addition to their ability to generate sales, Superbreak claim to offer a high standard of operational and accounting support to its contributing units. For its own marketing decisions, the company is able, through a daily analysis of bookings for each hotel featured on each page, to monitor the sales performance of every aspect of its product portfolio; a near perfect form of research, from which to make future strategic and tactical decisions.

While Superbreak did not invent short-break holidays, and did not pioneer tour operation methods, they took well tried operational principles and applied them on a larger scale than other independent contractors in the British domestic market to exploit a growth trend. In particular they single-mindedly developed a distribution strategy with travel retailers, which has given them a particular marketing advantage over their competition in the mid-1980s.

Chapter summary

This chapter sets out a deliberately broad view of marketing inclusive tours and product packages, intended to stress the similarities which exist between the major contracting firms and producer organizations increasingly interested in marketing their own packages. As product suppliers, such as accommodation interests, surface transport companies, and the larger managed attractions, grow in size and are large enough to justify their own central marketing departments, they are increasingly able, and increasingly likely, to assemble and market their own packages to improve their utilization of their high fixed cost assets. The bigger independent contractors take far greater risks, of course, especially in contracting air transport charters, for which there are significant penalties if the contracts cannot be met because of inadequate demand.

All marketing packages set out to solve the natural inefficiencies inherent in matching demand and supply, especially in the leisure sector; all are intended to optimize utilization rates for available capacity which would not otherwise be sold.

The pressure on managers to sell their programmes is enormous and puts great emphasis on the day-to-day tactical management of demand. On the other hand, the chapter stresses the strategic dimensions involved in marketing packages, which are likely to become more significant over the next decade, assuming the rapid market growth of the 1970s and 1980s slows, and the emphasis of competition shifts from price to other aspects of the marketing mix.

Finally, it is interesting to speculate that a tour operator's brochure demonstrates all that an operator knows about the aspirations and needs of his targeted customers. What appears in print, therefore, represents the state of the marketing art as it is understood by operators of packages at any point in time. As discussed in Chapter 17 the brochure is the tangible representation of the product portfolio and prices; it is a principle form of promotion, and the way it is distributed to customers represents a most important strategic marketing choice.

Epilogue:
Prospects for travel and tourism marketing in the year 2000

Throughout this book there are numerous comments on the probable directions that marketing may take in the travel and tourism industry, between the mid-1980s and the year 2000. The object of this concluding chapter is to bring together the most important of these, and to indulge in some speculation about trends. At the time of writing there is little more than a decade left to the end of the century, and one can be fairly confident that most of the trends which will be significant then, are already at work in travel and tourism markets around the world today.

Historically, most trends of major and lasting significance in consumer marketing either began and developed from the research and development of leading professionally managed organizations, or emerged as powerful new ways to do business, through the perception, initiative, and determination of entrepreneurs who changed the mould of current patterns of thought.

In the first category, for example, and of obvious future relevance to travel, is the tremendous growth in the use of credit cards around the world, made possible by the systematic development of information technology and effective marketing over the last two decades. Credit cards originated in the USA, and the first to offer extended credit facilities appeared in Britain in 1966, as *Barclaycard*, a brand name of Barclays Bank. Its early success was closely monitored by three major competitors, Lloyds, Midland, and National Westminster Banks, who joined together to launch and market the *Access* card in 1972 (McIver and Naylor: 1980: p. 220). With some 25 million credit cards of all types already used in Britain alone, the growth in ownership and use of such cards is so well established that it needs little further comment. It represents a classic marketing development with profound implications for the future conduct of business, and for the ways in which consumers understand, and are willing to use credit facilities. In the travel trade press of the mid-1980s there are frequent examples of new ways in which credit card systems are forming links with travel and tourism suppliers, while the data base potential (see below) of card ownership records for direct response marketing, appears immense and certain to expand greatly by the year 2000.

In the second category of pioneering breakthroughs by mould-breaking individuals, the list of innovators in the travel and tourism business is long. It includes internationally famous names, such as Billy Butlin, Walt Disney, Ray Croc (McDonald's Fast Food Chain), and Charles Forte. Another good example of the pioneer is the Frenchman Serge Trigano, chairman of Club

Mediterranée, who changed the traditional concept of holiday villages and customer behaviour in the 1950s and 1960s, by developing and promoting a style and spiritual philosophy of freedom on holidays, which is still highly relevant in the last part of the century. Club Med, with Trigano still its chairman, is now a global product selling over a million and a half holidays a year around the world in the mid-1980s; it recently enrolled its ten millionth 'GM' (gentil membre) as its customers are known.

In contemplating the next decade and beyond, it must be expected that other entrepreneurs will emerge to break the mould in the future, as they have in the past; many would consider the world a poorer place if it were not so. They are likely, however, to find it much more difficult to break into mature markets and develop against strong competition, than their forerunners did in the strongly growing markets of earlier decades.

In the ten prospects discussed in this epilogue, the intention is to highlight probable directions for travel and tourism markets, relevant both to systematic marketing professionals and to innovative lateral thinkers. The prospects are those which appear probable, assuming that no major economic or political catastrophe emerges to change the structure of the world order as we see it toward the end of the 1980s.

Growth and maturity in tourism markets

Against the trend of general speculation in developed countries about the massive potential growth prospects for travel and tourism markets, the first prediction for the year 2000 is that many markets, which grew so rapidly in the 1960s and 1970s, will continue to grow, but at a much slower rate over the remaining years of the twentieth century. More attention should be focused on the number of nights and the level of real expenditure by tourists, than on the number of visits. Holidays abroad by the British, for example, doubled between 1978 and 1986 to reach a total approaching 20 million in the late 1980s. In the heady growth years of the mid-1980s, major tour operators were able to double the volume of holidays on offer from one year to another. But the penetration of holidays abroad among the top socio-economic groups, and down into the middle and lower income groups, may now be approaching saturation level. The implication is that future growth lies at least as much in increasing the frequency of travel by repeat holiday takers, as in securing first-time buyers. If this is true, average length of stay for many forms of visit is likely to fall. Frequent travel leads to increasing consumer sophistication and expectations, and future travellers are likely to be more demanding than at present.

In the USA, the domestic travel market is estimated to have doubled during the 1970s to some one billion trips of 100 miles or more away from home, but this growth has already slowed in the 1980s and there are few predictions of future large volume growth on a regular annual basis. At a conference in London examining trends in the 1990s, the Director of the US Travel Data Center reviewed research showing that the US market began to show distinct signs of maturity around 1979. Looking ahead, he expressed his view that 'US resident travel demand will continue to grow only as fast as the overall economy' (Frechtling: 1986).

Growing and declining market sectors

Maturity of markets does not imply stagnation. On the contrary, it implies continuous and extensive change as producers react to increased competition with high levels of investment in new products designed to maintain and increase their market shares, and capture new segments. Obviously, just as there will be new products in the growth phases of their life cycle, there will also be declining products, which are losing market share and volume, and some of these will disappear by the end of the century. This is the normal experience of all mature markets and there is no reason to suppose that travel and tourism is different.

In Britain, the growth products are likely to be short, packaged stays in hotels and other forms of accommodation, for leisure purposes; city and historic town tourism for short stays focused on shopping, entertainment, heritage and cultural attractions, as well as for conferences and exhibitions; travel and stays associated with activities and hobbies; visits to farmhouses and high quality self-catering cottages; products which focus generally on healthy activities, such as walking in scenically attractive settings; and visits to new and developed visitor attractions. The growing number of relatively affluent and active mobile retired people in the population, in the age range 60–80, provides many travel market opportunities to be developed over the coming years. All of these growth areas have been the focus of recent investment and seem certain to grow strongly by the year 2000.

The declining tourism products in Britain and Northern Europe will continue to be mainly those for which warmth and sunshine are regarded by customers as highly desirable elements of a satisfactory experience. For main summer holidays, increasingly professional tour operators will continue successfully to package the desired product components around the recently built Mediterranean resorts in Europe, often at lower prices than their Northern counterparts, and the markets will continue to switch their preferences accordingly. On recent evidence, these packages are likely to mean growth more for sophisticated forms of self catering accommodation, than for the conventional style of hotels built throughout the 1970s.

The results of this deep-rooted structural change have led to a significant loss of volume in most seaside resorts in Britain and Northern Europe since the 1970s, in many places accom-

panied by a deterioration in product quality. There is often a vicious spiral in travel markets, of low prices, low standards, and low demand followed by a further lowering of price as the principal means of promoting what is clearly hard to sell. Such tactics lead inevitably to lower standards and the logical result, if underlying market circumstances do not change, is business failure.

The contribution of marketing to securing growth or arresting decline in conditions of change, lies in the speed with which it is possible to detect emerging trends ahead of the competition, take the initiative to steer a business using the 4 Ps in the most cost effective way, and move it in a direction to which targeted customers will respond. Once decline becomes firmly established, massive investment is normally the only route out, but it is not a route usually available to the declining businesses themselves.

Market segments; product differentiation

Maturing markets mean increasing competition for market share, and greater use of marketing research and experimentation to find strategic ways to segment existing large volume markets, and to differentiate products. Such developments are classical marketing responses to mature market conditions and are likely to place increased emphasis on the positioning and branding of operators' products, more to enhance or protect share than to stimulate overall market growth. As Frechtling put it, 'Travel marketers must pay more attention to the characteristics of the market and how they change than they have, and trust less in a booming market to validate all marketing decisions' (Frechtling: 1986).

The process of product differentiation is already well developed in the 1980s, reflecting the existence of different segments in the market. There are, for example, separate products based on age and stage in the life cycle, such as those for the over-55s, those in the age group 18–35, family holidays, and special products for schools. There are separate product groupings according to activity, ranging from beach type holidays to walking tours; special interest packages for every type of activity from photography and bird watching to sailing, golf and pony trekking; and products featuring particular types of accommodation such as cottages, farmhouses, and villas as well as caravans, chalets and hotels. The list is endless, and in it there is great scope for operators to experiment and innovate in order to discover new products which are better able to capture emerging consumer interests.

Even within broad groupings traditionally described as segments, such as business travellers to hotels, the process of further sub-division has led to the development of executive rooms and executive floors with their own check-in and service facilities, and products which differentiate between the service offered to loyal customers carrying privileged user cards (see Chapter 23), and others given less personal attention.

Lastly, on the key issue of segmentation, new forms of product differentiation are likely to be based on life styles and consumer interests, which are not necessarily related to economic or demographic characteristics at all, but to mental attitudes. There are, for example, groups in society who are not content to participate in the standardized packaged experiences provided by most tour operators, especially in third world countries, where the needs of air-conditioned itineraries and accommodation constraints often tend to insulate visitors from the societies they visit. Conventional packaged tours can create a totally false impression of destinations for visitors, and a totally false impression of visitors for the host community. There is a school of thought emerging in the 1970s, summarized and developed recently (Krippendorf: 1987), which argues strongly for a new philosophy of tourism to be reflected in products, which will promote and facilitate sympathetic 'encounters' as they

are known, between tourists and residents of the host community, for the mutual benefit of both parties.

Associated with this last point is the apparent scope for developing new forms of tourist products, which provide participative, creative or recreative experiences, intended to make a significant contribution to the mental well-being of visitors. These are quite different from traditional forms of mass tourism, which mostly provide only temporary passive relief or escape from the pressures and chores of modern living. These new forms may be related to one or more aspects of a concern for health, exercise, education, and a concern for the natural environment in all its forms.

Although large organizations are expected to increase their shares of overall travel markets, the developments noted above are also likely to provide ample opportunities for smaller businesses and entrepreneurs to discover and exploit specific niches. These niches will be based on identifying particular customer needs, for which it is possible to develop specific product expertise, in market sectors too small to be economic for larger operators. The scope for small businesses able to provide a distinctively individual service and welcome to their customers, appears certain to increase, not diminish.

Enclosed and controlled tourist environments for visitors?

One may discern two diametrically opposed management philosophies at work in travel and tourism in the 1980s concerning the nature of destination products, both of which appear likely to intensify and become more divergent by the year 2000. These are the philosophy, which aims to deliver marketing designed products within purpose-built, enclosed, and closely controlled environments; and its opposite, in which products are delivered with the minimum of control by the supplier over the visitor's experience at the destination.

Within the first category of full environment control are Disney World and the large-scale theme and heritage parks now to be found in many parts of the world. In these, the visitor experience is fully planned and managed from the point of entry to an enclosed site to the moment of departure. As Walt Disney put it, 'I don't want the public to see the world in which they live while they are in the Park. I want them to feel they're in another world' (Walt Disney Productions: 1982). Looking back about a hundred years, one may speculate that the seaside resorts of Northern Europe performed essentially the same 'other world' function for late nineteenth century populations of industrial cities, as theme parks perform today – they take people out of their normal surroundings and associated concerns, and expose them to strikingly different, attractive, purpose-built, high quality environments. In other words they provide experiences as far removed from their customers' everyday life, as it is possible to achieve within affordable prices. The emphasis on quality of service, as well as on infrastructure and surroundings, is also a vital part of the 'difference' which is created.

Modern examples of controlled destination environments are found in most parts of the world. They include resort hotels, resort villages, vacation islands, cruise ships, holiday parks, sports and activity centres, and adventure camps for young people. Wherever master planning of resorts occurs, as in the Languedoc Rousillon region in the South of France, or at Scheveningen in the Netherlands, the principle of environmental planning and control operates. The same principle of managed, purpose-built environments, operates also at a different level in first class lounges for travellers, in executive suites in hotels, in modern museums, and in themed shopping precincts or malls. In the mid-1980s the rationale for creating purpose-built,

controlled environments appears likely to become more, rather than less persuasive by the year 2000. It must be stressed, however, that the marketing orientated planning and control typified by Disney World, is radically different from the resource based, product orientated control, philosophies, which dominated so much of the public sector planning for tourist destinations in many areas in the 1960s and 1970s.

Arguments in favour of uncontrolled, or so called *authentic* destinations and experiences, are also strong. They are based on the view that more educated and experienced travellers do not need, and increasingly reject, the packaging of the environment usually involved in the first approach. Instead, they seek the opportunity to experience the natural quality of destinations for themselves, at first hand, and on their own terms. Climbers, fell walkers, anglers, and yachtsmen are obvious examples; so too are experienced skiers who use helicopters to reach otherwise inaccessible off-piste slopes. In Australia and New Zealand there is growing interest in two-option vacations, which involve a mixture of genuine exposure to wilderness for a short period of time, followed by the luxury of haute cuisine and highly sophisticated accommodation as a contrast. Visits involving small groups seeking to experience the life style of the residents of a destination, living in the same type of accommodation and eating the same kind of food, are other examples of the same trend.

In practice, the philosophy of exposure to uncontrolled 'authentic' environments, however attractive it appears, is presently available only to a very small number of people. It is likely to remain a minority form of tourism available either to the very rich, who can use modern transport and equipment to reach the natural environment of their choice, and others, such as students, with enough time and a willingness to forego comfort and convenience to achieve their experiences.

Market dominance by large organizations

Market growth generally has been accompanied by the emergence of large national and international corporations, which have successfully brought their standardized operations and marketing methods to destinations in many countries. Large-scale operators in the 1980s are found among international airlines and surface transport operators, hotels and other accommodation interests, fast-food restaurants, tour operators and multiple outlet retail travel chains. Both in Britain and in the USA, the largest six or so operators in each main sector of travel and tourism are already large enough to dominate market trends and strongly influence customer expectations of products, prices, and satisfactions. These large corporations are likely to secure greater shares of the markets in which they operate by the year 2000, and there is no evidence that limits to economies of scale have yet been reached. Similar patterns are likely to emerge among larger tourist attractions, in which economies of scale, especially of management and marketing, are likely to become more important.

For the customer, of course, the evidence of large-scale operations and standardization is certain to be effectively disguised by careful market segmentation and product differentiation, and there is no suggestion in this book that the future lies with homogeneous mass produced products; quite the reverse. Paradoxically perhaps, the new information technology already in the industry, and available mainly to larger operators because of the high initial capital costs of installation, is likely to confer new flexibility in marketing, which will greatly facilitate the segmentation process noted earlier and help bigger operators to 'think small'. The same technology is also expected to facilitate the efficiency with which managers are able to control large-scale multisite organizations, through the process of subdivision into market focused, profit centred operations (strategic business units), discussed in Chapters 10 and 12.

Information technology

Any view of changes by the year 2000 must relate to the marketing implications of developments in information technology (IT). While this vast subject has multiple implications for most aspects of managing and controlling service operations, the IT revolution has already brought about extensive changes in the practice of marketing in travel and tourism over the last decade. Three related dimensions of information technology in particular seem certain to develop and provide marketing opportunities over the years to the end of the century.

Inventory management

The first dimension is concerned with the sophistication of technology available for reservations, sometimes known as *inventory management*. In all sectors of the industry except attractions, for which advance bookings by the general public are either not relevant or are very much less important, computerization has served to increase customer convenience; to improve operational productivity through speed of access to products; to reduce the number of staff involved; and to reduce the unit costs of making individual bookings. Through interactive, on-line computer links between different suppliers, it is now common for different elements of the overall tourist product to be brought together in ways impossible until recently. Air transport can be linked with hotel inventories and car rental capacity to produce international bookings in seconds. The consumer credit developments noted earlier are also relevant in making it possible to achieve simultaneous automatic credit transfers for transactions.

The speed of developments is rapid. For example, until as recently as 1982, Britain's second largest tour operator took half a million bookings by telephone. By 1987, after a rapid development of on-line links with retailers over a four-year period, its computers handled some two million bookings, dealing with over 100,000 on a peak day, a figure unthinkable without a computerized inventory. Its major competitor had by that time established a four-year lead in the application of its systems. In particular, computerized inventory management has also made it possible for many operators in travel and tourism to greatly improve the efficiency with which they can identify unsold capacity, and supply information about it to retailers and customers, especially within the vital period of 48 hours before the available service is scheduled to be performed. This information can then be the focus of precisely targeted sales promotion, leading to rapid processing of the late and last minute bookings, on which so many operators now depend for their marginal sales revenue and profitability.

Flexible channels of distribution

The second and related dimension of IT was covered in Chapter 19, which discussed the marketing implications of computerized data bases comprising detailed information about existing and prospective customers. It was noted that 'data based marketing' is now a commonly used term to cover various forms of direct response marketing, which have been growing very rapidly in the 1980s. As more suppliers shift emphasis in their budgets towards targeted direct response marketing, there is an obvious danger of consumer overload as unsolicited product offers pour through letter boxes and over the telephone, as well as via radio and television. In the outlook period to 2000, strongly negative reactions from customers seem unlikely to be very significant in travel and tourism, although the skills required to product cost-effective direct response materials will undoubtedly become more sophisticated.

In the struggle for market shares, repeat customers, already very important in the travel and tourism industry, will be seen as even more important (assuming product satisfaction). Their details, retained within a data base, will provide a powerful advantage in enabling marketing managers to aim personalized, direct response marketing messages at them.

As noted in Chapter 19, one of the main arguments in favour of direct response marketing is that commission on sales through retail outlets is, for many operators, the most expensive element within their marketing budgets. But retailers are only one of several choices for producer organizations in travel and tourism, and the new technology is likely to make it increasingly possible, convenient and cheap, for individuals to book and pay by credit transfer for travel arrangements, either direct from an adapted TV set in the home, or in other places with public access, such as banks, post offices, transport terminals, and tourist information centres. It will also convey similar potential convenience and cost savings for all large corporate customers who might seek to bypass travel agents for the bulk of their needs. IT developments, linked to the positive advantage of not having to transport products physically to the point of sale, indicate that some of the greatest changes in travel and tourism marketing will occur in the channels for travel distribution by the year 2000.

Any reading of the travel trade press makes it clear that any shift of distribution away from the traditional network of retail travel agents, towards more flexible channels made possible by computer linkages, will involve a fierce struggle for power between principals and retailers. Retailers will obviously endeavour to close their ranks to defeat the actions of principals of whom they disapprove, but the balance of advantage appears likely to swing toward direct marketing and alternative channels, given their many advantages and cost saving potential.

Management control

Traditional dis-economies of scale, associated with businesses growing too large to be managed efficiently, appear likely to be less of a constraint to business growth in the future. At the time of writing, the full implications of information technology are by no means clear, and it is interesting to note a recent review of air transport in Europe, which suggested that, 'what has happened to date [in the applications of IT] is only the start of a revolutionary development, which will transform the way airlines operate in the future. Pricing and inventory management, the automation of marketing and alternative distribution systems will become vital components of airline profitability and survival over the next few years' (Wheatcroft and Lipman: 1986: p. 156). What is true for airlines, appears also to be true for tour operators, all forms of accommodation, and the larger managed visitor attractions. It is not difficult to predict that IT developments will increasingly be the basis for effective conduct and control of marketing by the year 2000.

Marketing professionalism

Towards the end of the 1980s it is easy to suppose, especially for students coming new to the industry, that the professional application of marketing skills discussed throughout this book is well developed in travel and tourism. It is not so. Judged by organizational changes and the frequency of marketing appointments, as well as the evidence of marketing activity on both sides of the Atlantic, an appreciation of the role of marketing in the travel and tourism industry has existed for little more than a decade. Ten years is a very short time indeed for a major new management philosophy to take root across a very fragmented service industry and change the conduct of business.

At the University of Surrey, one of the first academic institutions in Britain to offer post-graduate courses in travel and tourism, marketing was built into the programme at its inception in 1972. For undergraduate courses leading to a first degree in hotel and catering management, marketing appeared for the first time as a separate course only in 1977. As an external examiner for other postgraduate tourism courses and for the Hotel, Catering and Institutional Management Association, this author has observed at first hand, the way the subject has developed and changed. Initially, for lack of other materials, academic courses leaned heavily on standard marketing texts developed for fast moving consumer goods in the 1960s and 1970s. In the USA it was only in 1980 that the Harvard Business School offered its first MBA (Master of Business Administration) Course in Marketing of Services. Marketing courses in hospitality management programmes in the USA also originated in the 1970s, growing strongly in the 1980s.

Thus, in terms of both the practical and academic understanding and development of the subject, marketing in travel and tourism must be regarded as being still in the early stages of its professional development. By the year 2000, assisted by innovations in information technology previously discussed, improved marketing research and learning through data based marketing, there are likely to be important developments in the body of knowledge about the subject. These can be expected to produce radical improvements in the way in which strategy and tactics are understood and planned, and in the cost effectiveness of marketing practice. As always, developments in the subject will generally occur first in the most competitive, professionally led organizations, and filter down through the rest of the industry over time.

Larger marketing budgets

Marketing budgets, which have to be planned months ahead of the sales they are expected to generate, will always contain unavoidable risk. There cannot be guarantees that money spent on marketing activities will produce the hoped-for results. These truths will not change by the year 2000, but the growing professionalism of marketing management will reduce the level of risk and, as a consequence, the proportion of sales revenue allocated to marketing budgets will tend to rise by the year 2000.

Excluding commission payments to retailers, and any bulk purchase discounts offered, expenditure on marketing in most sectors of travel and tourism appears to be low in the 1980s; frequently under 5 per cent of sales revenue. In conditions of surplus capacity, leading to significant under-utilization of beds, seats, and visitor capacity at attractions, the *only* reason why budgets should be less than say 20 or even 30 per cent of revenue for *marginal* sales, is fear, based on ignorance, that the money will be wasted.

With better data-based evaluation of marketing expenditure, confidence in achieving results will increase. Larger marketing budgets will result. Perhaps, by the year 2000, the time honoured cliché that 'half my advertising is wasted, but I don't know which half', will have been exposed at last as the nonsense it already is.

A more productive interface between financial and marketing management

In the mid-1980s, in this author's experience of both industry practice and academic courses, there appears generally to be a traditional but artificial separation between the role and functions of accountants and finance managers on the one hand, and those responsible for marketing on the other. The distinction, so widely observed in the travel and tourism industry, reflects the relatively recent introduction of marketing in many organizations, and the fact that its full potential influence is not yet accepted in many organizational structures.

The same separation has been equally evident in the academic world, where it is still quite common in programmes preparing students for entry to management careers in hospitality and travel and tourism, to find courses in marketing and courses in accounting and financial management, existing side by side, taught in parallel, but rarely crossing traditional subject boundaries. The way in which pricing, budgetary control, feasibility studies, and marketing principles are often taught in separate courses, must provide the source of endless confusion for students. The growing use of integrating case studies, especially those using interactive computer based business simulation models, is breaking down the barriers in the 1980s, and this trend seems certain to accelerate.

It is evident to all marketing managers, if not always to financial managers and accountants, that the core of finance and of marketing are inextricably linked. This is true both in the strategic context of investing in a product/market portfolio relevant to long-run customer needs, and in the tactical sense of generating sufficient demand for perishable products on a daily basis to meet the need for adequate cash flow and return on assets employed.

Most commercial businesses, and many in the public sector too, operate on narrow margins between costs and revenues. Revenue flows in practice mean customer flows. In conditions of strong competition, customer flows for most businesses will generally be inadequate without targeted marketing activity to stimulate demand. Thus, the best budgetary control system, the best financial appraisal, and the most efficient borrowing arrangements, have little value unless marketing managers are able by their strategic and tactical use of the four Ps, to generate the sales revenue and cash flow patterns, on which financial estimates are based. In American parlance, marketing is about the 'bottom line'.

In mature markets and stronger international competition, stimulated by more professional management in the last part of the twentieth century, marketing as a management function seems certain to gain in influence over financial management in all sectors of travel and tourism. But the issue is not which of two management functions should predominate, but rather one of management integration around customer orientated objectives. One may predict that organizations in travel and tourism over the next decade will increasingly follow the management style set in Britain by British Airways, where Sir Colin Marshall, Chief Executive since 1983 and a leading exponent of the marketing approach, stated recently 'I look at marketing as the art, which provides the means of understanding the customers and the customers' needs. From that, you are able to fashion the specific programmes which are likely to produce the best customer response. Too frequently . . . people tend to think of marketing as being only one or perhaps two sub-sets of what marketing is really about – they see it as market research, or advertising or selling' (Marshall: 1985 p, 34).

Marshall's view leads to integration in management functions. The potential scope for more productive links and integration between financial and marketing disciplines appears immense over the next two decades; it seems certain to change many current board-level attitudes and organizational responses.

Marketing the margin

In expressing the view of marketing which underlies this book, the Preface notes:

What the rigorous application of the modern marketing concept can do . . . is provide the route to achieving the marginal extra business, on which the difference between profit and loss so often depends in the travel and tourism industry. Systematically applied, the marketing process can also secure marginal increases in the cost effectiveness of promotional and related budgets.

The book aims to justify the relevance of that view to current and future marketing operations, both at strategic and tactical levels. This epilogue, in identifying probable marketing developments in travel and tourism, emphasizes the increasing relevance of *marketing the margin* to the conditions marketing managers are likely to face by the year 2000.

The importance of the margin is succintly put in *A Passion for Excellence*, whose authors express the view in the context of general management, that:

'Excellence is a game of inches, or millimetres. No one act is, *per se*, clinching. But a thousand things . . . each done a tiny bit better, do add up to memorable responsiveness and distinction . . . and loyalty . . . and slightly higher margins' (Peters & Austin: 1986: p. 46).

Influencing and managing the direction, speed, and effectiveness of customer orientated responses, especially at the margin, is the principal preoccupation of marketing managers in the fascinating highly volatile, international business of travel and tourism.

Bibliography

One hundred and twenty-five useful references

Abell, D. F. and Hammond, J. S., *Strategic Market Planning*, Prentice-Hall International, New Jersey, 1979.

Alderson, W., 'The Analytical Framework for Marketing', in Lawrence R. J. and Thomas, M. J. (Editors), *Modern Marketing Management*, Penguin, London, 1971.

Allport, G. W., in Murchison, C., (Editor), *Handbook of Social Psychology*, Clark University Press, Worcester, Mass., 1935.

American Society of Travel Agents, *The Dilemma in Developing Printed Materials for Travel Agents*, ASTA, New York, 1974.

Ansoff, H. I., *Corporate Strategy*, Penguin, London, 1968.

Argenti, J., *Practical Corporate Planning*, George Allen and Unwin, London, 1980.

Baker, M. J., *Marketing: An Introductory Text*, 4th edition, Macmillan, London, 1985.

Bartels, R., *The History of Marketing Thought*, 2nd edition, Grid, Ohio, 1976.

Beaumont, M., Paper to the *International Conference of National Trusts*, Bath, 1986.

Boyd, H. W. and Larreche, J. C., 'The Foundations of Marketing Strategy' in Cox, K. K. and McGinnis, V. J., (Editors) *Strategic Planning Decisions: A Reader*, Prentice-Hall, Englewood Cliffs, 1982. pp. 3–17.

Brent Ritchie, J. R. and Goeldner, C. R., (Editors) *Travel, Tourism and Hospitality Research: A Handbook for Managers and Researchers*, John Wiley and Sons, New York, 1986.

British Tourist Authority, *Museums – Lessons from the USA*, BTA, London, 1983.

Broadbent, S., *Spending Advertising Money*, 2nd edition, Business Books, London, 1979.

Burkart, A. J. and Medlik, S., *Tourism: Past, Present and Future*, 2nd edition, Heinemann, London, 1981.

Burkart, A. J., 'The Role of a Reservation System in the Marketing of Tourism Services', in *HCIMA Review*, No. 4, Spring, 1976.

Buttle, F., *Hotel and Food Service Marketing: A Managerial Approach*, Holt, Rinehart and Winston, London, 1986.

Chisnall, P. M., *Marketing: A Behavioural Analysis*, 2nd edition, McGraw-Hill, London, 1985.

Christopher, M., *Marketing Below the Line*, George Allen and Unwin, London, 1972.

Christopher, M., *The Strategy of Distribution Management*, Heinemann, London, 1985.

Coffman, C. D., *Marketing for a Full House*, Cornell University Press, Ithaca, New York, 1970.

Cossons, N., 'Making Museums Market Orientated', in Scottish Museums Council, *Museums are for People*, HMSO, Edinburgh, 1985.

Cowell, D., *The Marketing of Services*, Heinemann, London, 1984.

Cox, K. K. and McGinnis, V. J., *Op cit*

Daltas, A. J., 'Protecting Service Markets with Consumer Feedback', in *Cornell Hotel and Restaurant Administration Quarterly*, May 1977.

Davidson, J. H., *Offensive Marketing*, Pelican, London, 1975. (New edition 1987.)

Davies, A. H. T., 'Business Planning in the Thomas Cook Group', in *International Journal of Tourism Management*, Vol. 2, No. 2., June 1981.

Donelly, J. H., 'Marketing Intermediaries in Channels of Distribution for Services', in *Journal of Marketing*, Vol. 40, January 1976.

Doswell, R. and Gamble, P. R., *Marketing and Planning Hotels and Tourism Projects*, Barrie and Jenkins, London, 1979.

Economist Intelligence Unit, 'The Role and Functions of an NTO Abroad', in *International Tourism Quarterly*, No 2, 1983.

Edwards, A., *International Tourism Forecasts to 1995*, (Special Report No. 188), Economist Intelligence Unit, London, 1985.

Eiglier, P. and Langeard, E., 'A new Approach to Service Marketing', in *Marketing Consumer Services: New Insights*, Report 77–115, Marketing Science Institute, Boston, 1977.

English Tourist Board, *Britain's Zoos: Marketing and Presentation – The Way Forward to Viability*, ETB, London, 1983.

Forte, C., *Forte: The Autobiography of Charles Forte*, Sidgwick and Jackson, London, 1986.

Frechtling, D. C., 'Key Issues in US Tourism Futures', in *Tourism Management*, Volume 8, No. 2, June 1987.

Gater, C., 'Database Key to a Direct Hit', in *Marketing* 2 October, (Journal of Inst. of Marketing) Maidenhead, 1986, pp. 41–42.

Gee, C. Y., Dexter, J. L. C. and Makens, J. C., *The Travel Industry*, AVI, Westport, Connecticut, 1984.

Greene, M., *Marketing Hotels and Restaurants into the 90s*, 2nd edition, Heinemann, London, 1987.

Haines, D., 'Pictures in Advertising Research in the UK and USA', in *Market Research Society Newsletter*, No. 214, London, January 1984.

Hart, N. A. and Stapleton, J., *Glossary of Marketing Terms*, 3rd edition, Heinemann, London, 1987.

Heape, R., 'Tour Operating Planning in Thomson Holidays UK', in *Tourism Management*, December 1983.

Heneghan, P., *Resource Allocation in Tourism Marketing*, Tourism International Press, London, 1976.

Holloway, J. C., *The Business of Tourism*, 2nd edition, Macdonald and Evans, Plymouth, 1985.

Housden, J., *Franchising and Other Business Relationships in Hotel and Catering Services*, Heinemann, London, 1984.

Howard, J. A. and Sheth, J. N., 'A Theory of Buyer Behaviour' (1967), reproduced in Enis, B. M. and Cox, K. K., (Editors), *Marketing Classics*, 3rd edition, Alleyn and Bacon, Boston, 1977, pp. 161–185.

Hudman, L. E., *Tourism a Shrinking World*, Grid, Ohio, 1980.

Hussey, D. E., *Introducing Corporate Planning*, 2nd edition, Pergamon Press, Oxford, 1979.

Jeffries, D. J., 'The Role of Marketing in Official Tourism Organizations', Paper to 23rd Congress of AIEST, in *Tourism et Marketing*, vol. 13, 15, Bern, Switzerland, September 1973.

Joyce, T., *What Do We Know About How Advertising Works?*, J. Walter Thompson, London, 1967.

Kotas, R., (Editor) *Market Orientation in the Hotel and Catering Industry*, Surrey University Press, London, 1975.

Kotler, P., *Marketing Management: Analysis Planning and Control*, 5th edition, Prentice-Hall International, London, 1984.

Kotler, P. and Cox, K., (Editors) *Marketing Management and Strategy, A Reader*, Prentice-Hall Inc., New Jersey, 1980.

Krippendorf, J., *Marketing et Tourisme*, Lang and Cie, Berne, 1971.

Krippendorf, J., *The Holiday Makers*, Heinemann, London, 1987.

Levitt, T., 'Improving Sales through Product Augmentation', in Doyle, P. *et al.*, *Analytical Marketing Management*, Harper and Row, London, 1974, p. 10.

Levitt, T., 'Marketing Myopia', in *Harvard Business Review*, Vol. 38, July/August, 1960.

Levitt, T., 'Marketing Intangible Products and Product Intangibles', in *Harvard Business Review*, May/June 1981, pp. 37–44.

Lewis, R. C., 'The Positioning Statement for Hotels', *Cornell Hotel and Restaurant Administration Quarterly*, Vol. 22, No. 1, May 1981, pp. 51–61.

Love, J. F., *McDonald's: Behind the Arches*, Bantam Press, New York, 1987.

Lovelock, C. H., *Services Marketing: Text, Cases and Readings*, Prentice-Hall, New Jersey, 1984.

Luck, D. J. *et al.*, *Marketing Research*, 3rd edition, Prentice-Hall, New Jersey, 1970.

Maas, J., 'Better Brochures for the Money', in *Cornell Hotel and Restaurant Administration Quarterly*, Vol. 20, No. 4, 1980.

Marshall, C., 'Marshalling Marketing Forces', in *Marketing*, 6th June, 1985.

Mayo, E. J. and Jarvis, L. P., *The Psychology of Leisure Travel*, CBI, Boston, Mass., 1981.

McCarthy, E. J., *Basic Marketing, A Managerial Approach*, 7th edition, Irwin, Homewood, Illinois, 1981.

McIntosh, R. W., *Tourism; Principles, Practices, Philosophies*, (4th edition, with Goeldner, C. R., Wiley, New York, 1984), Grid, Ohio, 1972.

McIver, C. and Naylor, G., *Marketing Financial Services*, The Institute of Bankers, London, 1980.

Medlik, S., *The Business of Hotels*, Heinemann, London, 1980.

Medlik, S., *Profile of the Hotel and Catering Industry*, 2nd edition, Heinemann, London, 1978.

Medlik, S. and Middleton, V. T. C., 'Product Formulation in Tourism', in *Tourism and Marketing*, Vol. 13, AIEST, Berne, 1973.

Middleton, V. T. C., 'Tourism Marketing: Product Implications', in *International Tourism Quarterly*, No. 3, 1979.

Middleton, V. T. C., 'The Marketing Implications of Direct Selling' in *International Tourism Quarterly*, No. 2, 1980.

Middleton, V. T. C., 'Product Marketing: Goods and Services Compared', in *Quarterly Review of Marketing*, Vol. 8, No. 4, July 1983.

Middleton, V. T. C., 'Marketing in the Hospitality Industry' in Cassee, E. and Reuland, R., (Editors) *The Management of Hospitality*, Pergamon, Oxford, 1983.

Middleton, V. T. C., 'Profitability Through Product Formulation Strategies', in *The Practice of Hospitality Management II*, AVI Publishing, Westport, Conn., 1986.

Middleton, V. T. C., 'UK Outbound', in *Travel and Tourism Analyst*, December, 1986, pp. 17–27.

Murphy, P. E., *Tourism: A Community Approach*, Methuen, New York, 1985.

Nykiel, R. A., *Marketing in the Hospitality Industry*, CBI Publishing, Boston (USA), 1983.

Ogilvy, D., *Ogilvy on Advertising*, Pan Books, London, 1983.

Peters, R. and Austin, N., *A Passion for Excellence*, Fontana, London, 1986. (Follow up of Peters, R. and Waterman, R. H., *In Search of Excellence* 1982).

Petersen, C., 'Promotions Boom in Confusion', in *Marketing*, September 1978, pp. 61–66.

Pickering, J. F., *Industrial Structure and Market Conduct,*, Martin Robertson, London, 1974.

Piercy, N., *Marketing Organisation, An Analysis of Information Processing, Power and Politics*, George Allen and Unwin, London, 1985.

Rathmell, J. M., *Marketing in the Service Sector*, Winthrop, Cambridge, Mass., 1974.

Reneghan, L. M., 'A New Marketing Mix for the Hospitality Industry' in *Cornell Hotel and Restaurant Administration Quarterly*, August 1981, pp. 31–35.

Rodger, L. W., *Marketing in a Competitive Economy*, 2nd edition, Hutchinson, London, 1968.

Rooij de, N., 'Mature Market in Europe', in *Travel and Tourism Analyst*, May 1986.

Sasser, W. E., Olsen, P. R. and Wyckoff, D. D., *Management of Service Operations: Text, Cases, and Readings*, Allyn and Bacon, Boston (USA), 1978.

Schmoll, G. A., *Tourism Promotion*, Tourism International Press, London, 1977.

Scottish Museums Council, *Museums are for People*, HMSO, Edinburgh, 1985.

Seibert, J. C., *Concepts of Marketing Management*, Harper and Row, New York, 1973.

Shaw, S., *Air Transport: A Marketing Perspective*, Pitman, London, 1982.

Stanton, W. J., *Fundamentals of Marketing*, 6th edition, McGraw-Hill, London, 1981.

Swinglehurst, E., *Cook's Tours: The Study of Popular Travel*, Blandford Press, Poole, 1982.

Taylor, D., *How to Sell Banquets*, Northwood, London, 1979.

Thomas, M., *Pocket Guide to Marketing*, Blackwell, London, 1986.

Torkildsen, G., *Leisure and Recreation Management*, 2nd edition, Spon, London, 1983.

The Tourism Society, *Handbook and Members List*, London, 1979.

US Travel Data Center, *The 1986–87 Economic Review of Travel in America*, Washington, DC., 1987.

Wahab, S., Crampon, L. J. and Rothfield, L. M., *Tourism Marketing*, Tourism International Press, London, 1986.

Walt Disney Productions, *Walt Disney World: The First Decade*, Florida, 1982.

Wheatcroft, S and Lipman, G., *Air Transport in a Competitive European Market*, Economist Intelligence Unit, London 1986.

Wilmhurst, J., *The Fundamentals and Practice of Marketing*, 2nd edition, Heinemann, London, 1984.

Wood, M., (Editor) *Tourism Marketing for the Small Business*, English Tourist Board, London, 1980.

White, R., *Advertising*, McGraw-Hill, London, 1980.

Zehnder, L. E., *Florida's Disney World: Promises and Problems* Peninsular, Tallahassee, Florida, 1975.

Index

Numbers in *italics* refer to figures